For John Williford
with all best wishes,

Richard Brooks?

Jan. 17, 2002

In Irons

In
Irons

Richard Buel Jr.

Britain's Naval Supremacy and the
American Revolutionary Economy

Yale University Press   New Haven and London

Published with assistance from
the Annie Burr Lewis Fund.
Copyright © 1998 by Yale University.
Printed in the United States of America

Library of Congress Cataloging-in-Publication Data
Buel, Richard, 1933–
In irons : Britain's naval supremacy and the American
Revolutionary economy / Richard Buel, Jr.
p. cm.
Includes bibliographical references and index.
ISBN 0-300-07388-7 (alk. paper)
1. United States—History—Revolution, 1775–1783—
Finance.   2. United States—History—Revolution,
1775–1783—Naval operations, British.   3. United
States—Commerce—History—18th century.
4. Agriculture—Economic aspects—United States—
History—18th century.   5. Great Britain, Royal
Navy—History—Revolution, 1775–1783.   I. Title.
E215.B84   1998
972.3′1—dc21   98-21281
CIP

A catalogue record for this book is available from the
British Library.

The paper in this book meets the guidelines for
permanence and durability of the Committee on
Production Guidelines for Book Longevity of the
Council on Library Resources.

10 9 8 7 6 5 4 3 2 1

For Marilyn

CONTENTS

PREFACE

Let me begin with a confession. I have always been fascinated by the sea and have from an early age been an avid sailor. That may explain why, in the face of prolonged interruptions, I have persisted with this project for more than a decade and a half. My love affair with the sea and sail has influenced my approach to the revolutionary economy in many ways, including the book's title. Besides the ordinary penal meaning associated with placing someone "in irons," the phrase has a nautical meaning. When a sailing vessel tacking to windward attempts but fails to come about, it can stall bow to wind, losing its momentum and its ability to steer, and remain unable to proceed until it falls off the wind far enough for its sails to fill again. Today the common phrase for this condition is "in stays."

The intellectual roots of this book reach back to a study completed nearly two decades ago. While exploring Connecticut's experience during the Revolutionary War, I realized that many of the state's difficulties stemmed from economic problems that afflicted New England and the entire Confederation. These problems arose either directly or indirectly from Britain's unchallengeable control of the seas. When I looked for secondary literature that explored this subject, I was surprised to find none. While naval historians have not been bound by the convention that their subject matter ends at the high-water mark, their focus nonetheless has remained the sea. Economic historians, for their part, are drawn to orderly data series rather than to the statistical chaos that the Revolution produced. Most recent economic histories of the period have concentrated on the pre- and postwar eras, deemphasizing—if not altogether omitting—an account of the war economy. The bicentennial had the effect of confirming rather than correcting this bias. The revolutionary economy has recently been identified as "among the least studied [subjects] in American history."[1]

Because I am not trained as an economic or naval historian, I recognize that I am unlikely fully to satisfy those who are. What follows, then, is a book with two goals. First, I hope to identify some of the major sources relevant to the subject. Second, I hope to give a general though by no means comprehensive account of the war economy. I shall argue that the most distinctive feature of that economy was the initial collapse of the agricultural sector, followed by a modest revival. Here, I diverge from those who have focused on the industrial sector, emphasizing the expansion of home industries. My reason for taking a different tack lies in the conviction that agriculture held the key to the outcome of the war while domestic manufacturing and subsidiary forms of economic activity, such as retail shopkeeping, did not. Though home industries protected domestic consumers against extreme hardship, they failed to relieve the revolutionaries of reliance on Europe for military essentials like arms and clothing. I also argue that access to overseas markets was critical to agriculture.

A word is in order about the numerical quantities that I have assigned to a range of economic phenomena hitherto unmeasured. Those figures which come directly from the surviving records are subject to clerical error, theirs and mine. In addition to difficulties in deciphering eighteenth-century notations, the accounts of that period were seldom kept systematically. Merchants then saw no anomaly in appending to an account rendered the phrase "errors excepted." In the same spirit, I would characterize the calculations that I have derived from these records as "provisional." Other figures—such as the tonnage estimates—rely heavily on inference from assumptions about which I have tried to be explicit in the notes and the appendix. Again, I do not regard them as the last word on the subject. Rather, my intention is to focus on a range of phenomena and the evidence pertaining to them. Those who follow me are invited to do better. My hope is that this book, beyond providing tentative answers to the questions raised in the text, will lead others more fully to explore the neglected relationship between naval warfare and the revolutionary economy.

ACKNOWLEDGMENTS

I am grateful to the Guggenheim Foundation, the National Endowment for the Humanities, and the John Carter Brown Library for fellowships that initially enabled me to pursue the research for this study, and to the Colonel Return Jonathan Meigs First (1740–1823) Fund at Wesleyan for continuing support. The Meigs Fund was created by Dorothy Mix Meigs and Fielding Pope Meigs Jr. in memory of that soldier of the Revolution whose home was in Middletown, Connecticut, from 1740 to 1787.

Over the course of a decade and a half I have benefited from the hospitality and assistance of countless individuals in the many libraries and depositories I have worked. Most of these institutions are listed in the abbreviations pertaining to locations and manuscript collections preceding the notes. In addition, I am obliged to the staff of Olin Library at Wesleyan University, and particularly to Joan Jurale and the late Steven Lebergott.

I have benefited from the assistance and counsel of several friends and colleagues. Stanley Lebergott and Thomas Truxes helped me address some problems in economic history; Jonathan Dull and Michael J. Crawford advised me on matters relating to naval history. Melissa Da and the late Susan Frazer speeded my passage through some eighteenth-century French manuscripts. My sister, Anne Clelland, and Claire Potter read through and commented on an early version of the whole manuscript; Richard Grossman and John J. McKusker read and commented on parts of it. I am especially indebted to Stanley Engerman, who read the whole manuscript twice, once in an early draft and again after an extensive revision. Elizabeth Frost Knappman, Otto Bohlmann,

Heidi Downey, and Marilyn Buel helped me to sharpen the argument and make it more accessible to nonspecialists. My wife, Marilyn, also created the circumstances that allowed me to get back to work on the project after a prolonged interruption. To her I dedicate the volume with love.

In Irons

PROLOGUE

Few colonial Americans were surprised by the outbreak of hostilities in the spring of 1775. Though more lamented than welcomed the approach of armed conflict, no informed colonist could have mistaken the potential for war that existed from the summer of 1774 onward. Certainly those harboring peaceful illusions should have abandoned them after the "powder alarm" of September 1. Following rumors that British troops, recently reintroduced into Boston, had shed American blood in their seizure of gunpowder stored in the Medford magazine, twenty thousand New England militiamen marched eastward from the interior.[1] When they learned that the rumors were false, the men quickly turned back. However, the British realized that they could not implement Parliament's recently passed Coercive Acts—which closed the port of Boston, altered the Massachusetts Bay charter, authorized the quartering of troops on the civilian population, and allowed the governor to remove the trial of capital crimes to England—without resorting to force. They also realized that the New Englanders would respond in kind. Thomas Gage, commander-in-chief of the British Army in the colonies and governor of Massachusetts, had sent a clear signal that the controversy between the mother country and her colonies had entered a new phase when, in response to the militia's marching, he had ordered Boston fortified against land assault.

The colonists could contemplate the prospect of war with the mother country rather than craven submission because of their rapid growth and Britain's apparent economic dependence on them. In the interval between the conclusion of the Seven Years' War (1754–63) and the beginning of the Revolutionary War, immigration had swollen the population of the mainland colonies by almost a quarter of a million souls, about 125,000 of them directly from the British Isles.[2] America's gain seemed to be the mother country's loss. Even more important, America's trade had become the centerpiece of Britain's economy. Threatened by the unprecedented debt accumulated during the Seven Years' War, Britain's solvency seemed to depend on maintaining a commercial connection with the American colonies. While the ministry and people of Great Britain might initially agree that coercing America was practicable, the burden of supporting an increased military establishment three thousand miles away without the benefit of the colonies' trade would change their minds soon enough.[3]

The first Continental Congress had recommended entering into an "Association" gradually to suspend all trade with Great Britain, beginning with nonimportation and nonconsumption at the end of 1774. The following spring the second Congress moved to cut off exports in the wake of the eruption of fighting at Lexington and Concord.[4] Incensed at the mother country's shedding of its offspring's blood, it also committed the continent to the military defense of Massachusetts. Congress acted as organizer rather than instigator of the *rage militaire* that spread throughout the mainland colonies during 1775. The growing enthusiasm for war fed on calculations about the strategic advantages that America would enjoy in a showdown with Britain as much as on the moral indignation of the moment.[5]

Strategically, Britain had the more heroic military task of conquering the colonies. All the colonists had to do was defend themselves from attack. In addition, it seemed as though Britain would have to act quickly or not at all. The longer the conflict lasted, the more likely it was that other European powers would come to the colonists' aid and the more likely it was that Britain's economic and political system would buckle under the strain imposed by hostilities. Finally, any military advantage that the mother country might initially enjoy would be canceled out by the difficulty of sustaining its armies on a distant and hostile continent.[6]

While Britain could expect to be strapped in replacing lost manpower, the rapidly growing colonial population could readily replace men lost to battle or disease. And while Britain would encounter problems in provisioning its armed forces, American farmers could easily feed an army.[7] The last thing the patriot leadership expected was a provision shortage. They did not have access to the statistical information which shows that on the eve of the Revolution the mainland colonies were annually exporting sufficient flour and wheat to feed a force of 240,000.[8] Nonetheless, they believed that the size of their armies and their ability to provision them would be their long suit. During the Seven Years' War the British had experienced difficulty maintaining their forces in North America without colonial assistance.[9] Though Britain could conceivably deploy a large force for a short time, no one thought that it could mobilize more than 100,000 men in a campaign. The North Americans appeared to have the decisive advantage in both numbers and access to provisions.[10]

Recent studies of the Revolutionary War remind us that America's actual military mobilization fell far short of her manpower potential.[11] Even in the early phases of the war, when troops proved relatively easy to raise, Washington repeatedly found himself dangerously short of men. In 1777 the continent formed a "permanent" army of long-term recruits for the duration or for three years, but Washington continued to experience difficulty procuring replacements to compensate for normal attrition during the rest of the war. Rarely throughout the struggle was the Continental Army to enjoy the numerical superiority in battle that the leadership had initially expected.

The discrepancy between military potential and the actual size of the army emerged from the hardships of army life, uncertainties about victory after the defeats of Long Island and New York in 1776, and a progressive war weariness. However, army recruitment seemed more dependent on morale than did economic production. Though farming was hard work, Americans were *routinely* producing sizable agricultural surpluses by the early 1770s. No matter what happened on the battlefield, one still had to make a living. The productivity of a diffuse, agricultural society should have remained roughly constant except in the limited areas directly affected by military operations. The colonists assumed as much and dismissed the idea that Britain's navy could significantly affect the American economy.[12] Had the revolutionaries doubted their economic advantage over Britain they would have been much less enthusiastic about their military prospects in 1775 than in fact they were.

I

THE GRAIN ECONOMY
OF THE REVOLUTION

War shattered the assumptions that Americans had made about the economic and manpower advantages they would enjoy in a showdown with Great Britain. Folklore has romanticized the army as a small and embattled band of patriots neglected by a society whose liberty it tried to defend. The army took the initiative in creating this image, which shifted responsibility for the length of the war onto other shoulders. Lack of public virtue, apathy, and the poor organization of civilian support plagued the revolutionary army.[1]

THE ARMY'S DISTRESS

Folklore has passed on an equally romanticized though less distinct image of the revolutionary economy. Most people who have heard of the terrible winter of 1777–78 at Valley Forge, Pennsylvania, realize that the army's suffering had an economic source. But how many realize that that winter was simply the first of four hard ones that culminated in the mutinies of January 1781; or that the Valley Forge winter was in some ways the easiest of the four? The hardships of 1777–78 originated in the location of the camp. Southeastern Pennsylvania had seen

extensive military operations the preceding summer and autumn, operations that disrupted the normal workings of that region's economy. A
shortage in meat rather than bread accounted for the army's distress.
Though the flow of flour occasionally proved insufficient, the army did
not face across-the-board shortages during the winter of 1778.[2] Moreover, the army's proximity to the grain regions of the Susquehanna
Valley in Pennsylvania and the Chesapeake region of Maryland and the
exertions of state authorities there meant that bread could be used to
compensate for the lack of meat, particularly pork. Thus the commissary
increased the daily flour ration from one pound to a pound and a half in
April, when the region's mills began to grind again and the condition of
the roads had improved after the spring thaw. The commissary also
alleviated the meat crisis by driving cattle from New England across
northern New Jersey to the army, once it again became feasible to cross
the Hudson.[3] Meat would not again be scarce until 1780.

During the two winters after Valley Forge, flour became the commodity in chronically short supply. The shortage could not be alleviated
by the substitution of other grains because it was part of a general
shortage of grains. The replacement of wheat flour with rye, oats, and
barley, which were also used as food for draft animals ("short forage"),
would have affected the quartermaster's ability to transport supplies
overland and thus the mobility of the army. Corn provided the likeliest
substitute for wheat flour, but both cornmeal and rye flour lacked the
keeping qualities of wheat. In addition, this or any other substitution
threatened the army's morale, because the troops preferred wheat flour
to all others, though substituting other grains for wheat was obviously
preferable to going hungry. According to Washington, the grain shortage in general and the flour shortage in particular prevented him from
taking the initiative and on several occasions threatened the army with
dissolution. Matters moved from bad to worse in the summer of 1780,
when the army confronted both a flour shortage and a meat shortage,
which lasted into the spring of 1781. Not until the harvest of 1781 did
the provision shortage ease to the point where the army's very existence
no longer hung in the balance.[4]

The correspondence of the commissary general of purchases, Jeremiah Wadsworth, and his subordinates confirm the picture of agricultural dearth followed by a modest easing of shortages. Wadsworth found 1778–79 to be years of acute scarcity. When Ephraim Blaine succeeded to Wadsworth's office at the end of 1779, he experienced comparable difficulties into 1781. Throughout both men's terms the commissary agents and quartermasters repeatedly complained of the "real" shortages that they confronted.[5] Only when Robert Morris accepted the position of financier general of the Confederation in 1781 and started contracting for army supplies did the sense of recurrent crisis at last wane, though even then problems remained.[6]

How can we be sure that the complaints of the commissariat and quartermasters were not covers for incompetence rather than reflections of real scarcity? In June 1778, General Horatio Gates commented on the anomaly of an army starving in a land "flowing with Plenty & Abundance." The following spring he offered Washington a sinister explanation for it: "I cannot persuade myself there has been any Natural Scarcity of this Article [flour]; Avarice and Monopoly, must have Caused the emptiness of our Magazines of Bread."[7] Suspicions of malfeasance and malpractice focused on the officers in the commissariat and quartermaster departments; in July 1779, Congress authorized the states to investigate their activities.[8] Pressure from the states and Congress led to the resignation of many of the commissary staff but not to an increase in supplies available to the army.[9] Nonetheless, historians continue to entertain suspicions about the administrative competence of the supply services.[10] Such judgments have worked to suppress efforts at assessing what the revolutionary economy was actually producing. While the statistical record is admittedly incomplete, what there is of it nonetheless deserves to be taken into account.

THE ROLE OF GRAINS IN AMERICAN AGRICULTURE

The surviving evidence about the wartime agricultural economy is fragmented at best. In texture it resembles the minute samples of the ocean floor that eighteenth-century mariners were accustomed to picking up with their leadlines when taking soundings on the continental shelf.

Though the small particles of sand, shells, or mud that attached to the waxed declivity at the end of the sinker hardly provided a comprehensive picture of the ocean floor, skilled mariners who knew what to look for could use this meager evidence to determine their position. The survey of the colonial farm economy that follows enables us to make analogous inferences for the revolutionary period from the statistical information that survives. It seeks to clarify the role that grain in general and wheat and flour in particular played in the colonial productive system.

The site of most agricultural production in the late colonial period was the family farm. In 1775, this system successfully fed a domestic population of close to two and a half million.[11] At the same time, it produced sizable surpluses of flour made from wheat, rice, corn, and rye, as well as meat. Every farm family kept some form of livestock, but cattle were prized far more than swine because they yielded dairy products and muscle power in addition to flesh. Farmers primarily interested in supplying the immediate protein needs of the family could let their cattle take care of themselves during the part of the year when grasses naturally grew. They would have to make some provision for feeding their stock either with hay or fodder from their grain crops during the rest of the year, though. Those who specialized in producing meat surpluses for the market used grain supplies to a greater extent. Getting full value for an animal brought to market required fattening, and stallfeeding with grains had become the customary means. Meat viewed from either perspective was often little more than stored grain.[12]

If grain culture was the crux of the agricultural economy, the principal grain crops of the colonial economy were wheat and corn. Farmers could grow both during the same year, planting and harvesting them at different times as a hedge against possible disaster. One crop might succumb to a drought that the other escaped; a storm might catch one in a more vulnerable stage than the other; or one might be afflicted by a parasite that the other was spared. The logic of crop diversification led farmers to grow other grain crops as well: rye, primarily for human consumption, and barley, oats, and buckwheat for feeding humans and animals.[13] However, when forced by the lack of available land or competing schedules to choose between these crops, farmers preferred to grow wheat and corn, though for different reasons.[14]

Wheat emerged as the premier grain for the market because it produced a flour with unsurpassed keeping qualities combined with high nutritional content. When baked, it yielded the lightest, most easily digestible bread and pastry. The high value of wheat flour in relation to volume made it possible to transport it profitably to more distant markets than was the case with rye flour or cornmeal. Wheat flour also suited the army's need for tasty, light, long-lasting provisions, and troops regarded it as a normal perquisite of army life.[15]

Rye flour and cornmeal were as nutritious as wheat, but they made coarser breads. Corn also took longer to mill into meal than wheat did to grind into flour. In consequence, millers paid cash for wheat but not for corn. Rye, whose growing season overlapped with that of wheat, was a hardier plant. Farmers grew it on marginal soils as a hedge against the failure of more desirable crops. Because corn was less susceptible to spoilage when transported on the ear or as kernels, it had less market reach than wheat flour. As a result, wheat fetched half again as much as rye and more than twice as much as corn in commercial markets. However, when grains were in short supply, the price of rye and corn could approach that of wheat.[16]

Colonial farmers grew corn as well as wheat because of corn's other attributes. Though corn was less prized in the market, it yielded more grain per acre than wheat, and its stalk and leaves, called "stover," provided excellent forage for livestock.[17] Corn also grew in a wide variety of soils and in fields that had been only partially cleared. Finally, corn was more resistant to drought and disease than wheat or the other grains. Its versatility and usefulness in feeding both humans and stock made it the leading grain produced and consumed in the colonial domestic economy.

This agricultural system was a success in the sense that the overseas export of farm commodities did not lead to domestic shortages. Though local food deficits occasionally arose, they were met by the transfer of domestic surpluses. So far as I know, there are no recorded instances of starvation in the late colonial period. That enables us to derive rough estimates about quantities produced based on population and trade statistics for 1770. In that year the total population of the colonies had been slightly in excess of 2 million. A population of that size would have required about 19.3 million bushels of grain to feed it throughout the year.[18] The colonial economy in 1770 also exported the equivalent of roughly 5.7 million bushels of grain,[19] bringing total production of all grains for human consumption to about 25 million bushels.[20] Exports came to 22.7 percent of all grains consumed by humans, but exported grain enjoyed a significance out of proportion to its limited share of total production for reasons that will become apparent from the analysis of the market that follows.

While Americans consumed most of the grain produced in the colonial economy, few households were self-sufficient. Instead, they traded with their neighbors for what they did not produce themselves. Farmers who produced more grains than they needed in any year would exchange their surpluses locally with other farmers who had different surpluses, with local laborers who supported themselves by selling their labor, or with the local storekeeper, who might also be the miller. Satisfying the domestic demand for breadstuffs, then, depended on trade between neighbors. The colonists recorded these myriad transactions as credits and debts in their individual account books. Debts and credits could remain outstanding for years before being settled. Trading based on book credit attached a higher premium to maintaining equilibrium between local supply and demand and to preserving a cooperative spirit among neighbors than to expanding production beyond the immediate needs of the locality.[21]

Colonists also traded grain surpluses long-distance, responding to impersonal demand beyond the community. Some of the long-distance trade catered to regional and urban, domestic demand. As the urban areas matured, they increasingly relied on producers in their expanding hinterlands for grain and other agricultural supplies.[22] In the early 1750s, the most densely populated towns of eastern and southern New England had begun importing substantial quantities of flour and rice from the middle and southern colonies to compensate for grain deficits that developed in their region.[23] Other urban areas followed their example, though their greater proximity to grain regions enabled them to tap supplies closer to home. Total urban demand for grains on the eve of the Revolution came to just under 6 percent of the 1770 production for human consumption.[24] Assuming that at least half of this demand was satisfied through long-distance channels, the proportion of grains produced for consumption beyond the local market probably accounted for about a quarter of total grain production consumed by humans.[25]

The colonists organized the long-distance grain economy differently from their local economy. New mechanisms were required to enable it to respond sensitively to variations in demand, and these in turn gave it a greater dynamism than the community-centered, local economy possessed.[26] The contrast between the local and long-distance grain trade is best illustrated by looking at the flour milling industry.

Nearly every area of European settlement had a local gristmill to which farmers brought grain to be custom ground. The limited capitalization of most custom mills, the need to process rye and corn as well as wheat, together with seasonal factors affecting the water supply, restricted the volume of the wheat flour that could be produced by them. The production of flour for long-distance exchange and particularly for export centered in merchant mills that were larger, more heavily capitalized, and increasingly specialized.[27]

The difference between a merchant and custom mill was one of degree as much as kind. Most merchant mills had started as custom mills, and the colonial and state governments often compelled merchant mills to set aside certain days for custom work. Mills that acquired the designation "merchant" did so because they catered to the demand of merchants in the principal ports. These merchants enabled certain millers to specialize in flour by placing orders for large parcels of it and paying in cash. That in turn allowed the millers to offer cash to the primary producers and grain brokers who delivered wheat to their mills. Cash became the badge of this export-oriented economy for the simple reason that farmers would thresh and haul their grain to landings and mills and even increase their wheat acreage to obtain it.[28]

Cash gave farmers choices they did not enjoy when they traded with neighbors alone. Beyond opening up access to a range of products that could not be produced locally, it freed one from the web of mutual indebtedness and allowed more choices in the selection of trading partners. In other words, it allowed producers to seek the best bargains in that wider, impersonal market of which the export of agricultural surpluses formed the principal part. Of course, few in this age would have welcomed total release from the support and obligations that the community conferred. Local producers could participate in both economies through the mediation of a storekeeper or miller who traded goods produced in distant locations for local surpluses. The storekeeper found cash just as useful in commanding those exotic consumer goods in distant markets as the farmer might. So the merchant miller's ability to offer cash for wheat served to draw wheat to the mill site whether it came directly from the farmer or indirectly from the local merchant, often over considerable distances. Cash became the instrument that regulated the orderly flow of wheat toward the larger merchant mills, allowing them to respond sensitively to signals about distant demand transmitted by the merchants in the commercial centers.[29]

Merchant mills dotted the water courses most resistant to seasonal droughts, which plagued the operations of the smaller, custom mills. The most important merchant mills were close to landings where watercraft could transport the flour produced to distant markets at minimal cost. Early in the eighteenth century Philadelphia emerged as the center of an expanding trade in flour produced by merchant mills along the Delaware and nearby Wissahickon Rivers. Later on, a large concentration of merchant mills appeared on the banks of the Brandywine River, near its junction with the Delaware. This location was particularly advantageous because it gave riverine access to the entire Delaware–northern Chesapeake producing area, as well as to the Philadelphia market. The Brandywine milling complex confirmed rather than challenged the premier role that Philadelphia had come to play in the long-distance flour trade. On the eve of the Revolution the city accounted for roughly 56 percent of the wheat and flour exported by the North American colonies. A similar proximity of mill sites to river systems and emerging trading centers accounts for the rise of New York and to a lesser extent Baltimore as secondary centers of the flour trade at the end of the colonial period.[30]

Grain Production in the Primary Producing Areas

The merchants who organized the continental commissariat responsible for feeding the army understood the workings of the long-distance grain economy of the late colonial period. Though they had occupied marginal positions in this system during the prewar period, they tried to keep as much of it intact as possible to support the Revolution. Naturally men like Jeremiah Wadsworth hoped the preeminent emporium of the prewar grain trade would help them out. But when in 1778–79 Wadsworth turned to his deputy commissar for purchasers in Philadelphia—the recent immigrant from England, John Chaloner—he was disappointed. Chaloner had entered into a partnership with another Philadelphia merchant, James White. The firm's records show that it was able to purchase only 3,344 barrels of flour on continental account made from wheat harvested in 1778. In addition the firm bought 4,666 bushels of wheat of that harvest plus a small parcel of loose bread, for a total of just over 4,000 barrels of flour. The partnership was even less successful with the harvest of 1779, purchasing only 3,364 barrels of flour between August and March 1780, when their continental activities ceased. In the early 1770s Philadelphia had exported the equivalent of over 300,000 barrels of flour a year.[31] Chaloner and White had experienced difficulty in scraping together a little more than 1 percent of the flour annually available in the city's prewar market.

Were the difficulties faced by the commissariat part of a general shortage? Two flour ledgers kept by Levi Hollingsworth of Philadelphia suggest that they were. Hollingsworth was one of eleven sons born to a prominent Cecil County landholder in northeastern Maryland. Levi began his career as a Bay sloop captain, but the father soon established him as a flour merchant in Philadelphia. In that capacity he became the leading figure in an extended mercantile family. Two of his brothers, Jesse and Henry, married into prominent milling families in the area. Thomas joined Jesse in establishing a merchant partnership in Baltimore, where they acted as Levi's correspondents.[32] Henry remained closer to home, taking charge of a store at Head of Elk, which Samuel and Zebulon now and then helped him run. The store stood at the northernmost point of navigation on the Chesapeake, from which vantage point they could supervise the movement of supplies over the short land carriage to Christiana Bridge, at the head of a navigable tributary of the Delaware.

Levi's access to the northern Chesapeake through his brothers had made him a major player in Philadelphia's flour economy before the war. He received flour from individuals, usually millers, which he either bought himself or sold to third parties for money or goods, charging a commission for his services. While he remained active in the provisions trade throughout the Revolution, between 1777 and 1780 when imports were scarce, he ran a local flour exchange in the city. Only occasionally during the war did he or his brothers encourage millers to produce flour by organizing contracts at specified cash prices.[33]

Table 1.1 tabulates estimates of the flour that Hollingsworth received during the harvest years (mid-August to mid-August) of 1776–81 and compares them with estimates of the amount of flour he handled from harvest 1773. The table suggests that the war years saw a considerable decline in the amount of flour coming to the Philadelphia market and that the worst shortages occurred in 1778–79. Figures for harvest 1777 are omitted because the British occupation of Philadelphia disrupted Hollingsworth's business from September 1777 through June 1778. The small quantities of new flour that came to him during the few weeks before the British occupation and the two months between the enemy's departure and when harvest 1778 became available do not permit meaningful comparison with full harvest years. However, other data drawn from the hinterland that Hollingsworth serviced before the war suggest that harvest 1777 was particularly thin.[34] His business records confirm the claims of commissary agents that, at least between 1778 and the beginning of 1781, they were victims of Philadelphia's market.[35]

The Hollingsworth data is at best suggestive. How significant, after all, are the accounts of one man when we are unable to ascertain what share of the market his business commanded? While exact measurements elude us, there are indications that if we have no choice but to take our bearings from the tip of the iceberg, the Hollingsworth accounts are not a bad place to look. First, Hollingsworth's prewar volume came to roughly 6 percent of Philadelphia's total wheat, bread, and flour exports.

Table 1.1. Estimated Flour Received by Levi Hollingsworth
During Harvest Years 1776–81

Amounts expressed as a percentage of flour received from harvest 1773
(superfine, common, middlings, and stuff).

Harvest year	1776	1777	1778	1779	1780	1781
Estimated percentage	48.5	—	14.4	16.7	52.8	67.8

Sources: Flour Ledger, 1774, no. 595, Flour Ledger, 1777–80, no. 598, and Flour Journal, 1777–81, no. 540, in Hollingsworth Family Papers, Business Records, HSP. For procedures, see appendix.

Then, though Hollingsworth failed directly to supply Chaloner and White with any wheat or flour from the 1778 harvest, he was their third largest supplier of 1779 wheat and flour.[36] The citizenry of Philadelphia certainly regarded Hollingsworth as significant enough to arrest for withholding during the severe shortages that plagued the local market that year.[37] He also emerged from the war as one of the city's more successful merchants, and it seems unlikely that he would have done so well had the sharp decline of his receipts for flour from 1777–79 been a personal rather than general misfortune.

Did Philadelphia's experience reflect widespread production declines in these years, or was the dearth evident in its market simply a local anomaly? It is not hard to see why Philadelphia's position as the foremost flour market of the mid-Atlantic states should have slipped in 1777–79. The British occupation of the city between September 1777 and June 1778 inevitably disrupted its flour trade long after the enemy evacuation. Before we can tie the fortunes of Philadelphia's market to actual levels of farm production, we need a more direct way of assessing that production.

Milling accounts provide a closer measure of actual production, as millers were the key intermediaries between the farm and the long-distance market. Indeed, many of Levi Hollingsworth's correspondents were millers. Most of the surviving mill accounts either come from small customs operations or are incomplete.[38] There is one significant exception, though, and that is the records of the prosperous Brandywine miller Thomas Lea. Lea had married the daughter of Joseph Tatnall, a Quaker entrepreneur credited with spearheading the expansion of the Brandywine as a milling center by constructing a mill race on the north side of the stream in the early 1770s. Tatnall in turn was a distant relative of Thomas Shipley, another Quaker who had constructed a mill race on the south bank of the stream in the 1760s. The Leas joined other prominent Quaker families—including the Canbys, the Mortons, and the Pooles—in forming a milling oligarchy that would dominate the area for well over a century.[39]

Thomas Lea's Daybook and Journal covers the interval from February 20, 1775, through September 27, 1783. It purports to record all his business transactions on a day-by-day basis throughout the war, and is to my knowledge the only such record that survives. On closer inspection it turns out that the Daybook and Journal is incomplete, but a separate Ledger covering 1773–87 allows us to fill in some of the omissions. Taken together the two documents provide us with an unparalleled, though not unproblematic, view of economic activity in the Delmarva Peninsula, between the lower Delaware and the northern Chesapeake, during the war years.[40]

Lea's accounts record the flow of grain through his establishment during the war. The pattern that emerges from them, as tabulated in table 1.2, is congruent with the experience of Hollingsworth for the period 1776–82. But the values in the mill account, as well as the total of the mill and custom accounts for 1774–75, deviate from the pattern of prewar prosperity followed by decline identified in the sources previously discussed. Harvest 1774 appears to have been a lean one at Lea's mill compared with harvest 1775, even after correcting for the fact that the 1774 accounts cover no more than half the harvest year. Lea may have responded to the threat of Congress's nonexportation in 1775 by processing, in a way that does not find reflection in the surviving records, as much grain as possible from harvest 1774 as quickly as possible.[41] Entries for freights paid by the mill and for the number of bushels of wheat measured in the surviving accounts for that harvest suggest considerably more activity for the harvest year. The relatively modest flow of wheat from harvest 1775 is probably related to the construction of a

Table 1.2. Amount of Wheat Brought Each Harvest Year to the Mill of Thomas Lea, Brandywine Creek, in Bushels

	1774	1775	1776	1777	1778	1779	1780	1781	1782
Mill account*	2519	11960	24000	7974	7420	7533	20460‡	51761	49084
Custom account†	35	118	989	995	6215	—	790	6571	187
total	2554	12078	24989	8969	13635	7533	21250	57939	49271

*Bushels of wheat bought by the mill for grinding on Lea's and his partners' account. †Bushels of wheat brought to the mill as "custom" grain. ‡8020 bushels of this wheat ground by Joseph Tatnall; see appendix.
Source: Thomas Lea's Daybook and Journal, February 20, 1775–September 27, 1783, supplemented by Thomas Lea's Ledger, 1773–87, both in HSD.

new facility to which there are many references in the Daybook and Journal. The expansion of the mill's wheat account during harvest 1776 suggests an effort on Lea's part to earn a return on his recent investment as well as to respond to wartime domestic demand. The overall drop in the mill's wheat account between 1777 and 1779, and the robust expansion, beginning in 1780 and consummated in 1781–82, parallels our measures of Philadelphia's market discussed above.

The bulge in total wheat received at the mill during harvest 1778 requires explanation. The best way to read the display in table 1.2 is to construe harvest 1777 as an anomaly and to compare harvest 1778 with harvest 1776. Harvest 1777 was anomalous because Washington shut down all the Brandywine mills for most of the harvest year to deny the enemy access to the region's supplies while the British remained in Philadelphia.[42] Lea did not begin to collect wheat from harvest 1777 until July 1778. A dramatic expansion took place in the mill's custom work between October 1778 and August 1779. It depended principally upon the custom grinding of 4,071 bushels for Francis Wade, a military purchaser. Wade disappeared from the mill's accounts after harvest 1778 with the collapse of the supply services.[43] Viewed from this perspective harvest 1779 emerges as the bottom of the production cycle. The Lea records point unambiguously to a dramatic revival in production during 1781. Here the abrupt decline in price accompanying the sharp increase in the volume of wheat brought to the mill confirms that we are looking at more than an atypical development particular to one mill or group of millers.[44]

Though the Delmarva Peninsula in particular and the northern Chesapeake in general may have fared marginally better than did the Philadelphia area in the harvest of 1778, the evidence from the Lea accounts suggests that the harvests of 1778–80 were thin compared to that of 1781.[45] This region's experience, then, roughly paralleled the ebb and flow of Hollingsworth's fortunes in Philadelphia. Since under normal circumstances Philadelphia served as an emporium for the entire region, the congruence of the two series is not surprising. But we are still seeing only measures of wheat brought to market rather than actual production at the farm level. To find a better measure of the latter we shall have to turn elsewhere.

The northern grain-producing region in the Hudson-Mohawk valleys had no tradition of commercial dependence on Philadelphia before the Revolution. Did its grain economy during the war resemble that of the Pennsylvania–northern Chesapeake region? Though the evidence for the war economy of this region is even more limited than that which survives from the Philadelphia-Chesapeake region, the few business records that remain suggest that it did. The most significant of these is the Livingston Manor rent ledger for the war years.[46]

In 1686 the governor of New York, Thomas Dongan, had issued Robert Livingston a patent to 160,000 acres of land along the Hudson. When he died in 1728, 141,000 acres of the original grant, known as Livingston Manor, passed first to his eldest surviving son and then in 1749 to his grandson, Robert Jr. (1708–90). At the time of the American Revolution slightly more than three hundred farm families held leases to manor lands. Most had their principal rent specified in bushels of wheat. Since the rent ledger begins in the 1760s, it provides us with a useful comparison between prewar and wartime behavior. Though it measures only rents paid rather than total production, the two were not unrelated.[47]

The total rent due in any year as specified in the leases for manor lands came to 7,215 bushels of wheat. Even in the best of years the lord of the manor never received more than 80 percent of what was owed him, nor

Table 1.3. Rents Received Between 1773 and 1783 from Tenants of
Livingston Manor

Amounts expressed as a percentage of rents due by calendar year.

1773	1774	1775	1776	1777	1778	1779	1780	1781	1782	1783
78.5	75.4	73.8	45.2	39.3	32.6	29.4	34.1	73.7	56.6	72.2

Source: Livingston Manor Rent Ledger, 1767–1784, Livingston Family Papers, reel 53,
New-York Historical Society.

did he expect perfect compliance. Initially the proprietor had had to
supply tools and stock and to suspend rent for a number of years to
attract tenants. He was willing to do so because he valued the improvements that tenants produced more than the immediate income they
might yield. Fending off assaults on the manorial title by Massachusetts
interests during the 1750s and the rent riots of 1766 led him to place the
good will of his tenants ahead of the punctual collection of rents, as long
as tenants showed a willingness to settle and the arrears did not exceed
the value of the improvements. A few tenants paid regularly, and about
an equal number were always delinquent. The rest paid in varying
amounts, depending on their agricultural fortunes. This is why the
ledger is the richest source of information about economic activity in
the upper Hudson Valley during the revolutionary period.

Table 1.3 tabulates by calendar year the percentage of total rents in
wheat received from the tenants of Livingston Manor during the war.[48] It
suggests that the fortunes of the Hudson were similar to those of the
Delaware-Chesapeake grain region. In both production seems to have
bottomed out somewhere in the 1778–79 period, and then to have revived in 1781. In both there seems to have been a genuine shortage of
wheat and flour in the same years that the army experienced the greatest
deprivation.

Grain Production in Less Specialized Regions

The regions that specialized in producing surplus wheat in the late colonial economy may have experienced a pattern of declining production

followed by modest revival during the war years, but what about the other areas of the colonial economy?

Every region produced some grain surpluses. Though New England in the late colonial period had ceased to be self-sufficient in grains and its farmers no longer cultivated wheat as a major staple, some continued to grow wheat for export, for the local market, and for personal consumption. At the beginning of the war, Joseph Trumbull relied heavily on Connecticut wheat to supply the troops around Boston. In 1775 the army did not find Connecticut wanting as a breadbasket because producers had concluded from the 1774 military reoccupation of Boston and the Medford alarm that the demand for bread was likely to be high in the region during the following year and acted accordingly. Jeremiah Wadsworth, in charge of the Connecticut end of Trumbull's supply line, complained that the problem was less one of finding flour than of restraining the impetuosity of local producers. "Our farmers still clamor about the flower [*sic*] and are determined to get every man his own and make me their Pack-Horse."[49]

However, Connecticut's bountifulness lasted only through the harvest of 1775. The harvest of 1776 was seriously compromised by the massive militia mobilization of that summer, which also interfered with seeding the crop for 1777. By the autumn of 1776 the commissariat was turning increasingly to the Hudson Valley and the Delaware-Chesapeake regions for supplies of bread.[50] Congress's reorganization of the procurement services during 1777 confirmed the trend. William Buchanan of Baltimore replaced Joseph Trumbull as commissary general.[51] Buchanan lasted less than a year, being replaced in April 1778 by Trumbull's former deputy, Jeremiah Wadsworth. The new commissary general realized immediately that he would have to turn elsewhere for the army's bread, leaving his home region to specialize in meat.[52] That autumn he found himself sponsoring the shipment of flour by sea from the mid-Atlantic states to New England, despite the risk of enemy seizure, to alleviate a regional grain shortage.[53] Attempts to revive New England's wheat production in subsequent years made little headway.

Of the remaining secondary grain producing areas, that of New Jersey was the most significant. During the colonial period New Jersey had been a divided colony. West Jersey facing on the Delaware was part of Philadelphia's hinterland, and its economic fortunes were tied to that city. East Jersey had been part of New York's hinterland. The portion of the state east and south of the high ground known as First Mountain, which runs from modern Paterson southwest into Somerset County, fared particularly badly during the war. It had been a major source of flour for the New York market before 1776, serviced by merchant mills located at New Brunswick and in northern Monmouth County. American forces were not strong enough to secure the area against repeated British incursions after 1776, such as the surprise raid by the 72nd Queen's Rangers under Colonel John Simcoe's command on October 26, 1779, against supplies warehoused for the army at Raritan. This portion of the state came to resemble a no-man's land where no government's writ ran and banditry flourished.[54] The resulting insecurity felt by the local population discouraged producers from aiming much beyond survival.

This was also the case in the no-man's land around New York City in modern Westchester County. The American and British armies competed for what surpluses these areas afforded with periodic foraging expeditions. But in this competition the British had the additional advantage of a well-stocked market in New York so that whatever was available more often than not ended up in their hands rather than in those of the Continental Army.[55]

At the end of the colonial period the southern Chesapeake, including the tidewater and piedmont, had been following the lead of the northern Chesapeake into cereal production; some estimated that the region exported the equivalent of more than 40,000 barrels of flour per year.[56] One might have expected that, with the wartime interruption of the tobacco trade, the transition to wheat culture, already evident before the beginning of the war, would have accelerated. Virginia seemed to have considerable potential as a wheat producer, and at the beginning of 1778, the commissariat assumed that it, together with Maryland and Delaware, could cover any shortages arising from deficiencies of supply in the more northerly states. However, their high hopes for the Virginia harvest of 1778 were dashed. The commissary blamed their disappointment on the Hessian fly, which had spread from Long Island in 1777 and whose full force began to be felt in 1778.[57] Thereafter Virginia became a corn economy until late in the war.

The correspondence of James Hunter Jr., who ran a commission store at Fredericksburg, records this change. Before the war Hunter had traded tobacco for foreign goods. After the commencement of hostilities he tried to fill orders placed with him for wheat and corn by the deputy commissary of purchases in Virginia, William Aylett. Up to the beginning of 1778 his accounts mention batches of flour, though with decreasing frequency. Thereafter, such references entirely disappear from his correspondence until the harvest of 1781. In the interval, corn rather than flour received his attention. The diary of Robert Honeyman, a recent immigrant to tidewater Virginia who observed the revolutionary struggle with more detachment than many, also reflects this change. In describing a provision shortage affecting Virginia during 1778–79, he refers to the rising price of Indian corn. Though wheat did not entirely disappear from the Virginia economy during the war years, its poor quality reduced its value in relation to corn.[58]

Virginia's shift from wheat to corn during the war years might have occurred even without the intervention of the Hessian fly. The records of Robert Carter of Nomini Hall illustrate why. Carter was the grandson of Robert "King" Carter, the richest and most prominent Virginian among his generation during the early years of the eighteenth century. Carter had been the first member of Virginia's Creole aristocracy to realize that the family's fortunes depended on the acquisition of new lands. As a consequence, his grandson Robert inherited an enormous landed estate when his father, Robert Jr., died young. At the time of the Revolution he owned over 70,000 acres of land in seven Virginia counties stretching from the Northern Neck, where most of his holdings were concentrated, to Richmond. No one in Virginia was in a better position to produce wheat surpluses. He had raised wheat before the war, and in 1773 he invested heavily in building a new merchant mill capable of grinding 25,000 bushels a year.[59]

Carter's correspondence in 1775 and 1776 suggests a heavy involvement in both wheat and flour through the harvest of 1776. Thereafter, references to both decline dramatically. That does not mean that Carter's plantations entirely eschewed growing wheat or that he had no further dealings in that grain.[60] However, during the fall of 1776 he twice limited his overseers' discretion in planting wheat. At the beginning of 1777, he ordered several others to plant Indian corn and oats rather than wheat.[61] For the next four years corn remained Carter's principal grain crop. In 1780 his wheat production had fallen to the point where he doubted he could supply his family's needs from the current crop. Only in 1781 did Carter authorize the planting of substantial quantities of the grain. The first mention of a parcel of wheat remotely resembling what had been routine in 1775 comes in connection with the prospective harvest of 1782.[62]

Carter had reasons for shifting to corn from wheat well before the Hessian fly took its toll. He responded to the prospect of declining access to overseas markets by quitting the long-distance market for flour. Carter saw isolation from foreign markets as a threat to his capacity to provide the customary annual clothing allowances to his extensive slave force. To cope with the situation he pursued a wartime strategy of striving for self-sufficiency in the manufacture of clothing, though with mixed success.[63] Having "his people" make their own clothing freed him from having to depend on outside sources of supply, but it also required a redeployment of his resources.

Carter was too much of an entrepreneur to withdraw entirely from the marketplace. He had a substantial stake in a Baltimore ironworks, whose products remained in high demand throughout the war. Indeed, iron proved to be one of his more successful hedges against wartime inflation. However, since adjustments had to be made to the shrinking prospects for international trade, he preferred producing tobacco instead of wheat for export, since tobacco had a longer storage life. He placed his remaining acreage in corn and small grains other than wheat. The Hessian fly simply confirmed the wisdom of a choice made before the appearance of that infestation. Even if the fly had never materialized, Carter's plantations would not have been able to provide grain for the army during the critical war years, except when the troops were close enough to provision them with corn.[64] To the extent that other large plantation owners acted as Carter did, Virginia could not live up to either the commissary's expectations or its potential as a bread basket for the continent. The same influences shaping Virginia's grain production also affected North Carolina.[65]

Could wheat grown in the frontier areas have been used to supplement short supplies in the more established grain producing regions? The British invasion of 1777–78 had less effect on the backcountry's wheat production in Pennsylvania than it had on exposed areas like Chester County.[66] However, any special advantage that interior areas derived from their location was canceled out by the difficulty of collecting surpluses from widely scattered settlements. It was much more expensive to assemble parcels of grain where the population was spread out than where it was concentrated nearer the coastal seaports. The difficulties faced by the commissariat increased still further as the deepening grain crisis affected the price of all cereals and thereby increased transportation costs.[67]

The isolation of interior areas also failed to insulate them from the effect of market forces. Word about price increases traveled quickly over long distances. Interior producers learned that demand was rising when purchasers for the quartermaster and commissary departments, seeking to lessen competition in the more developed areas, approached them. Instead of a free hand with producers, public purchasers found themselves contending with distillers, who were prepared to stay ahead of the market to assure access to customary supplies. Farmers here, as elsewhere, had little incentive to sell for anything but the highest price because of the steady decline of the currency and the expectation that prices would rise still further. Continental purchasers found it difficult to procure grain unless they gave in to market forces, even to the point of allowing producers to claim in their contracts the rise of the market to the time of delivery. When such terms were refused they found the farmers reluctant to honor past contracts and unwilling to enter new ones.[68]

The interior producing areas had earlier behaved as isolated regional markets at best. Under the pressure of the grain crisis of 1778–80 they achieved partial integration with the larger national market that the commissariat was trying to create.[69] However, they did so only when circumstances permitted. It did not take much to neutralize what little potential the interior had for cushioning the more settled areas against shortages. One Indian raid could throw a frontier on the defensive, making it hoard its supplies for local needs. The threat of another raid usually ensured that the entire region would remain neutralized.[70]

THE RICE ECONOMY OF THE LOWER SOUTH

On the eve of the Revolutionary War rice ranked fourth in value among colonial exports, with South Carolina and Georgia exporting between them about 150,000 barrels annually—the equivalent of approximately 37 percent of colonial grain exports, largely to southern Europe.[71] Enslaved Africans grew the entire export crop in tidewater plantations along the Atlantic coast. Roughly 14 percent of total rice exports came from Georgia, the rest from South Carolina.[72] While rice possesses excellent keeping qualities and high nutritional value, its bulkiness made it expensive to transport except by water.[73] Still, 150,000 barrels of rice could have supplied the basic grain ration for over 160,000 men per year, allowing for wastage.[74] Despite the enormous cost of transporting it to the northern theaters of operations, rice was occasionally used to reduce the army's dependence on flour in times of shortage.[75] Could the commissariat not have made more of this resource?

Several problems plagued harnessing peacetime rice production in the deep South to wartime needs aside from the difficulty that large plantation owners encountered in providing their enslaved laborers with annual clothing allowances.[76] The producing areas along the coastline were especially vulnerable to the enemy's naval superiority. The approach of any British force understandably strengthened the impulse of the slaves to run away, while actual raids destroyed whatever remained of the overseer's discipline.[77] Then, because rice was produced almost entirely for the export market, the peacetime price of clean rice in the Charleston market depended primarily on the availability of shipping. Since Charleston's merchants acted as the agents of entrepreneurs in other ports rather than conducting enterprises on their own account, they began the war without sufficient tonnage to transport the crop to overseas markets.[78] Congressional nonexportation in 1775 also discouraged rice production.

Nonetheless, South Carolina experienced a tenuous, wartime boom after the failure of General Sir William Howe's attack on Charleston in May 1776. Local entrepreneurs quickly realized that a profitable commerce with the French and Dutch West Indies was possible in small, fast sailing vessels. The production of both rice and indigo picked up as imports from the islands and even from Europe became more available in Charleston than in other parts of the continent thanks to the combined enterprise of American and French adventurers. Charleston briefly became a continental center for the wartime island trade, attracting such ambitious commercial agents as Elkanah Watson from Boston, Abraham Livingston from New York, and Jacques Plombard from the French West Indies.[79]

However, the deep South's distance from the principal centers of military demand in the north compromised the region's capacity to contribute to the war economy. Southern staples could move north only by sea. The deep South's wartime prosperity also depended on the northward focus of enemy operations. After Britain began operations against Georgia and South Carolina at the end of 1778, its so-called southern strategy, the coastal waters between New York and Charleston became infested with enemy privateers. This happened just when the North most needed the rice of the deep South to relieve its grain shortages. Shipments were attempted both on private and on public account, particularly during the spring of 1779; enough vessels got through to southern New England to persuade Horatio Gates, the commander-in-chief of the Eastern Department, that the substitution of rice for flour might temporarily solve the provision problem of the troops under his command. However, the loss rate on these voyages remained high and contributed to the stifling of any remaining potential the region possessed for supplying patriot needs.[80] The invasion of Georgia and South Carolina also progressively disrupted the slave economy of these two states.[81] The failure of the French expeditionary force under D'Estaing to take Savannah in October 1779 sealed the fate of the region six months before Charleston actually surrendered and brought an abrupt end to what was left of the rice economy. The completion of the British conquest of Georgia and South Carolina in 1780 meant that the deep South would not contribute to the revival of agriculture that took place in the more northern states in the last years of the war.

FRENCH PROVISIONING PROBLEMS IN 1778–79

The problems that John Holker, the agent for France's Royal Marine, encountered in supplying D'Estaing's expeditionary force during 1778–79 confirm the commissariat's claim that it confronted real shortages in these years.[82] Beginning in 1778 the French and the continental commissariats competed for supplies in North America, with the French enjoying a decisive advantage. French officials possessed specie and bills of exchange on Europe, and they had few scruples about outbidding continental agents. If supplies were available, the French succeeded in getting them and the American army went short.[83] Yet during the first two campaigns of the alliance (1778 and 1779), the French remained as hobbled by the American economy as the continental commissariat.

When Jeremiah Wadsworth became commissary general in 1778, he assured Congress that he would be able to provide for an army of 81,000 men, which he estimated would require 203,000 barrels of flour.[84] In fact, throughout 1778 he never had to provide for more than 43,000 in the army and should have been able to feed them together with the navy with roughly half that amount of flour by cutting back on wastage. The Convention Army, which General Burgoyne had surrendered at Saratoga, did become an additional, unwanted responsibility after the British abandoned attempting to provision it on learning of D'Estaing's approach to North America in the spring of 1778. During the following autumn its presence in the Boston area together with the French expeditionary force's two-month refit there taxed the region's resources to the limit.[85] Congress urged D'Estaing to turn to the Chesapeake for the resupply he sought. It ordered Wadsworth to collect 18,000 barrels of flour in the Bay for the French expeditionary force in hopes of easing the pressure on New England's limited grain supplies.[86] Instead, D'Estaing took some five thousand barrels from Philadelphia together with more than two thousand barrels that his especially appointed agents collected for him in the Boston area. His action compounded Wadsworth's difficulties in New England and simply postponed to the next spring—the short season in an agricultural economy—compliance with the original requisition. A congressional committee appointed to estimate military demand and available supply reported the following May that given D'Estaing's needs, the continent would come up about 10,000 barrels short until wheat from the new harvest became available in the middle of August.[87]

During the summer of 1779 the shortage was absorbed by the reduction of manpower levels in the army, and, thanks to the timely arrival of a large French convoy of merchantmen in the West Indies, by the curtailment of American grain shipments to the islands.[88] Meanwhile, the new crop promised well, and the commissary expected to procure 200,000 barrels of flour, which would permit the army to expand for combined operations with the French.[89] Nothing heroic could be attempted before the next harvest in July, however, which may have figured in D'Estaing's decision to linger in the West Indies until the end of the summer. In the interim the agent commissioned by Holker to buy flour for the French fleet in the Delaware valley had to suspend his activities after running afoul of the popular committees around Philadelphia.[90] Seriously embarrassed and doubtful that the incident would soon be forgotten, Holker looked beyond Philadelphia and its environs for a source of future supplies.

Maryland was Holker's best hope since that state, incensed by Virginia's sale of western lands that Maryland regarded as the property of all the states, had resolved to sell provisions to the French independently of congressional authorization.[91] Nonetheless, French agents proceeded cautiously until October, when, just before D'Estaing's expected arrival, Holker learned that his Baltimore agent, William Smith, had lent the flour he had collected to the continental commissariat to help them out of their difficulties. Afraid that he would be caught empty-handed when D'Estaing demanded flour for his force, Holker now put pressure on Smith to lay in as large a supply as possible.[92]

The consequent aggressiveness of French purchasing agents in Maryland contributed to a precipitous price rise for wheat and flour in the greater Chesapeake from October through December. In the Philadelphia market, prices would ordinarily have stabilized or declined as the new harvest became available; instead, the price of common flour more than quadrupled from August to December.[93] In Virginia the same thing seems to have happened, though the time interval was longer. News of French purchases put upward pressure on prices throughout the entire region, leaving continental agents outbid on every side.[94] By the end of December the Continental Army was in a woeful plight, and in response to Washington's representations of their distress, Maryland's government ordered that all flour purchased by anyone other than a continental agent be seized throughout the state. The government claimed that impostors posing as French agents had exceeded the limit of 8,000 barrels of flour that the state had previously set on French purchasing.[95]

There is no way to know for certain how much flour had in fact been collected for the French, but it could not have been more than 20,000 barrels and was probably a good deal less.[96] However, there is no doubt that the activity of French agents in procuring a comparatively small parcel had set off a general scramble among speculators that had an immediate, devastating impact on prices in the entire region. Twenty thousand barrels of flour came to no more than 11 percent of Maryland's prewar exportable surplus and to less than 5 percent of the entire region's prewar surplus.[97] For a parcel of that size to set off such a price explosion suggests an extraordinary constriction in normal supplies, not just in Maryland but throughout the entire region. State embargoes on the export of provisions played little role in this price rise because there was no effective way to stop the wheat or flour flowing from Virginia to Maryland or from Delaware to Maryland if it had been available. Indeed, the general rise in wheat and flour prices across state lines highlights the ineffectiveness of these embargoes. That the regional economy could not absorb a demand on its production that came to no more than a twentieth of its prewar surplus points directly to a general collapse in the principal grain region of the infant republic.

THE BEGINNING OF THE WAR

Why did key agricultural surpluses that American farmers had routinely produced in the late colonial period become unavailable in the late 1770s? One possibility is that the wartime diversion of men from the farm to the armed forces curtailed production. Only when the soldiers returned from the army could normal production resume. Another possibility is that the market failed to attract agricultural surpluses when and where they were needed. Both the availability of labor and the operations of the market contributed to the ups and downs of revolutionary agriculture. However, the force levels of the army suggest that manpower shortages could have affected agricultural production critically only in the second and third years of the conflict. During the worst years of agricultural shortages, 1778 to 1780, the army shrank steadily, indicating that influences besides the availability of labor were critical. That is why I concentrate on factors affecting the long-distance markets, both domestic and overseas, and note only in passing the effect that raising the army had on production.

DIMINISHED ACCESS TO OVERSEAS MARKETS

The Revolutionary War began with Britain and its colonies agreed on one point: America should halt its overseas trade. The revolutionaries initially regarded their trade as a weapon with which to avoid full-scale war. The colonists had previously developed nonimportation and nonconsumption as strategies for resisting Parliament's attempts to raise an American revenue in the Stamp Act (1765) and Townshend Duties (1767). Commercial pressures had contributed to the repeal of the Stamp Act (1766) and the partial repeal of the Townshend Duties (1770). Both efforts had convinced Americans that the mother country was dependent on their trade.[1]

In October 1774, the first Continental Congress launched a continental nonimport, nonexport, and nonconsumption association. Nonimportation and nonconsumption of British goods went into effect on December 1, 1774. The ban included imports from Great Britain, Ireland, and the British West Indies. Many in the first Congress had wanted to ban exports simultaneously with imports. Both measures together would exert more pressure on Britain than implementing each sequentially. However, nonexportation was unpopular among those who still cherished the hope of reconciliation with the mother country, and Congress postponed it until September 10, 1775.[2] The delay allowed plenty of time for petitioning the Crown and appealing to the people of Great Britain. It also signaled that the American cause was not to be misunderstood as rooted in a desire to escape overseas debts.

The British government responded aggressively to Congress's association. In November 1774, the king's speech opening Parliament proclaimed Massachusetts Bay to be in a state of rebellion. Parliament responded with a bill that would punish all of New England by restricting its commerce and fisheries: The Restraining Act limited New England's trade to Britain and its dependencies and barred it from the North Atlantic fisheries after July 20. The bill became law at the end of March 1775, three weeks before Lexington and Concord. Another Restraining Act affecting the commerce of all the continental colonies except New York, Delaware, North Carolina, and Georgia quickly followed. Americans did not learn of these acts until June 1775, but they fully expected the Royal Navy to blockade the American coast. Six months before, the Admiralty had instructed Vice-Admiral Samuel Graves to use his North American squadron to seize any arms, munitions, and powder being imported into North America without an express license from the Privy Council. It also reinforced that squadron with two additional ships of the line, bringing Graves's total force to twenty-five ships deployed along the coast from Halifax to Florida.[3]

Britain acted in response to colonial efforts to import powder from the West Indies and Europe. These had been launched as exceptions to nonimportation by individual colonies in the wake of the first Congress. However, heavily armed ships of the line were better suited to overawing the Bostonians than patrolling the coast, and several of Graves's smaller vessels, more appropriate for enforcing the king's orders, were in disrepair. The British naval effort against the powder trade did not get fully under way until after Lexington and Concord. By that time most of the light craft dispatched the previous autumn had made it safely back to home port. This explains why the navy failed to seize one vessel carrying powder before the outbreak of hostilities in April.[4]

In the spring of 1775, the British government finally realized how determinedly the colonists had been scavenging for powder in Europe and the West Indies. It then brought diplomatic pressure to bear on the western European states and issued a new Order in Council authorizing the seizure of all unlicensed powder shipments in "British" vessels. The Royal Navy's increasing aggressiveness toward New England shipping took no one by surprise after the outbreak of hostilities on land. Everyone expected colonial trade to be the first casualty of the combined pressures exerted by the British Navy's patrols and nonexportation when the latter was put into effect.[5]

The Royal Navy's dependence on the mainland for provisions complicated its efforts to control the colonists' importation of munitions during the early days of the war. With the outbreak of hostilities this source of supply began to dry up, creating shortages that also affected the king's troops. In response the navy started stripping New England's coastal islands of livestock and seizing coasting vessels carrying provisions to Massachusetts Bay. By the autumn of 1775 the navy had become embroiled in an escalating struggle with most of New England's coastal communities that culminated in attacks on several towns.[6] New York escaped this treatment because it continued to provision a small naval force led by the sixty-four-gun HMS *Asia* there. But the pressures that Britain's navy and army brought to bear against New England dissolved any lingering reluctance in Congress to stop exports. In September the full association went into effect as originally planned.

British military activity in Massachusetts Bay, the continued occupation of Boston, and the concentration of the Royal Navy there from 1775 into March 1776 seriously disrupted that region's maritime life, especially its fisheries. The ports immediately proximate to Boston undoubtedly felt more vulnerable than did the remoter outports in Massachusetts Bay. But in the end the British Navy torched distant Falmouth (now Portland, Maine) rather than nearby Gloucester. Southern New England's coastal trade also suffered from the resourcefulness of Captain James Wallace. He used Newport as a base for his fleet, which included two twenty-gun ships, an armed sloop, a brig, and several shallow-draft, armed tenders. This force menaced the communities in Narragansett Bay and terrorized the town of Newport into supplying Wallace's fleet with provisions throughout the autumn and winter, allowing him to prey on the shipping and property of the mainland.[7]

The southern New England governments responded to the military crisis by following Congress's lead. Each of the governments restricted their shipping and the export of certain goods. Massachusetts embargoed all voyages but coastal ones in the summer of 1775. Shortly after the battles of Lexington and Concord, Connecticut banned the export of provisions in vessels; the ban soon expanded to West Indian goods as well. Rhode Island waited until March 1776 to require all vessels clearing its ports to obtain the governor's permission in advance.[8]

Colonial commerce did not come to a halt, though. Officially sanctioned voyages from lesser ports, like New London, to the West Indies and Europe for military supplies continued, though not all were successful.[9] Only Cape Anne and Salem, Massachusetts, kept records of the degree to which their seaborne trade had been curtailed by British and American restrictions. Cape Anne claimed that its eighty fishing schooners had been idled, that the British had taken ten of its thirty merchantmen, and that only six vessels had succeeded in completing a voyage. Salem reported the loss of all income from its fifty fishing vessels and six coasters, noting that only ten of its sixty "sale [sic] of shipping" had been "Improved" during the preceding year.[10]

During 1775, the Royal Navy exerted less pressure on the remainder of the continent's coastline, but the Continental Association exacted a comparable toll from its commerce. The difficulties that American merchants could be expected to have in notifying their British correspondents of nonimportation forced Congress to implement it gradually. The association provided for a two-month grace period during which a merchant who received banned goods was given several options. Besides sending them back, he could have them stored for the duration of the association or sold under a committee's supervision, with anything over first cost going to the relief of occupied Boston.[11] This had the effect of postponing full nonimportation to February 1, 1775. Nor did the ban on imports after February 1 halt the shipment of all cargoes from Britain. Local committees in the Chesapeake, for instance, construed the association as permitting the continued shipment of convicts and servants, though the market for their services quickly became saturated.[12]

Surviving records kept by "naval" officers in several southern ports show that Maryland and North Carolina took Congressional nonimportation seriously. Entry records from two ports, Annapolis, Maryland, and Roanoke, North Carolina, yield congruent measures of the effectiveness of nonimportation. During the two-month grace period, more vessels entered both ports in violation of the association than conformed to it. After February 1, 1775, however, about three-quarters of the vessels entering each port conformed, mostly by entering without cargoes—"in ballast"—from British ports. Many of the remainder—also in ballast—conformed by entering from foreign ports. More than half of the vessels entering Annapolis from Great Britain and Ireland after February 1, 1775, carried some servants, convicts, or passengers. Compliance among arrivals from Great Britain, Ireland, and Europe after February 1 was substantially higher than among arrivals from the West Indies. While the Annapolis data fail to reveal the sanctions imposed on violators, the Roanoke records indicate that they were forced to clear out with the portion of their cargo that the committee deemed unacceptable, though they were given—and took—plenty of time to do so.[13]

The only liberty that seems to have been tolerated with the association as it affected direct imports from Britain was the admission of cargoes of salt, perhaps because indigenous sources of this necessity had yet to be discovered and the committees of inspection regarded it strategically as comparable to gunpowder.

Clearance records have also survived from Maryland's Patuxent, Annapolis, and North Potomac districts, from the James River in Virginia, and from Roanoke, North Carolina.[14] The Upper and Lower James River had accounted for about 30 percent of total tobacco exports to Great Britain in the late colonial period. The tonnage of the vessels and number of hogsheads of tobacco clearing for Great Britain during the life of the James River Naval Office record for 1775 is about in line with what had cleared for the same destinations in 1772, the last year covered by Customs 16/1. However, almost 20 percent of the vessels listed in the 1775 series managed to clear twice during the nine-month period, suggesting an urgency to export as much tobacco as possible before nonexportation took effect.[15]

Only 7 percent of the vessels clearing from North Potomac did so more than once, and there appear to have been no multiple clearances from Patuxent between December 1 and the implementation of nonexportation. In both these latter districts, though, there were other signs of a last-minute flurry of activity. Patuxent cleared more than 1,000 tons of shipping between September 7 and 19, almost half of it after September 10, as compared with 728 tons in June, 150 in July, and 658 in August. The comparable figures for North Potomac were 680 tons in June, 924 in July, 1,675 in August, and 2,098 before September 19, a quarter of which cleared after the 10th.[16]

The Annapolis district records support the conclusions derived from those of North Potomac and Patuxent. The amount of wheat, flour, and bread exported from the Annapolis district to European destinations in the six and a half months for which clearance records survive is without precedent. The Annapolis district cleared the equivalent of more than 145,000 barrels of flour and bread during the seven-month life of the record. During the banner year of 1769, Maryland as a whole had exported roughly 160,000 barrels of bread and flour or their equivalents to off-shore destinations.[17] The clearances to European ports from Annapolis also increased by 64 percent, suggesting that many European-based houses were trying to make the best of a good thing.

Roanoke is the only port for which significant clearance records survive beyond September 10—the implementation date for nonexportation. Between September 10 and November 30, 1775, 503 tons of shipping was cleared for overseas destinations from that port; after that the record ceases. Between September 10 and October 3, three vessels totaling 158 tons cleared, apparently in violation of the nonexportation provisions of the association. However, next to one of these violators is appended the note: "This Vessel was cleared out before the 1st Ins [September 1] with a different Cargo, which a violent Storm on the 2nd prevented from being carried to Sea."[18] The two other clearances were probably permitted on similar grounds. No other violations subsequently appear in the record. This same storm also may account for the slippage previously observed in implementing nonexportation at Patuxent and North Potomac. The remaining vessels clearing from Roanoke did so in conformity with nonexportation, though one vessel, which listed a British port as its intended destination, cleared in ballast. The total tonnage clearing from Roanoke for non-British destinations in the period after September 10 came to only 18 percent of what had previously cleared for overseas destinations in a comparable interval of time.[19]

The Roanoke data are too thin to base any firm conclusions on. But it is striking how similar Roanoke's figures are to Salem's and Cape Anne's estimates of the toll taken by the Royal Navy on their commerce. The association had an impact on the southern colonies that was similar to the restraint that British naval activity imposed on New England. The commerce of each shrank to between 16 and 20 percent of its prewar level. This similarity may be less of a coincidence than might at first appear. Though North Carolina was one of the few colonies initially exempted from the Restraining Acts, the privilege it enjoyed along with New York, Delaware, and Georgia grew less meaningful after the summer of 1775 as naval commanders in the West Indies, European waters, and even as far away as the coast of Africa were ordered to seize any colonial vessel found trading with foreign ports as well as those carrying ammunition or armaments.[20] Most all vessels clearing from North Carolina during the autumn of 1775 understood that they ran roughly the same risks as New England vessels, though they did not have to cope with the concentration of naval force that the New Englanders faced in Massachusetts Bay. Parliament's declaration that all vessels entering or leaving American ports after March 1, 1776, would be liable to seizure simply formalized a situation that had existed for some time.[21]

REOPENING OVERSEAS TRADE

Despite the association, Congress had realized from the beginning that totally ending trade was as politically impractical as it was economically undesirable. As Thomas Johnson Jr., a member of the second Continental Congress, wrote in June 1775, "I have no idea of fighting long without attempting to Trade." If nothing else, the colonist's dependence on outside sources for such commodities as salt, powder, medicines, textiles, and arms forced Congress to acknowledge the importance of foreign commerce. The delegates devoted a great deal of attention during the autumn of 1775 to how the colonies represented in Congress should manage that trade.[22] Once news of the Prohibitory Act arrived, Congress moved toward opening colonial ports to the rest of the world while continuing to boycott British commerce.

Congress approached this fateful decision cautiously. Such an action amounted to a repudiation of the principles on which the empire had flourished for more than a century. The delegates found it easier to agree on licensing private ships of war to cruise against the British. They saw this measure as a symmetrical response to the activities of the Royal Navy and agreed to it in the last week of March 1776. Opening colonial ports to the vessels of all nations except Britain appeared to be the first, seemingly irrevocable, step toward independence. Congress did not embrace the measure until April 6, 1776, and then with obvious reluctance. But it had little choice unless it wanted indefinitely to cooperate with Britain's throttling of the American economy.[23]

Fortunately for the revolutionaries, the announcement came at a time when the Royal Navy was preoccupied with concerns besides restraining American commerce. The success of Washington's little fleet of commerce raiders operating out of Massachusetts Bay during the autumn of 1775 had quickly demonstrated that if the British failed to protect their supply lines, the revolutionaries would appropriate them.[24] The navy also had to respond to the appeals of anxious royal officials for assistance in defending those loyal to the Crown.

The navy did receive considerable reinforcement in the western Atlantic at the end of 1775.[25] However, military operations during 1776 would compel it to assume the additional mission of escorting army transports in three major force deployments as well as supporting the army in its campaign against New York. Then, as American armed vessels put to sea, the Royal Navy came under pressure to provide British merchantmen with convoys. At any given time, only a portion of the navy's strength in North American waters was available for blockading the more than one thousand miles of coastline that stretched from Maine to Georgia.[26] Cold fronts periodically sweeping across the continent regularly blew those that could be spared for this duty off station. In addition, the vessels patrolling the coast had to retire periodically to refit, since the mainland no longer provided a convenient source of provisions and naval supplies. In contrast, the navy's ships stationed in the West Indies had a freer hand and used their newly granted authority to seize colonial vessels making for the islands to greater effect.[27]

How successful was the navy in blocking the revolutionaries' attempts to establish commercial contact with the non-British world? The question is highlighted by the charge of two naval historians writing from the perspective of the Battle of the Atlantic in World War II that Britain had been negligent in using its undisputed naval supremacy during the early phases of the Revolutionary War. While it was clearly beyond British capabilities to seal off the entire continent, the published prize lists from the early phase of the struggle suggest that the British posed a real threat to the revolutionaries' ability to conduct overseas commerce.[28] However, prize lists in themselves fail to tell us what portion of the attempted voyages the British succeeded in interdicting.

In principle, only the maritime records of the newly constituted states could supply this information. But even fewer such records survive for the period after March 1, 1776, than for the period immediately preceding it. I have located three such fragmentary series that are relevant to measuring the impact of the British blockade on American efforts to renew commercial contact with the outside world. One, the continuation of the Roanoke series mentioned above, records ten clearances and nine entries during the winter months up until the beginning of April, all to and from the Caribbean islands or coastal ports. After Congress had opened American ports to foreign shipping, though, only one vessel appears in this record, and it is a coastal clearance rather than an entry.[29] We might be tempted by the Roanoke series to conclude that British naval pressure, at least along the Outer Banks of North Carolina, was stunningly effective. That impression, however, is seriously qualified by the other two series—from Philadelphia and Rhode Island—suggesting that we are seeing no more than the termination of this record at Roanoke.

Of the two other series, Rhode Island's is the only continuous, though far from complete, set of state records that survives as a whole for the Revolution. The Rhode Island records list the state's clearances from March 5, 1776, onward in what appears to be a reasonably comprehensive fashion, but they provide only fragmentary information about entries. In contrast, the records of the naval officer of the port of Philadelphia contain the only comprehensive tabulation of entries between September 1775 and late August 1776 that survive from that period, but they are not accompanied by clearance data.[30]

The Philadelphia entry figures give a graphic picture of the impact of the Prohibitory Act on that port's commerce. Between September 6, 1775, and March 1, 1776, a total of 8,866 tons of shipping entered at Philadelphia, much of it in ballast to conform with the requirements of both the Restraining Act and the Association. About 87 percent of the tonnage and 77 percent of the vessels entering the port during the above period were locally owned and had presumably been instructed to return home for want of more suitable alternatives. Many of the other vessels were owned by New Englanders evading the blockade of their coast. Total entering tonnage amounted to roughly 34 percent of Philadelphia's normal peacetime entries over that half-year interval.[31]

After March 1, 1776, until the series terminated on August 27, only

2,586 tons of shipping entered, less than a third of the tonnage recorded for the preceding period. In this latter period, only 17 percent of the entering vessels were locally owned, and the entering tonnage owned by Philadelphians shrank from 7,708 to 460 tons. Obviously the Prohibitory Act had a tremendous impact on Philadelphia's commerce, though it did not stifle it completely. Another significant trend is evident in the entry figures from April 26 to August 27, 1776. Roughly 70 percent of the vessels and 72 percent of the 902 tons of shipping entering Philadelphia in this five-month interval had cleared from non-British ports, suggesting that Congress's opening of American ports was having the desired effect.

One should note, however, that at least 2,426 tons of the shipping entering Philadelphia during the preceding seven-month period before Congress opened American ports, or roughly a quarter of the total, had also cleared from non-British ports in defiance of the Restraining Act. More significantly, the increase in the percentage of entries from foreign ports after April 6 accompanied a dramatic decline in the total tonnage entering. Philadelphia failed to benefit from the sprinkling of French arrivals before the French alliance, some of considerable tonnage bearing important military supplies, since most avoided the port.[32] Even at destinations that the French did not consciously avoid, their entries hardly balanced the tonnage lost as a result of Britain's declaration of war against American commerce. Thus, as Robert Honeyman noted, the French vessels in the Chesapeake failed to bring in the supply of foreign commodities that the region had been used to before the war.[33]

The Rhode Island data confirm the picture we have sketched of Philadelphia's commerce, but this time largely from the perspective of clearances. The maritime records beginning in March 1776 tabulate the state's commerce from the eve of James Wallace's withdrawal from the Narragansett Bay area, when the patriots had become aware that he was about to move his station but before Congress had actually opened American ports to the commerce of other nations, until the end of the war.[34] The earliest records, from March 5 to 30, 1776, show the clearance of seventeen vessels, of which only three made for foreign ports. But beginning in April this ratio changed abruptly. Of the fifteen vessels clearing in April, eleven made for foreign ports, including two for Europe; the rest cleared for coastal destinations. In May the foreign clearances slackened briefly; out of twenty-one, seven were for foreign destinations, including one for Europe. Then in June they rose again to comprise 50 percent of all clearances. After April, though, foreign clearances seldom exceeded domestic clearances in number. The portion of the records that gives the tonnage of vessels clearing suggests that only 36 percent of total tonnage cleared for overseas destinations.[35]

The Rhode Island records confirm that the commercial enterprise of the patriots persisted despite Britain's determined efforts to suppress it. The explosion of foreign clearances as Wallace was in the process of retiring to Halifax suggests that the revolutionaries were also astute in picking the moment and making the most of it. However, while trade resumed under wartime conditions in 1776, just as it did in Philadelphia, it did not exactly thrive. We are in a position to compare Rhode Island's peacetime trade during the last years of the empire with its trade during 1776. Customs 16/1 gives a detailed picture of entries and clearances between 1768 and 1772. Though Rhode Island was relatively free from British naval surveillance between April and December, total clearances in 1776 came to only 36 percent of average annual clearances during 1768–72 and total tonnage in 1776 to 48 percent of the prewar average.[36]

Entries are as important as clearances to complete the picture of the revolutionary economy. In most northern ports during the late colonial period, tonnage clearing exceeded tonnage entering by about 10 percent. However, southern ports, which shipped tobacco, rice, and other staples directly to Europe in vessels owned by Europeans, often recorded more tonnage entering than leaving. The imbalance between entry and clearance tonnage reflected each region's overall balance of accounts with its overseas trading partners. If the value of the colony's imports exceeded the value of its exports, it had to collect additional remittances to pay for them.[37] One way that the New England economy had done so was through the constant building and employment of newly constructed vessels.

Rhode Island's fragmentary entry records for the period support the conclusion that the Revolutionary War dramatically accentuated the discrepancy between clearances and entries, reducing the flow of imports to American ports. The first series of entries spans the period June 19 to November 25, 1776.[38] It lists only 27 arrivals during a period in which there were 136 clearances, which translates into five times as great a discrepancy between the estimated tonnage of clearances and entries as had been characteristic in peacetime. What kind of a measure of the British navy's effectiveness in shaping American commerce is this? The failure of the entry list to note several coastal vessels that regularly cleared at two- to three-week intervals as well as three vessels that cleared twice for foreign destinations point to the record's limitations.

Though flawed, the entry data are not entirely useless. Four vessels of the total of sixty-eight clearing for off-shore destinations are listed as reentering during 1776. Moreover, seven captains of these vessels show up as subsequently clearing in other vessels for foreign destinations during 1777. That still leaves four-fifths of the clearances for overseas destinations unaccounted for after taking into consideration the three vessels that cleared a second time without appearing in the entry record. It is not plausible that the British captured them all. One finds only occasional references to the seizure of Rhode Island vessels in the prize lists of this period.[39] So what happened to them?

Most of the vessels that cleared in this phase of the war were unarmed and under one hundred tons in burthen. The owners may have been seeking to dispose of them in the neutral ports of the Caribbean, or, . short of that, to refit them as armed vessels from the proceeds of the outward voyage. Such a strategy was being pursued by others at the time, and it would help to explain why so few vessels show up in the lists of enemy captures or in the entry figures.[40] Some Rhode Island captains may also have made for ports in other states after hearing that the British had occupied Newport on December 7, 1776. Thereafter, Massachusetts and Connecticut were not under the pressure Rhode Island experienced in having an enemy naval base at the entrance of Narragansett Bay. Rhode Island privateers preferred to dispose of their prizes in the state's Admiralty Court, but they sometimes sent them to the safer and more lucrative markets of Massachusetts.[41] One way or another, Britain managed to hobble the state's commerce far more than the opening of

American ports to foreign shipping helped it. During 1776, only one foreign vessel is recorded as entering and only two as clearing in Rhode Island's naval records.

The Attempt to Create a National Domestic Market

During 1776 and 1777, as the colonies' overseas commerce shrank, prices for foreign goods, particularly West Indian, rapidly rose in North America. The revolutionary leadership initially assumed that the colonies were doing the mother country more harm by denying it the benefit of America's markets than Britain could ever do by preying on the colonies' trade.[42] They also assumed that the major European powers had an interest in recognizing the independence of the United States and that eventually they would take the necessary steps to share in America's trade, even if that meant going to war with Britain.[43] Since the revolutionaries lacked diplomatic influence in the great European capitals, they realized that they would have to wait for others to take the initiative. As a stopgap they proposed to sponsor a bold economic revolution at home. They hoped that this revolution would at least temporarily do away with the need for contact with the outside world that great-power intervention was some day sure to restore.

In place of a colonial economy—in which American surpluses were exchanged for overseas imports—the congressional leadership proposed to create a national market that they hoped would be responsive to domestic rather than foreign demand. With both the Royal Navy and the Continental Association sealing off American producers from the rest of the world, there seemed to be few alternatives to focusing on the domestic market.

In June 1775, shortly after the commencement of hostilities, Congress began to issue money on the common credit of the states. It was reasonably confident that its bills of credit would circulate, because cash shortages had plagued the development of the colonial economy. The absence of an adequate circulating medium in the early years of settlement had inhibited economic progress by limiting capital formation and the development of markets. Although these problems had to some extent eased in the late colonial period, liquidity in the face of wide-spread indebtedness remained a problem.[44]

Congress's action flowed more immediately from the need to raise and support an army once the shooting had started. The colonists knew from their experience with warfare in the colonial period that armies could be supported only by the exertions of a great many individuals besides the soldiery. They also had learned the value of markets in organizing these exertions. Colonial bills of credit had created local markets for labor and provisions. These markets had assigned a monetary value to each individual's contribution, whether in person or in kind, sufficient to command the donor's consent. Individual colonies had had considerable success in mounting military efforts through such means before the Revolution, giving value to the bills of credit by laying taxes to retire them. And there seemed to be no reason why the policy could not be implemented on a continental scale provided each of the states undertook to sink its share of the debt through taxation.[45]

Initially, Congress's currency lived up to expectations. People eagerly sought the bills, which held their value despite the accelerating volume in which they were issued—6 million by the end of 1775 and 15 million on the eve of formal independence—and the parallel action of many of the states in issuing their own currencies. The value of continental bills began to sag only after the defeat of the Continental Army at Long Island and New York in August and September 1776 raised questions about whether the Revolution would succeed. David Ramsay, the historian of revolutionary South Carolina, claimed that his state was unaffected by these concerns and that the depreciation there did not become a serious problem until 1778. Still, once begun in earnest, the slide in value proved irreversible, except briefly after news had been received of the Franco-American alliance in the summer of 1778.[46]

Most scholars have concluded that the depreciation arose from the issuing of too much money, both state and continental. They point out that Congress had no authority to limit the money supply through taxation beyond asking the states to comply with continental requisitions. The new, weak state governments, for their part, feared taxing their citizens lest they alienate their constituents. Both Congress and the states preferred to rely on the market to mobilize resources, whatever the cost. So both issued more and more money to less and less effect, fueling vicious inflation. By the end of 1777, the combined total of all currencies came to an unprecedented $72 million.[47]

This explanation fails to capture the complexity of the forces fueling the decline in state and continental currencies. It ignores how British naval supremacy was shaping American economic behavior early in the Revolution. The interruption of normal commercial relations with the outside world limited the uses to which the new money could be put. Imports were still available, but at inflated prices that discouraged consumption. Producers initially accepted the currency in the expectation that it would store value for the future. However, once the currency started losing its value producers were under pressure to part with it for something of more stable value. The most eligible investment, given the continued shortage of imports, was domestic produce—often the very products the commissariat needed to buy in order to feed the army. Farmers, when they realized that their reward for producing surpluses would be limited to investing their depreciating currency in goods like the ones they were producing, understandably lost interest in producing them. Thus the commercial restraints shaping American economic activity encouraged a neglect of agriculture while inflating the price of supplies. These commercial restraints were a significant factor—neglected in the accounts that stress only the money supply—in forcing both the states and Congress toward printing more and more money.[48]

The revolutionary leadership repeatedly recommended limiting the money supply through taxation as the remedy for the situation. Their emphasis on taxation reflected their sense of the most politically feasible solution to the problem rather than the best solution. The revolutionaries considered several other strategies for halting the depreciation, though none of them proved to be within their power to implement.

One plan was to borrow a substantial sum overseas against which Congress or the state governments could have drawn bills of exchange. The governments could then have sold the bills on their overseas funds for their domestic currencies, as many of the colonial governments had sold drafts on their Parliamentary subsidies in England during and after the Seven Years' War. Even better, they could have offered to exchange domestic bills of credit for loan certificates bearing interest in bills of exchange drawn on Europe. This is what Congress tried to do with its initial subsidy from the French Court in 1777.[49] The strategy allowed one to service a far larger debt than would otherwise have been the case. But it made the revolutionaries beholden to a foreign government without conferring any immediate advantage on their overseas patron. No foreign government, no matter how interested they were in sustaining the American rebellion, was likely to supply the revolutionaries with that kind of fund. Not only was the sum required growing larger by the day, but a government that did put up sufficient funds was unlikely to retain any control over its client. If there were to be foreign subsidies in excess of the first small loans proffered the revolutionaries by France and Spain in 1777 and 1778, they would take a different form.[50]

Another solution to the currency problem was to expand the new nation's commerce with the outside world. Many assumed that an ample supply of imports would effectively lower the price of both imports and domestic produce in relation to the value of the money. Robert Morris spoke for the leadership in predicting that "when we get plenty of goods the money will rise [?] . . . as the prices [of commodities] decline." Implicit in Morris's comment was the assumption that diminished opportunities for consumption were hurting the demand for continental money. If there had been a wider array of imports, the demand for money would have kept pace with its supply, halting the accelerating process that fueled the depreciation.[51] Because trade and the demand for money were thought to be linked, Congress had from the beginning behaved as though the credit of any currency it issued would to some extent depend on the continent's commerce with the outside world. By September 1777, Congressman Henry Laurens had concluded that the market for continental money "will continue to decrease until we can open our Ports & obtain a free exchange for the Products of our Land."[52]

The revolutionary leadership understood what needed to be done; what eluded them was a way of doing it. If our estimates of the revolutionaries' initial success in establishing a commercial connection with the non-British world have any validity, the problem was not going to solve itself. The revolutionary economy simply could not continue on between one- and two-fifths of its former overseas trade. The continuing decline in the value of the paper money made this clear. A radical solution was needed, and Congress initially hoped that it would come from the European powers. In 1776, Congress spent more than two months off and on debating a model commercial treaty to offer foreign powers, particularly the French. The American commissioners in Paris were instructed to propose an alliance in exchange for recognition and support in the form of military supplies, money, and naval assistance in the western Atlantic. Naval assistance was valued as much for commercial as for military reasons.[53] Naval intervention resembled a foreign loan, but at least the United States would have its trade to give in return.

THE IMPACT OF RAISING THE ARMY

Despite Congress's concern with trade and diplomacy at the beginning of the conflict, it had no choice but to devote more energy to raising and sustaining the army than to any other single matter. Supporting an army had initially lured Congress into the realm of currency finance, and throughout the war the army consumed resources with the expectation of producing little besides the defense of the Revolution. Next to money, the resource it consumed most was manpower. Whether men lived or died, entering the ranks diverted them from production in an economy that depended principally on labor for its outputs. The impact of military mobilization on wartime agriculture can best be appreciated by examining the ways that labor constraints interacted with other factors to limit the colonial farmer's capacity to respond to the peacetime demand for wheat surpluses.

We have already seen why farmers grew both wheat and corn rather than exclusively wheat. Compatible schedules for each crop meant that there was little to be lost and much to be gained from cultivating both.[54] Apart from different planting and harvesting times, wheat and corn also diverged in the labor that each required. Overall, corn was less demanding than wheat. Corn could be sown without elaborate soil preparation, whereas wheat fields had to be carefully cleared before planting. Winter

wheat was easier to tend, since corn had to be hilled, hoed, and har-
rowed while wheat required only a single weeding. But the planting
and harvesting schedules of corn were much more flexible than those
of wheat.[55]

Winter wheat had to be planted in a two-week period at the end of
summer. Because corn grew more quickly than the other grain crops, it
could be planted over a six-week period from mid-April to the beginning of June. More important, one could harvest corn at one's convenience, since there was no danger of its going to seed and it could stand
in the fields until well after the first frosts. Winter wheat, on the other
hand, had to be reaped in a ten-day period at the beginning of July when
the kernels had ripened but before they had begun to sprout. This
restricted harvest time limited how much acreage could be planted.
Since a skilled worker with a sickle could cut no more than one half acre
per day, the average farm laborer could reap no more than forty bushels
per harvest, assuming a yield of ten bushels to the acre and two days of
the harvest lost to sabbath observance and weather. The introduction of
scythes in the mid-eighteenth century increased a laborer's cutting capacity, but the stalks still had to be gathered for binding into sheaves.
Wheat that could not immediately be sheaved was vulnerable to mois-
ture and rain. When a farmer planted wheat, then, he always had to
calculate how much labor was likely to be available at harvest time.[56]

The constraint that available labor placed on the expansion of peacetime wheat production in turn raises the question of how the drain of
men from farms to the army affected production of wartime wheat.[57] In
1790, Henry Knox, one of Washington's key subordinates during the
Revolution and the first secretary of war under the new federal constitution, calculated the number of noncommissioned officers and men furnished by the several states to the Continental Army between 1775 and
1783. His figures can be used in estimating the impact that raising the
army had on the wheat harvests that appear in table 2.1.[58] The calculations are based on the extravagant assumption that every private and
noncommissioned officer serving with the army, including militia serving for more than half a year, came from a pool of potential farm laborers

Table 2.1. Estimated Annual Wheat and Flour Production Forgone
Because of Army and Militia Service

Includes only men from North Carolina to present-day Maine

	Men under arms	Bu. of wheat forgone	Bbl. of flour equivalent	Remaining prewar surplus
1775	32,625	1,305,000	253,891	350,945
1776	78,425	3,137,000	610,311	−5,475
1777	51,175	2,047,000	398,249	206,587
1778	39,225	1,569,000	305,253	299,582
1779	36,700	1,468,000	285,603	319,233
1780	33,825	1,353,000	263,230	341,606
1781	25,600	1,024,000	199,222	405,614
1782	15,250	610,000	118,677	486,159

Source: Henry Knox's estimates of men raised during the Revolutionary War, May 10, 1790, in Walter Lowrie and Matthew St. Claire Clarke, eds., *American State Papers: Military Affairs* (Washington, D.C., 1832–61), 1: 14–19.

that cost the revolutionary economy forty bushels of wheat for each year of service.[59] Commissioned officers, camp followers, and naval personnel are excluded from the calculations, as are the crews of privateers.[60] For purposes of comparison, table 2.1 translates lost wheat into lost flour expressed in barrels.[61]

The 1776 mobilization had the potential to wipe out all the prewar exportable surplus of 604,836 barrels of flour. Further, because of discrepancies between the harvest and calendar years, the repercussions of the campaign of 1776 would have been felt well into 1777. However, 1776 and 1777 were not the shortage years, at least in wheat. The commissariat encountered problems only when the number of men under arms had begun declining. After deducting the customary 25 percent to accommodate officers, camp followers, and wastage, there still should have been enough wheat and flour to provide for 83,204 men annually once the harvest of 1777 came in, assuming that labor shortages at harvest time alone affected production. That was 27,000 more than the number of full-year equivalents Knox recorded as actually being under arms, even counting the navy and Burgoyne's Convention Army, which had surrendered in mid-October.[62]

Is there a way to account for the time lag between peak mobilization and the chronic grain shortages at the end of the decade? Perhaps farmers initially found substitutes for the labor they lost to the army. Alternatively, the commissariat may have succeeded in carrying over flour surpluses accumulated in a year of plenty. The keeping qualities of fine flour made this possible, and it seems certain that the bumper crop of 1775 helped tide over the army through 1776. When carrying over wheat surpluses ceased to be an option, perhaps the commissariat managed to mix the flour of such grains as corn and rye with wheat flour, in effect substituting them for wheat. Finally, the radical fluctuations in force levels that characterized the Continental Army before the "permanent" army formed in the middle of 1777 undoubtedly helped the commissariat make ends meet despite the inroads that mobilization made on production in 1776 and 1777.

The cumulative effect of these strategies certainly cushioned the impact of the mobilizations of 1776 and 1777, but they do not explain why things got worse from 1778 to 1780 as the army steadily declined in size. However, it is possible to argue that raising the army had a delayed impact on agricultural production by emphasizing another aspect of grain culture.

Farmers were limited in the number of acres they could sow not only by the availability of labor but also by the tendency of all grain crops to exhaust the soil. The Chester County, Pennsylvania, tax lists for 1760 demonstrate the enduring effect of this constraint.[63] Since Chester County was close to the Philadelphia market, the continent's principal grain emporium, its farmers had incentives to specialize enjoyed by few others. Nevertheless, local farmers sowed less than 10 percent of their total land in grain crops (referred to as "corn"), or about 25 percent of their improved land. Planting more than twenty acres in grains was rare. Only those who owned more than two hundred acres of land did so. Neither the availability of land on the larger farms nor a sufficiency of labor on smaller family farms (relative to the acreage cultivated) seems to have significantly influenced the proportion of lands devoted to grains.[64] Instead, farmers kept three-quarters of their improved land fallow, or planted with grasses instead of grains, to sustain the productivity of the remaining quarter.

In addition to affecting how much of each grain one could plant and exerting constant pressure on farmers to diversify into crops whose schedules did not overlap, the availability of labor held the key to the preparation of new lands for cultivation. However, soil exhaustion also set a limit to the amount of improved land a prudent farmer could sow in grains independently of the availability of labor. Significantly, the amount of cleared land in Chester County never exceeded 50 percent of the total. Still, the cereal productivity of the late colonial period depended to some extent on the continuous opening of virgin lands. Thus it is possible that the principal effect of the mobilization of 1776 was its impact on the preparation of new lands. If that were the case, it would not have manifested itself until several years later. One can also speculate that the extraordinary migration of Europeans to British North America in the late colonial period saturated the labor market just as the war broke out, cushioning the initial impact that mobilization might otherwise have had on productivity in the agricultural sector.[65]

However, neither of these factors helps us much in explaining the expansion of production observed after 1780. That expansion occurred independently of any renewed immigration from overseas, though it did coincide with the continued reduction of the army. A possible slowing of soil exhaustion during periods of peak mobilization may also have had an indirect influence on the expansion of flour production observed after 1780. Several years of fallow time should have given cleared land in the wheat regions a chance to recover its fertility in part. But the declines in production associated with the late 1770s as well as the surge in production during 1781 delineated in the previous chapter are too abrupt and dramatic to be attributed solely to the loss and restoration of soil nutrients or a decline and resumption in the clearing of new lands, though these processes undoubtedly played some part in the collapse and revival of wartime agriculture.[66] Emphasizing soil exhaustion fails to qualify significantly the principal impression conveyed by table 2.1 that labor shortages arising from the mobilization of the army provide a progressively less plausible explanation for agricultural shortages after 1777. For, in addition to the steady decline in the ranks of the army, these years also saw a large new generation of American males come of age and enter the ranks of the adult labor force.

THE FRENCH CONNECTION

The revolutionaries responded to the impact that the military mobilization of 1776 had on the revolutionary economy by creating a "permanent" army—one in which men enlisted either for three years or for the duration—in 1777. Congress took this action as an economy measure, in part to eliminate the effect that rotating short-term enlistees through the ranks was having on agricultural production. Members of Congress also realized that their efforts to create a national market with the continental currency would not free them from dependence on European sources of supply in clothing and arming the Continental Army. In the absence of a decisive military victory over the British, their best hope for a speedy resolution of the conflict lay in the involvement of other European nations. They assumed that the recognition and intervention of a power like France would quickly prove decisive, first in freeing the American economy from the vise in which the Royal Navy held it, and then, more significantly, in producing an international settlement that would restore peace.

High Hopes Dashed

The French court and the United States signed a commercial treaty and a secret treaty of alliance in Paris on February 6, 1778.[1] Before that, only a few French vessels had arrived in American ports. With the exception of the ships used by the French dramatist and unofficial agent of the court Caron de Beaumarchais in channeling military supplies to the Americans, and the vessels fitted out by Reculès des Basmarein et Raimbaux Cie., most had been small craft sailing from the West Indies.[2] In 1778 a stream of larger vessels began appearing in the Chesapeake and other American ports. Many had sailed from France for the West Indian islands the previous autumn, loaded with goods for the continental market. By anticipating the dispatch of a French naval force to the western Atlantic, adventuresome French traders hoped to buy American staples, particularly tobacco and indigo, while prices remained low.[3] Once transatlantic trade resumed under the protection of the French navy in North American waters, the price of these staples would rise.

Profits lured French entrepreneurs to act in advance of France's expected naval deployment. Some French syndicates armed their merchant vessels and procured commissions authorizing them to defend themselves against capture. The largest of these vessels was the former East Indiaman *Fier Roderique*. Beaumarchais's firm, Hortales, Roderique & Cie., bought it with a subsidy supplied by the French government. The *Fier Roderique* carried more than fifty-four heavy guns, an armament that would make even a British frigate hesitate to attack. Such a ship could protect smaller, unarmed vessels that accompanied it.[4] Many French vessels, however, sailed for America without armed escort.

American merchants were enthusiastic about the renewal of overseas trade. As Boston merchant Paschal N. Smith confidently predicted to one of his correspondents, "America will receive more advantage from Commerce, than she has for sometime past." During the spring of 1778, American merchants started shifting their assets into currency for the first time since the beginning of the depreciation. During the colonial period, merchants had used cash to facilitate the exchange of European manufactures for American produce. Accordingly, they assumed that the value of money would rise as demand for it increased. News of the Franco-American alliance halted the relentless depreciation of paper currencies that had begun in 1776. The value of Congress's bills of credit briefly rose during the spring and summer of 1778 with the expectation that the Franco-American alliance would bring the war to a speedy end and give Congress ample opportunity to sort out its finances.[5]

British officials were alert to the strategic implications of French commercial intervention. In the autumn of 1777, the Royal Navy began routinely searching French vessels in European waters for contraband and seizing those that appeared off the North American coast. And to the extent that their resources permitted, they attempted to strengthen the blockade of the American coast. Early in 1778 several British line-of-battle ships joined the customary frigates in patrolling key entry points, such as the Delaware and Chesapeake, eager to capture prizes of greater value than small American merchantmen. They were able to participate in the blockade because of the cessation of troop movements during the winter.[6]

News that France and the United States had entered an alliance and that a naval force under the command of the Comte D'Estaing was on its way to North American waters again forced the British navy to concentrate or risk destruction in detail. This compromised the British navy's blockade of the continent and brightened the prospects for Franco-American commerce by making it possible for the vessels of both countries to enter and clear with relative impunity during the spring and summer of 1778. Moreover, when D'Estaing actually appeared off the coast at the end of June, he seemed to be admirably positioned to strike a mortal blow against Britain's commerce and naval supremacy in the western Atlantic, as well as to seize an immense quantity of booty in New York, including the French trading vessels that already had been taken by the British. During his first three weeks on the American coast he captured more than twenty merchantmen and several smaller men-of-war. In late July, when the French and Americans moved against Newport, the British scuttled three frigates together with six lesser-rated men-of-war and three galleys.[7]

France's naval advantage proved short-lived. The news that Britain had dispatched reinforcements under Admiral John Byron—reinforcements that more than matched D'Estaing's forces—meant that D'Estaing had to neutralize what remained of British naval power in North American waters quickly or go on the defensive. When D'Estaing's efforts to bring Admiral Richard Howe's squadron to a decisive engagement off Newport aborted in a summer northeaster of unusual power, injuring both fleets about equally, he lost the advantage. Byron himself had sighted the battered French fleet as it made its way back to Rhode Island on August 19. Alone, his squadron dispersed by the same storm, he made for Halifax without engaging the French. Nonetheless, D'Estaing concluded from his sighting of Byron that British naval reinforcements had arrived and that he had best retreat to a safer, better equipped port to refit. His withdrawal to Boston bitterly disappointed the patriots. It also underlined the limitations of French naval power in the western Atlantic to both the revolutionaries and to French entrepreneurs.[8]

Though Byron's timely arrival tipped the balance of naval power back in Britain's favor, D'Estaing's presence in Boston left the Royal Navy concentrating as much of its resources as possible in Massachusetts Bay during the autumn. This had less effect on Britain's attempt to interdict Franco-American commerce than might have been expected. Well before France's formal entry into the war the British government had begun recruiting private interests to help the navy isolate France from America. Early in 1777, possibly in response to American armed vessels using French ports to provision and sell prizes, the Admiralty started commissioning private vessels to seize rebel shipping. In June of that year it had extended the privilege to Bermudian and West Indian merchants. The initial commissions limited those who possessed them to seizing American vessels and English vessels trading with the United States. The searching of French vessels for contraband remained technically the duty of the navy. By the end of the year, though, private ships of war—some acting without commissions—were making as many seizures of French vessels as the Royal Navy, at least to judge from the number of appeals coming to the High Court of Admiralty. Inevitably overzealous captains not only took French vessels but violated France's territorial waters as well.[9]

Private "commissioned" vessels provided an effective complement to regular naval forces. They cost the Royal Navy nothing directly, and they were cheaper to arm and fit than regular vessels of war. While their loss would not affect the naval balance of power significantly, their modest size allowed them to hide more effectively in the immensity of the sea. British privateers could operate in seas under the naval domination of a hostile power as effectively as American commerce raiders had been doing since March 1776.[10] Britain had already mobilized a sizable privateering fleet in the eastern Atlantic and the Caribbean before the formal announcement of the Franco-American alliance. The government, confident that plenty of eager volunteers would respond, now moved quickly to enlarge the scope of its commissions to include all vessels trading with the rebellious colonies. Local officials in North America also sought to issue privateering commissions to a few New York loyalists, though over the vociferous protests of the naval commanders who feared the effect this would have on their capacity to man the fleet.[11]

THE TOLL EXACTED FROM THE FRENCH

Britain seized well over a hundred French merchantmen before war was declared. There is in the Archives de la marine antérieures à la révolution, in Paris, a register of French vessels taken by the British before the official commencement of hostilities in mid-June 1778. It lists 134 French vessels captured on the high seas in addition to 21 seized in British ports. Most of the vessels mentioned were from the Atlantic ports of Bayonne, Bordeaux, and Nantes. Though the register appears to have been compiled for the purposes of pressing claims against Great Britain, it seems unlikely that it contains a complete tally of France's maritime losses before mid-June 1778. Not only does it fail to mention the loss of any vessels from La Rochelle, one of France's principal ports trading with the French Caribbean, but it also omits mention of losses from almost all of the less prominent Atlantic ports.[12]

French merchants complained bitterly of their losses and of the role that Britain's privateers played in them, but that hardly constitutes a reliable measure of the blockade's effectiveness.[13] What percentage of

French vessels intending to trade with the United States actually succeeded in doing so? Only the largest British men-of-war could have taken on such heavily armed vessels as the *Fier Roderique*. Nonetheless, two circumstances stacked the deck against French vessels trying to elude the force of the British blockade.

French captains had to run the British gauntlet twice to complete their voyages. Many of those arriving in American ports during the brief interval when Britain had relaxed her surveillance of the American coast in response to the threat posed by D'Estaing were seized as they tried to clear later in the year. In addition, French captains were handicapped by their ignorance of the coast. Unlike many of the West Indian islands and most of the western coast of Europe, much of continental North America makes a bad landfall, especially south of Cape Cod. In an age before the average mariner could determine longitude accurately, the direct westerly approach, though easiest and safest, invited attack by enemy cruisers. Approaching North America from the islands reduced this hazard but could increase the difficulty of determining one's position in relation to the continent.[14]

The list in the Archives de la marine does record the losses of the largest French house trading with the United States in 1777–78. Twenty-four of the fifty-two vessels from Bordeaux that appear in the list of captures made before the war formally began, or 53 percent of the forty-five vessels for whom ownership is specified, were the property of Reculès des Basmarein & Raimbaux. In addition, this house was involved in at least fourteen other vessels that were captured after February 1, 1777. Unlike Hortales, Roderique & Cie., which received subsidies from the government, relieving it of the need to raise capital, Reculès des Basmarein & Raimbaux had mobilized the resources of an array of French investors during 1777 and 1778. Whereas Hortales, Roderique & Cie. dispatched nine vessels to North America early in 1777, Basmarein & Raimbaux sent out sixty-five in the eighteen months between spring 1777 and autumn 1778.[15]

In spring 1778, after the first reports of heavy losses were received, the firm applied to the French government for assistance. Initially it had asked for a loan which the finance minister, Jacques Necker, had refused on the grounds that the treasury could not afford it. Eventually Basmarein & Raimbaux settled for the right to fit out a frigate-sized vessel with which to prey on British shipping. In June the government issued a privateering commission to the twenty-four-gun *Vengeance,* which sailed from Bordeaux. When the *Vengeance* failed to redeem the firm's fortunes, Basmarein & Raimbaux poured even more of its dwindling resources into equipping the larger *Marquise de Lafayette,* but again to no effect. In February 1779 the firm's creditors, alarmed by its mounting losses, forced the company into bankruptcy, and Pierre de Basmarein fled to England.[16]

Though Reculès des Basmarein & Raimbaux had invested heavily— some would have said recklessly—in the American trade during 1777–78, much of the money was not its own. It had succeeded in selling shares in its many ventures to an eager monied public convinced that the riches of Britain's former colonial trade were there for the taking. In this manner it briefly became the largest French firm interested in exploring the unfathomed potential of the American trade. However, the commerce of the new republic attracted as wide a sample of French entrepreneurs as the war did military adventurers. The most meaningful way to distinguish between them is to focus less on the size of their capital than on their relationship to the government, though the two were not unrelated.[17]

Figures like Jacques-Donatien Le Ray de Chaumont, the flamboyant Beaumarchais, and Jean-Joseph Carié de Montieu of Nantes had connections at Court. This type of entrepreneur either was involved in manufacturing or entered into partnerships with prominent manufacturers capable of delivering services valued by the government.[18] The insiders benefited from a certain amount of cronyism in the form of contracts with the Crown for goods and services. While Beaumarchais's two-million-livre subsidy remained unique, most insiders had access to what were known as *affrètements royaux,* or royal charters. Deficiencies in the military transport services forced the Crown to charter large quantities of shipping from French merchants in such principal Atlantic ports as Bordeaux and Nantes to sustain operations in the western Atlantic and to provision the islands. These charters amounted to a subsidy because the Crown guaranteed payment for the freight and vessel regardless of the outcome of the voyage. In addition, the Crown usually provided convoys for its charters while a portion of each vessel was retained by the owners for their use. However, the Crown chartered only large, armed vessels belonging to the wealthiest shipowners.

In their relationship to the government, Basmarein & Raimbaux occupied an anomalous position. Though Pierre de Basmarein, the head of the firm, had married into a West Indian fortune and had enjoyed royal patronage under Louis XV, he had lost favor in the succession. His heroic sponsorship of Franco-American commerce should be seen as a bid to recover his former status.[19] While he used connections made in the previous reign to recruit capital for the firm's North American ventures, Necker's rebuff signaled to Pierre that he was not likely to succeed. Basmarein & Raimbaux's impetuosity in entering the American trade also precluded their benefiting from royal charters. Though the government had started expanding on royal charters during 1777 as it sought to reinforce the West Indies, it did not resort to them on a large scale until 1779, after it became clear that the war would be a prolonged one.[20] By that time Basmarein & Raimbaux had no ships to charter.

The associates of Basmarein & Raimbaux were not the only French adventurers to fall victim to Britain's commercial depredations in the early phases of the war. Sabatier fils & Després, a house involved in textile manufacturing in Montpellier, made extensive private investments in the American trade and suffered heavily as a consequence. The merchants of Nantes, about whose trade unusually complete records survive, also experienced especially heavy losses in the initial years of the war, before the institution of effective convoys. And the fortunes of Bordeaux seem to have paralleled those of Nantes. The heavy losses taken by both ports at the beginning of the war were typical.[21] Combined with the bankruptcy of the largest concern involved in the American trade, they deflated the optimism with which French investors had initially viewed America and consequently the degree to which the government could rely on them unaided.

The Maryland merchant Joshua Johnson, writing his brother from Nantes in spring 1779, commented on the general absence of "Arrivals from America." He then went on to describe the effect that these developments were having on French entrepreneurs: "The frequent miscarriage of these ships has sickened the Merchants very much, many is [sic] retiring from Business to the Country until the War is over." Johnson added that "they are so sick of American business that their [sic] has only one French ship cleared for America from Bordeaux for these three Months and I only know of two or three from hear [sic]." The preceding year's losses had led to an astronomical rise in the rates that insurance underwriters would accept for adventures to America. With premiums running at 80 to 90 percent of the value insured, venturers had no choice but to forgo this way of limiting risk, which was a further discouragement to the trade.[22] Finally, though Johnson did not mention the matter, the continent was unlikely to benefit from royal charters while D'Estaing's expeditionary force remained in the Antilles.

Johnson's report failed to do justice to the tenacity of French entrepreneurs. Sabatier fils responded to the loss of five of the seven vessels in which they had had an interest during the summer of 1778 by considering a suspension of their North American operations. But they already had six new ventures under way by the time they were in a position to tally those losses. Once involved in the trade, disengagement was neither simple nor easy. The losses only gradually affected the behavior of entrepreneurs. Some, like the Meulan family, stopped investing in North American ventures after losing thirteen of the twenty-two vessels in which they had taken a four-fifths interest from Basmarein & Raimbaux. The value of trade between Nantes and North America declined precipitously between 1778 and 1779, suggesting that the de Meulans were not alone.[23] Those French-based entrepreneurs who did not withdraw explored new strategies for staying in business.

The most obvious remedy was to instruct their captains to wait for convoys, but it took time to implement a full convoy system. In April 1778 the French government responded to Britain's increasing naval pressure by instituting limited convoys to forty leagues off shore in both Europe and the West Indies. These were more effective in getting vessels out than in. During the autumn of 1778 British privateers seized a fleet of sixty West Indian vessels and three East Indiamen on their way home just after the merchantmen had parted from their naval escort. France responded by instituting *convois obligatoires* in early 1779, though with mixed results. The following year all eleven vessels of one outgoing convoy escorted by several armed merchantmen were seized by an English fleet of eighteen sail, and an incoming convoy from the islands escorted by three French frigates lost fourteen of forty-eight vessels when it encountered two of Britain's seventy-four-gun line-of-battle ships. These events led the French navy to pay greater attention to escorting merchant fleets throughout the remainder of the war, but rarely was a French vessel of force available to protect ships making directly from the islands or France to North America.[24]

Though convoys were designed to limit losses, occasionally they increased them. Off Cape Saint Vincents on August 9, 1780, an armada of thirty-two Spanish and French vessels captured almost all sixty-four merchantmen in a British fleet under the escort of the seventy-four-gun HMS *Ramillies* and two frigates. Although convoys reduced the cost of insurance, armaments, and manning, the savings had to be balanced against indirect costs. Convoys slowed commerce because all the vessels had to rendezvous before they could proceed, and then only as fast as the slowest sailor permitted. The delays increased the expense of a voyage. Moreover, when convoys arrived, the price of the commodities carried in the escorted merchantmen usually fell as local markets became saturated.[25]

French investors tried arming their merchantmen as an alternative to convoys, but that strategy provided no firmer guarantee against seizures. In 1778, several French vessels with armaments comparable to a frigate's were taken on the American coast. Finally, some entrepreneurs tried using vessels especially constructed for speed, exploiting French superiority in nautical design. A mixture of all three strategies promised the best results. French venturers in the autumn of 1778 attempted to profit from the disasters experienced the year before. Among the ships sailing in convoy to the islands that autumn was the five-hundred-ton *Souci,* consigned to Simeon Deane in Virginia, where it was expected to take on tobacco for the return voyage to Europe. The *Souci* represented an innovative attempt to adjust to wartime conditions without sacrificing the prewar scale on which the tobacco trade had been conducted.[26]

The *Souci* had sailed from Bordeaux partially loaded with salt and dry goods, picking up an additional cargo of sugar and rum in the West Indies, but not so much as to compromise its sailing abilities. In January it made for the Chesapeake, carefully timing its arrival for when the British were least likely to be patrolling the entrance to the Bay. Nevertheless, the *Souci* barely managed to escape a swarm of enemy corsairs at the Virginia Capes. Though the *Souci* found refuge under the fort at Portsmouth, Deane realized that the corsairs would be waiting for the ship to leave and that a large cargo of tobacco would compromise the vessel's trim. Accordingly, he sought to increase its armaments before dispatching it back to Europe. The arrival of three British frigates in the lower Bay in March, however, further complicated the task of clearing the coast. The vessel was still trapped in Portsmouth in late May when a raiding force, led by Sir George Collier, destroyed it on the 29th, bringing this experiment to an abrupt and unprofitable end.[27]

Sabatier fils & Després, which held a major share of the *Souci,* thereafter loaded goods on someone else's vessel rather than investing in both ship and cargo. This strategy diminished the risk more effectively than either waiting for convoys or arming large vessels. French merchants in the American trade increasingly consigned goods on either American or French vessels with American captains or pilots. Such vessels enjoyed a significant advantage in making directly for the American coast, bypassing the islands. The new route not only allowed them to get cargoes to the American market in a more timely fashion but also permitted them to bypass seas that by the end of 1778 had become a major theater of warfare. After D'Estaing's arrival in the Caribbean in December 1778, a French merchantman on its way to North America via the islands ran almost as much risk of having its crew pressed by the French navy as it did of being captured.[28]

The Limitations of the American Market

Threading one's way though British cruisers and negotiating an unfamiliar coast were but two of the difficulties for French merchants attempting to trade with America. The cargo still had to be sold.

European goods often traded at eight to ten times their original cost, while West Indian produce sold at considerably lower though still highly advantageous rates. However, the high prices discouraged sales, especially when there was even a hint of a new development in the war. Weak demand made it impossible to sell goods wholesale without extending credit, which exposed the seller to losses from the depreciating currency even if the buyer agreed to an exorbitant price. The alternative was to retail imports oneself. This required time. It also limited one's exposure to the market unless one established a network of stores in the country, as the Scottish tobacco factors had before the war. It was several years before any French merchants could set up such stores.[29]

Selling imports did not address the problem of what to do with the proceeds; one certainly did not want to hold the depreciating currency any longer than necessary. There were few possibilities for converting it into hard money or bills of exchange, particularly at the beginning of the alliance. On the other hand, the high cost of American staples shocked French merchants.[30] Getting to America and selling one's cargo turned out to be relatively easy; finding something to send back to Europe on satisfactory terms proved much more difficult.

Different languages and cultures complicated the problem. Before the arrival of the first French consuls in the summer of 1778 there was no one to whom French captains and merchants could turn when they encountered difficulties.[31] French investors had to rely on American intermediaries, whom they blamed when things went wrong. During 1778–79 the number of French consuls and vice consuls steadily increased, as did the number of bilingual French and Americans. But French entrepreneurs encountered other problems as time progressed. For instance, they had expected that their consuls would have jurisdiction over disputes between French nationals in North America. The Franco-American commercial treaty recognized the right of each power to appoint consuls but had left their "Functions" to be clarified by a subsequent "Agreement." Not until 1789 did the two countries enter into a convention that brought "all differences and suits between the subjects of the Most Christian King in the United States" under the jurisdiction of French consuls.[32] Until then nothing prevented a Frenchman from seeking refuge from justice in the bewildering complexities of the American legal system. In a dispute between a French merchant and an American merchant, there was no alternative to the American courts unless the American agreed to submit to French consular jurisdiction.[33]

Despite these obstacles, more and more French firms established themselves in America, but the process was a torturous one that engendered distrust of Americans. Simeon Deane, for instance, was rumored to have had six hundred hogsheads of tobacco on hand with which he could have loaded the *Souci* on May 12, before Collier attacked. The French investors saw Deane's failure to act as willful obstruction rather than as a strategy to divide risk and avoid provoking an assault before the *Souci* was in a position to defend itself. Sometimes American agents did victimize the French. In 1778, John Langdon sold goods belonging to Le Ray de Chaumont in Portsmouth, New Hampshire, on scandalously disadvantageous terms. Though the consuls acknowledged that most American merchants wished to establish a good relationship with their French counterparts, they advised their countrymen to rely on French houses as much as possible.[34] However, that was often easier said than done.

By 1779, French investors had more options for conducting their business independently of Americans. The networks had to be extensive because Britain's continued naval supremacy in the western Atlantic made it impossible to predict where their ventures would arrive. The vessels in which the Meulans and Basmarein & Raimbaux shared an interest had initially been expected to pick up tobacco. Those that made it through the British blockade, however, had ended up scattered along the Atlantic seaboard, often far from the Chesapeake. By the autumn of 1779 Sabatier fils & Després could specify their agents of choice in all the principal ports not occupied by the British, as well as in North Carolina and the Chesapeake.[35] This gave them options they had previously lacked, though it hardly addressed the obstacles they faced in acquiring return cargoes.

The New England economy, for instance, provided few exports for Europe besides masts, a trade that had limited practicability under wartime conditions. New England fish could have commanded a market, but fish remained in short supply because of the threat the British navy posed to the fisheries. When available, fish was expensive. Limited quantities of New England's salted meat sold in the provision-short West Indies throughout the war, but Britain restricted access to the island trade. Salted meat would play a role in the direct trade with Europe only if there were a French army to be fed in America, and there seemed to be no prospect of that in the early years.[36]

Only the Chesapeake and the South had staples wanted in Europe. South Carolina and Georgia produced rice and indigo, while North Carolina, Virginia, and Maryland produced tobacco. Of the three, European investors were principally interested in tobacco. Many of France's difficulties stemmed from this preference.[37]

Prior to the Revolution the farmers-general had bought more than twenty thousand hogsheads of Chesapeake tobacco a year. The tobacco was used to make snuff, which an eager French public purchased despite the high duties concealed in the price. The farmers-general struggled to maintain this revenue source throughout the war. They had to worry about American prices as much as supplies because the Crown limited the price of snuff in the home market. None of the contracts they negotiated with large-scale suppliers could be executed because the price of Chesapeake tobacco continued to rise well beyond what it could be sold for in France. That left France's once powerful tobacco monopoly haggling over what little American tobacco independent French and American merchants managed to bring to Europe.[38]

Before the war Chesapeake planters had depended on British ships for access to the Europe market. Since most American tobacco was consumed in Europe, access to that market was the major factor in determining the staple's commercial value. The war created a shipping shortage in the Chesapeake because the region could not replace the British vessels that had formerly been deployed in the tobacco trade.[39] The shortage should have depressed the price of tobacco in the Chesapeake, making it attractive to French adventurers, like the investors in the *Souci*. However, they failed to appreciate the effect that the war would have on American tobacco production.

Cuts in tobacco production began in 1776, long before enemy operations became a serious problem for the region in 1779. Vulnerability to seaborne raids discouraged many a planter along the exposed coast well in advance of actual depredations. Those in less exposed positions also abandoned the crop because they assumed that the war would limit their market. Reduced production raised prices and encouraged the few who continued to produce to hold out for more. Tobacco could be withheld from the market with less risk of spoilage than experienced with grain, making it an attractive inflationary hedge during wartime. Prices rose in the Chesapeake despite a shipping shortage, primarily in response to declining production.[40]

The war also affected the price of American tobacco indirectly by increasing the cost of assembling tobacco cargoes. During the colonial period, tobacco was brought to local inspection stations attached to warehouses scattered throughout the Bay area. Ships from Europe could take on cargoes of known quality at these "tobacco ports." Fortifying and defending all of them in wartime seemed impracticable, but failing to do so made them dangerous places to assemble cargoes. Instead, prudent merchants laboriously collected tobacco in small parcels in the countryside and then transported them to the few areas considered secure enough for launching their ventures. They incurred additional costs because of the risk and expense in transporting even the smallest shipment of so bulky a commodity by water or land.[41]

Matthew Ridley, speaking from the perspective of the Chesapeake, and the French firm of Lony et Plombard in Charleston advised against tobacco ventures almost from the beginning of France's commercial involvement with America.[42] Had the French been able to concentrate on the Chesapeake, some of the problems that they encountered in the tobacco trade might have been diminished. But the entrance to the Bay could be easily blocked by large men-of-war, and the risk remained, once inside, of enemy capture. Short of a permanent French naval presence there, merchantmen making for the Chesapeake had either to sail in convoys shepherded by ships such as the *Fier Roderique* or risk capture.[43] French merchants regarded North Carolina as a safer destination, particularly after the Royal Navy took station off the Capes of the Chesapeake and Charleston. North Carolina was almost as close to French bases in the Caribbean as Charleston. The narrow channel at

Ocracoke Inlet, the only navigable access to the North Carolina Sounds in the eighteenth century, was less vulnerable to enemy warships than was the Chesapeake. Its proximity to Cape Hatteras also made it more hazardous to place under naval surveillance than the approaches to Charleston and the Chesapeake.[44]

Though North Carolina could provide a safer haven for shipping, its location compounded the problems of speedily and cheaply assembling a return tobacco cargo. The coast of the southern states also presented special navigational problems for strangers. The Gulf Stream passes within 140 miles of Charleston and very close to soundings (the hundred-fathom line); farther north, the Gulf Stream and the continental shelf diverge as the latter narrows. At Cape Hatteras, incoming French captains, lacking chronometers for establishing longitude at sea according to a newly developed method, had as little as twelve miles of soundings before running on a less than perfectly visible shoreline. In winter, when enemy cruisers were least likely to be present, bad weather increased the problems of navigating this area of the American coast.[45]

The continued depreciation of the American currencies compounded the difficulties of the French. Many French merchants responded to the rising currency price of American staples, such as tobacco, by backing off in the hope that more advantageous bargains could be found in the future. Usually they incurred losses by doing so. The longer they held currency to buy a return cargo, the greater the loss. Though Joshua Johnson spoke primarily for himself in this regard, he concluded a letter to his brother in 1779 by declaring that "the great Reason why People [in France] will not make adventures to America is owing to the immoderate depreciation of your Money."[46]

While a declining currency complicated business for French entrepreneurs in America, it imposed an additional burden on those investors who persisted in viewing the decline as a potential windfall. They took Congress's pledge to honor the continental debt seriously and acted as if the currency would eventually rise in value as much as it had fallen. The slight appreciation of the continental currency in the first months of the Franco-American alliance encouraged foreign investors to persist in their hopes. If the United States had possessed a fund into which foreign merchants could have safely deposited the proceeds of their sales, that fund would have provided an alternative to finding return remittances to Europe and simplified operations. It also would have attracted foreign investment to the new nation. French officials unsuccessfully pressed Congress to create such a fund, but in the meantime French entrepreneurs behaved as though Congress's loan office certificates provided one.[47]

John Holker, agent for the French navy and consul-general in Philadelphia, also acted as agent for several French syndicates, including one involving his father, that subscribed large sums to the loan office debt. He argued that the continuing depreciation enhanced the attractiveness of the investment by increasing its potential yield. As a short-term strategy, putting currency in the loan office, where interest was still paid, had obvious advantages. However, it did not protect one against a general devaluation.[48] On March 18, 1780 Congress announced that the currency debt would be reduced to its current specie value, which was less than one-twentieth of face value. The action infuriated French investors. Repudiating the nominal value of the debt deprived them of the windfall profits they counted on to compensate them for losses incurred in exchanging European goods for American currency. Prominent French investors pressured their government to ask Congress to exempt French holders of American currency from the repudiation. Congress refused, and the French creditors would have to wait until after their own Revolution had begun before the United States made good on its pledge to redeem its loan office debt, even at liquidated specie value.[49]

AMERICA'S DISAPPOINTMENT WITH FRANCE

American merchants found dealing with the French as difficult as the French found dealing with the Americans. Americans had been accustomed to British merchants, who shared their culture, offered comparatively high-quality merchandise at bargain prices, and provided them with long-term credit. French merchants were ignorant of American customs, offered high-priced but inferior merchandise, and proved reluctant to extend any credit.[50] The French were also inept at selecting goods for the American market, ignoring the difference between the fall and spring markets, and sending luxury goods instead of cheaper ones. As a result, an American agent accepting a cargo for a French principal usually found that it took a long time to dispose of the consignment. Religious differences nourished mutual antipathy. Anti-French prejudices made Americans resistant to French goods and made French agents uncomfortable in North America. Prejudice also led to brutal fights between gangs of French and American sailors in the continent's ports.[51]

There was more in the American response than prejudice, though. Americans also felt that the alliance failed to address their commercial needs. In the early days, most French vessels had made for ports where they could load tobacco, rice, and indigo. These were southern ports remote from the principal theaters of the war. French trade failed to stimulate the regional economies further north, on which the Continental Army depended. The area with the greatest wartime economic potential was the Delaware–northern Chesapeake. The produce of its farms held the key to a successful resolution of the war. The region failed, however, to attract a commerce commensurate with its importance, particularly after the first year of the alliance, largely because of Britain's naval superiority.[52]

French maritime activity in the Chesapeake lessened after 1778 but did not cease. Beaumarchais, for one, remained committed to collecting the tobacco that Congress and the Virginia legislature pledged to deliver in exchange for the military supplies that he had brought to America. On August 25, 1778, the *Fier Roderique* cleared the Chesapeake Capes with its first convoy back to France before the tightening of British naval pressure on the mid-Atlantic. By October the ship had arrived safely at Rochefort.[53] Beaumarchais had intended to send it back to Virginia quickly in the company of a dozen merchantmen, but during the winter of 1779 it was diverted to convoy duty along France's Atlantic coast. Then, by order of Admiral La Motte-Picquet, the *Fier Roderique* was assigned to a convoy to the West Indies. D'Estaing commandeered the vessel into his fleet on July 6, 1779, for the Battle of Grenada, in which it took a place in the French line of battle and suffered considerable damage, losing its captain and 10 percent of its crew.

The *Fier Roderique* did not return to the Chesapeake until late November 1779. Sickness, the difficulties that Beaumarchais's agent, Théveneau de Francy, experienced in collecting the tobacco he had been promised, and a severe winter imprisoned it and most other vessels in the Chesapeake until the next spring. After two months of preparation, during which the price of tobacco rose to unheard of heights, a convoy of eighteen vessels sailed on June 14, 1780. That convoy reached Bordeaux on August 9, losing only one vessel. By this time the *Fier Roderique* had so deteriorated that it was not worth refitting. British operations in the Chesapeake between October 1780 and Cornwallis's surrender at Yorktown in October 1781 subsequently created additional difficulties for French entrepreneurs interested in the Bay.[54]

Between 1778 and 1780, frigates and occasionally larger French warships made runs from the Chesapeake and the Delaware to provision French forces in the West Indies. They usually escorted smaller supply vessels. These vessels were considered as much in the king's service as the frigates were, though like the royal charters they carried some freight from the islands. However, they constituted at best an occasional and unpredictable presence. France did finally commit a few frigates to the Bay after the British surrender at Yorktown, but too late to be of much benefit to the struggling community of French merchants in the region.[55]

The French entrepreneurs who persisted in the Chesapeake-Delaware did so by adjusting to wartime challenges just as Americans did. In August 1779 the Terrasson brothers, Barthélemy and Antoine, who had been sent by their well-established, provincial father to act as agents for his European associates in the New World, had set up a firm in Baltimore with another French adventurer. Terrasson et Poey responded to the difficulties plaguing all who dealt in tobacco by proposing to trade with the West Indies rather than with Europe. Almost simultaneously, Sabatier fils in France had come to similar conclusions about the advantages of mounting a provisions trade between the mid-Atlantic region and the Caribbean similar to the one that had developed during the early years of the war between the deep South and the islands.[56]

These responses failed to address the American economy's need for direct access to the European market. Instead, they duplicated a commerce in which Americans were already engaged. Since island markets were notoriously thin, they seemed to threaten an unwelcome competition. Given the shortage of shipping that existed throughout the war, there was no danger that French vessels in the West Indian trade with North America would crowd out American ones, whatever momentary inconvenience might be encountered in a specific port. Indeed, a thriving commerce with the West Indies seemed the most eligible way for Americans to gain access to European imports. Since the beginning of the war the islands had served as a way station for the westward movement of such strategic commodities as powder, arms, and uniforms. There was no reason why they could not perform a similar function for a wide array of consumer goods. Still, buying from and selling to Europe exclusively through the islands burdened the exchange process with crippling additional expenses.

Only New England enjoyed direct commercial contact with France throughout the war. Since the region lacked a ready supply of commodities that could find a market in Europe, the development surprised French officials. Yet, if we may believe the French consuls' reports, French merchants imported immense quantities of goods through Boston. Holker worried about the development because he felt the region lacked the means to pay for the goods, but the arrivals continued throughout 1779 and into 1780. In 1781 a sizable fleet under official French convoy from Europe entered Massachusetts Bay. French merchants increasingly focused on New England as the war progressed, and an otherwise peripheral economic region succeeded in placing its stamp on the emerging Franco-American commercial connection.[57]

The vigor of New England's privateering helped to pay for the imports. And after 1778 and throughout the rest of the war, British pressure on South Carolina's and Georgia's food exports to the islands increased West Indian demand for New England salt provisions.[58] In the end, though, French commercial activity in New England was less a product of what the region had to offer than a consequence of Britain's naval effort against Franco-American trade. During 1778, French vessels had conspicuously better luck getting in and out of Massachusetts Bay than their counterparts had elsewhere along the coast.

Massachusetts Bay extends three hundred miles between Cape Sable and Provincetown, distinguishing it dramatically from the comparatively narrow channels that give access to most of the rest of the continent's bays, sounds, and estuaries. This feature made it impossible to blockade Boston and its environs. In addition, fog was much more likely to shroud Massachusetts Bay than the Chesapeake, the Delaware, and the southern coastline. Fog was a blockade runner's friend because it increased the chances of slipping past enemy patrols. Finally, it was much more difficult to take station close to shore in Massachusetts Bay, since doing so exposed a ship to the risk of being caught by a northeast storm. Admiral Byron learned this in the autumn of 1778 when he tried to pin the French down in Boston with his squadron and in the process ended up losing the sixty-four-gun line-of-battle ship HMS *Somerset.* In the Delaware or Chesapeake, blockading ships could usually find a lee shore under which to take shelter. Even if the navy accepted the risks involved in a close blockade of Massachusetts Bay, an incoming vessel could always make for a more easterly port, such as Newburyport or Portsmouth, New Hampshire.[59]

Massachusetts Bay also presented far fewer navigational problems than did the other principal destinations, with the possible exception of the approach to Charleston from the West Indies. Massachusetts Bay's extension over four degrees of latitude allowed a number of options for those arriving from Europe. The route in from the West Indies was almost as simple as that from the east, thanks to Block Island Soundings, an expanse of distinctively dark green mud covering approximately two degrees of longitude and one of latitude off the southern New England coast. Once one picked up this mud on the leadline, even an inexperienced navigator could fetch the entrance to Massachusetts Bay with relative ease.[60]

Nothing in the course of the war changed Massachusetts Bay's distinction as offering the safest ports of entry, and Britain's commitment to operations against the South after 1778 gave French merchants additional incentives to shift trade northward. Holker was aware of how far the British naval threat had deflected the French trade from its principal objective. He tried to resist what was happening, first with exhortations and eventually by inserting penalty clauses in contracts specifying where goods might be landed. But this kind of pressure did not reverse the effect of Britain's seapower. Many of France's imports to New England eventually found their way to the middle states. But transportation costs increased their price still further, limiting their impact to marginally alleviating pent-up demand along the Hudson and in the mid-Atlantic states.[61]

Without access to French money and goods the Continental Army would not have been able to reclothe and rearm itself as the war continued, so the French commercial connection was in a sense vital to the success of the Revolution.[62] Nonetheless, the private activities of French merchants throughout the war, as distinguished from those sponsored by the French government, remained only marginally relevant to America's revolutionary economy.

A few French entrepreneurs like the Terrasson Brothers demonstrated extraordinary ingenuity as well as tenacity in adjusting to the challenges of the war economy. Always willing to consider innovative commercial strategies, they dissolved the partnership of Terrasson & Poey in Baltimore during the summer of 1780 to explore new ways of making the tobacco trade pay. During the following autumn, mounting British pressure in the Chesapeake led Antoine to move to Philadelphia, where his brother shipped any tobacco he was able to procure. The following spring Antoine was able to respond to La Luzerne's concerns about providing for expected reinforcements for the French army by directing Barthélemy to purchase Chesapeake flour. After it was learned that there would be no reinforcements and La Luzerne canceled the purchases, Antoine took ship for Havana with some of the firm's flour while Barthélemy moved to Philadelphia. Antoine's speculation met with enough success to enable him to go on to Cádiz, where he arrived early in 1782. From there he proceeded to France, where he negotiated with French suppliers a series of contracts designed to minimize the cost of the goods, their shipment overseas, and their distribution in the American market.[63]

Antoine's aggressive salesmanship in Europe together with a network of correspondents—mostly minor French adventurers whom Barthélemy managed from Philadelphia in the Chesapeake—had by mid-

1782 strategically positioned the brothers to take advantage of whatever commercial opportunities either war or peace might bring. Nor were the Terrassons the only French success story in the mid-Atlantic region. Others secured a foothold by pooling their capital with American firms, as was the case with LaCoste and Bromfield of Fredericksburg. Still others, like LaCaze and Mallot of Philadelphia, were resourceful and lucky enough in the war economy to emerge as aggressive purchasers of American shipping in 1782.[64]

The failures, however, far outnumbered the successes because the major French capitalists, those best equipped to meet the challenges of war, preferred to play it safe and follow where the government led rather than to master the difficulties entailed in trading with America on their own. The experiences of Beaumarchais, who after 1777 gradually retired from Franco-American trade, and Chaumont, who went bankrupt in 1781, provided a cautionary lesson for them. Royal charters continued to play some role in subsidizing imports from France to North America while Rochambeau's expeditionary force remained on the continent. But the aftermath of the war, both in France and America, suggests that the long-term effects of relying on state favors penalized French enterprise more than benefited it.[65]

In the end, the energy of most of the Frenchmen who did venture to America failed to compensate for their lack of capital and ensured that the French commercial connection at the conclusion of the war would remain one of unfulfilled potential. Though there was a large French community in Philadelphia, the French consul there complained that the city contained only two French merchants of any real credit. Stephen Girard would amass one of the great fortunes of the postwar era and would shape the development of Philadelphia and eventually the republic in significant ways. But no mercantile firm of French derivation exercised a comparable role during the Revolutionary War, least of all Girard's. His successes took place after the conclusion of hostilities and depended on his having committed himself to an American future.[66]

As the end of the war approached, French officials became more critical of the Franco-American relationship. They were acutely aware that Great Britain was in a better position than France to reap the rewards of the coming peace and were correspondingly pessimistic about the future of Franco–American trade.[67] Neither French nor American merchants emerged from the Revolution entirely satisfied with what the war had brought them, and both had reservations about the future of the French connection.

CONTENDING WITH ALBION'S MIGHT

Developments during 1778 underscored that the new nation's best defense against the economic dislocations brought on by the Revolution lay in its own exertions. From the very beginning Congress had realized that opening American ports to foreign vessels would not be enough. The harbors also had to be fortified. Congress accordingly recommended that each colony provide for the defense of its deep-water ports. Most responded by immediately building new fortifications or by strengthening existing ones. Where ports lay on important river systems, like Philadelphia and New York, revolutionary authorities tried to limit enemy access by creating floating chains, underwater chevaux-de-frise, and other navigational obstacles.[1]

THE CREATION OF THE AMERICAN NAVIES

The development of a naval force followed from the decision to defend the continent's deep-water ports. No one supposed that the revolutionaries would be in a position to challenge Britain's naval supremacy gun for gun, ship for ship. But specially armed vessels could provide protection against the enemy's lesser men-of-war, which merchant vessels were much more likely to encounter as they entered or cleared American ports. If nothing else, a naval force could maintain surveillance over the enemy's warships, notifying incoming vessels of hostile movements and safer routes. Commissioning armed vessels to scout the enemy's movements and escort merchantmen in American waters seemed both desirable and feasible from the beginning.[2]

Rhode Island was the first state to organize a naval force to defend its trade. The people living on Narragansett Bay quickly realized that they had less to fear from Captain James Wallace's twenty-gun sloop of war—the HMS *Rose,* which was patrolling the Bay—than from its armed tenders. Tenders posed the greater threat because they could pursue local craft into the shallow tidal waters from which larger vessels were excluded. Since the maritime economy of Narragansett Bay depended as much on small-tonnage coasters as on the larger vessels that conducted the region's overseas trade, many Rhode Islanders wanted Wallace's tenders checked. In mid-June 1775, Rhode Island armed several commercial vessels and commissioned them to "protect the trade" against the Royal Navy.[3] Strong as Britain was at sea, it was not omnipotent.

Massachusetts had considered a similar course in early June but declined to act after learning that the people of Machias had seized a small British man-of-war on the Maine coast. Preoccupied with the siege of Boston, the revolutionary government of Massachusetts moved slowly in response to local initiatives. It did not encourage the towns to fit out armed vessels until mid-October, and only at the end of 1775 did it begin to create a sizable state navy. By contrast, Connecticut, which suffered from Wallace's tenders almost as much as Rhode Island did, acted decisively at the beginning of July 1775 and commissioned two vessels of its own.[4]

By the end of 1775 most of the other colonies had followed New England's lead. In July, Pennsylvania's Committee of Safety had assumed responsibility for the naval defense of the Delaware. Pennsylvania also built the first specially designed vessels for its navy rather than just pressing existing vessels into state service. Early in 1776, Massachusetts surpassed Pennsylvania by authorizing the construction of ten 100-ton sloops of war. Six of these were actually built and put into commission. Virginia followed Massachusetts' lead and, with Pennsylvania, assembled one of the largest of the state navies. South Carolina's navy, initially smaller than those of the three leaders, eventually reached the size of Massachusetts' and Connecticut's navies combined. New England continued to enjoy a naval advantage over the rest of the nation, however. Its greater commercial tonnage allowed the governments to take private vessels of war into public service whenever they were needed. Maryland organized a more modest state navy, which at times cooperated with Virginia in defending the Chesapeake. Rhode Island and New Hampshire organized navies of moderate size. North Carolina, Georgia, and New York made half-hearted efforts toward establishing navies. British conquest affected the programs of Georgia and New York more than any others. Only New Jersey and Delaware made no naval effort at all.[5]

Building a Continental Navy proved more controversial than forming the Continental Army. British naval power seemed much less vulnerable to direct challenge by the revolutionaries than did the British army. Britain had emerged from the Seven Years' War (1756–63) as the dominant naval power in Europe in contrast to the colonists, who had little experience either in building large warships or in maintaining them. The revolutionaries assumed, as Thomas Paine had argued in *Common Sense,* that Britain would be able to deploy only a fraction of its navy in the western Atlantic. Most of it would have to be reserved for protecting the kingdom and British commerce and possessions in other parts of the world. But this simplified the task Americans faced in confronting Britain's naval might on paper more than in fact.[6]

The most critical problem for Americans was manning a naval force. They benefited from the surplus of jobless seamen caused by the Restraining Acts. However, these sailors respected the Royal Navy's reputation for aggressiveness in battle even more than they hated the practice of impressment. The army had attracted a flood of enthusiastic recruits in the opening days of the war, but seamen were reluctant from the beginning to join the state or continental navies. This may help explain why Congress remained divided over the wisdom of trying to form a Continental Navy long after an irreversible commitment had been made to the army. New Englanders generally backed a national navy as a supplement to their local naval efforts. Delegates from the mid-Atlantic region voiced skepticism about whether the cost of such a naval force could ever return comparable benefits. They did so even though navigation of the Delaware River and the Chesapeake was much more vulnerable to British naval control than was the New England coast.[7]

Congress gradually accepted the wisdom of establishing a naval force, even one that could not directly challenge Britain's command of the sea. In early October, news of two unarmed vessels carrying ordnance from England to Quebec underscored the use to which a continental navy might be put. If the vessels could be intercepted, their cargoes would prove a godsend to the patriots. Congress authorized Washington to commission New England armed vessels for the mission. It simultaneously voted to fit out two fourteen-guns brigs in Philadelphia—the *Cabot* and the *Andrew Doria*—for the same mission. Washington dispatched a fleet of small armed vessels from Plymouth and Beverly in Massachusetts, but they failed to intercept the ships Congress had in mind. However, the fleet captured another ship carrying ordnance and numerous other supply vessels, including eleven merchantmen that had to be returned because they were not in the ministry's service. Thus Congress was moving toward some naval involvement when news arrived of the burning of Falmouth (Portland, Maine) in mid-October. That resolved most remaining ambivalence over expanding the continent's naval force. Any residual reservations vanished with the British destruction of Norfolk, Virginia, on New Year's Day, 1776.[8]

By the end of January 1776, Congress had acquired and outfitted a fledgling navy of seven vessels, all under the command of Ezek Hopkins of Rhode Island. Once the first step was taken, the naval ambitions of Congress quickly expanded. In December 1775, when Congress concluded that the British government preferred a military showdown to a negotiated settlement, it commissioned the building of thirteen frigates capable of carrying heavy enough armaments to do battle with comparable British warships. The merchantmen available for conversion into the men-of-war that comprised Hopkins's fleet had not exceeded 300 measured tons; the larger of the frigates were projected at 500 to 700 measured tons. As the war progressed, Congress commissioned the building of two more frigates and a line-of-battle ship of more than 2,500 measured tons that was designed to carry seventy-four guns. Finally it purchased several frigates from France and even borrowed one, together with two smaller, armed vessels; all three were manned and sometimes officered by Frenchmen. The largest and most famous American fighting ship was a 900-ton French Indiaman, the *Bonhomme Richard* (42 guns [hereafter, the number of guns is designated by a number in parentheses]). In all, the continent commissioned fifty-eight vessels, representing a major effort by a society whose naval experience before 1775 had been confined to privateering.[9]

Congress conceived of the Continental Navy as a deep-water force. Its principal rationale was defensive, but Britain's naval superiority ironically made an offensive capability the continent's best defense. Robert Morris, an influential member of Congress's marine committee, underscored the point early in 1777 while outlining the purpose of a projected expedition against British West Florida. "It has long been clear to me that our Infant fleet cannot protect our own Coasts; and the only effectual relief it can afford us is to attack the enemies [*sic*] defenseless places." If the American navy could force the British navy "to defend their extensive possessions at all points," this would further divide "their force," relieving the pressure that Britain could apply to the North American coast.[10]

Deep-water navigation required vessels able to manage the extreme conditions periodically encountered on the high seas. Ideally such vessels would be built with seasoned timber; they would be of considerable draft so that they could carry enough sail to maximize their speed without overturning; and those carrying larger armaments would be double-decked. Most of the "clumps" that had been the workhorses of the peacetime trade were ill suited to such wartime use.[11] Whether converting merchant vessels or building from scratch, a deep-water navy was difficult and expensive to construct, especially in wartime.

Apart from the tight labor market, which affected the shipping centers as much as the countryside, chandlery, cordage, and sails became scarce once the war began. Though these items had constituted more than half the cost of the average merchant vessel before the war, the colonies had continued to rely on overseas sources. Consequently, prices rose after 1774 with the dramatic reduction in North America's commerce. Cannibalizing merchant vessels abandoned as unsuitable for wartime use remained an alternate but limited source of supply. Revolutionary America was better endowed with wood and iron, the main components in a deep-water man-of-war. Still, combining even these materials proved costly. Colonial America's iron industry was centered in the mid-Atlantic states, while New England had only three internal sources of iron, one of which lay inland along the New York border.[12] A deep-water navy also required constant administrative oversight if it were to be properly maintained.

Given the expense and problems involved in assembling a naval force, the newness of the revolutionary governments, and the awesome advantage enjoyed by the British navy, it seems surprising that so many of the states built deep-water navies. Why did they not defer in such matters to Congress?[13]

The new state governments could not put much stock in Congress's naval effort because they had little control over its deployment. If they wished to command the loyalty of their constituents, they had to demonstrate a capacity to defend them against the enemy, or at least a willingness to try. The initial success of the revolutionaries in finding areas where the Royal Navy's power could be challenged undoubtedly acted as an additional impetus. Economic incentives also were at work. A deep-water navy was much more likely to pay for itself through its captures on the high seas than could a navy confined to defending the coast. It also could help procure vital supplies from overseas. In the initial years of the struggle, many vessels taken into the state and continental navies found themselves carrying and fetching cargoes or running other sorts of errands only tangentially related to the defense of the nation's coast or commerce.[14]

All of the state governments realized that their resources were limited, and that led some to take a strictly defensive view of their navies. Those lacking the maritime resources of New England and preoccupied with economy chose the galley as the mainstay of their fleets. Though galleys carried sails—indeed, some were ship rigged—and were sometimes large enough to undertake ocean voyages, their principal form of propulsion was long oars known as "sweeps." Usually they carried one or two exceptionally heavy cannon—eighteen- to thirty-two-pounders rather than a larger number of six- to nine-pounders most common in American men-of-war. These guns normally were mounted on the bow rather than amidships, though one of Virginia's galleys mounted sixteen cannon and several others mounted ten. Galleys were somewhat narrower and of much shallower draft than deep-water vessels, and they were invariably single decked. They could also be assembled with considerable speed. The first one commissioned by Pennsylvania's Committee of Safety was slapped together in three weeks.[15] There was less carefully to select seasoned timbers for a vessel whose only function was to carry a battery of cannon in protected coastal waters.

All of the state navies except New Hampshire's used galleys, and the vessels initially dominated the naval forces of Pennsylvania and the southern states. Most of New England's coastline, especially from Cape Cod northward, is directly exposed to the open sea and therefore to the full force of the cyclonic storms that periodically sweep the Atlantic coastline. South of Cape Cod the coastal topography changes dramatically. A series of sounds, bays, and estuaries challenge the mariner's navigational skills but also afford a measure of shelter. Much of the protected water of the Atlantic coastline south of New York is shallow. Deep-water access to these areas is often limited to narrow and shifting channels. Galleys of light tonnage and draft seemed especially suited to defending them.

To be effective against a vessel of superior armament, however, galleys had to be able to fire without being fired upon. There were two options. One was for the galleys to present as small a target as possible by firing from the bow instead of from the beam. The more reassuring choice was to rely on the superior range of their large guns. Galleys were best suited to defending channels surrounded by large expanses of shallow water where they could take station out of range of an adversary with limited options for maneuver. An adversary able to maneuver could easily close the distance and destroy the galley. Narragansett Bay and the Connecticut coastline had shallow areas, but they usually were not proximate to the locations one most wanted to defend. Rhode Island and Connecticut built several galleys, but they proved less useful than expected.[16] The protected waterways of New England offered a good deal more room for deep-water vessels to maneuver than did the more southerly sounds and estuaries.

The Limits of American Naval Power

The revolutionaries' courage in committing themselves to carrying on a naval struggle against Great Britain should not be confused with their effectiveness. The first mission that Congress assigned the newly constituted continental fleet under Ezek Hopkins was to clear the Chesapeake of enemy cruisers, a task designed in part to placate Southern opposition to a navy. Congress quickly learned that issuing orders and having them carried out were two different things entirely. The Naval Committee had given Commodore Hopkins a way out by instructing him only to enter the Chesapeake if the enemy there were "not greatly superiour" in strength.[17] Even before departing the Delaware in mid-February 1776, Hopkins decided to make for the Bahamas.

In Hopkins's defense, everyone realized that the Chesapeake was a potential trap. Had Hopkins committed the continental fleet to extensive operations there, a powerful British force could have been drawn to the Capes, bottling up his fleet indefinitely and neutralizing at one stroke Congress's naval initiative. Going fishing in the Bahamas for powder and ordnance, which were still in critically short supply, seemed the more prudent course. Hopkins did manage to procure some of both before returning to New London. However, he forfeited the political and tactical value of making a token appearance in the Chesapeake.[18] A momentary show of force there or anywhere else on the American coast would, at the very least, have forced British cruisers to concentrate on their blockading stations, creating greater opportunities for American and foreign vessels to slip by them.

Hopkins had reason to be wary about risking his untrained fleet, even against an inferior British force. A chance encounter early on April 6,

1776, demonstrated why. Hopkins and his seven vessels were returning from the Bahamas when they stumbled on the twenty-gun HMS *Glasgow* in Block Island Sound as it made its way with dispatches from Boston to New York. Though outgunned by more than three to one in the amount of metal it could throw, the *Glasgow* escaped to Newport after inflicting heavy damage on the continental fleet, which limped into New London.[19]

Captain James Wallace's abandonment of the Rhode Island station shortly after this incident allowed Hopkins to move his fleet to Providence, where he argued that his Rhode Island connections would facilitate its refit. Still, he was unable to man more than two of his vessels before the British seized Newport in early December 1776. The enemy's unchallenged control of Aquidneck Island until August 1778 left the remaining vessels in Hopkins's fleet, in addition to the two continental frigates being built on Providence River, in a difficult position. They had to choose between running down a narrow channel past a substantial enemy naval force or rotting in idleness. Both of the new frigates, the *Warren* (32) and *Providence* (28), eventually got out during the first half of 1778, but one of the larger vessels in Hopkins's original fleet, the *Columbus* (20), did not.[20]

By then Congress had dismissed Hopkins. He had been subjected to a congressional investigation after the engagement in Block Island Sound but had retained his command. The Marine Committee recognized the difficulties of conducting any action, let alone a fleet action, without proper training. Congress was less forgiving after the seizure of Newport neutralized a major portion of its naval program. When Hopkins botched an operation that should have destroyed a British frigate grounded in Narragansett Bay in March 1777, Congress relieved him of his command.[21]

Disappointing as its achievements may have seemed during its first year and a half, the continental fleet still had accomplished something. Any challenge to British naval power, no matter how minimal, benefited the American cause. The small armed vessels that Washington had commissioned to cruise from Massachusetts Bay against military transports in 1775 eventually took thirty-eight prizes. The two vessels of Hopkins's fleet that did manage cruises in the autumn of 1776 put the enemy on the defensive in the Maritime provinces. Both initiatives forced the Royal Navy to divert some of its resources from blockading the coast to protecting its own vessels. Admiral Richard Howe responded to intelligence about Congress's naval-building program by having his frigates cruise off the principal American ports in pairs. This in turn qualified the scope of the blockade that he could mount.[22]

The Continental Navy also helped persuade Admiral Howe to put his naval resources at the disposal of his brother, Sir William Howe, commander of Britain's land forces, during the campaigns of 1776 and 1777. Given the difficulty and expense of replacing British military manpower in America, neither Howe wanted further losses—four troop transports were taken by American armed vessels directly after the evacuation of Boston. The amphibious nature of the operations that the British launched against Charleston, New York, and Philadelphia made naval support particularly important. Again, blockading the coast took second place to supporting the movements of the army through 1777. The Howes chose to subordinate their naval effort to the land campaign for another reason as well. If foreign intervention was to be forestalled, time was of the essence: a decisive victory over Washington's army seemed far more likely to bring the rebellion to a speedy end than would the slow workings of a blockade. In the autumn of 1777 the fleet was again tied down in opening the Delaware so that Henry Clinton's army of occupation could be supplied by sea. All of these developments rebounded to the advantage of American commerce.[23]

Whether the Continental Navy fully justified the resources it consumed is another matter.[24] None of the frigates authorized at the end of 1775 got to sea until 1777, and eight of those rendered no service while incurring considerable expense during that year. Four never would make any direct return on the capital invested in them, since they were destroyed or captured before they could put to sea. The navy also lost a continental frigate and three other vessels in the defense of Philadelphia. In Massachusetts Bay, the new frigates *Hancock* (32) and *Boston* (24) took HMS *Fox* (28) in early July 1777, only to lose it and the *Hancock* to the HMS *Rainbow* (24) and HMS *Flora* (32) two days later.[25]

The navy's other vessels fared only slightly better. The frigate *Raleigh* (32), in company with the *Alfred* (24), overtook a convoy of West Indiamen while on their way to Europe to complete the *Raleigh*'s armament. However, they were unable to capture more than a few of the merchantmen before being driven off by the convoy's armed escort.[26] The frigate *Randolph* (32), sailing out of Philadelphia, lost two masts made of rotted timber on its first cruise, forcing it to limp into Charleston for repairs. In September the *Randolph* eventually captured a small fleet of merchantmen off Charleston. According to historian David Ramsay, the prizes were worth half a million dollars, a substantial enough sum but hardly much of a return on the entire capital that had so far been laid out on the navy.[27]

The year 1778 began with a devastating series of losses. In February, the *Randolph* blew up while engaging a British warship of superior force, HMS *Yarmouth*. In early March, the *Alfred,* returning from Europe with the now fully armed *Raleigh,* was taken in the West Indies by two British vessels of inferior armament after the *Raleigh* failed to support her consort properly. And later in the month the British captured the frigate *Virginia* (28) trying to get out of the Chesapeake after its rudder was disabled on a shoal. All these losses forced the Marine Committee to become cautious about protecting its dwindling resources.[28]

Prospects in the western Atlantic subsequently brightened with news of the French alliance and the arrival of D'Estaing's expeditionary force in American seas. With them came two frigates purchased in France, the *Deane* (32) and the *Queen of France* (28). In addition, the *Warren* and the *Providence,* at last free of the blockade of Narragansett Bay, were in a position to join the *Boston,* the *Raleigh,* and the newly constructed frigate *Alliance* (32), together with the *Ranger* (18), to form a significant naval force. The Marine Committee wanted to put it at D'Estaing's disposal. France's expeditionary force was short on frigates, and the continent's navy could have kept D'Estaing better informed about the strength and disposition of Howe's fleet. Miscalculations about British naval strength contributed to D'Estaing's unpopular decision to abandon operations against Newport and retire to Boston.[29] However, the French commander showed no interest in Congress's offer. If he had, he would have been disappointed, as most of the navy's vessels were immobilized by equipment and manning problems.

D'Estaing's arrival in Boston in September to refit simply made matters worse by putting the limited resources of the Navy Board there under additional pressure. If the Continental Navy had no fleet to offer its ally, the least it could do was provide the French with the naval stores they needed. At the end of September 1778, the *Raleigh* did finally manage to embark on a cruise, but it was promptly driven on to the Maine coast by part of the stronger British force shadowing D'Estaing.[30]

Only in 1779 did the Continental Navy begin to yield benefits that seemed comparable to what it cost. The newly completed frigate *Confederacy* (32) replaced the loss of the *Raleigh* in the autumn of 1778. While manning and equipment shortages prevented all the commissioned vessels from putting to sea simultaneously, they eased in November 1778 after the French departed from Boston. For much of the following year small fleets of continental vessels offered American commercial vessels welcome relief by putting British cruisers on the defensive. The Continental Navy also experienced a brief streak of good fortune. In March 1779, in the course of a cruise against British privateers, the continental ships *Warren, Queen of France,* and *Ranger* intercepted a convoy of ten vessels en route from New York to Georgia and managed to seize seven transports as well as their armed escort. The following July the *Providence,* the *Queen of France,* and the *Ranger* intercepted a large Jamaican fleet off the Grand Banks, taking eleven rich prizes—eight of which got safely into Boston. These coups were to some extent neutralized by the loss at the end of July of the *Warren* and two sloops of war in the abortive Penobscot expedition. Fortunately, after lying idle for almost three years in the Connecticut, the *Trumbull* (28) finally got past the bar at its mouth to replace the *Warren.* The year 1779 also marked a high point for operations in European waters, with John Paul Jones's cruise around the British Isles culminating in the *Bonhomme Richard*'s (42) capture of HMS *Serapis* (44). Finally, the navy's activities contributed to the success of American privateers operating in northern waters during 1779.[31]

There was a price, however. From May through July the British conducted a series of raids along the coast to which the Continental

Navy made no response. Moreover, pressure on American commerce resumed after the failure of D'Estaing's assault on Savannah in October 1779. Despite this unwelcome development, the navy appeared to be holding its own and, equally important, paying its way during much of the year.[32]

Instead of being the prelude to greater things, however, 1779 was the high-water mark in the navy's fortunes. At the end of the year the Marine Committee ordered three of its frigates to Charleston to help defend the city against the British. When Charleston surrendered on May 12, 1780, two of them, along with the *Ranger*, fell into the enemy's hands after the remaining one was sunk as a navigational obstruction.[33] That left the continent with only four vessels of frigate strength—the *Alliance*, the *Confederacy*, the *Deane*, and the *Trumbull*—along with the newly launched *Saratoga* (18). A dismasting immobilized the *Confederacy* throughout much of 1780. The *Trumbull* managed a brief cruise that yielded no prizes before retiring to refit after an inconclusive engagement with a British letter of marque. Both the *Confederacy* and the *Trumbull* would be lost the following year while convoying merchantmen off the Capes of the Delaware, and the *Saratoga* foundered with the loss of all hands.[34] By mid-1781 the Continental Navy was capable of little more than running errands and raiding commerce for the remainder of the war.

The fortunes of the state navies paralleled those of the Continental Navy. Some of the galley fleets had an initial success in defending strategic waterways. Pennsylvania's thirteen galleys engaged the *Roebuck* (44) and *Liverpool* (28) in the Delaware on May 8–9, 1776, after which the two British frigates retired.[35] The following year the galleys participated in a heroic defense of the Delaware against an armada of more than two hundred vessels seeking to make its way up the river to Philadelphia. In this extended struggle the British lost the ship of the line *Augusta* (64), as well as the *Merlin* (18), both of which had run aground off Fort Mifflin. The former evidently was damaged by American shells, and the latter was burned by the British to keep it out of American hands. Overall, however, the galleys contributed only marginally to the battle. Most of the credit for temporarily halting the British advance upriver belongs to the gallant men from the army who manned Forts Mercer and Mifflin. When Fort Mifflin finally fell on November 15, Pennsylvania's navy and remnants of the continental fleet tried to retire up river. A few galleys got past the British position in Philadelphia, but most were destroyed, together with what deep-water vessels remained, either by their crews or by the enemy. The galleys that did make it upriver were dismantled on George Washington's recommendation.[36]

Despite their modest success in capturing three enemy vessels off the Georgia coast in 1778, the galleys declined in reputation with the loss of the Delaware. They lost further prestige in the Chesapeake when Virginia's galley fleet proved powerless to oppose Sir George Collier's armada as it ravaged the lower Bay in May 1779, destroying or capturing 130 vessels. Only one galley came to grief in this raid, but afterward the Board of War resolved to sell the rest. Some were put back in commission in 1780, but virtually all of them, along with whatever deep-water vessels Virginia had at its disposal, met destruction from the repeated British incursions that began on October 20, 1780, and culminated in Benedict Arnold's raid on Osborne's Landing near Richmond on April 27, 1781. Maryland also responded to Collier's raid by selling off its galleys during 1779–80.[37] Similarly, South Carolina's galleys proved of little use in the defense of Charleston.

The states' deep-water naval vessels eventually went the way of their galleys. Those of Connecticut and Massachusetts were effective commerce raiders until the enemy captured them. Most of Massachusetts's deep-water navy, as well as New Hampshire's one warship, were lost in the disastrous Penobscot expedition of 1779. Massachusetts kept a small deep-water fleet operational until the end of the war, but Connecticut, New Hampshire, and Georgia all abandoned theirs in 1779. None of Pennsylvania's deep-water fleet survived the fall of Fort Mifflin in 1777.[38] Charleston's surrender cost South Carolina's navy two of the frigates that it had recently acquired in Europe. Despite the effect of the British conquest on the state's credit, South Carolina managed to charter a Dutch-built vessel constructed to mount cannon customarily deployed on a seventy-four-gun line-of-battle ship. The *South Carolina* was the most heavily armed warship flying the American flag during the Revolution. Under the command of the controversial Alexander Gillon, it participated in a number of raids in European and American waters during 1781–82. But it failed to yield the profit hoped for before succumbing to three British frigates off the Delaware at the end of 1782. Virginia rebuilt a small naval force after the French drove the British out of the Bay, but it proved effective only against enemy corsairs.[39]

OBSTACLES TO CREATING EFFECTIVE NAVIES

Disappointing as the state and continental navies were, their poor performance cannot be attributed to lack of gallantry or skill on the part of the men involved. Although a few were incompetent or lost their nerve —as was to be expected in a service that had no traditions, professional standards, or esprit de corps—many more displayed extraordinary heroism and military prowess. The duel between the *Bonhomme Richard* and HMS *Serapis* in European waters on September 23, 1779, became celebrated in national folklore because the American vessel took a Royal Navy adversary with superior armament.[40] American captains challenged Britain's naval superiority on many other occasions as well. At the end of 1776, Lambert Wickes defiantly carried the American flag into British seas, and during 1777 he sent enough captured British vessels into French ports to precipitate a diplomatic crisis between France and Britain. In early 1778, John Barry audaciously harassed British ships traversing the lower Delaware to Philadelphia, and later in the war, while in command of the frigate *Alliance,* he took five vessels from a Jamaica fleet.[41] American captains and crews, both within the continental service and without, repeatedly demonstrated courage and resourcefulness. But several structural factors limited the effect of their heroic efforts.

Competition with American privateers for seamen and supplies hobbled the Continental Navy. Privateers could always find crews because privateering offered more money in exchange for less rigorous and less dangerous service. The navy subjected its crews to strict discipline because they had to engage British naval vessels as well as raid commerce. They were more likely to be injured or killed in combat and, if captured, to be incarcerated in Britain. Privateers could relax discipline because they seldom engaged vessels of superior force while they assumed that vessels of inferior force would strike without a fight. And privateersmen, if captured, ran a much better chance of being exchanged quickly. Reports of taking lucrative prizes throughout the war, and especially at its beginning, made privateering seem like the best chance to make good money with the least amount of danger and work. The men who joined such ships did not even have to wait for a capture to realize a return. Any crew member could sell his share in prospective captures, either in whole or in part, to eager investors before the cruise got under way.[42]

At the beginning of the war, the Marine Committee had high hopes for recruiting volunteers from captured warships and merchantmen. It assumed that Royal Naval crews would welcome release from military slavery. The committee also hoped to entice British merchant seamen into the American navies by releasing those captured and paying the wages due them. If the naval services had met with greater initial success, the committee might have succeeded. However, the foreigners who participated in the nation's maritime life during the Revolution, including deserters from French warships and merchantmen, did so largely on private vessels of war and letters of marque.[43]

The British navy also had to compete with private ships of war, but it possessed the time-honored remedy of impressment. That option was not so available to the Continental Navy. When in 1780 the *Deane* and the *Trumbull* attempted to seize men out of two Philadelphia privateers, the *Holker* and the *Fair American,* the Board of Admiralty ordered them returned. To counter the competition for mariners the Continental Navy resorted to other expedients: signing men on for a cruise rather than a calendar term; offering large bounties to sailors who manned its vessels for these cruises; and drawing on convicts and British prisoners of war, despite their dubious political loyalties.[44] State navies faced similar problems but had even fewer resources.

A more fundamental problem arose from capital shortages, especially late in the war. The Continental Navy benefited from embarking on a large building program in 1776, when prices were still reasonably low and Congress's credit intact. As the currency progressively lost value, however, building new vessels became more expensive. This is one reason why Congress turned in 1778 to purchasing frigates abroad. In 1779, after Congress had exhausted its credit at home and overseas, the Continental Navy's principal resource was its captures. This proved to be an irregular one at best, not only because the number of prizes declined with the waning strength of the navy but also because of difficulties encountered in efficiently distributing the proceeds of the few prizes that were taken. A prize, no matter how rich, brought into Boston would contribute relatively little toward the navy's bills in Philadelphia because of the difficulty in transferring the funds and because of price differentials. Throughout most of the war, prices in the mid-Atlantic markets remained considerably higher than those in Massachusetts Bay. The proceeds of a prize sold in New England would buy far less in Philadelphia than if it was sent into the Delaware and sold. The preference prize masters showed for New England ports increased both the cost and time required to repair damaged vessels or to fit them out for new cruises outside New England. Relying on captures for income also meant that losses were less likely to be replaced. Significantly, the only addition to the navy's list after the launching of the *Saratoga* in 1780 would be the *General Washington* (20), captured in 1782, and the *Duc de La Luzerne* (20) purchased with French aid the same year.[45]

Privateers also lived by their captures, and their owners labored under the same difficulties in building and fitting these vessels as the continental and state navies. Still, it cost a good deal less to fit a privateer for one voyage than it did to build and maintain a large warship for the duration. If a privateering venture failed to pay the expected return one could dissolve the syndicate. Privateers like Blair McClenachan's *Holker* persisted and brought riches to their sponsors; unsuccessful ones were taken by the enemy or abandoned to rot in a safe haven, or they found commercial niches as letters of marque. A continental frigate, however, was much more difficult to abandon because of the enormous investment it represented and because of the dishonor that doing so might bring upon the government. Though many state and continental vessels ended up carrying strategic cargoes, the cost of their armaments and fits meant that they could not do so economically.

Privateers also fared better than the navy because no one expected them to engage the British navy. No stigma attached to private ships of war that avoided combat with adversaries of superior force. Only the navy bore the burden of having to engage a truly formidable adversary. That considerably reduced the life expectancy of any continental vessel. Most lasted less than two years. Both of the frigates that survived the war had special features: the *Deane* enjoyed the technical advantage of having been built in France, and the *Alliance* was fitted with a copper bottom.[46] Continental men-of-war needed a special edge if they were to survive.

Many American frigates had been built too rapidly, with unseasoned timbers and defective masts and spars.[47] Repeated dismastings also suggest that they may have been overrigged. These problems were corrected with time, but there were two other stark differences between American and British men-of-war that time could not redress.

The Royal Navy began coppering its smaller men-of-war in 1778 and moved on to its line-of-battle ships in 1779. By 1782, almost all British war vessels had received copper bottoms, giving them an undisputed advantage in terms of speed and serviceability. The American economy did not produce sufficient copper for this purpose, so whatever ships were coppered had to get the material from Europe either by importing it or going there themselves. Very few did.[48]

The navy's greatest handicap derived from inferior armaments. At the beginning of the war, no continental vessel carried anything heavier than 12-pound cannon, and some, like the *Confederacy* and the *Queen of France,* carried mostly 9- or 6-pounders. They were no match for British vessels armed with 18- and 24-pounders. Later, heavier cannon were bought in Europe. The *Bonhomme Richard* boasted a half-dozen 18-pounders but had to settle for 12- and 9-pounders to complete its armament. With these the vessel battled the *Serapis,* which was equipped with twenty 18-pounders, twenty 12-pounders, and ten 6-pounders. The *Alliance* brought home from Europe a set of 18-pounders, which the Marine Committee authorized it to mount in 1780 if the Commissioners of the Navy Board in Boston thought it could bear them.[49] Still, for most of the war the navy's larger vessels were outgunned as well as outsailed.

The disadvantage in gunnery in turn controlled the Continental Navy's deployment. If the Eastern Navy Board issued orders for the fleet to concentrate, it risked the navy's destruction by a more powerful enemy. The Continental Navy could not be stationed at strategic choke-points, such as the Capes of the Chesapeake and the Delaware, for fear of attracting a superior enemy force. Nor could it afford to tarry long in any area of the open sea. Instead of concentrating its force, which was the principal tactic of Europe's state navies, the Continental Navy's safest course was to disperse. The strategy made its vessels additionally vulner-able to British capture or destruction when they encountered enemy warships on the high seas and doomed the Continental Navy to playing a marginal role in the struggle.[50]

Despite repeated opportunities for doing so, the Continental Navy never succeeded in cooperating with various divisions of the French navy that appeared on the American coast after 1777. Neither the conti-nental nor the state navies played any role in establishing the momentary naval supremacy necessary to make the siege of Yorktown a decisive victory.[51] The marginality of both compromised the political will to maintain them. Individual ships might occasionally distinguish them-selves, but to no strategic effect. Indeed, the navy's losses often served to enhance the enemy's naval strength. Thus the *Hancock,* the first conti-nental frigate to be captured, had, as HMS *Iris,* participated in the cap-ture of the last frigate to be lost, the *Trumbull.* Though continental vessels occasionally took Royal Navy vessels of inferior armament, they failed to bring in any frigate-sized vessel in American waters.[52]

Both the continental and state navies had more success raiding com-merce, but that by itself hardly justified the expense and commitment of scarce resource involved. Commercial depredations could just as well be executed by letters of marque or privateers, as Salem-based Jonathan Haraden's exploits in the *General Pickering* showed. One could clear local seas of enemy privateers without a navy, as Silas Talbot's 1779 adven-tures with the *Argo* off the southern New England coast demonstrated. American privateers would attack their British counterparts if there was a payoff, such as bounties for guns and prisoners and full rights to the captured vessel. Privateering fleets were as effective as the navy in commerce raiding, to judge from the capture of nineteen ships in a convoy bound from Britain to Quebec in 1780.[53] However, seizing merchant vessels, whether they were of comparable or inferior strength, did not have much effect on the overall balance of naval power. The insurer, Lloyds of London, released statistics about the number of merchant vessels and privateers captured by both sides during the war. These showed a loss of 2,208 British merchant vessels to the belligerents (the United States, France, Spain, and eventually the Netherlands) balanced by the capture of 1,106 enemy merchant vessels. While Lloyds's lists are not wholly accurate, they allow one to get a sense of comparative recapture rates. They suggest that the British recaptured 39 percent of the vessels they lost while the allies recaptured only 2.5 percent of the merchant vessels Britain seized. American and allied commerce raiding took its toll, but Britain continued to rule the seas.[54]

All the states' navies struggled against the same difficulties as the Continental Navy. All experienced crippling manning difficulties. All had to contend with chronic shortages of suitable naval stores and bare treasuries. All were powerless to counter any determined concentration of naval force by the enemy. When it became clear that the state navies yielded little in either protection or booty commensurate with their cost, they gradually disbanded.[55]

The Response of American Merchants

American merchants had realized from the beginning that if the new nation was to have an overseas commerce, it would not get very far relying on the naval efforts of the continent, the states, or foreign allies. In the early years, when the procurement of strategic commodities—like powder, salt, and arms—was vital, and the risk of navigating the seas seemed particularly high, Congress and the states sponsored much of the trade for strategic supplies. The usual procedure was to charter a private vessel at public risk and issue a permit exempting it from the Continental Association. Because the New England states produced little that Europe wanted to buy, the official and unofficial commerce of the region focused on voyages to the south and to the West Indies to obtain the remittances needed to pay for European imports. Robert Morris, as chair of Congress's secret commercial committee, sponsored some enterprises on public account directly to Europe because the middle Atlantic region had access to flour and tobacco.[56] While nonexportation remained in effect, publicly sponsored enterprises—either by the states or the continent— were the rule rather than the exception. Once Congress opened the continent's ports, though, most state governments recognized the advantage of encouraging private entrepreneurs to supply the continent's needs. Still, the character of that commerce, whether public or private, continued to be shaped by the enemy's superiority at sea.

The increased risks of seaborne commerce increased the costs of exchanging American produce for foreign commodities in several ways. For a time, the fear of seizure did almost as much to diminish the supply of foreign goods as had American-imposed restrictions on commerce. Some American merchants initially responded to the outbreak of war by retiring or at least thinking about it. The mariners who manned the merchantmen occasionally suffered a similar loss of nerve. But the lack of alternatives drove nearly all seamen and most merchants back into seaborne commerce. Seamen failed to adjust well to land routines, and merchants lacked secure investments to live on. In addition, the dream of turning wartime shortages to commercial advantage served as a lure. American merchants had been accustomed by their peripheral position in the British Empire to taking risks before independence and were unwilling to let the greater perils of the war blind them to new opportunities.[57] However, all pursued whatever strategies they could to lessen those risks.

The most obvious strategy was insurance. Marine insurance in eighteenth-century America was still an individual rather than a corporate enterprise. Ports with substantial commerce usually had one or more insurance offices that wrote policies, posted them, and settled balances between the insurers and the insured for a fee. The actual capital was put up by individuals or partnerships, who signed their names at the bottom of the policies—hence the term underwriter—for the posted rate. No money changed hands at this point. The contract simply stipulated that the insured would pay the insurers the stated premium on their subscriptions whether or not the vessel came to grief. If the vessel did not complete its intended voyage, the amount of the premium was deducted from the amount for which the underwriters were liable. Balances between the insured and the underwriters customarily remained unsettled for some time, especially in cases of distant losses, where proof was required before underwriters would honor the policies. If no one subscribed at the rate initially posted, those seeking insurance had to offer more favorable terms or do without.[58]

This mode of writing insurance had disadvantages. For one thing, insurance was not always available. Not only were insurers sometimes reluctant to insure, but at others they could not due to lack of capital. Then, both the insurers and the insured remained vulnerable to each other. Underwriters, for example, could be victimized by fraud. An owner who had received intelligence that made the loss of a vessel seem likely or certain could take advantage of the underwriters by posting a policy before the news became public. On the insured's side, there was no way to guarantee that an underwriter would be able to pay the sums he had underwritten. In the event of a default, the insured's only recourse was to sue for breach of contract. But that was not much of a remedy if in the interim the underwriter had become insolvent.[59]

Eighteenth-century marine insurance left rates especially sensitive to adverse news of captures and to changing perceptions of the disposition of naval forces in the seas mentioned in the policy. Those seeking insurance often complained that underwriters exaggerated risks. But insurance would have quickly disappeared if the rates at which underwriters were prepared to subscribe their capital had not exceeded the actual capture rates being experienced among the insured. Frauds and capital shortages contributed to rising rates, but it was captures that pushed them to between ten and eighteen times what they had been during peacetime.[60]

One solution to the high rates that American entrepreneurs encountered during the war was to seek insurance elsewhere. In the late colonial period some American merchants had routinely insured in Britain. As the conflict drove up costs, merchants came under more pressure to find lower rates in other North American ports, in Europe, or in the West

Indies, where outbound vessels could avail themselves of the protection of convoys. Many became proficient in shopping around for the lowest rates. Additionally, merchants in different ports might agree to cover each other's risks with insurance to protect themselves against sudden fluctuations in local rates.[61]

Still, problems remained with insuring away from home. Usually one had to defer to the judgment and discretion of one's agents. Moreover, during wartime Americans found themselves at a disadvantage competing in the strained capital markets of Europe. When disputes arose, they were vulnerable to local favoritism. Sending the required proofs of loss overseas could be time consuming and bothersome. And the insured sometimes had to accept payment on undesirable terms when contracts were honored. Where cash was short, American insurers might tender a commodity like molasses to satisfy claims. One merchant found to his horror that his French underwriters paid him not in cash but in notes of long date secured by other vessels still at sea.[62]

The uncertainties and difficulties involved in having others insure one's venture led merchants to explore schemes for self-insurance. One strategy dating from early colonial times was to distribute ownership as widely as possible. Merchants, whose partnerships before the outbreak of hostilities had resembled joint stock companies, began to offer shares in privateering and trading ventures to their fellow merchants and to accept such offers in return. Instead of two or three partners in a venture, shares were now broken down into eighths, sixteenths, thirty-seconds, and even sixty-fourths. The actual owner of a vessel might retain a half share in the venture to maintain control, covering his risk with insurance. Others would participate in the enterprise at a more modest level. Expanding the number of participants in the enterprise helped to raise capital in short supply as well as to distribute risk more evenly. However, expanding the number of investors also made management of the enterprise more difficult, particularly if they did not all reside in one place.[63]

There were other ways to share risk that did not involve an outright pooling of capital. For instance, a merchant ordering a parcel of goods from overseas could instruct his agent to divide the goods among several vessels coming to America. Then a syndicate that provided the goods might agree with a different syndicate of vessel owners to become joint venturers in a voyage, splitting the proceeds proportionately to what each had invested. Alternatively, one syndicate might promise to pay another a certain sum if its vessel were lost in exchange for a reciprocal pledge. Finally, two merchants from the same port, who had been fortunate enough to have their vessels arrive at a common foreign destination, might load their return cargoes on each other's vessels.[64]

The most obvious strategy for minimizing the risk of capture during wartime was to arm. Any armament, no matter how small, diminished the chance of being taken, because enemy cruisers came in all sizes. In certain conditions, a small whaleboat of less than ten tons mounting one gun could take a large, richly laden but unarmed vessel of three hundred tons. If one had no way to defend oneself against a hostile vessel that could fire on one with impunity, the only alternative was to strike. Armaments, though, forced one to sacrifice cargo space. Cannon were not so much bulky as heavy, but their weight limited the amount of cargo one could stow. They also required additional men, and enlarged complements did directly displace cargo. It made no sense to ship armaments without additional crew both because of the expense involved in procuring the guns and because enemy cruisers preferred to board a merchantman rather than cannonading it, in order to conserve the value of the prize. The best protection against being taken was to have enough manpower and firepower to deter the attempt in the first place.

Speed and versatility also diminished the risk of capture. A fast sailor capable of making to windward could often escape pursuit by a larger, heavily armed vessel. Captains were frequently advised to clean their hulls in foreign ports through careening before returning to North America. Despite the difficulty and expense of obtaining naval armaments, American vessels under pursuit often jettisoned cannon to make them faster. Some merchants felt that arming smaller vessels was pointless because "it adds but little to their safety and must prejudice the sailing." The speed of any vessel could also be enhanced by loading it with a less-than-capacity cargo, and American captains usually elected to preserve their vessel's sailing trim in this way.[65]

The size of a vessel also affected the likelihood of capture. Smaller vessels were much more versatile in eluding cruisers than were larger ones. Shallow draft vessels could escape from larger vessels of force by taking refuge in coastal waters. Large vessels were also visible at a greater distance than small ones. This gave small vessels a special advantage at first light. Robert Morris advised Congress's agent in the West Indies, William Bingham, to instruct French masters making for the American coast to be sure that they were "lying hull down" (without any sails set) at daybreak. A vessel following this advice would be able to "see the Enemy when they cannot see her." In addition, enemy cruisers usually pursued the largest vessels in a convoy as they scattered, on the assumption that the larger vessel would make the more valuable prize.[66]

The shift to smaller vessels was difficult and costly. Because New Englanders had their commerce curtailed earlier than the rest of the colonies, they enjoyed a head start in adjusting to a war footing. When they realized that their larger, slower tonnage was vulnerable to enemy capture, the more enterprising merchants tried to sell them in other ports, such as St. Johns, Newfoundland, Quebec, and Philadelphia. Unsalable vessels were cannibalized to "dress" the smaller or faster ones that remained. Philadelphia merchants had less opportunity to unload their unsuitable tonnage both because the New Englanders had already saturated the market and because the Continental Association excluded Philadelphians from the larger British market after September 10, 1775.[67] But Philadelphians were no less assiduous in abandoning their large vessels. One of the rare pieces of statistical information about Philadelphia's maritime activity during the war, apparently taken from naval records that no longer survive, shows that the average tonnage of vessels clearing the port in 1779 stood at half the prewar figure. Levi Hollingsworth's flour inspection book suggests that this decline, as reflected in the average size of cargoes that came under his scrutiny, occurred well before the occupation in 1777–78.[68]

As the conflict progressed, American shipbuilders responded to wartime conditions with what became known as the "new construction." What was new were not the principles of making fast sailors, already embodied in Bermuda and Virginia sloops and schooners, but their general application to commercial activity. Clumps dominated prewar seaborne commerce because they offered the most stowage per measured ton. Clumps characteristically had rounded bows, a broad beam, and minimal deadrise (that is, their bottoms proceeded outward almost at right angles from the keel before turning upward toward the deck). "Sharp" vessels of the new construction had longer, narrower hulls that tapered upward from the keel at a noticeable angle. Faster they certainly were, but their speed was purchased with drastically reduced cargo space.[69]

Merchants preferred the new construction because it made it more likely that a vessel would complete its voyage. Sharp vessels could also be insured at much lower rates than clumps. Ports that had been serviced predominantly by British shipping before the war enjoyed the advantage of not having to write off their stake in clumps when converting to a war footing. Perhaps this is why a port like Baltimore benefited from insurance rates markedly lower than those prevalent in Massachusetts Bay, at least during the late 1770s.[70]

PAYING THE PIPER

Every risk-avoidance strategy that American merchants pursued was designed to encourage commercial enterprise under wartime conditions. By stressing speed, arming, and downsizing, American merchants made it easier to find investors to cover the costs of fits, conversions, and the new construction. When new vessels were appropriately armed and manned, they were also insurable at lower rates.[71] Still, these adjustments were not necessarily beneficial to the society as a whole. A few individuals managed to accumulate quick wealth in privateering. Some merchants emerged from the conflict far richer than they had been before it began.[72] But most were not so lucky. The overall effect of the war-imposed adjustments was to increase the cost of exchanging domestic produce for foreign imports for almost everyone.

The rising expense of manning vessels highlights some of the costs involved. The demand for skilled seamen by privateers and the navies made it particularly difficult to engage crews for purely commercial ventures. Sailors preferred service on vessels where they received a share in the proceeds of captures. This was not just because a rich prize could be infinitely more lucrative than the highest wages. While the value of goods of all kinds continued to rise against money, a crew's share in a prize offered them more protection against inflation than wages did.[73]

Commercial venturers also found themselves bidding for crew members by advancing wages and by increasing the crew's "privilege" (the portion of the cargo that sailors had an interest in). And owners were forced to yield to the reluctance of crews to undertake prolonged voyages. That reluctance sprang from the threat posed by depreciation, as well as from the difficulty of getting back home in case of capture or discharge.[74]

Historians traditionally have regarded seamen as singularly exploited compared with other legally free laborers. Did the war enhance their bargaining power? Some individuals undoubtedly benefited from wartime circumstances, but they were few. Seamen's wages hardly kept up with the depreciation of the currency, and a single share of a prize, no matter how rich, did not amount to a personal fortune after deductions were made for expenses. Further, the chance of becoming ill, of being wounded or killed by enemy fire, or of being captured remained substantial. Capture could, in turn, involve a choice between long periods of imprisonment under dangerous conditions or serving on board an enemy man-of-war. And the likelihood of being shipwrecked while navigating dangerous winter seas to avoid enemy cruisers was considerably greater than during peacetime.[75]

Merchants shared parallel frustrations with seamen, whose hard lot the war failed to ameliorate. Initially, privateering seemed to offer merchants a panacea for their problems. The kinship that privateering bore to piracy had given some merchants momentary reason to abstain. While lucrative prizes continued to tumble in, as they did in the early phase of the war, privateering quickly became accepted as a means of financing the changes that the war imposed on the way American merchants did business. But privateering soon proved to be a mixed blessing. Once British merchant ships began to arm, form convoys, or take refuge under neutral flags, the returns on their investments dropped as the risk rose and the cost of equipping suitable vessels increased. Privateering persisted, especially in New England, because of the absence of a regional staple suitable for the European market. Seizures on the high seas often yielded products that could serve as remittances. The frequent resort to export embargoes also encouraged privateering because they applied only to merchantmen. The difficulty that French merchants experienced in making remittances from America to France sometimes led them to take shares in North American privateers.[76]

Over time, most merchants realized that privateering provided at best only a partial substitute for commerce. A prize might yield as much trouble as profit if it were not brought into a port where the backers resided. Even then the cargo might prove ill suited to the place. A ship sailing from Canada with lumber for the West Indies, seized and brought into Massachusetts or New Hampshire, was the proverbial carrier of coals to Newcastle. A privateering center might find itself awash in luxuries, such as wine and West Indian produce, but lacking in essentials, such as salt. In 1777, Boston was deluged with prize flour; a year and a half later it had no bread. Privateering, even when it was most successful, still had limitations.[77]

As the war dragged on, merchants came increasingly to compromise between privateering and commerce by investing in letters of marque. Letters of marque increased the chance of high returns to both investors and crew, and not incidentally reduced the costs of manning and insurance. Since they had a dual mission of carrying commercial cargoes and seizing enemy shipping, they often had less armament than a privateer of comparable burthen and considerably fewer crew members. Though there was no uniform rule, crews of letters of marque sometimes got a smaller share of a prize than did privateersmen because they were paid wages. By way of compensation, though, smaller crews made each member's share worth more. Investors could also hold the line against wage demands through the distribution of share rights.[78] The Massachusetts Council Papers, which distinguish between commissions issued to privateers and letters of marque, reflect a growing preference for the latter over the course of the war. By 1779, letters of marque had taken a decisive lead.[79]

The transformation of privateers into letters of marque did not solve all the merchants' problems. Investors still had to bear the direct costs of converting merchantmen into armed vessels and the indirect costs of the larger complements involved. The direct costs proved staggering because of the inflated price of skilled labor and armaments in the principal ports, not to mention the costs of duck, cordage, and chandlery, which remained in short supply during the war. Since speed was as important in a letter of marque as in an ordinary commercial vessel, investors preferred the new construction, despite the astronomical costs involved. Some syndicates had vessels built in France to avoid the high costs of wartime America as well as to avail themselves of superior French technique.[80]

Investors quickly overcame their reluctance to foot the bill in these ventures once they realized that the costs could be passed on to others. Thanks to the general reduction in tonnage accompanying the war, a fast, well-armed vessel could command premium freights. In June 1781, a partner in the Maryland firm of Wallace, Johnson, and Muir predicted that the freight from just one round trip of a vessel newly completed for them in France would pay off the entire cost of its construction. Freights varied according to value and bulk, with the most valuable, least bulky commodities bearing the least charge, proportionately. A captain would carry tea and handkerchiefs for as little as 10 to 12 percent of what their sale would gross in America. Bulkier commodities commanded higher freights, if the captain accepted them at all. Flour to the West Indies during the war usually fetched a freight of between 25 and 33 percent, payable in the commodity shipped. The rate could rise to as much as 50 percent in well-armed, "fast sailors," in which one could place one's property without insurance, when demand exceeded available tonnage. Tobacco, the bulkiest wartime staple in relation to intrinsic value, routinely commanded a freight of 50 percent.[81]

In addition to freight one also had to pay "primage." This traditional fee of less than 1 percent had in peacetime been analogous to tipping the captain for taking care of one's goods. In wartime it became a premium paid to get him to accept them, and on occasion it rose to as much as 5 percent.[82]

Lucky captains benefited from these circumstances, as did a few strategically placed entrepreneurs who retained their ability to maneuver within the wartime constraints on commerce. For example, while freights from Europe were extraordinarily high, they remained considerably cheaper for the few in North America who could arrange to have them paid in advance overseas.[83] Owners might also enhance the return on a voyage through various strategies for self-insurance, thereby avoiding the high premiums that would otherwise be paid underwriters. Fragmentary evidence suggests that traditional insurance increasingly lost favor among merchants as the war progressed, though only the fortunate benefited.[84] The comparative good fortune of the few did not compensate for the burdens borne by the majority of the population. For many producer-consumers, withdrawing as much as possible from the long-distance market often was the most attractive course. This response, however, made it more difficult for merchants to pass along the cost of doing business to the consumer, and it further taxed their ingenuity in meeting the challenge posed by Britain's naval power.

INTRACTABLE FETTERS

More deadly to American merchants than the loss of their ships and cargoes to Britain's naval power was the enemy's ability to seize major ports on the North American coastline. This, together with the continued depreciation of the continental currency, throttled the potential of the revolutionary economy and dramatically limited the revolutionary leadership's options in carrying on the struggle.

AMERICA'S PORT TOWNS

America's principal ports evolved as anomalies on the colonial landscape. Only a fraction of the North American colonial population resided in towns of more than 2,500 persons. The "urban" sites that did develop were scattered throughout the British settlements, apparently without regard to the size of the jurisdiction in which they emerged. For example, in 1775, Virginia was the largest mainland colony, with a population pressing 500,000, yet it lacked a major city. Its capital, Williamsburg, did not rank among the top twenty centers of population in the thirteen colonies. Its population expanded to accommodate the seasonal attendance of the Burgesses when the legislature was in session, but as a town it performed few economic functions other than providing the site for a local market.[1]

The first towns in colonial America were established as administrative and military centers. They grew principally in response to immigration flows. In the eighteenth century the continent's largest towns emerged as commercial centers. The four biggest—Boston, New York, Philadelphia, and Charleston—had developed in locations with strategic advantages for reducing the cost of processing and exchanging exports for imports. They ranged in size from 12,000 to 40,000 inhabitants, and they dominated the overseas trade of their respective regions. A major share of each region's exports passed through these ports. Smaller ports also contributed to the flow of staples overseas, either by funneling them toward the commercial center of the region or by exporting them directly to foreign markets. By 1775, sixteen smaller towns with populations between 3,000 and 10,000 were active in overseas trade.[2]

All of the top twenty centers of population on the eve of the Revolution, with the exception of Lancaster, Pennsylvania, were seaports. And all had evolved in response to expanding overseas demand for American produce during the eighteenth century. These towns in turn nourished the growth of numerous smaller towns in the interior, which channeled American staples toward the secondary and primary commercial centers, while receiving imports from them to be distributed to inland consumers.[3]

Expanding exports enabled an increasing quantity of imports to flow into British North America, and the major port cities handled more imports than they did exports. This dominance in the import trade made them gateways for the introduction into provincial America of a range of commodities from the larger Atlantic world.[4] The gateway ports' disproportionate involvement with imports in turn provides us with a clue about the commercial functions they performed that lesser ports were unable to do as well.

America exported agricultural surpluses possessing low value in relation to volume. It imported comparatively high-value, low-volume commodities in return. Thus a vessel arriving in a European port with

American produce was unlikely to be able to fully reload with the proceeds of its cargo. While the unused cargo space pushed down freight rates on voyages from Europe, the resulting savings failed to balance the cost of underutilized shipping.[5] Partially filled vessels arriving in America raised substantially the unit cost of overseas imports. Locating the exchange process in a major port made it possible to recover some of this cost in several ways.

As collection centers for the bulk commodities of their regions, the gateway ports could provide incoming vessels with full return cargoes, lessening turnaround times (limiting demurrage, in commercial terminology). More important, many of the ports' merchants acted as wholesalers who distributed imports to the interior, facilitating the rapid disposal of incoming goods to retailers and consumers. The efficiency with which the larger ports disposed of incoming goods made British merchant capitalists willing to finance full cargoes of imports on credit. In addition, the larger ports provided services that supported the exchange process, such as navigational aids, safe anchorage, wharfage, warehousing, court houses, naval offices, customs houses, insurance, and the ready sale of bills of exchange drawn on distant commercial centers. Finally, merchants could obtain what they needed for refits, including cordage, chandlery, duck, and spars, not to mention cooperage, carting, seamen, and provisions, at prices considerably below those in the lesser ports.[6]

A hierarchy of towns linked the gateway ports to outlying regions by selling imports and collecting exports. Lancaster helped connect Philadelphia with the Pennsylvania backcountry; Newport, Providence, New Haven, New London, Middletown, and Norwich linked New York to the hinterland of Rhode Island and Connecticut; and Georgetown, Wilmington, and Savannah helped connect North Carolina's and Georgia's expanding economy with that of Charleston. The economic integration of each of the gateway regions depended to some extent on carting. This was particularly true of Philadelphia's trade with its hinterland, which centered around Lancaster.[7] However, water transport ultimately proved more critical in determining the market reach of the gateway ports.

Small vessels plying the coastal and inland waterways linked the regional gateways to secondary and tertiary towns along the coast and principal rivers far more efficiently than horse- or ox-drawn wagons could, particularly over substantial distances. In effect, the gateway ports served as regional foci for the coastal trade. Superior water communication with an unusually rich hinterland explains why Philadelphia surpassed Boston as the premier gateway city of the continent in the mid-eighteenth century. Except for a short, seven-mile overland stretch between Head of Elk and Christiana Bridge, Philadelphia enjoyed uninterrupted water access to both the northern Chesapeake and the Delaware River areas.[8] Furthermore, its location midway on the Atlantic coastline allowed for easy communication with the other secondary and primary ports of the continent.

New York's emergence as a gateway port derived from similar advantages. Its location at the junction of the Hudson River with the Atlantic, besides providing an unrivaled harbor and a deep water passage 140 miles to the northward, gave it protected coastal and riverine access to eastern New Jersey, southern New England, and Long Island. Boston continued to perform gateway functions for northern New England after 1760, but its market reach in southern New England progressively shrank as New York's expanded. Charleston's dominance over the expanding lower Carolinas and Georgia continued unchallenged. However, British-based factors interested exclusively in a staple trade in indigo and rice restrained that port's development as a general entrepôt until the last years of the colonial era.[9]

Historians have also distinguished between two tiers in the North American staple trade: a primary economy centered on the exchange of domestic surpluses for European imports and a secondary economy centered on exchanges with the West Indies. Trade with the islands was secondary in the sense that it took a good deal less capital than did trade with Europe. As a consequence, many more merchants could participate in it. The West Indian trade was also secondary in a legal sense. The Navigation Laws did not accord it the same preferential status that staples exported directly to the British home market received.[10] The key difference between the European and West Indian markets, however, was that the former drove the latter. Those areas that enjoyed a favorable balance of trade with Europe, such as the Chesapeake and the deep South, were slow to develop an extensive West Indian trade. Those that had an adverse balance of trade with Europe, such as the colonies north of the Chesapeake, depended on the West Indian trade to make up the difference.[11] As a result, the northern colonies developed a complex commerce that in turn encouraged urbanization.

The disproportionate location of gateways in the northern colonies becomes more understandable once these ports are also seen as sites where the primary and secondary economies were integrated. Thus in 1772, Philadelphia enjoyed the largest trade with the West Indies as measured by clearances, while Boston took the lead when it came to entries.[12] However, the West Indian trade remained less centralized than the European trade. Boston found itself closely rivaled by Piscataqua (modern Portsmouth, New Hampshire), as well as Newbury, Massachusetts, and its other principal outport, Salem (including Marblehead), in clearances to the West Indies. Only when it came to entries did all four ports yield to Boston, on which they continued to depend as a gateway for European imports. Similarly, Rhode Island enjoyed a large trade with the West Indies but had only a modest direct trade with Europe. Though Rhode Island's entries and clearances for the islands remained more in balance than did those of the Massachusetts outports, Newport and Providence continued to depend on Philadelphia, New York, and Boston to conduct a significant portion of their European trade.[13]

The merging of primary and secondary economies with a growing internal trade played a role in colonial urbanization that is demonstrated by the one apparent exception to the rule. The tobacco regions of the Chesapeake and of North Carolina alone lacked a regional commercial center, even though tobacco accounted for 90 percent of the Chesapeake's exports to Europe and 50 percent of the continental colonies' exports to the mother country.[14] The absence of urbanization in the Chesapeake can be explained by the organization of the tobacco trade. Most of the crop was marketed in Europe by British entrepreneurs whose vessels annually visited the Bay to pick it up from producers situated along the region's extensive system of rivers.

Only after 1713 did small "tobacco ports" begin to emerge. They did so in response to the rising demand for Virginia tobacco, which in turn was fueled by the expanding purchases of a French tax monopoly, and the institution of tobacco inspection laws. However, these ports had an interest in limiting the hinterland they served in order to preserve the distinctive reputation of their own particular variety of tobacco. Because British agents involved in exporting tobacco served a limited market of slave-owning consumers, they were less concerned with maximizing the consumption of European goods in the Chesapeake area and in North Carolina than were the colonial merchants in the gateway ports. A few tobacco ports, such as Annapolis, evolved into growing towns because their role in the tobacco trade dovetailed with their other functions; Annapolis was the seat of Maryland's provincial government and was briefly a craft and distribution center. After the Revolution, when entrepreneurial control of the tobacco trade shifted from Britain to America, the marketing of Virginia tobacco became more centralized in such towns as Fredericksburg, Petersburg, and Richmond.[15] During the colonial period, however, the export of tobacco failed to stimulate the emergence of a gateway port like those that had come to dominate the rest of the continent's trade.

Nonetheless, the Chesapeake did see significant urban development in the late colonial period. After 1750, Baltimore and Norfolk emerged not as tobacco ports but as sizable grain exporting centers, the former to southern Europe and the latter to the West Indies. Both evolved rapidly after midcentury in response to the rising demand for grain throughout the Atlantic world and the willingness of farmers in the northern Chesapeake and Delaware region to satisfy that demand. Baltimore sprang up as a milling and shipping center because of its location. It had access to the developing backcountry of Pennsylvania, as well as the eastern and western shores of Maryland and Virginia. In addition, proximity to waterpower sites permitted Baltimore to have an adjacent milling center comparable to the one on the Brandywine, which supplied the Philadelphia market with much of its "superfine" flour.[16]

Norfolk grew even more dramatically as the result of its West Indian trade. Because of the threat of spoilage due to heat and the limited size of its markets, the islands required a constant flow of limited supplies of grain. Norfolk is several hundred miles closer to the West Indies than is Baltimore, and was then the most northerly ice-free port. Norfolk's advantage over Charleston, whose backcountry also supplied the islands with grain, lay in a larger hinterland with superior riverine communications.[17] Norfolk's emerging prominence helps explain why—after Philadelphia—the Lower James cleared more tonnage for the West Indies in 1772 than did any other naval office on the continent.

BRITAIN'S SEIZURE OF THE GATEWAYS

Before 1775, commerce far more than politics accounted for the pattern of urbanization that evolved in the colonies. British occupation of all the gateway ports at one time or another during the Revolution—and of New York for all but one year of the war—disrupted the elaborate division of labor that had emerged in the late colonial economy between primary, secondary, and tertiary towns. In occupying them the British destroyed many of the efficiencies that had contributed to the prosperity of the late colonial period.[18] Whenever a gateway port fell to the enemy, the integration of its regional economy collapsed. Whatever routes remained open to the flow of commodities were shaped in ways that would prove as penalizing for the revolutionary economy as the British navy's efforts to interdict American commerce on the high seas.

Of course, seizure of the continent's gateway ports often benefited secondary ports. Thus the outports profited briefly at Boston's expense even after March 1776, when the British abandoned the city. Simultaneously, Providence leapt to the forefront of Rhode Island's trade, challenging Newport's former primacy, and from April to December 1776 it dominated Rhode Island's foreign trade. Providence's advantage became permanent following subsequent occupations of Newport, first by the British from the end of 1776 to mid-October 1779, and then by the French from July 1780 to May 1781. Similarly, Baltimore flourished during and after the British occupation of Philadelphia and benefited from Norfolk's destruction in January 1776.[19]

The improving fortunes of some secondary ports did not necessarily redound to the advantage of the continent's economy, however. This was because the share that smaller ports gained in the overseas trade came at the cost of an overall inefficiency in the wartime economy. Occupied gateways also made excellent bases from which to strike at what remained of any region's trade. Insofar as commodity flows persisted despite the obstacles encountered, their diminished volume adversely affected the revolutionary economy's productivity.

Of course, the British could no more fully interdict the coastal trade than they could the continent's overseas trade. Water transport never entirely ceased. For instance, throughout most of the war, the inland water route between Philadelphia and the northern Chesapeake remained open and was, compared with the lower Delaware and the actual seacoast, comparatively safe. However, it did not take much to compromise the value or efficiency of many of the continent's water transportation routes. Though Pennsylvania's thirteen galleys had driven the British frigates HMS *Roebuck* and HMS *Liverpool* down the Delaware River from Wilmington on May 8 and 9, 1776, the engagement led to the abrupt termination of the movement of small parcels of wheat from local producers to Thomas Lea's mill on the Brandywine. Lea still processed large consignments, which he received from wheat jobbers, but only because either he or the jobbers—it is not clear which—were prepared to assume the risks entailed in transporting wheat by water. Isolated farmers no longer would do so.[20]

After the summer of 1778 the danger from enemy cruisers in Chesapeake Bay led a Baltimore merchant to instruct his captains to anchor in a shallow inlet on the seaward side of the Capes (access to the Bay lies between Cape Henry and Cape Charles) when approaching the Chesapeake. The captain was to inquire about enemy cruisers before venturing in unless he happened to be in the company of a heavily armed vessel. In a worst-case scenario, cargoes could be landed at one of the minor ports on the eastern shore such as Sinepuxent and carted to a stream emptying into the Bay, where they then could proceed to the western shore by a small vessel called a shallop. Powder and arms runners had established the route in the earliest days of the war to circumnavigate the British blockade, and the route remained open throughout the war.[21] Alternately, a vessel could wait at the Capes for a suitable convoy.

In either case, the movement of goods slowed and the cost of the exchange increased.

The mid-Atlantic region was not unique in its vulnerability to this kind of pressure. In New England the mere report of a British man-of-war off Cape Cod could deter coastal voyages between Boston and points south and west. While the British occupation of Newport lasted, merchants moving goods westward from Massachusetts Bay preferred land carriage at least to Norwich, Connecticut, instead of attempting to sneak past Narragansett Bay by water. The British occupation of New York limited the trade between New England and the Delaware River Valley to a fraction of its former volume. The diminished traffic at times made it difficult to sell a bill of exchange in Boston on Philadelphia and vice versa. The dangers of coastal navigation led merchants to limit their sea risks to importing from overseas. Once goods were safely landed, merchants usually preferred carting to an additional sea passage.[22] The coastal trade did not provide sufficiently lucrative returns to justify the additional risk by water.

Land carriage, often over enormous distances, came increasingly to dominate the revolutionary economy's transportation system. In 1777, when Charleston was the preferred port of entry for French vessels from the West Indies running the British blockade of the mainland, carts often took cargoes overland from South Carolina to destinations as far away as Philadelphia. Carting from Boston to Philadelphia also became frequent, despite the exorbitant expense. The costs of wagon transport ran roughly ten times that of water transport per ton-mile. On the heavily traveled routes, the cost of land transport rose even further as teams competed for limited forage.[23]

In addition to the direct costs, there were several hidden ones. A typical wagon could carry little more than a ton at a time over long distances—considerably less if it also had to haul its own forage. Accordingly, shippers had to break up cargoes into small parcels. This made it more difficult to place one person in control of the operation, and it encouraged pilfering by the drivers. Land carriage also was likely to be a good deal rougher on containers than was water carriage. Barrels were widely used because they could be moved short distances with minimal effort;

but barrels tend to shake apart in wagons without springs. Once a barrel had sprung, its contents could leak or be damaged by the weather. Finally, each team of horses could normally travel only twenty miles a day, and an ox-drawn wagon somewhat less. This was when seasonal conditions were favorable and the streams that had to be negotiated were few and far between. In winter, sleighing took the place of carting and sometimes permitted greater speed. However, land carriage in any form often became impossible, especially in the late autumn, when heavy rains came, and in the early spring, during mud season. Of course, seasonal conditions and storms could impede a sailing vessel's progress as well. Still, throughout most of the year, depending on wind and current, vessels could often make as many as one hundred miles in twenty four hours.[24]

The British seizure and evacuation of the continent's gateway ports also shaped the larger patterns of the continent's overseas trade. Early in the war French and American entrepreneurs had flocked to Charleston because they assumed that as long as the British focused on the northern half of the Confederation, it would be the best base on the continent from which to trade with the islands. But Charleston lost its attraction as a wartime gateway after a disastrous fire in January 1778. In addition, the state government's penchant for responding to the least British threat by embargoing shipping became habit after the British shifted operations southward at the end of that year.[25] During 1779, after the seizing of Charlestown had clearly emerged as a British objective, the port's commerce progressively shrank until the town's surrender in May 1780 permanently eliminated it and the region it served as players in the revolutionary economy.

The British evacuation of Boston in March 1776, on the other hand, enabled Massachusetts Bay to emerge as the preferred northern destination on the continent. The attributes of Massachusetts Bay—the same qualities that drew the French to it—quickly made it the privateering capital of the revolutionary Confederation. It was near the principal shipping routes from the western Atlantic to Europe, and the topography of the Bay made it less likely that prizes would be retaken as they approached the coast and more likely that an inexperienced prize master

Table 5.1. Estimates of Tonnage Libeled in the Admiralty Courts of
Massachusetts Bay, 1776–82

	1776	1777	1778	1779	1780	1781	1782
Massachusetts Bay	23,492	23,491	19,838	26,270	17,303	16,382	14,186
Middle District		14,325	18,983	17,308	25,471	17,114	15,871	14,051
Boston		2,555	13,748	15,855	25,471	12,226	13,574	9,677

Sources: Notices of vessels libeled, in *Boston Gazette,* 1776–82.
Note: Where tonnage is not given in newspaper reports, values are assigned according to type and rig; whaleboats, 5 tons; two-masted boats and shallops, 15; galleys, 30; sloops, 50; schooners, 70; brigs, brigantines, and snows, 120; ships, 150.

would bring in his charge safely. In addition, the state's many private ships of war usually afforded some protection to friendly vessels. Finally, the Bay's navigational assets made arrivals in late winter, before enemy cruisers normally ventured forth, feasible. The Bay's reputation as the safest landfall on the continent forced Congress's Marine Committee to threaten captains with being cashiered if their prize crews failed to bring captures into the port nearest to the spot they were taken.[26]

Britain's success in shutting down the economy of the deep South simply confirmed Boston's status as a gateway for the continent's overseas trade. Of course Boston shared the favorable attributes of Massachusetts Bay with its outports, to which much of the metropolis' tonnage—and many of its inhabitants—had fled during the British occupation. Once the British departed, however, the city had little difficulty luring back this tonnage over the ensuing year. The British undermined the economies of the smaller coastal towns by striking at the fisheries.[27] Boston's rapid recovery finds reflection in the distribution of tonnage libeled (an action of condemnation in Admiralty law) in Massachusetts's Admiralty Courts as detailed in table 5.1. Over the course of the war, the middle district, which sat in both Boston and Salem, accounted for an increasing percentage of the total tonnage tried in the state's courts. At the same time, Boston's share of the middle district's libels expanded to the point where by 1779 it had completely eclipsed

Salem. Although Salem reclaimed some portion of the court's activities in subsequent years, this hardly compensated for the loss of its fisheries on which outport prosperity had formerly depended. The ease with which Boston reclaimed its dominance in New England's economy suggests that the war enhanced rather than diminished the town's regional hegemony.

Still, Boston emerged from the war poorer than it had been in the late colonial period. Similarly, Providence, New London, and New Haven acquired no more advantage from New York's occupation than did Salem, Newburyport, or Portsmouth over occupied Boston. Though Philadelphia lost much of its commerce to Baltimore in 1778–79, Baltimore lacked the attributes of a great mercantile center and failed to displace Philadelphia as the primary entrepôt of the region. Throughout the war Baltimore relied heavily on the capital of Philadelphia merchants.[28]

Boston came closer to replacing Philadelphia as *the* gateway of the continent than did Baltimore. New England merchants had established connections with southern Europe and Holland in the late colonial period. After the British evacuation of Boston in 1776, Massachusetts Bay reestablished a direct though limited commerce with Europe. The state's privateers provided the necessary remittances to pay for European imports that mid-Atlantic merchants often lacked. Massachusetts Bay never saw its commerce restricted as severely as the commerce of the other major regions. As a consequence, the price of imports was lower in Boston than in Philadelphia through most of the war.[29]

Still, serious problems remained in the northern regional economy. Boston's yielding to Philadelphia as premier gateway port in the late colonial period was a by-product of a less richly endowed hinterland. Though the British occupation of New York City suddenly added the grain-rich Hudson Valley to Boston's trading area, this development favored Boston proper a good deal more than it favored the northern regional economy. So long as the British controlled the mouth of the Hudson River, the valley remained fifty overland miles from western New England's nearest waterways. New York producers could cart goods to Fairfield or the Connecticut River, then ship by water to Norwich, Providence, or New Bedford (Dartmouth)—where they had the choice of carting again or continuing by water around Cape Cod to Boston. While the Boston market still remained open to them, access was hardly as cheap as during peacetime.[30]

After the British occupied Rhode Island in December 1776, the economic integration of the Hudson Valley into the New England regional economy grew more problematic. Coasting captains continued to make for destinations east of New London, often successfully. Still, eluding British cruisers depended on speed and the ability to take refuge in shallow waters. The Rhode Island records reveal sustained maritime activity during these years, but in vessels averaging less than fifty tons of burthen. Larger vessels might have continued trading between Fairfield and Norwich at the head of Connecticut's Thames River, but the British occupation of Long Island and their base at Lloyd's Neck forced Americans to use smaller vessels in Long Island Sound. The reduced tonnage and heightened risk of water transportation were reflected in rising insurance and freight costs. These in turn made carting increasingly competitive, a sure sign that the economic integration of the region was seriously compromised. Boston failed to replace Philadelphia fully as the principal continental gateway for European imports because transportation difficulties hobbled further distribution.[31]

Rather, to the extent that the British succeeded in compromising Philadelphia's gateway functions, Dutch St. Eustatius in the Leeward Islands took over its economic role.[32] In effect, the gateway for the continent moved offshore. During much of the conflict the exchange of European imports for American staples centered on St. Eustatius, to the extent that it centered at all.

"Statia" had long entertained such ambitions. The Dutch West India Company originally settled the island as an isolated patroonship, but it quickly became a center for the informal—often illegal—trade (*kleine vaart*) that grew up among the European colonies in the Caribbean basin. During the late seventeenth and early eighteenth centuries this trade network expanded to North America, despite the attempts of the West India Company and the major imperial powers to restrict it. By the mid-eighteenth century Statia had emerged as the leading island entrepôt in the Caribbean. At the beginning of the Seven Years' War, the

Dutch authorities secured its status by making it a free port. During that war the island played a crucial role in the illegal trade between New England and France's Caribbean possessions. After the war it continued as a focal point for trade with the non-British islands, and on the eve of the Revolution it had emerged as the preferred port of call for American vessels seeking military supplies.[33]

Still, Statia had to compete with the other Dutch islands in the Antilles, as well as with Surinam, the Danish islands (principally St. Croix), and, until French entry into the war, with the French Islands. The active involvement of several Amsterdam firms in sending sizable quantities of war materials to Statia at the beginning of the Revolution explains the island's early prominence. These merchants perceived a commercial advantage in the independence of Britain's North American colonies. They were also strong enough at home to defeat British attempts at bullying the Netherlands into breaking off commercial contact with the revolutionaries. In November 1777 they forced a reluctant Stadholder to respond to the British navy's search and seizure of Dutch vessels near Statia by instituting armed convoys. Statia's privileged connection with Amsterdam, reputedly the best stocked and cheapest market in Europe, had political as well as economic implications.[34]

The widening of the war in 1778 made Statia the nearest neutral port to the continent prepared to sponsor trade with Britain's former colonies. After France became a belligerent, much of the mid-Atlantic and New England commerce with Europe passed through this tiny island, whose annual production of sugar would load no more than a medium-sized vessel. The dry goods and military supplies that came from Amsterdam to Statia in neutral vessels did not have to bear the cost of wartime insurance. American exporters of such staples as tobacco and flour could cut the cost and risk of transporting their commodities by carrying them to St. Eustatius instead of shipping them directly to Europe or to the French West Indies. Statia's proximity to the continent also gave American merchants price information about their staples that might be as recent as two weeks old. Information from Europe took a minimum of two months in its westward passage. Finally, after France entered the war, Britain could no longer station a significant naval force off Statia to seize vessels arriving from Europe and America. The leeward position of the island would not allow them to do so without compromising the security of their more valuable possessions to windward, such as Barbados, St. Lucia, and Grenada, not to mention their incoming convoys from Great Britain.[35]

St. Eustatius had so much going for it during the last two years of the 1770s that it also became a gateway for France's Caribbean colonies. It was the only island market in which an American merchant had the choice of selling locally or forwarding a cargo on consignment to Europe. In the summer of 1780, when Congress found itself unable to comply fully with Cuba's request for flour shipments from the continent, Robert Morris offered to dispatch three ships to Statia to make up for what the continent was reluctant to supply. St. Eustatius's magnetism as a market in which to exchange European manufactures for American and West Indian staples was powerful enough to attract even British merchants. Not only was a buyer or seller less likely to be disappointed by the resources of its market, but the number of vessels bound out and back to the continent permitted the routine formation of fleets in which lesser craft received protection from those with greater armament.[36]

However, funneling so much of the mid-Atlantic region's trade through St. Eustatius dampened demand on the continent in several ways. American commodities had to compete in a restricted arena for European and West Indian produce; doing so depressed the price of their staples in the exchange process. In addition, there was still the danger that the arrival of too many American vessels might break the Statia market. Merchants and producers, therefore, hesitated to commit all their assets to this trade. If Statia had been closer to a large continental population concentration, as Philadelphia was, it would have been in a better position to absorb temporary gluts without a dramatic drop in prices. Though other neutral islands, like St. Croix, were close to Statia, their proximity meant that their markets were likely to be affected by Statia's market.[37] Finally, Statia's central role in the revolutionary economy did not solve the problem of distribution once goods arrived in North America, though its proximity to the continent did assist captains in finding the best routes back to a home port.

Sowing the Seeds of Monetary Collapse

Merchant adventurers not only had to cope with the inefficiencies of having the economic integration of their regions disrupted by the British seizure of American gateway ports, they also had to come to terms with a radical depreciation of the continental currency. The two processes were related. The inefficiencies that the British imposed on the revolutionary economy limited the access that American producers had to overseas imports just as effectively as did the seizure of vessels on the high seas. A declining supply of imports and the forced flow of investment into domestic produce initially fueled the depreciation, and the British occupation of the key gateway ports contributed to the process as much as the blockade.

Congress had fewer alternatives than it would have liked for combating the falling value of its currency. Nonetheless, it explored all of its options. One was to use a small subsidy, procured by its commissioners in Europe from the French Court, to pay interest in bills of exchange on the face value of any sums of continental currency subscribed to the loan office. Congress embarked on this policy on September 9, 1777, but the plan's reception was disappointing, despite the promised return of 6 percent. The offer expired on March 1, 1778, after which currency subscribed to the loan office received less favorable treatment.[38]

Congress also tried to enhance the domestic demand for its money by getting the states to do two things. First, it recommended that they open their courts to creditors. The courts had been closed in most jurisdictions as part of the debtors' holiday with which the Revolution began. Second, it urged the states to confiscate and sell off loyalist estates and deposit the proceeds in the continental loan offices.[39] Neither of these efforts was likely to have much effect as long as Congress continued to issue ever-increasing amounts of currency. The key to restoring the value of the bills of credit seemed to lie in limiting, if not reducing, the quantity in circulation.

This was easier said than done, since almost half the currency outstanding by the end of 1777 had been issued by the states. During the summer of 1777, following the recommendation of a regional convention that met in Springfield, Massachusetts, Congress urged the states both to refrain from emitting any more bills of credit and to withdraw what they had issued from circulation, either through loans or taxes. Coupled with this recommendation came Congress's first requisition on the states for $5 million.[40] The sum represented only 13 percent of the total continental currency outstanding. Congress knew, given the interval needed for state implementation and collection, that the measure would not finance the war effort from current receipts, let alone reduce the currency debt. It was intended instead as a gesture of good faith and a demonstration of how the pledge implicit in the initial issue of continental bills of credit by the thirteen states collectively would be honored. Unfortunately, the recommendation had the contrary effect. It dramatized the problems that the scheme would encounter when projected on a continental scale, though it had worked well on a colonywide basis.

Congress had forwarded its requisition to the states in late November 1777, just after submitting the Articles of Confederation to them for ratification. The draft of the Articles specified a metric for determining each state's share of the continent's debts, but Congress wisely refused to wait for ratification to launch this first experiment in taxation. The Articles would not be implemented until March 1781, and the metric specified in them for apportioning the common debt was immediately discarded as unworkable.[41] Congress could address the issue of justice between the states without reference to the Articles of Confederation because in 1778 the uneven distribution of continental currency produced by the war seemed like the most pressing problem. In the early years of the conflict most of the continent's resources had been expended in the North, where the enemy had pressed its operations. The diminished trade between the states during wartime did little to redistribute the currency more evenly. This circumstance seemed to make it easier for those states where the greatest disbursements had been made to raise large quotas. However, it made the compliance of states remote from the centers of the war, such as South Carolina and Georgia, problematic.[42]

Congress tried to manage these difficulties by assigning quotas to the states in proportion to "their present circumstances and abilities" rather than according to an estimate of what a state's final proportion of the common debts of the United States might be. Thus Connecticut drew a quota far larger than its share of the common expenses because Joseph Trumbull had relied on the state while serving as commissary general. To meet possible objections of hard usage from the people, the requisition specified that all monies paid to the continental treasury in excess of its eventual quota would be carried to the state's account with the continent at 6 percent interest. Assuming an eventual appreciation of the currency, anything that the state overpaid in the near term would redound to its benefit in the longer term. Connecticut would receive credit in a future settlement with the other states for the face value of the currency it raised even though the money had lost much of its real value. Few problems were expected in collecting the bills through taxation while they were widely distributed throughout the population. As Governor Trumbull approvingly observed to Connecticut's Congressional delegation: " 'tis easier paying taxes when this is the case than it will be when speculators and others have accumulated the bills."[43]

In effect, the states that had been closest to the fighting could earn credits against a prospective settlement of accounts with the other states at bargain rates. States that had been least touched by the war would not be so favored. As Congress withdrew bills of credit from circulation by subsequent requisitions, the money would appreciate in value as it became scarcer. Those states, as well as the individuals within them, who would not or could not act with dispatch, would eventually have to pay a higher price for retiring their share of the currency debt.[44] It was even possible to conceive of the remoter, laggard states having eventually to pay a premium above par to comply with the terms of a requisition. However, debtor states would also have the option of postponing payment to their creditors until a final settlement took place at par.

The notion of a final settlement between the states pointed toward a decentralized procedure for redeeming the continent's revolutionary debt. Although it took account of the revolutionaries' reluctance to vest Congress with any revenue powers, in retrospect it appears impractical because it could not be implemented during the Confederation period (1781–17). Well before 1781, disagreements surfaced about what should be admitted as a continental expense. The prospect of a final settlement between the states also drew unfavorable comment from both foreign and domestic observers, who saw in it the potential for civil war.[45] But who is to say that it might not have proved practicable given the comparatively modest size of the nominal debt at the end of 1777, assuming that the depreciation had actually stabilized at about 3:1, as it appeared to during the most critical part of that year's campaign?

We shall never know, because Congress's plan never got a fair trial. This was not merely because of the states' reluctance to ratify the Articles of Confederation, or because of practical difficulties associated with implementing the requisition. Rather, news of the alliance with France, welcome though it was, forced Congress to choose another path incompatible with placing the Revolution on a sound financial basis.

With little prior notice, Congress learned in April 1778 that a powerful French expeditionary force was making for the coast of North America to undertake combined operations against the British. If Congress adhered to the policy of keeping war costs within its means, it might not only fail to win the military decision that French intervention seemed to promise, but it might also lose credit with its new ally and tempt the French to abuse the alliance. On the other hand, if Congress exerted itself to the utmost through the one means at its immediate disposal—currency finance—it surely ran the risk of accelerating the depreciation and perhaps bankrupting itself for good. In the end, Congress showed its revolutionary mettle by preferring the latter course, no matter what the risks, and chose to go for broke in 1778 instead of cutting back.[46]

Congress had moved in that direction even before news of the alliance became official by appointing Jeremiah Wadsworth commissary general of purchases. In June 1777, Congress had tried to control the runaway costs of procurement by undertaking an elaborate reorganization of the commissary department. The new system had prompted Joseph Trumbull to resign as commissary general; William Buchanan from Maryland was his successor. Perhaps the change was partially responsible for holding the depreciation at 3:1 throughout the summer and early autumn, before it slipped to 4:1 at the end of the year. Under Buchanan's management, however, the commissary department proved better at limiting disbursements than at procuring supplies. The army barely had enough provisions to cover its operations for the remainder of the year. When it went into winter quarters at Valley Forge, it had insufficient stocks to carry it through the season. The ensuing debacle discredited both Buchanan and the new organization of the department.

When Congress approached Jeremiah Wadsworth about taking the job, he insisted that procurement take precedence over economy. In accepting Wadsworth, Congress implicitly agreed to print as much money as was necessary to clinch victory, regardless of its effect on the value of the currency.[47] If the gamble paid off, there would be time enough afterward to clean up the nation's finances.

The gamble did not pay off, as Chapter 3 has shown, and the Franco-American alliance brought financial disaster in its wake. During the campaign of 1778 the continent almost tripled its currency debt. Once Congress had embraced the policy of unrestrained currency finance, it proved impossible to reverse.[48] The increasing issuance of money helped fuel a depreciation that precluded the public from borrowing back currency. That in turn precluded limiting the quantities in circulation while meeting the costs of the war.

In the autumn of 1778, Congress tried to cancel several currency emissions made in 1777 and 1778 on the grounds that the British had counterfeited them. The proposal inspired schemes to dump the recalled currency in South Carolina, much to the injury of that state's economy. Eventually, Congress backed away from the idea of making the canceled emissions subscribable only to the loan office, allowing holders to exchange their bills for other currency issues. Most preferred the latter alternative to the former. Continental money still circulated in the marketplace, whereas loan office certificates came in large denominations designed to obstruct their circulation.[49]

During the winter of 1778–79, Congress spent crucial months embroiled in mutual, noisy recriminations associated with the Lee-Deane controversy, rather than coping with the currency debacle. The Lee family had orchestrated Silas Deane's recall from France, where he had acted as one of Congress's commissioners. In attempting to make Deane a scapegoat for all that had gone wrong with the war, Congress dramatized the continent's apparent helplessness in coping with the economic consequences of the Revolution.[50]

THE VANISHING DOLLAR

By 1779, the depreciation of the currency started to have consequences beyond just compromising Congress's ability to manage the war. At a more fundamental level it began to erode all public authority. It also threatened the very lineaments of revolutionary society by undermining the bonds of trust between citizens. For instance, the depreciation increased tensions between creditors and debtors. Many state legislatures had attempted to resist the depreciation by passing tender laws, which specified the value at which state and continental bills were receivable for debts in order to protect the currency's credit. When Congress called for an end to the debtors' holiday, tender laws proved useful to debtors in victimizing their creditors without enhancing the currency's value. So long as advantage was taken of enemy creditors, whether loyalists or Britons, few could publicly object. Virginia encouraged such actions with respect to British creditors on the grounds that since the mother country was responsible for the depreciation, its people should bear the cost.[51] However, encouraging injustice against the enemy risked promoting similar, less desirable forms of behavior among one's own people.

Thus, those who had the misfortune to reside in the larger seacoast towns had to live not only with the threat of enemy occupation but also with the reluctance of farmers in the hinterlands to bring their produce to market. The depreciation gave country people reason to believe that the longer they waited, the more their farm surpluses would be worth. The hapless urban dweller, dependent on the city market and unused to having the terms of trade between country and town tilted in the former's favor, complained bitterly of withholding and extortion. In addition, the depreciation had the subtle but sustained effect of diminishing the sanctions of the legal system on criminal behavior, particularly those involving fines and the posting of bonds. The depreciation was not the only cause of the increasing lawlessness that came to characterize revolutionary society. The brutalization of men in the armed services and in privateering deserves the principal credit for the rising incidence of armed robbery.[52] Still, the depreciation played a significant part in reducing the moral tone of American society, and in so doing it made Congress's task of rescuing the Revolution all the more difficult.

At the beginning of 1779, heroic taxation looked like the best antidote for the disarray into which the Revolution seemed to have fallen. But by then a new constraint hampered Congress in dealing with the depreciation. Congress's repeated reaffirmations of its intention to establish the full faith and credit of the bills that had already been issued pointed to an intention to appreciate the currency as radically as it had already depreciated. In Chapter 3, I alluded to the role that these pledges played in sparking currency speculation by French and American merchants who bought depreciated continentals to subscribe to the loan offices. They did this expecting a radical appreciation to benefit them at the expense of the public. Congress could not have been ignorant of the popular hostility to redeeming the money at par, supported by the claim that the depreciation was a fairer tax on the population at large than any available alternative. Congress must also have realized that a rapid appreciation would place debtors at a dire disadvantage in relation to their creditors and was likely to prove as disruptive as the depreciation had been. Congress, then, had reason to fear that any attempt to check the depreciation through taxation might backfire.[53]

Seen in this context, Congress's resort to massive requisitions on the states in 1779 bears the mark of desperation. It began the year with a $15 million requisition, increased that amount by $45 million in May, and capped the year with another $30 million in October, bringing the total for 1779 to $90 million.[54] Although Congress's actions failed to arrest the depreciation, the threat of an equally dramatic appreciation seemed real enough. The massive requisitions were not the only factor affecting the currency's value. A peace brokered by friendly European powers could also have favorably affected its value. In February 1779, Ambassador Conrad Alexandre Gérard had informed Congress that the Spanish Court had presented Britain with an ultimatum that would lead either to peace or to Spain's entry into the war. Gérard's request that

Congress appoint and empower peace commissioners produced a brief appreciation in the Philadelphia area in mid-February. When Britain spurned Spain's ultimatum and Spain entered the war in June, the currency still looked as though it could be rescued by either of the two allied naval powers inflicting a decisive defeat on the British fleet.[55] Once an appreciation started, for whatever reason, a speculative stampede to the loan offices might develop.

The requisition of May 1779, which posed the greatest danger of setting off a whirlwind appreciation, caused Congress to think through the implications of its plan. Even if all the states complied immediately with Congress's request, six months to a year would elapse before the money could be collected. The danger arose not from tax revenues, which under the best of circumstances would flow in slowly, so much as from the eagerness of investors to lend money in response to an anticipated appreciation. Full loan offices, of course, would allow Congress to pay its bills for a change. Congress could also check any tendencies toward a radical appreciation by issuing warrants on these offices for withdrawals to balance the funds flowing into them. After state taxation took effect, the recently constituted Board of Treasury would still have the power to balance receipts with withdrawals. Instead of forfeiting authority through bankruptcy, Congress hoped to reaffirm its leadership over the Revolution with this response to the currency crisis.[56]

However, no appreciation ever took place. The Franco-Spanish naval effort in 1779 proved as abortive as had the combined operations between French and American forces in 1778.[57] More significantly, Congress's requisitions ignited a covert tax rebellion under the cover of a popular committee movement to regulate prices. The movement began during the spring of 1779 in Philadelphia as town dwellers attempted to counter provision shortages stemming from withholding by the countryside. Boston quickly followed Philadelphia's lead because its people faced a similar problem. During the summer, though, the movement suddenly and uncharacteristically spread to the countryside, which had long favored regulating the price of imports but had resolutely opposed regulating the price of country produce. Country folk now joined in the regulation because they feared the possibility of a rapid appreciation of the currency as much as urban folk feared the rising price of country produce. Price regulation through popular committees seemed an effective way of preventing a potential currency appreciation while at the same time halting the continued depreciation. However, regulation strangled efforts to raise tax money by bringing internal trade to a halt.[58]

The committee movement collapsed once the danger of an appreciation dissipated. In the early autumn of 1779, when it became clear to all that the rural face of price regulation was little more than a tax rebellion in disguise, the pressure to maintain the masquerade eased. A device that Congress had hit upon for continuing to finance the war during the campaign of 1779 also played a part. During the first half of that year Congress had more than doubled the number of bills of credit outstanding. Congress might have gone on indefinitely increasing the money supply, had not the size of the currency debt seriously threatened the credibility of its pledge to pay it off at par. In September, as the total approached $200 million, Congress realized that it had no choice but to halt further issues or forfeit all credibility in relation to its repeatedly declared intention to redeem the debt at par. For some time before that Congress had been employing the fiction that its requisitions were producing large enough revenues through loans and taxes to justify drawing warrants on the state loan offices. Since the loan offices had no money with which to pay these warrants, the warrants started circulating as a surrogate currency in place of money. Congress eventually issued warrants on the state treasurers, with no better results. Meeting the costs of the war through warrants avoided increasing the currency debt, but it led to a more rapid increase in prices than had been the case while they relied on the printing press. In November 1779, Congress began forwarding to the states detailed requisitions for "specific" supplies needed to carry on the war effort during the next year, in effect abandoning reliance on both its currency and warrants for procurement.[59]

Still, Congress's initial currency requisitions looked as though they had had some effect. From losing one half its value in the first three months of 1779—the fastest rate of depreciation ever—the currency lost less than 20 percent of its value again over the next three months. However, the official depreciation schedule for the war years suggests that the rate at which the currency lost value varied seasonally. Normally the depreciation accelerated between October and April and slowed during the remainder of the year, when the armies conducted their campaigns and economic activity was at its peak. People could pass off the currency rapidly during the campaign and thus benefit from the facility it provided in trade without suffering too much damage. Winter posed physical obstacles to the circulation of money. Traders demanded higher prices because they expected to hold the currency longer. The year 1779 was the only year, during which the old continentals circulated as current money, when the depreciation failed to slow down throughout the campaign. Instead, between July and October the currency lost 58 percent of its value, in part, one cannot help suspecting, because of the effectiveness of the committee movement in obstructing exchanges in the marketplace.[60]

If the committee movement deserves credit for accelerating the depreciation of the currency it proposed to save, D'Estaing's failure to strike an effective blow against the British during the autumn of 1779 administered the coup de grâce. Everyone realized that D'Estaing had no choice but to refit in Europe at the end of the year. After the difficulties the French had experienced in the comparatively thriving privateering center of Boston the preceding autumn, it was unlikely that they would find what they needed in the ruins of recently burned Charleston or recently evacuated Philadelphia. Nonetheless, everyone, including the British, expected the French expeditionary force to return to North America on its way home sometime during the autumn of 1779, since the route back to Europe from the islands lay along the Gulf Stream, paralleling the continent's coastline.

As autumn progressed, rumors spread of D'Estaing's imminent arrival. In early September, the sloop *Flying Fish* arrived in New England from the Caribbean and reported having sighted a French fleet with twenty-five ships of the line heading northward.[61] In October the British responded to such rumors by evacuating their forces from Rhode Island and concentrating in New York. Until early November it was still possible to imagine that D'Estaing might achieve a decisive victory, relieving British pressure on Georgia and South Carolina and breaking the stalemate that had developed in the northern theater. Such a victory might, in turn, help appreciate the value of the currency. Only in mid-November did the northern states learn of the disastrous failure of the Franco-American attempt to retake Savannah.

The news had a devastating effect on what remained of the currency's credit. Everyone who held it rushed to divest. Peter Colt, Jeremiah Wadsworth's principal agent in Connecticut, reported on November 18 that "Merchants & others . . . [wer]e determined to exchange their *Square Dolls* [continentals] for any kind of Produce." Less than a week later he wrote that "People are running, or rather flying thro the Country geting rid of their Cash at any rate." Under the circumstances, few were willing to accept that cash unless "they [were] sure of immediately vesting the Money in some other Articles of advantage."[62] By the beginning of 1780 the continentals had depreciated to one fortieth of the value they had possessed in 1775–76.

Merchants thought that the depreciation caused them more difficulties than the British occupation of the continent's gateway ports—unless, of course, they lived in a port that the British had seized. Only a minority speculated by subscribing to the loan office debt, but the depreciation affected every merchant who tried to launch a wartime enterprise. Though it might have appeared that merchants were getting richer as prices rose, the hyperinflation undermined their efforts to assemble capital by inflating expenses while eroding the very concept of credit. Among the more visible effects of the declining value of money were the higher wages and prices demanded by crews and outfitters. Crews also insisted that they be paid in advance, rather than out of the proceeds of the voyage, or be guaranteed their wages in hard money—or both.[63] All these costs increased the capital requirements of each voyage, which in turn seriously restricted the scale of American enterprise.

Thus the depreciation dictated that the majority of overseas ventures be directed to the Caribbean rather than to Europe. Just as crews were unwilling to commit to long voyages at fixed wages for fear that by the time they returned they would have lost to the depreciation most of what they had contracted for, so investors were loath to tie up their capital in lengthy ventures. Doing so simply increased the risk that the return cargo would not cover the cost of the voyage. Boston merchant William Palfrey was not the only one to complain that "a Vessell in which I was concerned came in safe yesterday, but all she has brought won't make me whole by 2 or 3000 £, besides the depreciation of the money." Finally, the depreciation compromised one's ability to buy protection through insurance. What security could underwriters give if, in the interval between the original posting of a policy and their payment of the claim, the currency lost a substantial portion of its value? Merchants could protect themselves against the depreciation by posting insurance policies in hard money, but the scarcity of specie made it unlikely that such a policy would be underwritten before 1781.[64] If the salvation of the revolutionary economy lay in the revival of overseas commerce, the collapse of the currency posed a major obstacle to its rejuvenation.

CREATIVE MISFORTUNES

In 1778, Britain sent the Carlisle Commission to America to head off the Franco-American alliance through a negotiated settlement to the conflict. When it became clear that such a settlement could not be reached, the departing commissioners threatened the Americans with a more destructive form of warfare. That autumn the Royal Navy raided Bedford, Massachusetts, and Egg Harbor, New Jersey. European intelligence sources warned Americans to expect far worse in the next campaign.[1]

THE CHANGING NATURE OF THE WAR

The eighteen months from autumn 1778 to spring 1780 were the darkest of the Revolution. Many had hoped that Britain—in the face of the new alliance—would withdraw from the continent and direct its military effort against the West Indies. Instead, it launched a major assault against the deep South. There a dense population of enslaved Africans near the coast compromised the region's ability to defend itself. During the campaign of 1779, the British subdued most of Georgia and positioned themselves to move on Charleston the following year.[2]

Meanwhile, because of supply difficulties, the Continental Army in the North proved unable to exploit the division of Britain's forces. Washington mounted only one major initiative during 1779: a punitive expedition against the Iroquois in western New York and Pennsylvania, led by General John Sullivan and designed to secure the frontiers of the two states. The rest of the army, aside from the southern units that were dispatched to meet the growing threat to Charleston, remained immobilized around New York. Continental detachments did storm two enemy strongpoints, Stony Point and Paulus Hook. But these victories failed to change either the local balance of power or the overall strategic picture.[3]

The widening of the war in June 1779 to include Spain as well as France had promising strategic implications for the future. However, its principal short-term effect was to plunge Europe into diplomatic ferment. Largely dependent on the good intentions of France, Congress found itself pressured by its ally to formulate the terms on which it was prepared to conclude a peace. The process distracted Congress's attention from its other pressing problems and led to bitter internal wrangling. Instead of establishing the republic's independence, the French alliance seemed to trap Americans in a new dependency the only alternative to which was surrender to the British.[4]

During 1779 the war worsened for civilians as well. Frontier violence, endemic since the war's beginning, increased with Sullivan's efforts to suppress it. Meanwhile, southerners found their lives disrupted by the movement of armies in their midst. Slavery, in conjunction with the dispersion of European settlement, enabled British forces to range more freely there than they had elsewhere. The patriots often found themselves having to divide their forces and engage in partisan warfare. This placed civilians in the South at greater risk than they had ever been in the North.[5]

Finally, the British intensified the pressure along the nation's coastline. The damage that the Royal Navy had inflicted on the shores of the Chesapeake and Connecticut during the spring and early summer of 1779 gave substance to the threats that the Carlisle Commission had issued. Raids had only a momentary effect on a region, though, unless a base were established nearby, as the British had done in both Savannah and the Penobscot region of Maine. The enemy could maintain a more continuous pressure by unleashing the loyalists against the patriots, transforming the struggle more than ever into a civil war, with all the fury and bitterness that this entailed. Loyalist raids along the coast inflicted misery on the patriot population and had serious economic consequences. In some areas, particularly Connecticut's coast, loyalists focused on taking hostages. Capturing prisoners reduced the number of men available for farming or other work and often plunged their families into financial distress.[6]

Loyalist privateering, however, hurt the American economy even more. Until the spring of 1778, Britain had refrained from unleashing the loyalists against American commerce. Three influences restrained it: the hope of conciliating the colonists, Britain's manpower needs in North America, and the Royal Navy's desire to monopolize the capture of American shipping. The navy had seized and libeled most of the vessels in New York's Vice-Admiralty Court before March 1778. Letters of marque, from ports other than New York, libeled the remainder.[7]

Neither the British army nor the Royal Navy thought that transforming New York into a base for privateering was consistent with satisfying their manpower needs. Governor William Tryon, on the other hand, was enthusiastic about the idea because he could charge a fee for issuing commissions. His pleas to London for authority to grant letters of marque acquired new cogency as the government confronted the realities of French naval intervention. The ministry finally decided to let Tryon have his way in June, though actual authorization did not arrive until the beginning of September. By then D'Estaing had lost the brief supremacy he had enjoyed in the western Atlantic. Though from the British perspective the immediate crisis had passed, that did not stop Tryon, who issued 105 warrants for letters of marque to the local Vice-Admiralty Court between September 8, 1778, and February 1, 1779.[8]

Many of the owners or masters taking commissions from the New York Vice-Admiralty Court had been active litigants before September 8, under commissions that had been issued elsewhere. They took out local commissions because they wanted the cooperation of local of-

ficialdom in condemning their captures. They and local owners receiving their first commission also needed the cooperation of the navy's station commander in New York to protect their men from impressment. Admiral James Gambier, who succeeded to the command in September after Admiral Richard Howe had returned to England, granted letters of marque immunity from impressment. The new policy proved controversial; Gambier was accused of acting out of personal self-interest and kept in retirement for the rest of the war.[9] But it did significantly increase the pressure brought to bear on both French and patriot maritime activity. With D'Estaing bottled up in Boston, privateers quickly supplemented the navy's blockade of the coast, particularly in key areas like the Capes of the Chesapeake. In August the navy's share of libels filed in the New York Vice-Admiralty Court fell to two-thirds of the total. By December the navy accounted for only one-third of the prizes brought before the court.[10]

The revolutionaries thought that loyalist privateering enhanced the effectiveness of Britain's seaborne efforts to throttle the American economy. American vessels that relied on speed, size, and shallow draft (rather than armaments) for defense now found themselves confronting an adversary who knew the coast as well as they did and could anticipate all their strategies of evasion. The new circumstances put American entrepreneurs to the unwelcome expense of arming virtually all their merchant vessels, blurring the distinction between merchantmen and private ships of war. Along with the commercial limitations of relying on privateering, the loyalist naval effort forced the patriot shift to letters of marque that began in late 1778.[11]

THE PHILADELPHIA MALAISE

One bright spot cheered the patriots in the midst of these depressing developments. In June 1778, the British had evacuated Philadelphia, enabling the revolutionaries to recover control over the continent's most significant gateway port. At the center of the principal grain region of the nation, the city seemed to have the potential for rejuvenating the revolutionary economy and providing the sustenance needed by the

army to win the war. Merchants and commissary agents expected a great deal from Philadelphia's market. As John Chaloner, looking for whiskey for the army, commented in July 1778, "The country is full, and a few West-India Men will reduce it [the price of whiskey] where it ought to be." Arrivals from overseas, facilitated by the establishment of French naval supremacy in the western Atlantic, would reduce the price of imports to the point where country people would flock to Philadelphia's market with their surpluses. Philadelphia then would reclaim its reputation for being the cheapest market in the region for both foreign imports and domestic produce.[12] The success of Boston's refugees in re-establishing their city's regional commercial supremacy encouraged such expectations.

Boston and Philadelphia had dramatically different recovery experiences, however. Boston's unrivaled advantages as a privateering center enabled it speedily to reacquire the needed vessels, not to mention appropriate staples, for overseas trade. Consequently, Boston attracted ambitious entrepreneurs despite continued attempts by the Royal Navy to keep the port under surveillance. Then, the bumper crops of 1775 protected the region against food shortages during 1776, shortages that otherwise might have slowed the return of refugees. Despite its reliance on food imports, Boston avoided major shortages until the winter of 1779, thanks to the prize goods and imports that could be used to tease surpluses out of the countryside.[13]

The British had cut a wider swathe of destruction around Philadelphia than they had around Boston, scattering Philadelphia's merchants more extensively. They fled to Maryland and Virginia or the interior of Pennsylvania with what they were able to salvage of their former capital. The British evacuation of Philadelphia brought them flocking back, but not with the same resources. Most had suffered from the seizure or destruction of the port's seaborne tonnage, and some had their capital locked up in complex ventures centered in the Chesapeake. The British had been able to seize and destroy many more vessels in the river and its tributaries before evacuating the city than they had around Boston. Philadelphia's merchants had greater obstacles to sur-

mount and fewer resources with which to reconstitute the city's market than had Boston's.[14]

D'Estaing's failure to send prizes taken in American waters into Philadelphia for sale was the first of several signs that all was not well. In late July, Chaloner noted that though some vessels had entered the Delaware, they had declined to come up the river, apparently because "Our barren City affords no Crop."[15] Farmers and millers directed their produce to Baltimore or the lesser ports along the Delaware rather than to Philadelphia that fall. Philadelphians even found themselves having to turn to Baltimore for supplies. But Baltimore's ascendancy proved momentary, because its arrivals tapered off as British naval activity increased around the Capes of the Chesapeake. It was left with the same scarcity of European and West Indian goods that plagued Philadelphia.[16] The trickle of imports reaching both cities failed to stimulate the bustling trade of the prewar years. Prices did not fall in response to a flood of European goods; instead, the tempo of activity at the wholesale level slowed. Merchants attributed the stagnation to the expectation that imports would soon become more plentiful. But in reality rural producers were positioning themselves to deal with continued shortages as it became apparent that D'Estaing's expeditionary force would not end the war quickly.[17]

At the beginning of the conflict, the price of West Indian goods in Philadelphia had soared while the price of European imports had remained comparatively firm.[18] In 1777, however, European goods joined West Indian imports in rising precipitously. The revolutionaries had hoped that ships from France and other friendly powers would satisfy domestic demand for imports once American ports were opened to the rest of the world. The patriots had accordingly concentrated on procuring military supplies and to a lesser extent on privateering. However, not enough ships arrived to satisfy domestic demand.[19] Though the price of flour in the Philadelphia market also began to rise during 1777, it did not begin to catch up with the price of imports until after the evacuation of the British in June 1778.

In July of 1778 flour in Philadelphia sold at roughly 50 shillings per hundred weight, double the price from a year before; in August, the price fell briefly in anticipation of the incoming harvest; then in the ensuing five months, when prices ordinarily stabilized, flour prices more than tripled. By contrast, the price of tea remained almost constant, while loaf sugar, West Indian rum, molasses, and, as far as can be ascertained, dry goods less than doubled. "Walsingham" attributed the sudden jump taken by provisions in the Philadelphia market to the actions of the ordinary farmer, who "must charge the extraordinary price of calicoes, tea, sugar, etc. upon the produce of his farm, or he will be a loser by his labor." Massachusetts farmers had responded to a town-inspired attempt by the legislature to regulate prices in January 1777 by withholding agricultural supplies from the Boston market until the price was right in relation to imports.[20] The farmers who had supplied the Philadelphia market copied the behavior of the Massachusetts farmers with a vengeance. In Philadelphia, however, the result proved catastrophic. Denied its customary flow of imports, Philadelphia's market lacked the resources with which to attract enough produce from the countryside to sustain the city's population.

How did the farmers acquire such power? Then, as now, the amount of merchantable surplus that any one farmer could produce was too small for an individual to affect the market. In addition, they seemed to have little choice beyond trading on the terms set by the metropolitan market or being excluded from its benefits. However, farmers of this era diverted only a portion of what they produced for sale, either locally or distantly, and that autumn the Philadelphia market had few benefits to confer on those who had surpluses. Nor were farmers likely to be influenced by indebtedness to city creditors. The British occupation had obstructed the extension of credit in the short term, while long-term creditors, if they had not already been paid, discouraged payment in depreciating currency.[21] Since old supplies of flour in the region had been destroyed or consumed, and enemy operations and the fly had taken their toll on new supplies, anyone in possession of fresh, clean flour in the autumn of 1778 could charge what he wished on whatever terms he chose. Many held out for hard money or its paper equivalent from grain jobbers. Before the grain crisis was over there would be reports of farmers bartering with millers who possessed the imports they desired without any regard for the needs of the city residents. In this way they equalized the difference that had emerged at the beginning of the war between the price of imports and domestic produce.[22]

The approach of winter put Philadelphia's market into hibernation. By this time local merchants had resigned themselves to waiting for the spring arrival of imports from the West Indies—for which demand was expected to be great—to check the gradual rise of prices for both foreign and domestic goods that persisted through the winter. In March 1779, when the first small fleet from the islands arrived, the price of flour did dip briefly. However, it began to shoot upward again in April, as did the price of both foreign and domestic goods.[23] An incident involving a French vessel, the polacre *Victorious,* which had arrived with the West India fleet, dramatized the new, alarming behavior of the Philadelphia market.

Because of a misunderstanding between the owners of the polacre and their appointed agent, Robert Morris, the cargo of the *Victorious* was withheld from the market while the other vessels in the fleet disposed of theirs. When the *Victorious* finally began to discharge its cargo in April, prices of both foreign and domestic goods began rising precipitously to new heights. This created the impression that the price of foreign goods was driving up the price of domestic goods. In May a committee charged with investigating the situation blamed the across-the-board price explosion on Morris, accusing him of deliberately withholding imports in the expectation of being able to force people to pay higher prices for his ship's cargo. The committee's report fueled a popular movement in Philadelphia to regulate prices in order to break the abnormal link that had emerged between the rising cost of produce and imports. Another committee formed not just to hold prices constant but to progressively lower them. Traders were allowed to bring commodities into the city, but they could not remove them.[24] The authority of the Philadelphia committee's regulation was backed up by the power of an angry, armed populace.

Philadelphia's regulation failed to have the desired effect. Producers in the countryside simply dug in their heels. As one of Levi Hollingsworth's suppliers wrote at the height of the committee movement, "Your regulators or mob has put a Stop to my sending flour until I know whether its mine or theirs." Philadelphia's merchants shared his discontent: according to them the regulation discouraged producers from bringing surpluses to the market by making trade all but impossible.[25]

Philadelphia's committee principally blamed the city's merchants for the crisis.[26] Though the merchants in turn criticized the committee movement, they were as interested as the regulators were in restoring the health of Philadelphia's market. The millers were suspected with more justice, for they did respond to local market conditions, as Levi Hollingsworth's correspondence shows. But a miller, who had capital tied up in his mill, would receive no return if the mill lay idle.[27]

More attractive alternatives were open to the farmer, who was the principal culprit. He could leave the wheat in the ground and plow it under to restore the fertility of the soil; he could leave it on the stalk and store it, though this course enhanced the risk of spoilage in the short term because of the fly; or he could feed it to his stock. All three options allowed him to avoid threshing, an onerous chore. A fourth option was selling grain to whiskey distillers. The miller was more vulnerable to the seizure of grain than was the farmer, whose stores were likely to be too small to attract much attention. That is why during the autumn of 1779 commissary agents complained about the farmers more than the millers. The only strategy that the commissariat could envision for getting grain into the mills was to provide the millers with cheap salt that could be bartered—to farmers who needed it—for grain.[28]

Withholding in response to the committee movement seems to have been the immediate cause of the acute shortages that afflicted the Philadelphia market in 1779, at least to judge from the manner in which the harvest of 1779 was disposed of. If Levi Hollingsworth's experience is any guide, most of it was brought to market after the beginning of 1780, and almost half of that after June 1.[29] Only the approach of another winter, combined with the Fort Wilson Massacre, checked the committee movement in Philadelphia. However, no one could be sure that regulators would not be back in even greater force during the following spring's season of scarcity.

At the end of 1779, Congress inadvertently helped dissolve the committee movement by aligning itself with popular pressures to have the state legislatures, rather than local committees, set uniform fixed prices. On October 20, a convention representing New Hampshire, Massachusetts, Rhode Island, Connecticut, and New York met at Hartford. It recommended that the nine northern states, including Virginia, adopt common price regulations and send delegates to meet in Philadelphia at the beginning of 1780 for that purpose. Congress endorsed the convention's call for uniform state price fixing laws on November 10, 1779. Before the end of the year, New Jersey and Maryland had acted to comply with the recommendations of the convention and Congress.[30] Others were expected to follow suit.

The political futility of regulation was not recognized until February 1780, after New York and Virginia had failed to send delegates to the Philadelphia convention. Most now realized that the unanimity needed for an effective regulation was missing. It took longer for Americans to become convinced of regulation's destructiveness. While every necessity remained in short supply, rationing shortages took precedence over stimulating production. Many states also continued to look to price limitations and embargoes as aids in complying with Congress's requisitions for specific supplies.[31]

After 1778, Britain may have faced a widening war, which clouded its long-term prospects in the struggle. But it could console itself with the financial problems it was causing the Confederation. The British had not only immobilized Washington's army, but, to judge from the Fort Wilson riot in Philadelphia, they had also brought American society to the verge of anarchy. Moreover, they had good reason to conclude that the staggering increase in the currency debt during the past year was alienating Americans from their revolutionary regimes. British intelligence reports confirmed a growing war weariness in the population that might rebound to the benefit of the Crown.[32] Congress seemed as bankrupt of ideas for handling this desperate situation as it was for funds.

MARCH 18, 1780

At this point, the British assessment of the war's progress was not far off the mark. From Congress's perspective the collapse of the currency could not have come at a worse time. During 1777, Congress had succeeded in raising a "permanent" army with considerable difficulty. Congress had given enlisted men the choice of signing up for three years or for the duration of the war. Substantial bounties offered by the states and local communities helped to fill the ranks. Now, those who had enlisted for three years were about to be discharged. Could they be replaced without a stable currency? The declining value of the dollar had diminished the credibility of any monetary incentives that either the continent or the states could offer to recruits. States with unsettled lands might still offer land bounties, but landless states had only a draft, which produced short-term recruits and bad soldiers. In practice, even the land-rich states depended on cash bounties.[33] Congress managed to collect some provisions for the army by requisitioning the states for specific supplies. But it needed a better currency than the continental if it expected to keep an army in the field.

To restore its credibility if not its credit, Congress would have to abandon the pretense that the continental currency's nominal value corresponded to its real value. Before the money had gone into the tailspin engendered by D'Estaing's defeat at Savannah, Governor Jonathan Trumbull of Connecticut had urged the president of Congress, Henry Laurens, to substitute the "idea of intrinsic worth" for "nominal value." Trumbull wanted the "present currency [to be] a legal tender to all intents & purposes, but . . . [to] let the quantity tendered make up the want of quality or value." After the Savannah fiasco Trumbull reiterated his plea for "establishing the currency as a tender, not for ideal and nominal, but real and intrinsic value."[34] By that time Congress's finances were in such disarray that ideas like Trumbull's attracted attention. Congress remained reluctant to repudiate its former policy. Still, until it abandoned the pretense that one day the old, devalued continentals would be redeemed at par, it could not maintain an army or mount much of a campaign.

On March 18, 1780—after extended debate—Congress agreed on a plan to reform the currency by revaluing old continentals at 40:1 specie dollar. In doing so, it renounced forever the objective of trying to appreciate the old continental back to par. In place of the former currency, which the states were to recall through taxation, Congress proposed emitting a new currency. Each state would issue one dollar of the "new emission" for every twenty dollars of the old that they retired. Thus, a limit of $10 million new dollars was built into the plan. The new currency also entitled the bearer to 5 percent annual interest. The states were asked to pay the interest on their assigned quotas of the new emission annually. Congress authorized each state issuing the new currency to retain six dollars of every ten in its own treasury to fill vacancies in its line regiments and to collect specifics; the remaining four dollars would be at the disposal of Congress. The states got a boost while Congress retained a revenue with which it might continue to direct the war effort.[35]

Despite high expectations for the plan, the new currency failed either to restore Congress's power or to stabilize in value. The credit of the new money depended on the states' unanimous and timely compliance, an expectation that proved unrealistic. Some had already responded to Congress's requisition for specific supplies by issuing their own currencies. Others did so after the announcement of Congress's new money scheme. The slowness with which Congress communicated its plans to the states invited deviations from the master plan. However, all the new state issues resembled the new continental currency in their claim to pass as the equivalent of specie and in their promise of annual interest.[36]

Inevitably, the value of the new state and continental currencies fell. All had to labor against the adverse effects of the fall of Charleston in May and Horatio Gates's defeat at Camden, South Carolina, in August. They also had to contend with the general atmosphere of mistrust engendered by Congress's abandonment of its repeated pledges to honor the nominal value of the old continentals.[37] Surprisingly, the new money remained in less demand than the old, though there was more of the old in circulation than the new. The efforts of the states to withdraw the old continentals from circulation may account for the anomaly. Still, some states ignored Congress's multiple requisitions, which were expanded as of February 1780 to include the raising of monthly quotas of $15 million of the old money. Though others, with varying degrees of energy, continued to try to withdraw it through taxation, the effect of state taxation should not have been uniform.[38] Seasonal factors may also have played a part in increasing the demand for the old emission. Between April and October 1780 the old continentals lost only 22 percent of their worth, giving them a firmness of value they had not enjoyed in 1779. However, the same factors should have had a comparable effect on the new currencies.

Americans preferred the old continental currency to the new, in part because of its character as a national medium equally current on both sides of a state boundary. Millers in the Delaware River region, for instance, continued to value the old currency because it made it easier for them and the farmers they dealt with to conduct interstate business and get around the state embargoes that obstructed the resumption of the flour trade. There was nothing to stop the new continental money from crossing state lines as well, of course. But since the interest due on the bills was the responsibility of the state issuing them, what was to prevent that state from discriminating between residents and nonresidents in making annual payments? Even if the nonresident were paid, he would still be put to trouble and expense in collecting what was his due.[39]

However, the most important difference between the old and new money lay in Congress's and the states' continued insistence that the new currency be considered the equivalent of coin. The old continental remained more versatile as a circulating medium than the new currency precisely because Congress had finally applied the principle of intrinsic value rather than nominal value to it. Its versatility ensured that it would remain in demand even as it continued to depreciate. Those seeking to use it as a medium of exchange complained of its scarcity, and in special situations some even preferred it to coin.[40]

FALSE STARTS

Though the new continental money failed as a currency, Congress's plan of March 18, 1780, marked a turning point. In the act of breaking faith with the public, Congress had taken a significant step toward restoring public and private credit. Both had been eroded by four years of denying that there was any difference between the nominal and intrinsic value of the revolutionary currencies. By revaluing the old continentals at 40:1, Congress had pointed the way toward reducing bloated currency debts, both public and private, to equitable specie values. This, in turn, opened up the possibility of doing justice to creditors without destroying debtors. Since the debts had been contracted at different times as well as different values, Congress's action also promoted the idea of interest "as the money value of time."[41]

State tender laws, which made paper currencies legal tender for public and private debts, had also sustained the myth that nominal value and real value were one. Tender laws had the additional effect of driving what little coin there was in the American economy into hiding or overseas. Congress's attempt to establish the specie equivalency of its new currency logically pointed to the retention of tender laws.[42] However, the rapid depreciation of the new money underlined the folly of such a policy. Though it would be almost a year before Congress recommended the repeal of all legal tender laws, it took the first, irrevocable step in that direction on March 1780.

Congress realized almost immediately that those who had enlisted for the war in 1777 would have to be paid the real value of their wages up until 1780. Otherwise, the arrival of new recruits from states serving under pay scales reflecting the depreciation would cause serious disturbances at camp. Subsequently Congress found it necessary to do "justice to the Creditors of these United States" by providing that those who were owed new emission money for the supplies they had furnished be paid in the older currency according to the "current value of continental Bills of Credit compared with Specie."[43] Taking their cue from Congress, several states began exploring the possibility of modifying or suspending their tender laws during the remainder of 1780 and into early 1781. Others started to experiment with their embargoes, which had been instituted to support price controls. As the states began to explore more liberal approaches to the marketplace, hard money—still in alarmingly short supply—and the credit that could be built on it began tentatively to resurface.[44]

Congress still had powerful reasons for clinging to the specie equivalency of its new currency. The plan of March 18, 1780, had been launched with the realization that the French might send an expeditionary force to America. A year of inconclusive warfare after D'Estaing's abandonment of the assault on Newport convinced American leaders that French assistance was indispensable. After Saratoga no British commander was again likely to commit his army in a way that precluded relief by the Royal Navy. This made it unlikely that the war could be won without French naval intervention, and the best way to ensure that was to admit a French army to the continent. When Washington cautiously signaled to Lafayette his approval of the idea in the autumn of 1779, the French government seized on the information in planning for the campaign of 1780. After the collapse of its attempt with Spain to invade Britain in 1779, the best place to seek a decision appeared to be North America. When the new French ambassador, the Chevalier de La Luzerne, had broached this possibility in January 1780, Congress had responded by pledging a force of 25,000 men to combined operations on the North American continent.[45]

In late April, Lafayette returned to America and confirmed that the expeditionary force was on its way. Though accorded a rapturous welcome in Boston, Lafayette was careful not to share his knowledge widely, hoping that Rochambeau's army would arrive while the bulk of Britain's forces were deployed in South Carolina, leaving New York ripe for the taking. The French emphasis on secrecy led them to press for the creation of a special committee of Congress to coordinate arrangements for the coming campaign so that knowledge of their precise intentions would not have to be shared with so large a body. Concerns for secrecy may also have played a part in La Luzerne's decision to offer French specie for current money in the various state treasuries, at par with the new state and continental issues, and at 40:1 for the old continentals. Buying goods with American currency would draw far less attention to the intended movements of the French force than paying with bills of exchange and specie. La Luzerne also hoped to manage French purchases in a way that did not compete with American procurement while throwing France's weight behind Congress's recent monetary reforms.[46]

Though the Americans needed the French more than the French needed the Americans, circumstances conspired to place both parties on their best behavior. The French, sensitive to the danger that their intervention could backfire and drive Americans into the arms of the British, took the precaution of placing Rochambeau nominally under Washington's supreme command. The foreign minister, Vergennes, professed relief that a shipping shortage had forced a last-minute reduction in Rochambeau's expeditionary force. There would be time enough to send a "second division" after it became clear how the first had been received. The Americans, for their part, had to worry about their capacity to cooperate with their ally. Lafayette had been shocked by how small and ill-provided for Washington's army had become since his departure from America in the autumn of 1778. Though Congress had pledged to triple the army's size, reports of the special Committee of Congress at Camp made this seem unlikely. If the revolutionaries seriously disappointed their ally, the "consequence and reputation of these States in Europe [would be] sunk."[47]

With the stakes so high, Congress clung, however misguidedly, to the discredited policy of affirming the specie equivalency of its new emission money in an effort to influence the course of events that it hoped would decide the war. Though members of Congress were concerned most about manpower, shortages in supplies were to prove more immediately critical. The French expeditionary force arrived at Newport when Congress was reorganizing the commissariat. In place of its previous system, which had centralized responsibility for procurement in a commissary general, Congress proposed a new arrangement whereby the states would assume primary responsibility for collecting specific supplies requisitioned by Congress. The continental commissariat would simply receive, process, and distribute them. Because of the poor wheat harvest in New York in 1779, and the effect of the recent winter on New England's livestock, Pennsylvania held the key to the coming campaign.[48] It is therefore worth exploring in some detail how successful Pennsylvania's government was in raising the supplies that Congress required of it.

The severe winter of 1780 prevented the state legislature from responding to Congress's requisition of December 1779 until the following

March. Then it tried to purchase rather than seize what was requested. The government already confronted a low-level tax rebellion among the Quakers and other disaffected minorities over collecting its quota of the congressional requisitions of 1779. That made it impractical to implement Congress's plan of March 18. Instead, Pennsylvania's legislature authorized its own emission of £100,000. Acting independently allowed them to provide the state currency with additional safeguards against depreciation not enjoyed by the new continental money. The value of the entire issue was backed by properties confiscated from loyalists, properties that were valued at ten times the amount of currency issued. The state also promised to retire its new currency within four years and to pay 5 percent interest annually on any money outstanding. Finally, the government secured an informal pledge from Philadelphia merchants to receive the new currency as specie.[49]

Even before Pennsylvania's new currency went into circulation it became clear that the system of state-centered purchasing would work slowly, if it worked at all. Pennsylvania did not begin to buy supplies until April, after the purchasers had been selected and had received their commissions. The purchasing agents, in turn, had to wait over a month for the new state money to arrive, leaving them no alternative but to try collecting supplies on the credit of a currency with which no one was familiar.[50] The defunct continental commissariat, headed by Ephraim Blaine, was unable to do much to compensate for Pennsylvania's tardiness, since the only form of money available to his service was unpaid orders on the continental loan offices. Yet he had to try. This led to a situation in which Blaine's agents, the French commissary agent Ethis de Corny, and Pennsylvania's purchasers often competed for the same parcel of goods. De Corny immediately repudiated the agreement that La Luzerne had instructed him to make to purchase with the state's new money. Instead of state, continental, and French officials complementing each other's efforts, they undermined each other while the army's circumstances grew ever more desperate.[51]

The situation was further complicated by a transportation crisis. In the middle of June, Washington grew alarmed about the condition of his forces in New Jersey and West Point. In addition to collecting its quota of specifics, he ordered Pennsylvania to provide 250 teams for transporting supplies to camp. Transport had been the responsibility of the continental quartermaster, but the collapse of the currency had damaged that service as much as it had the continental commissariat. Congress's requisition for specifics had failed to be precise about what was to be done with the supplies once collected, besides depositing them with the continent's commissary officials. In April, Washington directed Pennsylvania to establish thirteen magazines throughout its extended territory. "President" Joseph Reed estimated that doing so would add 25 percent to the total cost of the requisition, though he intended to comply. But Reed balked on learning of Washington's additional requisition for 250 teams.[52] By then Washington had become desperate enough to send Henry Lee to seize the teams. Lee began to operate peremptorily, without state authority. Though the state government quickly authorized him to proceed, his modus operandi led some Pennsylvanians "to oppose Force to Force" and alienated the citizenry at large. To add to the general confusion, the state's militia, which Washington had summoned to reinforce the Continental Army, started arriving in Trenton—where no plans had been made to feed it![53]

Instead of responding effectively to the prospect that Franco-American cooperation presented for a triumphant outcome to the war, Pennsylvania had to strain its resources to prevent a fiasco from disintegrating into a full-fledged disaster. The militiamen, who had been slow in responding to Washington's calls, were ordered to remain on the alert at home. Those that had already marched to Trenton were ordered to camp outside the town to await Washington's orders. In this situation they could be supplied reasonably cheaply from Philadelphia without burdening the local populace.[54] However, the main body of the army, in northern New Jersey and the Highlands, had yet to be provided for.

A voluntary association of Philadelphia merchants stepped in to fill the void created by the ineffective workings of the state government. The merchants organized themselves into what became known as the Bank of Pennsylvania. In early June they had experimented with a "bank" to fill the ranks of the Pennsylvania line, successfully raising a substantial fund for bounties. After news of the surrender of Charleston arrived, several members of Congress asked the leading merchants behind the scheme to expand their operations and begin supplying Washington's forces in the field. The bank's sponsors responded quickly, opening a subscription to form a private bank. The subscription drew pledges of £300,000 from ninety-two merchants in amounts ranging from £1,000 to £10,000.[55] Subscribers had only to pay a tenth of the capital they had pledged immediately. On the basis of an initial £30,000, the bank began issuing notes in exchange for money received or borrowed.

The notes were to bear 6 percent interest and were to be used to buy and transport provisions to the Continental Army. Acceptance of the notes seemed assured because the money would make its way sooner or later to the circle of merchants who were the bank's subscribers. The bank also received congressional support of sorts. Once the subscription was completed Congress voted to deposit £15,000 in bills of exchange on its commissioners in Europe with the bank as a token of its intention to repay the subscribers for assuming public burdens, but presumably not before it had restored its credit.[56] In the interim, private credit would substitute for public credit.

Compared with the system of requisitioned specifics, the bank seemed a model of efficiency. It appointed two directors to manage the institution's affairs; a "factor," or agent, to purchase provisions; and two transfer agents in Trenton to ensure that the supplies purchased were forwarded promptly, in response to Washington's orders. The bank declared that it would try to supply the army with 3 million rations over the next six months. Robert Morris, one of the initiators of the association and one of its largest subscribers, managed to forward five hundred barrels of flour to the army on the day that subscribers were called to pay in the second portion of their pledge. The project had certainly started with éclat, and many, including Washington, concluded that the bank was the army's best bet for the forthcoming campaign.[57] The bank also enhanced the prestige of the entrepreneurs managing the enterprise and earned their activities immunity from public regulation.

Yet the bank offered Washington no more than a momentary respite from the supply difficulties that plagued him during 1780. An audited account of its agent, Tench Francis, passed by congressional authorities in 1784, suggests that it purchased and shipped to the army between 4,000 and 5,000 barrels of flour from June 1780 to April 1781, or roughly 25 to 33 percent of its stated objective. In a settlement of accounts dated November 18, 1786, the bank was eventually credited with shipping 5,436 bushels of corn in addition to 4,290 barrels of flour. It may have done more than the state of Pennsylvania over the same interval. Still, 5,000 barrels was what Congress expected Pennsylvania to deliver each month. It was not enough to support a mobile army of 30,000 that Washington and Rochambeau envisioned for an assault on New York.[58]

As a supplement to other sources of supply the bank could not but have helped so long as it did not interfere with other modes of procurement. President Reed claimed that it did interfere. He referred to the bank as an association of individuals "officially unknown to Governm't & holding no Communication with it" and complained that it had undermined Pennsylvania's attempt to deliver specifics. The bank had hoped that the "convenience the trading people would find in lodging their money" in it in exchange for "notes payable on demand" would enable the backers "to have the command of a vast fund for our purchases." Reed's open hostility to the bank, however, discouraged depositors and forced it to rely on its own stock rather than its credit in purchasing. The bank did help keep the army from disintegrating during the latter half of 1780, but it failed to live up to the high expectations entertained for it by either Washington or its backers.[59]

FATE'S KIND FROWN

Rochambeau arrived off the American coast in July just after Clinton had returned to New York with most of the men the British had detached for the siege of Charleston. This development deterred Rochambeau from proceeding directly to New York, as Lafayette had urged. Instead, he landed his force at Newport. After more than two months at sea, his troops were sickly, and Rochambeau's first concern was that they regain their health.[60]

Three days after their arrival at Newport, Admiral Samuel Graves sailed into New York with a reinforcement of six ships of the line, conferring naval supremacy once again on the British. Clinton and his naval counterpart at New York, Admiral Mariot Arbuthnot, immediately decided to launch an assault on Newport before Rochambeau could be reinforced from Europe. It took until the end of July to assemble the expedition. Though offensive operations were well beyond Washington's current capabilities, he responded to the movement of British forces eastward by marching his small army toward New York. Washington had gotten no further than Peekskill before learning that Clinton was returning to New York. In fact, Clinton probably canceled the attack on Newport after learning that the French had fortified their position there. Clinton also had trouble getting along with Arbuthnot, on whose cooperation he would have to depend in mounting such an operation. Whatever the reason, Lafayette pretended to his French colleagues that Washington had been responsible for the enemy's retreat.[61]

A superior British fleet still closely blockaded the French expeditionary force in Newport. There was not much likelihood of a relaxation of this pressure after British naval strength in New York doubled in September with the arrival of two additional squadrons. Though the British failed to make much use of their naval preponderance in the western Atlantic for the rest of the campaign, Rochambeau had to remain in Newport to support Ternay's squadron in the face of such a superior force.[62]

An acute supply problem also restricted the French expeditionary force's options. Rochambeau had come to America with transports carrying only two months of provision instead of the customary four. De Corny's efforts to provide in advance for the needs of the expeditionary force had fallen victim to the continued depreciation of the American currencies. Jeremiah Wadsworth, who had recently retired as commissary general for the Continental Army, became Connecticut's agent for helping the French collect supplies. However, Wadsworth was unable to render de Corny much assistance.[63] Faced with the likelihood of having to defend themselves against a British attack, French officials turned to the first American contractors promising to provide for their immediate needs. Josiah Blakely of Hartford and Gideon Delano of Dartmouth, Massachusetts, persuaded the French to pay one-third in specie and two-thirds in bills on France for all supplies delivered on schedule. Though Blakely and Delano provisioned both the army and navy, they did so at the expense of the Continental Army and at a rate that would rapidly consume all of Rochambeau's specie resources.

As long as Rochambeau expected to be reinforced and resupplied by a second division, the extravagance of Blakely and Delano seemed acceptable. However, once the threat of British attack receded—along with the prospect of being reinforced and resupplied—Rochambeau dismissed Blakely and Delano. He then turned to Wadsworth, who joined forces with John Church, Philip Schuyler's bilingual son-in-law, to solve his provisioning needs in an affordable manner.[64]

Wadsworth and Church brought unusual attributes to the partnership. Wadsworth could make use of the elaborate network of contractors and purchasers he had developed while serving first as Joseph Trumbull's deputy and later as commissary general in his own right. Church's fluent French reassured their clients, and his connection with Schuyler gave him access to the inner circles of upstate New York's leadership and, presumably, preferential access to that region's grain production. The partnership, which went by the name Wadsworth and Carter, refused to engage directly in supplying the French. Instead, they made contracts for them with third-party suppliers. They insisted that the French work exclusively through their partnership. Only by controlling American access to the French commissariat could they join agreements to buy what farmers were eager to sell with agreements to buy what they otherwise might have withheld or asked too much for. Wadsworth and Carter's exclusive agency also enabled them to husband the expeditionary force's limited monetary resources by making the less-desired American currencies part of the payment package.[65]

Blakely and Delano's recent spendthrift behavior continued to pose a problem, though, since now that the precedent had been set, it proved impossible to purchase without offering some specie in their contracts. Producers prized gold and silver above paper currencies because specie alone would store value until the war was over. Wadsworth and Carter attempted to stretch out the remaining French specie as far as possible by insisting that producers accept old or new continentals, or even the new state currencies, as a precondition to partial payment in specie. The partners also tried to buy back some of the specie that Blakely and Delano had squandered with bills on France. However, this simply depressed the value of the bills and added to the inflated costs that the French expeditionary force confronted in America.[66]

Wadsworth and Carter had recourse to another strategy when Rochambeau's specie supplies finally ran out in December 1780. Rochambeau had sent his son home in the late autumn to explain to the ministry his situation and to bring back an emergency resupply of funds. Meanwhile, Wadsworth and Carter made contracts in which bills of exchange served as noncirculating collateral for future payments of specie. The craving of American producers for gold and silver, together with the confidence that the French and Americans both had in Wadsworth and Carter, allowed them to pursue this course until late February, when the frigate *Astrea* arrived with enough coin to pay the French debt.[67]

France had sent Rochambeau's expeditionary force to America to save a revolution that it feared might be on the verge of faltering. Lafayette, who was his government's chief informant about the American situation—though not one it entirely trusted—had alerted it to the political implications of France's failure to win the war in 1778 and 1779. The absence of French victories enabled British propaganda to portray France as untrustworthy. The French did not care about American independence. Their real objective was to weaken their British rival by supporting the colonists, possibly in a prolonged, inconclusive struggle. In 1780, when Britain immobilized Rochambeau at Newport, Lafayette grew alarmed that French inactivity would make Americans additionally vulnerable to British propaganda. He concluded that a decisive blow had to be struck soon or there might not be another chance. Benedict Arnold's treason showed that Lafayette's anxieties about the prospects of the Revolution were not misplaced.[68]

Fortunately, Lafayette misread entirely the larger implications of Rochambeau's immobility at Newport. Not only did it mercifully postpone testing the American commitment to combined operations until the next campaign; it also allowed French provisioning to administer a shot in the arm to the New England regional economy. After five years of revolutionary disruptions, the steady purchasing of a friendly army was the next best thing to military victory. The Revolution would still experience some very bad moments. The mutinies in the Continental Line with which 1781 began seemed even more threatening than Arnold's treason of the preceding autumn.[69] Nonetheless, the French helped set the stage for abandoning pernicious expedients such as price fixing, legal tender laws, and embargoes. They did so by creating enough of a margin so that productivity no longer had to be sacrificed to allocative preferences. Moreover, the New England example would prove contagious. Unperceived and unheralded by most Americans, a new day was about to dawn.

7

THE SEEDS OF RECOVERY

Rochambeau failed to produce the immediate victory that both the United States and France had hoped for. Nonetheless, his arrival was a turning point in the war. Politically, it sent the heartening message that France intended to stand by the new nation.[1] And while Rochambeau's army remained on the continent, its need for provisions—together with purchases by individual soldiers—revived the economy of the neighboring region.

FRENCH PURCHASING

Eighteenth-century European armies expected to be paid in hard coin. The French expeditionary force had, accordingly, brought a sizable supply of specie to America. Americans recognized that the French army would not stay in the field, as the continental army had, without regular pay. Though the French government had carefully chosen its soldiers with an eye to making a good impression on Americans, if they were not paid, they might plunder the local inhabitants, as Continental troops had occasionally done in response to extreme hardship. This would damage the alliance perhaps beyond repair.[2]

Paying the troops promptly would also help to win over any Americans with reservations about the French alliance. At the beginning of the Revolution, most of the specie in America had either gone into hiding or been sent overseas to pay for arms and munitions. Rochambeau arrived just as Americans were giving up on their own depreciating paper currencies.[3] Because French troops had to spend their pay locally, they would inject welcome specie into the American economy.

The French supply services had far fewer specie reserves than the army and relied principally on drawing bills on government funds in Europe. Because bills were troublesome to keep track of, French officials preferred to issue them in large denominations. They were not useful in ordinary transactions involving smaller sums, and they did not circulate widely. American merchants used French bills to settle debts and establish credits between themselves. In this capacity, the bills helped draw imports into the heartland despite high transportation costs. Individual farmers were willing to sell to contractors who had access to bills on Europe because the credits they earned represented a claim to hard currency with which desired imports could be purchased. A contractor who accepted bills could command attractively priced imports and, when necessary, some hard currency with which to satisfy the claims of local producers who sold to him.[4] However, bills on France were primarily used to make remittances overseas.

Restrictions on the circulation of bills in turn affected their value. Although bills fared better than paper dollars, there was no fixed equivalency between them and specie. Since months could pass between the drawing of a bill and its presentation for payment, when the drawee might protest the bill, bills on Europe normally sold at a small discount.[5] But if the demand exceeded the supply of exchange, bills could rise above par—that is, merchants would pay more for them in local money than the face value of the bill at the official rate of exchange. Beginning in the spring of 1775, after nonimportation had gone into effect, sterling bills of exchange sank steadily in Philadelphia. Declining imports and continued exports flooded the colonies with more sterling exchange than was immediately needed. When exports ceased in September, however, the value of bills of exchange payable in sterling abruptly rose above par in Philadelphia and its environs. The number of merchants still seeking to retire outstanding sterling debts had increased in relation to the number able to draw on overseas credits.[6]

In 1776, the widening of the war prompted both aggregate demand for sterling bills and their supply to fall. Nonetheless, sterling exchange continued to be important in the northern European trade, particularly with Holland. Revolutionary leaders also sought to use it in providing for American prisoners of war until British authorities made it clear that they would accept only specie or provisions. By 1779, the diminished supply of sterling exchange together with the depreciation had driven its price in paper dollars to unprecedented heights, despite the increasing unwillingness of British merchants to accept the bills that American creditors drew on them.[7]

Initially, American merchants had little use for exchange payable in *livres tournois,* the national money of France. Britain's national money enjoyed a much better reputation for holding value. The Spanish "piece of eight," or dollar, was held in even higher regard than the English shilling and was used extensively in the island trade.[8] The developing Franco-American connection led only gradually to greater acceptance of French money. Initially, Congress had drawn bills of exchange on the subsidy provided by the French court to pay interest on the loan office debt in Spanish dollars rather than livres. These bills on the American commissioners were much more likely to be paid than were private bills drawn by French nationals, and they proved readily negotiable in France. Beginning in 1779, they—together with the disbursements of D'Estaing's expeditionary force in Boston during the autumn of 1778—helped spark the development of a small import trade from France to New England. This in turn created a demand for livre exchange in the merchant community. American merchants also gradually grew used to accepting bills on France in the French islands.[9]

The direct trade between France and New England remained small until the end of 1780, however. The severe winter of 1779–80 reduced the number of American vessels in France the following spring and summer. Only late in the summer of 1780 did Rochambeau's purchasing begin flooding the Boston market with French bills. New England merchants eagerly accepted them to pay for Dutch, Spanish, and French merchandise. However, the official French bills did not hold their value as well as sterling bills because the availability of livre bills outpaced demand. Consequently, French bills often sold at a large discount of about 25 percent and occasionally dipped below 30 percent.[10]

Commercial demand controlled the discount at which bills passed in Boston and Philadelphia, the two markets in North America where one could readily buy and sell exchange for local currency and specie. If a large number of vessels were preparing to depart for Europe from the port in question, the demand for bills drawn on France rose. Once the vessels sailed, demand promptly fell. Similarly, if the enemy made a major effort to blockade a port's commerce, exchange dropped as commerce declined. The difficulty that the British experienced in blockading Massachusetts Bay throughout the war enabled Boston to absorb a larger volume of exchange than Philadelphia. But that advantage did not always translate into higher prices for French bills in New England, for two reasons. First, the French issued more bills in New England than anywhere else. Second, distance was no barrier to merchants seeking the best market for exchange. Thus lower prices in Philadelphia usually led to an influx of buyers from Boston that diminished the differential, and vice versa.[11]

France's specie supply in North America also affected the discount at which exchange passed in Boston and Philadelphia. A dearth of coin forced French provisioning agents to issue more bills, both to buy supplies and to recapture some of the specie that had been spent by the army and the contractors. The arrival of shipments of coin from Europe raised the value of bills of exchange by temporarily relieving French officials of the need to issue them. Americans concerned about the value of exchange kept a sharp eye on French specie imports. But an arrival might not raise the price of exchange if the specie was destined for another region. Thus the specie shipment that entered Boston at the end of August 1781 did not lower the price of exchange in Boston once it was learned that it would be shipped overland to Philadelphia.[12]

Though relying on bills of exchange added significantly to the costs of French purchasing in North America, no alternative could be found.

Shipping large supplies of coin to North America was not a possible solution, because it was so expensive that it was self-defeating. Though only one of the nine specie runs by fast-sailing frigates came to grief during the war, and that only partially, it still cost about one livre for every four transported to the United States, making specie as extravagant an expedient as bills. Short of supporting their army by importing European goods—which at times sold for as much as ten times in America what they cost in Europe—there was no economical way for the French to maintain a military force in North America. They experimented with two small shipments of merchandise, but practical difficulties proved insurmountable. The army was unlikely to conduct operations in locations near the best markets. So the expeditionary force would remain separated from where the imports could be traded most advantageously for local supplies. France's finance minister, Jacques Necker, pushed the idea, but one suspects that he did so more to dramatize the extravagance of the war than as a practical way of honoring France's commitments.[13]

Insufficient Aid

The discount at which French bills sold made them especially attractive to American merchants, particularly New England merchants, seeking remittances on Europe. New England produced few products in demand there, except fish and timber. Britain's continued control of the sea, together with the magnetic force that privateering exerted over American fishermen, spelled the end to most of the fisheries. Much of the timber trade to Europe had been in naval stores. While wartime conditions enhanced demand, they also forced most of it to the islands. The war also discouraged any triangular trading by pushing the costs of freight and insurance to dizzying heights.[14] The French army's reliance on bills of exchange in buying supplies provided New England's merchants with a new way of making wartime remittances on Europe without the risk and expense of the indirect trade.

Bills would have been in demand as wartime remittances even if the New England economy had not labored under these disadvantages.

First, they were bulkless at a time when available shipping space was at a premium. Bills were also safe. Captains of the ships carrying them to Europe could sink them in case of capture with reasonable confidence that another of the multiple copies of a given bill would get through on a different vessel. Bills also helped redress the structural imbalance between the bulk and value of American and European cargoes that had plagued trade with Europe throughout the colonial period. By 1781, bills had pretty much eliminated the problem of filling a returning vessel with the proceeds of the outgoing voyage. Instead, American merchants faced the problem of finding a captain willing to accept freight in Europe for America at a reasonable rate.[15]

The Middle Atlantic states shared in some of the largess that accompanied the Franco-American alliance. During 1779, Philadelphia had benefited disproportionately from John Holker's drafts on his French correspondents—at least until his bills began to be protested. And though transportation costs, whether by land or water, were initially high enough to favor providers closest to the French army, New England could not supply all of their needs. The collapse of New York's grain production in 1779 had forced the French to explore shipping wheat from the Delaware to Rhode Island in the autumn of 1780, at least to the extent of loading several French supply vessels in Philadelphia. They also had to build magazines elsewhere in anticipation of the day that Rochambeau would leave Rhode Island to rendezvous with Washington's army.[16]

Southern New England derived a disproportionate benefit from French specie and bills of exchange, however. Proximity was critical in determining which region would get the biggest lift. The army's pay moved from camp toward the nearest commercial centers, where it could be exchanged to greatest advantage. French funds used to buy supplies flowed in a similar path. Rochambeau's selection of Wadsworth & Carter as his principal contractor ensured reliance on northern commercial networks while the French expeditionary force remained in New England.[17]

In peacetime, much of the money the French spent in the north would have circulated beyond the region through internal trade. But the cost of carting silver écus or pieces of eight remained prohibitive. Merchants might also have distributed the benefits of imported specie by drawing internal bills of exchange. The British conquest of Georgia and South Carolina, however, excluded the deep South from deriving any benefit from New England's relative good fortune. Further, the close blockade mounted by the Royal Navy against the French in Newport after July 1780 created an inviting opportunity for loyalist privateers in the waters between Boston and Philadelphia and further constricted the coastal trade between the two ports. Their diminished trade in turn complicated, though it did not completely inhibit, merchants in each port from entering the other's markets.[18]

Boston merchants acquired credits in Philadelphia by forwarding imports to the southwest, though generally not by sea. When the imports were sold, Boston's merchants were happy enough to accept payment in bills of exchange. For a brief interval in 1781, Philadelphians found that they could buy bills on France in Boston at an attractive price with old continentals. Massachusetts persisted in retiring the old currency through taxation, long after other states abandoned the attempt, giving them a higher value in relation to exchange in Boston than they enjoyed in Philadelphia. The resulting flood of paper into Boston, together with the accelerating depreciation of the currency after February 1781, soon forced Massachusetts to abandon its tax. Only as Philadelphia regained its status as a regional entrepôt toward the end of the war did it recover the power to attract exchange that it had previously enjoyed as the central gateway of the continent.[19]

Meanwhile, French bills played a major role in expanding the northern region's volume of direct trade with Europe. Livre exchange not only provided New England merchants with ready remittances overseas, but it also helped solve the problem of shipping shortages that had been particularly acute in 1779–80. So long as there was no convenient way to make remittances on France, few would send their vessels there. With the growing availability of exchange, American vessels suddenly materialized on the western coast of France during the winter of 1780–81. During 1780, Jonathan Williams had been able to get private freight on only two vessels bound for New England. Early in 1781, Williams could identify nine American vessels in French ports, four of which, together with the 1,200-ton *Marquis de Lafayette,* were bound for New England. Equally significant was Williams's new willingness to send out consignments on his own account to America. Previous difficulties with the flow of American remittances to Europe, the sale of tobacco cargoes in the French market, and the depreciation of the currency had stopped him from venturing on his own account during 1780. With bills in the offing, he was much more willing to risk his own capital in supplying the starved American market with European goods.[20]

French expenditures in New England between July 1780 and June 1781 also stimulated a vigorous expansion of imports into the region from non-French western European ports. French bills of exchange that arrived in Holland or other western European ports could usually be negotiated in Nantes and other French commercial centers. Alternatively, recipients of French bills outside of France could use them to order goods in France to New England by the first available ship.[21]

However, an expanding overseas commerce could not by itself surmount all the structural problems that continued to limit New England's wartime economic potential. The region lacked the capacity to become a major grain producer. The Hudson Valley, the most important granary in the area, remained at a disadvantage in sharing in the new commercial possibilities created by the arrival of Rochambeau's expeditionary force. Nowhere did the northern region's structural limitations, and New York's anomalous position within it, become more evident than in the way it responded to the arrival of the French at Newport.

In early August 1780, delegates from Massachusetts, New Hampshire, and Connecticut had met in Boston to coordinate the measures they expected to take in supporting combined operations with Rochambeau's force against the British in New York. The convention had recommended that the "several States" repeal all their land embargoes. New York had obliged the following autumn, even though by that time its leaders knew that combined operations would be impossible until the next campaign. Udny Hay, New York's agent for supplying provisions to the continental army, warned the state legislature that such a measure courted disaster. However, as he feared, "the clamors of the people . . .

hemmed in by the enemy from the whole of the outward trade they formerly enjoyed" and "restricted to a degree unknown to the other States, in the sale of the very articles they raised themselves" eventually prevailed with the lawmakers. According to Hay, speculators from Massachusetts and Connecticut responded to the repeal by buying up most of the flour and wheat in the state, offering in exchange "hard money" or "articles the people of this State were excessively in want of." Hay feared that the garrison at West Point would starve over the winter if six thousand barrels of flour were not immediately secured. He recommended that the flour be seized from the speculators rather than the producers, assuring Governor Clinton that such a measure would "be popular."[22]

Clinton was reluctant to act on Hay's recommendation but eventually responded to Washington's warnings of impending disaster and his endorsement of the plan. On December 15, 1780, Clinton notified the commander-in-chief that he had authorized Hay to impress four thousand barrels of flour. Clinton nonetheless tried to make the measure seem like something else, instructing Hay to replace or pay for what was taken, though he knew full well that the state had the means to do neither. His only hope for delivering these pledges was that Congress would miraculously come up with the necessary funds. Clinton had chosen this course, he explained to Washington, "to induce the Proprietors to part with it [their flour] with less reluctance and thereby render the Means more effectual." Washington replied by forwarding extracts of Clinton's letter to Congress, predicting that the "energetic Exertions of the State of New York" would keep the army from "dissolution" and recommending New York as an example for others to follow.[23]

There is no record of Congress ever enabling Clinton to honor the engagements that Hay had been instructed to make on his behalf. Instead, as had become customary since 1777, the victims of confiscation received certificates for what had been seized. Hay noted that the "excessive scarcity of money in the State" left no alternative, though for the same reason the recipients of the certificates would be unable "to receive any value for them." New York later claimed credit for "purchasing" out of the harvest of 1780 its quota of flour in Congress's requisition for specific supplies. But the "sales" generated considerable discontent because the seller got nothing tangible that he wanted or could use to advantage.[24]

Despite the difficulties and inefficiencies involved, a command economy worked better in New York than in other areas. Because the Continental Army was stationed at the lower end of the Hudson Valley and on the northwestern frontier, it actually seemed to be protecting the population that lived between Albany and the Highlands surrounding West Point. When the state or continental authorities impressed supplies in the Hudson Valley, those affected had the sense of at least getting something besides certificates or currencies that were good only for paying taxes.[25] Moreover, whatever supplies were collected could be quickly and economically transported by water to where they were needed. This was especially true of wheat and flour because of the proximity of the state's many milling sites to the river. The special circumstances of the state made it more feasible to provide for the American army coercively there than elsewhere.[26]

However, the British occupation of New York's lower counties also precluded the full incorporation of the state into the northern economy. New York would briefly benefit from the presence of the French army on the Hudson during the summer of 1781. In July, after the American and French armies had rendezvoused, Washington established a market in each camp to which anyone loyal to the Revolution could bring produce. That would, at the very least, have given New Yorkers access to specie distributed to the French as pay, had Rochambeau's army tarried for any time in the region. Within a month, however, their army had marched to Virginia. They did not return until mid-September 1782.[27]

The movement of Rochambeau's forces to the south hurt patriot New Yorkers, though there were compensations. Only the relaxation of British naval pressure on Newport and the southern New England coast in general had made it possible to separate Rochambeau's land force from its naval escort in the first place. This facilitated the westward movement of goods by water from Massachusetts Bay to the Fairfield, Connecticut, region before they had to be shipped by cart overland, cutting transportation costs between Boston and the Hudson considerably.

In 1780 some specie and European goods had reappeared in upstate regions, and that trickle increased during 1781. The resumption of long-distance trade in overseas imports stimulated a limited economic revival that led to the expansion in grain production noted in Chapter 1. But the modest improvement in patriot New York's fortunes also reminded local residents how much worse they had fared in the war economy than their neighbors had.[28]

New London and Norwich

The northern regional economy's difficulties cannot be blamed entirely on the British. The fortunes of New London and its hinterland during the war highlight some of the region's intrinsic limitations. Table 7.1 compares the tonnage libeled in the Admiralty Courts of present-day Massachusetts Bay as a whole with that libeled at New London. Massachusetts Bay libeled more tonnage in 1776 and 1777 than in any other comparable interval during the war. Thereafter, with the brief exception of 1779, when the conversion to letters of marque conspired with the unusual luck of the Continental Navy to bring in a rich haul of prizes, the tonnage condemned in Massachusetts's Admiralty Courts slowly but steadily declined. New London, whose total wartime captures came to only 15 percent of Massachusetts Bay's, stepped briefly into the privateering limelight during 1781.[29]

New London began to develop as a regional privateering center in 1779, when its cruisers libeled 5,280 tons of shipping in its Admiralty Court, or roughly 20 percent of Massachusetts's total in that peak year. However, in 1780 the tonnage libeled in New London's Admiralty Court fell by more than 60 percent, as could be expected from Britain's success in establishing overwhelming naval superiority in northern waters and her close blockade of Rochambeau's force in Newport. After the British abandoned efforts at blockading Rhode Island in January 1781, though, New London privateersmen had a banner year, libeling 7,725 tons of shipping, or roughly 50 percent of Massachusetts's total during the same interval.

Until September 1781, New London's success in privateering owed

Table 7.1. Estimates of Tonnage Libeled in Selected Admiralty Courts, 1776–82

	1776	1777	1778	1779	1780	1781	1782
Massachusetts Bay	23,492	23,491	19,838	26,270	17,303	16,382	14,186
New London	1,241	1,295	1,957	5,280	1,980	7,725	2,515

Sources: Notices of vessels libeled, in *Boston Gazette* and *Connecticut Gazette,* 1776–82.

much to the presence of a French squadron in Newport. Beginning in January 1781, when a storm dispersed the British blockading squadron, until the end of August, the French naval force enjoyed local superiority. During this period it attempted two sorties against British positions in the Chesapeake and one against the British base on the north shore of Long Island at Huntington's.[30] In addition, the French squadron provided a strategic umbrella for local commerce raiding along the shipping lanes southeast of Cape Cod. New London privateering also benefited indirectly from French spending in Newport, which provided some of the capital involved. In gross tonnage, New London's captures may have exceeded Philadelphia's during the period 1779–81.[31]

Yet New London's privateering failed to have much economic impact. Undoubtedly that was in part due to the raid that Benedict Arnold led against the town on September 6, 1781, just after the removal of the French naval shield.[32] During 1782, New London took only 2,515 tons of shipping—roughly 18 percent of Massachusetts's declining total— partially as a consequence of the losses sustained from Arnold's burning of the town and partially as a consequence of Britain establishing decisive naval supremacy in North American waters through most of 1782. The peculiar nature of eastern Connecticut's economy, however, must also bear some responsibility for the failure of New London's brief prosperity to stimulate the surrounding countryside to greater productivity.

In the mid-eighteenth century the region between the Connecticut and Thames rivers specialized in exporting salted meat. Initially the region's stock raisers had exported live animals to the West Indies by way of Boston. In the late colonial period, New London and Norwich began salting the meat and sending it in barrels to the islands.[33] Deputy commissary Henry Champion had used his central location in Colchester, Connecticut, to organize the meat-packing industry of the region. Each spring local stall-feeders bought stock from farmers so as to be able to supply packers along the Connecticut and Thames with fattened animals that were slaughtered in November and December and processed for export. When the war came, Champion expanded his local network, and he quickly became Joseph Trumbull's and then Wadsworth's chief supplier of meat during the term that each served as commissary general, though wartime salt shortages quickly forced the substitution of fresh beef for salted meat.[34]

Only at the end of 1779 did Champion encounter difficulties that threatened meat shortages comparable to the grain shortages that had developed somewhat earlier. He attributed his failing supplies to his inability to honor the huge debts that he had contracted in depreciated currency and the threat of a general price regulation. In late November, and again in December, he warned Samuel Huntington, the president of Congress, who came from nearby Norwich, that the "People through this Country are not making near half the preparation for winter feeding" that they should be doing, and that farmers were unwilling to "sell their lean Cattle to the Stallfeeders on trust." Champion argued that there was no real shortage of meat in the country and that Congress was solely responsible for the supply failure because of its inability to provide him with money and its advocacy of price regulation.[35]

Until this point, those who raised beef for the market had not withheld their produce in the way those who raised grain had, because stock raisers were under constant pressure to get rid of one generation of cattle in order to make room for the next.[36] Since it took four years for an animal to become ready for slaughter, stock raisers would maintain production in the face of declining incentives simply on the chance that the following year might be a better one. If Champion's assessment was correct, stock raisers had finally decided to the cut back on long-term production just before the onset of the extraordinarily severe winter of 1780. Some of Champion's informants may have been bluffing, and many more probably expected to thin their herds less than they actually did. But by failing to accumulate sufficient winter feed they unwittingly increased the effect of that extraordinary winter in reducing the amount of meat available to the army.[37]

No direct measure survives of how the winter affected Connecticut's herds, but we do have tax lists from Bucks County, Pennsylvania, that enable us to compare the size of its herds in 1779, 1781, 1782, and 1785. In 1773, Bucks County had the highest ratio of cattle to population of any Pennsylvania county. Between 1779 and 1781, according to the published tax lists, the county's herds dropped 17 percent. Individual townships fared differently. In 1781, Upper Makefield's herd was 18 percent larger than its 1779 herd. The same year, the herd of Lower Makefield had decreased to 43 percent of what it was two years before. Some of the latter's herd might have gone to Upper Makefield, possibly because of its proximity to Trenton, a center for the movement of supplies to the northern army. The years 1780–81 also saw repeated Indian raids on the state's frontiers. Still, Bucks County was unaffected, and those townships that saw the biggest decline in their herds were often those farthest from the frontier.[38]

Farmers with the largest holdings of cattle (ten or more) accounted disproportionately for the decline in the county's herd size, suggesting that those who specialized in raising beef had also been most vulnerable to the prolonged winter season. Some animals, particularly the younger ones, perished in the cold; others were slaughtered by owners when they realized they had to sacrifice part of their herds in order to save the rest. The cattle population in Bucks County continued to decline into 1782, but at the slower rate of 7.6 percent, as continued demand made inroads on diminished supplies. The county's supply of cattle did not begin to stabilize until after the war.[39]

If the winter of 1780 affected the size of the herds in Bucks County so dramatically, it seems likely that southern New England's herds suffered similarly. That winter's unusual length meant that most of the region's farmers had exhausted their supplies of fodder before the spring grasses emerged. Animals perished in the extreme weather, and New England farmers, like Pennsylvania farmers, felt pressure to thin their herds. Finally, those cattle that survived were lean, additionally reducing the short-term availability of meat.[40]

Rochambeau arrived in a region in which nature and man had cooperated to create a severe meat shortage. After an initial period of adjustment the French bought whatever meat supplies were available. Stall-feeders were eager enough to fatten cattle for anyone in a position to offer good money, and farmers were willing enough to sell to fatteners able to pay. However, what the French procured came at the expense of the Continental Army, which continued to suffer meat shortages until the French marched south to Yorktown. If the French had not been there, cattle raisers who chose to stay in the market would have had no option but to do business with the army's agents. A mild winter that conserved the herds despite the stock raisers' willingness to thin them might have left enough meat to provide for both the French and American armies. The combination of dramatically shrunken herds and the presence of the French empowered producers to hold out against the continent until their debts were paid.[41] As the Bucks County records suggest, the situation did not ease in the short term, because once the supply of beef was in serious imbalance with demand, it took several years before a new equilibrium could be established.

This is why the prosperity of southeastern Connecticut's two towns failed to stimulate their regional economy in a way that addressed the problems of the war economy. Privateering combined with internal migration from exposed coastal locations encouraged the accumulation of precious capital in both centers, though Norwich, twenty miles inland from Long Island Sound, probably benefited more than New London. Norwich became a minor industrial center during the Revolution, though not one capable of influencing the outcome of the war. Privateering also led to the development of a small service sector in both towns and enabled some urban consumers to compete with the French for limited meat supplies. Still, the wartime expansion of Norwich and New London failed to stimulate a significant increase in the production of meat because of the time required to rebuild herds after their reduction in the winter of 1779–80. Consequently, New London's brief prosperity led to an economic dead-end that aborted in a devastating British raid.[42]

The story of New England's economy, of course, was more than New London's story writ large. Northern New England was less affected by the severe winter of 1780 than southern New England and portions of Pennsylvania because its farmers were used to longer winters and kept smaller herds. By expanding their geographic reach, purchasing agents were soon able to tap additional meat supplies despite the weight loss involved in driving stock over greater distances. The region also continued, as before, to produce some grain in the coastal and valley areas of Connecticut and Massachusetts, quite apart from New York's. Meanwhile, New Hampshire and the upper Connecticut River remained a valued source of naval supplies.[43]

New London's story did epitomize the war experience of the region in a significant respect, though. While New England benefited the most from the French presence in America, it was unable to convert the stimulus that French capital supplied to the region into an economic revival capable of supporting the decisive military effort needed to win the war. That economic revival would occur elsewhere and would involve a more fruitful interaction between urban markets and their hinterlands than either Boston, New London, or Norwich were able to administer to their environs.

Revival in the Mid-Atlantic

Although Philadelphia had been the central gateway for the mid-Atlantic region at the start of the war, it had ceased to behave like one well before the British occupation in September 1777. The intermittent British blockade offers only a partial explanation for Philadelphia's decline as the entrepôt of the revolutionary economy. Equally important were the Quaker beliefs of many of the city's richest residents, who, in the face of conflict, preferred quiescence to heroic entrepreneurship. In addition, most people assumed that the enemy would attempt to take the city that appeared to be the capital of the Confederation. The British advance across New Jersey in December 1776 made clear that only through military resistance could Philadelphia hope to escape the fate that Boston and New York had experienced. Investment in river fortifications and state and continental warships grew accordingly. Who was to say that with sufficient preparation Philadelphia might not prove as impregnable to attack as Charleston had in May 1776?[44] Military expenditures, however, discouraged aggressive entrepreneurship both by competing for scarce capital and encouraging the belief that the time was not ripe for individual ventures. Most people still expected a short war and saw in the successful defense of the city the key to a quick victory.

A more promising prospect emerged with the British evacuation of Philadelphia in June 1778. Though the city was not impregnable, the British had had to fight extraordinarily hard to secure the one-hundred-mile river route to it.[45] Then, in response to the threat of superior French seapower, they had hastily abandoned Philadelphia in favor of New York, which could more easily be defended and reinforced. There was always the danger that the enemy might return, but the British withdrawal in 1778 offered some reassurance that so long as the Franco-American alliance remained intact, another occupation was unlikely. This allowed entrepreneurs to begin rebuilding the city's economy in earnest.

We have already examined some of the reasons why Philadelphia's recovery took more time than Boston's. The most important consequence of the delay was that the city's merchant leadership had to cope with the misconceived regulation of 1779. The best tonic for the committee movement was resumption of the port's trade to a level that would put Philadelphia's extensive service sector back to work. But that was unlikely before its merchant fleet had been rebuilt. The city's merchants had been striving since well before the British evacuation to replace the tonnage they lost when the port fell. Some had vessels under construction in the Chesapeake, others responded by investing in privateering. Privateering was easier to finance than overseas commerce since crews did not have to be paid or cargoes assembled. Though armaments were expensive, their scale could be adjusted to the resources of the investors and increased with each successive capture. Blair McClenachan's *Holker,* which captured more vessels than any other Philadelphia privateer during the war, started as a lightly armed vessel.[46] In addition, privateers promised quicker returns for roughly the same risk.

Initially, Philadelphia's merchants do not seem to have flocked to privateering. According to Pennsylvania's Letters of Marque Register,

Table 7.2. Tonnage of Vessels to which Pennsylvania Issued Commissions, from the End of the British Occupation of Philadelphia until the End of 1781, by Calendar Year

	Letters of marque				Privateers				Total
	Number	tons	known	extrap.	Number	tons	known	extrap.	
1778	23	1703	(22)*	1777	8	347	—	—	2124
1779	55	2345	(33)	3908	48	1587	(33)	2308	6216
1780	57	2145	(21)	5822	64	1874	(29)	3427	9249
1781	100	6078	(76)	7997	41	1870	(34)	2255	10252

*Figures in parentheses identify the number of vessels in the sample for which tonnage figures are given.
Source: Letter of Marque Register, July 31, 1778–August 12, 1782, Records of Pennsylvania's Revolutionary Governments, 1775–90, Pennsylvania State Archives, Record Group 27, reel 9.

only 16 percent of the tonnage and 26 percent of the vessels taking out commissions in 1778 were equipped as privateers. That proportion changed dramatically in the two subsequent years, as is shown in table 7.2. One of the effects of the regulation of 1779 may have been to direct greater attention to privateering by obstructing commerce.[47] Privateering would have had the additional advantage, as a labor-intensive activity, of offering employment to those most affected by the collapse of the city's market. By helping to get the unemployed out of town, it also provided insurance against a resumption of the regulation in 1780.

Table 7.2 also suggests that the city's merchants had managed to double their tonnage in letters of marque during 1779, despite the committee movement. Indeed, the violence at Fort Wilson between those who supported the regulation and its opponents grew out of the merchants' determination to put together winter voyages to the islands with the fleet of twenty-eight vessels that began arriving immediately after this incident. The populace's acquiescence in the suppression of the riotous militia and the subsequent abandonment of the regulation reflected a widespread realization that the prospect of finding adequate supplies would improve if the merchants rather than the committee were supported. The city's merchants understood that their credibility was on the line during the winter of 1779–80. One senses that they heaved a collective sigh of relief when they succeeded in significantly increasing the movement of imports into the city during the following year.[48]

Table 7.3 supplies the figures for arrivals from beyond the Delaware during 1779–81, as nearly as they can be reconstructed. Even at the peak of the recovery, in 1781, these arrivals amounted to little more than 42 percent of the tonnage that had entered from beyond the Delaware in the immediate prewar years.[49] Still, aggregate tonnage entering from beyond the Delaware doubled between 1779 and 1781. Privateering may have played a more critical role in this expansion than table 7.3 suggests, since an additional 3,170 tons of prizes not included in the display entered the Delaware during the peak year of 1780; 1,100 tons of those prizes were sold in the city after being condemned in neighboring Admiralty Courts.[50] This rich haul in prizes undoubtedly contributed to Philadelphia's doubling its involvement in letters of marque between 1779 and 1781, as detailed in table 7.2.

However, a comparison of table 7.1 with table 7.3 suggests that overall the capture of enemy vessels continued to play a less significant role in Philadelphia's wartime economy that it did in Boston's. During 1780, its best year for privateering, Philadelphia received only 37 percent of the tonnage in captures that Boston directly benefited from during the same year, its third worst in the war (see table 5.1). Philadelphia's recovery remained unique in the degree to which purposeful commerce dominated privateering in the port's economy. Privateering tonnage accounted for less than 25 percent of Pennsylvania's commissioned tonnage during 1781, and prizes accounted for only 23 percent of Philadelphia's entering tonnage that year.[51] The staples of the mid-Atlantic region facilitated the resurgence of Philadelphia's trade once the port had rebuilt its merchant fleet. Massachusetts Bay found it easier to replace tonnage but harder to turn that facility to commercial account because of the scarcity and inappropriateness of the region's staples in wartime.

Wholesale price information during this period allows us to observe how Philadelphia's expanding commerce affected its market. The winter of 1779–80 closed the port to overseas commerce until the ice broke in March—almost a month later than usual. When the Delaware did

Table 7.3. Estimates of Philadelphia Arrivals from
Beyond the Delaware, 1779–81

	1779		1780		1781	
	no.	tons	no.	tons	no.	tons
Prizes	42	3,545	47	4,520	44	4,235
Commercial arrivals	70	5,870	98	9,940	139	14,290
Total	102	9,415	145	14,460	183	18,525

Source: Reports of arrivals and notices of libels in *Pennsylvania Packet*; PRI.

finally reopen, arrivals from the West Indies had a different effect on the regional economy than they had had the previous year. During 1779, the price of all commodities had risen relentlessly throughout the year, though prices for local produce rose at roughly twice the rate of West Indian imports. In 1780, however, price increases moderated with little difference between the prices of imports and domestic produce. No commodity rose more rapidly in price during 1780 than it had in 1779. Beef led all other commodities in the 1780 index, as it had during 1779. In 1780 it increased in price only by a factor of 3.3 compared with a 14.7-fold increase in 1779, despite the effect of the winter of 1780 on herd size. The rate of increase slowed even more dramatically in key commodities of domestic consumption, such as common flour and middlings, a coarse flour sold only in the local market. Price increases of key West Indian imports also moderated in ways roughly congruent with the prices of domestic staples.[52]

Such price behavior suggests that during 1780 imports and domestic produce were again being drawn to each other in Philadelphia's market, as they had been before the war. The wheat harvest of 1780 was as critical to the restoration of the city's market as the increased flow of imports. It had been planted in September 1779, when farmers had little incentive to increase production, and some thought it a thin crop.[53] If farmers had withheld it, as they had withheld wheat from the previous harvest in response to the regulation, hyperinflation would have continued. Instead, the farmers seemed increasingly eager to send their grain to market. Millers who corresponded with Levi Hollingsworth offered more flour than they had previously supplied, provided cash was forthcoming to procure wheat at the mills.[54]

Though Philadelphia's market showed signs of renewed vigor, it still fell far short of its prewar condition. In 1780, 14,460 tons of shipping entered Philadelphia, roughly 32 percent of the 1770 tonnage entering from beyond the Delaware.[55] Baltimore shows a similar pattern for clearances—the only data that survive for that port. During 1780, 7,131 tons of shipping cleared for ports beyond the Chesapeake and North Carolina, or 32 percent of the tonnage that had cleared Patuxent in 1770 for the same destinations.[56] The commerce of both ports shared one other significant feature in 1780: 80 percent of vessels entering Philadelphia from overseas had come from the West Indies, a little more than half of these from St. Eustatius. Roughly the same proportions were observed by the 105 vessels that left Baltimore for foreign ports during 1780. Capital shortages aggravated by the continued depreciation of the currency past and present meant that the Caribbean would continue to be the focus of the mid-Atlantic region's commerce.[57] Ironically, the New England economy was less beholden to the islands in wartime than it had been in peacetime, because France's armed forces had provided it with other ways of making direct remittances to Europe.

THE CUBAN FACTOR

Describing the recovery of Philadelphia's market does not fully explain it. New London's sterile flowering as a privateering center between 1779 and 1781 demonstrates that there was no necessary connection between urban revival and rural productivity. Perhaps a lingering Quaker prejudice against privateering helped ensure that Philadelphia would never lose its commercial focus the way New London had. Philadelphia's hinterland also specialized in a staple more responsive to the marketplace than stock raising was. Instead of four years from calving to slaughter, flour produced from winter wheat took a little less than a year from planting to reach the market. Still, if dearth was to be replaced by plenty, farmers had to plant in mid to late September for the next harvest in early

July. Turning to spring wheat remained unappealing because its growing cycle competed more directly with that of Indian corn, and because spring wheat was more vulnerable to pests.

Two other hurdles—besides making a decision ten months in advance—stood in the way of expanding winter wheat production. First, the planting process, though not as laborious as the harvest, still came at a busy time. Farmers needed a good reason to plant the next wheat crop instead of doing other things, including threshing the recently harvested crop. Second, memories of the regulation of 1779 continued to affect production. Levi Hollingsworth's correspondents may have sent in more flour in the first half of 1780 than before, but they did so because they were pressured by debt or the threat of confiscation by state authorities trying to comply with Congress's demand for specific supplies.[58] Many also probably felt that the wheat or flour that they held was so old or of such poor quality that it would soon be unmarketable. Some producers undoubtedly responded to purchase offers from the Pennsylvania Bank. However, as we have already seen, the bank hardly constituted an economic force that would lead to a dramatic surge in planting and production. A more powerful stimulus was needed.

The price of wheat in the Philadelphia market during 1780 points to the existence of such a stimulus. Under normal circumstances, the price of wheat from harvest 1779 should have risen gradually to a peak in July, just before the new crop became available. It should have declined in August and September, as the new crop reached the market. At the end of the year, when transportation became more difficult and ice halted the mill races, it should have risen again.[59] Instead, the price of wheat, after rising 18 percent between April and May 1780, remained relatively stable through August and then shot up 47 percent in September before declining with equal abruptness in October to within 7 percent of what it had been in August. It finished the year with another, more customary rise, but it was well below its September high. The price of common and superfine flour also rose at this time before subsiding in October, but only by 10 to 15 percent.

Hollingsworth's records indicate that the price stability of flour during 1780 was achieved in the face of rising demand. The volume of

Hollingsworth's flour receipts roughly tripled between harvest 1779 and harvest 1780 (see table 1.1). If this was at all typical of what was happening to other flour merchants in the city, the expansion of supply would have had a dampening effect on prices had not demand been expanding in equal proportion. Despite occasional price irregularities, millers had until September made substantial progress in adjusting supply to demand. To judge from the difficulties that the American commissariat continued to experience in providing for the army, domestic military demand had little influence on prices in the Philadelphia market. At this juncture the commissariat relied principally on specific supplies collected by the states.[60] The demand that shaped the rise of prices in the Philadelphia market in September 1780 came from another source: the Caribbean.

Several developments made 1780 a better year than 1779 for the Caribbean trade. The most significant change was the dispatch of a large Spanish fleet to the West Indies, purportedly as part of a design against Jamaica, and its juncture in June 1780 with a French fleet sent to replace D'Estaing's force in the northern Antilles. The two fleets looked as though they would enjoy indisputable naval supremacy in the Caribbean, and Americans optimistically inferred many benefits flowing from the event.[61] In fact, the Spanish fleet had no intention of taking the offensive, and most of the French fleet retired to refit in Europe at the beginning of the hurricane season, shifting the naval balance back in Britain's favor. Mid-Atlantic flour producers were sensitive to what one of Hollingsworth's correspondents referred to as the "Transmogrification of [the] Fleets."[62] However, the Spanish military buildup in the Caribbean remained, creating the potential for an extraordinarily lucrative exchange of American provisions in the Havana market.

Wartime conditions modified Spain's earlier reluctance to have its colonies trade with the United States. Though the Spanish Court had initially maintained official neutrality, it had covertly favored the revolutionaries in various minor ways.[63] American leaders consequently expected greater support from Spain after it declared war against Britain in June 1779. Spain's government, however, would not formally recognize the United States or assist it in direct ways. It rebuffed John Jay as an accredited representative of the Confederation in the spring of 1780, rejecting his pleas that the United States be granted free navigation of the Mississippi and a free port on the Gulf Coast, and stalling over the acceptance of bills that Congress had drawn on its commissions in Europe. One year later, it released in New York the British troops captured after the successful siege of Pensacola.[64] Despite such unfriendly acts, Spain contributed significantly to America's independence. Spain's military ambitions in the Caribbean inevitably modified official economic policy in the Spanish islands. Faced with having to feed many new mouths, Cuba's governor, Diego de Navarro, in the late spring of 1780 instructed Spain's agent in Philadelphia, Juan de Miralles, to arrange for the export of flour from the continent.[65]

Unbeknownst to Navarro, Miralles had recently died. His secretary, Francisco Rendón, referred the matter to the new French ambassador, La Luzerne, who took it up with Congress. Congress and La Luzerne were too preoccupied with finding adequate supplies for Rochambeau and Washington to welcome yet another demand on the continent's meager resources. Still, Congress grudgingly permitted the export of a token three thousand barrels of flour to the Spanish islands, one thousand fewer than Rendón had requested. De Navarro, however, was taking no chances; he had authorized Miralles to inform the merchants that foreign provisions would be welcome in Cuba and to spread the word that he intended to "sanction the export of bullion from Cuba as payment to North [America]."[66]

The prospects of opening trade with Cuba held a great deal of allure for mid-Atlantic producers and merchants. Americans assumed that the Spanish islands were rich in specie because of the suspension of the annual flotas to Spain that had accompanied the widening of the European war against Britain.[67] That meant American grain would command unprecedented hard-money prices in the Cuban market. The prospect of importing bullion was particularly enticing. It was in high demand throughout the continent and uniquely suited to wartime commerce. Bullion paid little freight and kept a vessel light; under duress, a vessel could be run on the coast and still make a profitable voyage, provided the coin was safely removed. To avoid the risk of shipping the money, not to mention any restrictions that Spain might subsequently lay on its exportation, captains could also leave it on deposit in Havana as a fund against which bills of exchange could be drawn in making remittances to Europe.[68]

La Luzerne recognized the powerful incentives in such a trade and feared that encouraging it might disrupt all plans for Franco-American military cooperation during the remainder of the year. He accordingly advised Rendón not to make much of Governor Navarro's communications in public. Rendón complied by telling only a few influential traders about Cuba's new trade policy. Robert Morris, who had managed Congress's commercial affairs, undertook to supply the 3,000 barrels of flour sanctioned by Congress for Rendón, taking it from the magazines that the French had assembled in Maryland. Since the beginning of 1779, Morris had been sending the schooner *Buckskin* to Havana for intelligence purposes in a trade of wheat for sugar licensed by Miralles, so he was in a good position to execute this mission. He advanced his own capital in the venture without the benefit of a formal contract and arranged for the dispatch of three additional vessels to Statia to pick up flour and transport it to Havana.[69] The potential for trade between Cuba and the mainland was not lost on him; a better one could not have been conceived in heaven!

Morris's vessels sailed at the end of July, setting off a flurry of local rumors. By then reports from the islands supported the assumption that the French and Spanish together would take the initiative, after the hurricane season, against Jamaica, further enhancing the demand for American produce. Some expected the new opportunities to extend to the far reaches of the Spanish empire. The inferences drawn did not amount to confirmation of the rumors that Spanish Cuba would welcome American traders. This had to wait for a vessel testing the Cuban market to return to North America. A Havana correspondent of Rendón's wrote him on September 10 about the recent arrival of the *Fox* with 628 barrels of flour. The customs service had valued the incoming cargo at half-price to ensure profitability. Every effort was made to reload quickly as an encouragement to other venturers.[70] Yet the *Fox* could not have returned to the American coast until after the fall planting of winter wheat had been completed. Although mid-Atlantic wheat growers were aware of the improving prospects of the Caribbean market, these remained possibilities rather than guarantees.

During the late summer of 1780, producers interested in reaching the lucrative Cuban market fixed their attention on obstacles closer to home. Since the end of 1779, most of the states had responded to Congress's requisitions for specific supplies by seizing provisions at fixed prices and embargoing their export both across state lines and overseas. Pennsylvania, Maryland, and Delaware had been among the states pursuing such policies. Since their quotas involved large quantities of flour, all three had placed restrictions on the exportation of wheat or flour out of their jurisdictions without special permission of their legislatures.[71] Fortunately, the debacle accompanying the regulation of 1779, together with the collapse of continental price-fixing, had led the states to eschew price fixing as they collected specifics.[72] Embargoes, however, remained central to most of the state efforts to comply with Congress's requisitions, and they constituted a major obstacle to the resumption of overseas trade.

Nonetheless, some states had already begun to modify their embargoes. As early as October 1779, a convention of New England states meeting at Hartford had recommended that all restrictions on inland commerce be lifted. The following summer Maryland abandoned its inland embargo, and Delaware was not far behind. However, no one had suggested that overseas embargoes be discontinued. Though their respective export restrictions expired on different dates, Pennsylvania and Maryland had taken steps to coordinate their extension, however tentatively, well into the autumn of 1780. Delaware posed less of a problem because its embargo was not scheduled to expire until October 20. Pennsylvania and Maryland agreed not to modify their overseas embargoes until Delaware declined to renew its, again long after the next wheat crop would go in the ground.[73]

The farmers of the mid-Atlantic region acted without iron-clad guarantees, gambling on the trade opening up in the coming year. American agent Robert Smith's arrival in Havana undoubtedly encouraged them. They also realized that state officials were their servants as much as their masters and that they could exert more influence over their own state governments than over Spain's imperial policy. Farmers further surmised that their representative assemblies, which increasingly realized that trade embargoes were part of the problem instead of the solution, would be swayed by the profitability of the Cuban trade. The prominent Republican faction in Pennsylvania, which had sponsored the Bank of Pennsylvania, supported market-oriented alternatives to the ineffective "command" policies pursued by the Constitutionalists in the upcoming election. Whatever the outcome of the vote, producers in the region assumed that they would not be denied all access to such a lucrative market. The army's needs would decline in the winter while a trade capable of providing the local economy with a substantial influx of bullion or its equivalents would create the political pressures for at least modifying the embargoes. Everyone knew that if one of the three principal flour states, Pennsylvania, Maryland, or Delaware, dropped its overseas embargo, the remaining restrictions would be hopelessly compromised.[74]

The upward burst of wheat prices in the Philadelphia market during September 1780 reflected the attempt of millers to build wheat inventories for a lucrative flour trade with the Caribbean before the winter set in. Prices rose explosively during September because it was also the planting season. Ordinarily farmers would have divided their energies between threshing some of the wheat they had recently harvested and putting in the next crop, keeping prices level. But the sudden rise in wheat prices suggests that many more producers than usual were choosing to plant the next crop rather than thresh for the mills. At the same time, millers were reluctant to let their mills stand idle for the two or three weeks involved in planting. If either had been willing to change their behavior, the price rise would have been more modest, if it had occurred at all.[75] Only after the new crop was in the ground would farmers turn back to the increasingly enticing activity of satisfying the millers' demands. This, in turn, brought down the price of wheat.

The movement of Philadelphia's wheat prices was symptomatic rather than causative. The momentary inelasticity in the supply of wheat derived from an adjustment that the regional economy had to undergo to achieve an appropriate equilibrium between limited supply and expanding demand. While it is hard to conceive of a better signal for producers planting for the harvest of 1781, they acted more in response to the logic of the situation than to immediate price movements. Insofar as they were aware of the sharp increase in wheat prices, they knew that it would be at best temporary. More significant were their reasons for believing that the demand for wheat and flour would remain high into the next year.[76] Accordingly, they reacted to this prospect by expanding the amount of winter wheat they sowed. In doing so they laid the basis for a limited economic recovery in the following year that was to provide a necessary precondition for the victory at Yorktown.

8

TOWARD A
NATIONAL ECONOMY

Farmers in the mid-Atlantic states soon realized their dreams of profiting from the Caribbean trade. They were aided by Pennsylvania's October 1780 election, which brought the state's Republican faction a greater role in running the government. At the same time, a violent hurricane swept the islands, sinking two British ships of the line, severely damaging nine others, and destroying or disabling thirteen lesser-armed vessels. With Britain's power weakened in the Caribbean and its naval force in northern waters blockading Rochambeau in Newport, American ships could more safely sail to the West Indies from the Delaware and Chesapeake regions. The hurricane also created desperate food shortages in the French islands, raising the prices of American products for even greater profits.[1]

WARTIME BOOM

Delaware led the way in relaxing restrictions on trade. On October 19, before it heard of the hurricane, the state acted to lift its embargo on grain exports. As a result, flour began flowing to

Wilmington. There, at the beginning of December, seven Philadelphia vessels started loading for Havana, some in response to Francisco Rendón's prompting. Other states soon followed, realizing their inability to stop smuggling across state lines and fearing loss of business. Pennsylvania Governor Joseph Reed urged lawmakers to continue to provide for the army by coercion, but the new legislature refused to oblige. According to Reed, "After sitting several Weeks, they [the legislature] broke up, without entering into the subject farther" than to modify the embargo in a way that left shippers free to export provisions, provided they first tendered one-third of their consignments to the public.[2]

A complete record survives of Philadelphia entries from February 13, 1781, when the ice disappeared from the Delaware River, to December 16, when the port closed for the winter. During this period 139 vessels entered Philadelphia from beyond the Delaware, all but thirteen of which had cleared from off-shore ports. Commercial tonnage entering Philadelphia from beyond the Delaware in 1781 was 45 percent greater than in 1780, but entries did not begin to climb until April 1781, and over the course of the year vessels from Cuba accounted for only 42 percent of the overseas entries. The combined trade with the French, Dutch, and Danish islands continued to overshadow Philadelphia's trade with Havana. Does this mean that the city's merchants were less enthusiastic about the Cuban trade than the region's farmers had been the previous planting season?[3]

Politics caused some of the delay in the expansion of entries. The Republicans influenced the Assembly after the election in October 1780, but they still did not control the state government. Though the modification of the embargo at the end of 1780 was a step in the right direction, it fell far short of what merchants like Stephen Collins desired. In May 1781, Collins complained to his correspondent in Salem, Massachusetts, William Gray, that although flour was cheap and plentiful in Philadelphia, the requirement that he tender one-third of each cargo to the state, which would be paid for in depreciated state money, kept him from trading with the islands.[4]

Pennsylvania's failure to modify its embargo until the end of December also delayed the impact of the legislature's action. If a ship had not cleared before the end of December, it would not have another chance until late February, when the ice broke up and the roads become passable enough to assemble cargoes. Since a round trip to the Caribbean required at least six weeks, the first vessels that sailed to the West Indies under the new regulations could not return to the North American continent before April 1781.

Finally, the number and tonnage of entries returning from Havana were less reliable indicators of outward clearances than in other trades. The Havana trade—involving as it did the exchange of flour for bullion —did away with the expectation that a fully loaded vessel would return. Instead, Philadelphia merchants usually instructed their agents to send bullion back by the "best risk"—in other words, the fastest and most defensible vessel available. Vessels leaving Philadelphia with flour might return with a small cargo of sugar, or their captains might be instructed to sell them or seek freights to other parts of the world, such as Cádiz.[5] So the number of vessels entering Philadelphia from Havana fails to provide a precise measure of the size of that trade.

The difficulties that Pennsylvania experienced in enforcing its modified embargo provide a better measure of the stimulus the Cuban trade administered to the state's economy. Governor Reed complained that many merchants refused to take the state's currency in payment for the tendered third of their cargoes, except "at a *Depreciation destructive* of the Money & many wholly declin[ed] it." If forced, the merchants threatened to "unlade [their flour], send it over to New Jersey or the Delaware State, in small Craft, & re-ship it from thence." Reed felt that he had no legal authority to seize these cargoes. Calling the legislature into emergency session in May 1781, he requested summary powers. The Assembly refused and instead lifted the embargo entirely in early June.[6] By that time, a surge of entries from the islands had been under way for almost two months, with profits for all to see.

Britain's conquest of the deep South also played a role in stimulating the region's island trade. From the beginning of 1779, the enemy's southern strategy deflected pressure from the mid-Atlantic coast. As Britain progressively conquered Georgia and South Carolina, Philadelphia and the Chesapeake increasingly replaced Charleston as hubs of the Caribbean trade. This development eventually inspired a rising level of enemy activity in the lower Chesapeake Bay and Delaware River. In the late spring of 1780, loyalist refugees, most often in small barges and whaleboats, started harassing shipping in both areas. Their operations had a greater impact on the Chesapeake's economy than the Delaware's because assembling tobacco cargoes depended more on water transport than assembling grain cargoes did.[7]

The patriots in both places responded vigorously and effectively to refugee privateering. However, Baltimore had the harder task, because of the size of the Bay and the city's distance from the Capes gave refugees many more opportunities to evade its armed vessels. After the summer of 1780, loyalists in the Chesapeake also received support from British men of war in the lower Bay. The heightened aggressiveness of these British ships in late 1780—and particularly during early 1781—kept Maryland in a constant state of alarm. During 1780, 87 percent of Baltimore's 235 clearances occurred during the first two-thirds of that year; only 13 percent in the last third. In 1781, clearances dropped to only 38 as a result of continued enemy pressure. By July 1781, the state had become so traumatized that officials assumed the flotilla transporting the British army under Charles Cornwallis's command, from Portsmouth to York in Virginia, intended instead to attack Baltimore.[8]

Baltimore's decline contributed directly to Philadelphia's reemergence as the leading entrepôt of the Confederation's economy. British pressure on the Chesapeake increasingly led producers and merchants to reroute parcels of grain and tobacco to Philadelphia via the several inland water routes. It also led merchants and ship captains from other ports to prefer the Delaware to the Chesapeake as a destination. Baltimore-based privateers even sent their prizes to Philadelphia. During 1781, Philadelphia's entries rose to roughly six times the number and tonnage of Baltimore's entries for the same period.[9] The availability of shipping in turn enhanced the power of Philadelphia's market to draw supplies from the countryside.

During 1781, Baltimore's trade suffered almost as much from allied operations as it did from the British. Before the rendezvous of French and American forces at Yorktown in September, Maryland had to support the continental detachment under the Marquis de Lafayette's command in Virginia. Maryland was as inclined as Pennsylvania and Delaware to lift its embargoes. However, providing for Lafayette forced the state to reimpose restrictions on the inland export of its produce. Maryland officials also had to seize horses, wagons, and clothing, and impose embargoes on its shipping. Still, the state's citizens sent their goods to Philadelphia when the regulations were lifted—and sometimes even in defiance of them. Embargoes did, however, keep the price of flour in Baltimore lower than in Philadelphia.[10]

The British seizure of St. Eustatius on February 3, 1781, also helped Philadelphia. Anglo-Dutch relations had steadily worsened over the issue of neutral shipping rights, and most people realized that Britain and the Netherlands would soon be at war. Admiral George Rodney's attack on the island nonetheless came as a surprise. News of Britain's December 20 declaration of war against the Netherlands did not reach America until the following March. Rodney seized an enormous quantity of American shipping about to set out on their winter return voyage to the continent. Philadelphia lost much of the tonnage in the largest branch of its Caribbean trade. Contemporaries regarded this loss as a significant setback in Philadelphia's painful struggle to win back its eminence.[11]

Instead, during 1781 the number and tonnage of the vessels entering Philadelphia from Havana slightly exceeded that of those entering from Statia the year before. Cuba quickly replaced Statia as Philadelphia's key trading partner. Before Rodney's assault, some of the vessels that had formerly visited St. Eustatius had wisely begun making for the French and Spanish islands. Arrivals from other areas also strengthened Philadelphia's merchant fleet. Besides the redirection of some Chesapeake ventures toward the Delaware, New England, whose staples were not as suitable for the Havana market as the flour of the mid-Atlantic, also increasingly sent vessels to Philadelphia.[12] Both contributed to Philadelphia's brief wartime renaissance during 1781, and benefited from doing so. Still, most of the vessels entering Philadelphia during that year were of Pennsylvanian registry. This ensured that Philadelphia would benefit most.

Philadelphia's reemergence as continental entrepôt after the seizure of St. Eustatius was far from inevitable. Baltimore had failed to replace Philadelphia when the British occupied it in 1777 because of its limited facilities. Though Baltimore served as an entrepôt of sorts for the upper Chesapeake's tobacco trade, its commerce continued to center on St. Eustatius before the Dutch island fell to the British. After February 1781, other Caribbean islands in the hands of neutral European powers, such as St. Thomas and St. Croix, attempted to replace Statia for the remainder of the war. However, all failed to match Philadelphia during 1781 because none had as versatile a market. Havana was the best place to sell flour in the islands but not to procure dry goods. St. Thomas and St. Croix had dry goods, but flour sold at a discount there.[13] Nonetheless, St. Thomas and St. Croix might have offered the better alternative for North American traders in 1781 had Philadelphia not managed to do something about its money.

Philadelphia merchant Levi Hollingsworth complained about the currency. The depreciation principally affected a merchant's relation to the countryside. Within Philadelphia, barter exchanges recorded as book entries made the currency more a convenience than a necessity. Money played a much more central role in attracting rural surpluses to the urban market. In the country, the opportunities for barter were more restricted than in a market center, and cash, even depreciating cash, gave the producer the ability to seek better bargains and to escape indebtedness, provided he did not hold the money too long. Any kind of money, assuming it retained some value, therefore, remained more highly esteemed in the countryside than the city. But if cash suddenly and unexpectedly lost value, the integration of rural producers into the urban market could collapse.[14]

Philadelphia was not the only commercial hub to experience difficulties arising from the depreciation of currencies. As residents of a port aspiring to regain its credentials as a gateway, however, its merchants felt especially vulnerable on this score.[15] Philadelphia's merchants knew at first hand the liabilities of currency finance, since they could not escape the effects of both Congress's and their state government's experiments with it. They also sensed a political opportunity in the increasing discredit into which paper money, both state and continental, had fallen since 1778. The merchants had been successful in reestablishing themselves as a presence in Pennsylvania's state government during the October 1780 elections because of the demonstrated inadequacy of the existing regime. Though they failed to win a complete repeal of the tender laws or to lift the embargo entirely, they were at least a force to be reckoned with. The fortunes of the state's currency emissions during the first months of 1781 would strengthen their hand.[16]

Pennsylvania had been so careful in limiting the supply of money issued to procure Congress's requisition of specific supplies that the executive council had to dispense new emission continentals provided for by Congress's resolution of March 18, 1780, as a supplement. Pennsylvania should have experienced little difficulty in recalling the necessary old continentals since they were issued in Philadelphia, but the state had encountered widespread resistance to paying war-related taxes. Though state authorities ruthlessly attached the property of delinquents, the process failed to speed collections. In May 1781, David Rittenhouse estimated that only one-fourth of Congress's eight monthly requisitions to retire the old continentals had actually been collected.[17]

Desperate for funds, the Assembly authorized use of the old continentals as well as the new continental emission as legal tender. On December 23, 1780, it pegged old continentals to the new state and new continental currencies at 75:1 until February 1, 1781. Beginning then, and at the commencement of each subsequent month, the council was required to publish an official exchange rate. The Assembly thus signaled its expectation that some adjustment would be necessary to protect the state's and the continent's new money from being hurt by the old continental money's continuing decline.[18]

The Assembly's policy of publishing exchange rates reflected a fiction that only the old continentals were depreciating. Everyone knew, however, that the new state money enjoyed less credit than the old continentals. As one of Levi Hollingsworth's correspondents wrote, "I dare assure you there is not a man here that would not as soon have a Continental Dollar [as] one of Mr. Joseph Reed & [the Executive] Comm's silver Dollars." Everyone also knew that when the Assembly had pegged the old continentals at 75:1 specie dollar the market rate for old continentals had been closer to 100:1. In mid-November, the city's merchants, after some governmental prodding, had succumbed to the temptation of expanding Philadelphia's market by declaring their willingness to accept old continentals at 75:1. But their pledge assumed that the market value of the old continentals in relation to specie would stabilize. When the value of the continentals continued to fall, the merchants reneged.[19] That meant that the gap between the official value of old continentals in state money and their actual market value in relation to specie would continue to widen at least until February 1, when the law required the executive council to speak officially on the matter.

Though the old continentals had depreciated to 110:1 at the beginning of February, the council refused to act as the legislature had directed. Instead, it adhered to the exchange rate of 75:1 for a simple reason: at the time, Pennsylvania's executive council saw Congress's resolution of March 18, 1780, as the best way to establish an adequate currency. Therefore, the executive council wished to encourage compliance with taxes that the state had laid to retire the old continentals. The collection of these taxes was affected by the continuing depreciation, which gave taxpayers an incentive to postpone payment as long as possible. The Supreme Executive Council feared changing the rate at which old continentals passed for the new continental emission and state money because that would further discourage people from paying the old money into the state treasury.[20] Their determination to stick with the out-of-date official figure for exchange soon produced a currency crisis.

The crisis had two precipitating causes, neither of which in itself would have been sufficient to produce the effect that ensued. The first was news of the British seizure of St. Eustatius. Major defeats always lowered the value of the old continentals because they meant a longer war and therefore less potential resource with which to pay the currency debt at the war's end. The fall of St. Eustatius was no exception, particularly in view of the quantity of American shipping that the British had seized. In the two months between early March and early May 1781, the old continental fell from 125:1 to 175:1. The idea that old continentals were worth 75:1 specie or state money became preposterous, especially when in late April neighbor New Jersey proclaimed the value of old continentals to be 150:1. New Jersey's action led a great many people to send old continentals across the Delaware to Philadelphia, where the official exchange remained more favorable. The saturation of the Philadelphia market with old continentals had a positive side. Besides Pennsylvania's new interest in Congress's plan of March 18, 1780, many Philadelphians were collecting cheap continentals to send to Boston, where Massachusetts' more effective program of taxation still made them current for bills on Europe.[21]

The free fall of the old continental precipitated a wholly new currency initiative by the legislature. On April 7 the Assembly voted to emit £500,000 in paper currency, declaring that after June 1, 1781, the state would receive only gold, silver, and this latest emission in satisfaction of debts and taxes due it. The legislature had adopted this course in response to the "many and large arrearages and sums of money due this state from private persons." After pledging the faith of the state to retire the entire sum through taxation over the next five years, it set aside £200,000 to be exchanged for all previous emissions, both state and old continental at the official exchange. Shortly after the passage of this law the Assembly ordered the Supreme Executive Council to stop issuing currency under Congress's resolution of March 18, 1780, and to collect what was outstanding "on the best terms at which the same may be had."[22] It then blithely adjourned as if it had solved the state's currency problems when instead it had sowed the seeds of currency chaos.

The act of April 7 solved only one problem: by eliminating all but one paper currency after June 1, it offered a potential avenue of escape from the embarrassment of having the official exchange rate so widely out of kilter with the market rate. But the Assembly had failed to reckon with the continued free fall of the old continentals. Those hoping that the state's new currency would rescue them from their fiscal dilemma grew alarmed that continued adherence to an official exchange rate of 75:1

would prejudice the value of their most recent emission. On May 2, the president and council finally revalued the old continentals in relation to the new currency at 175:1, though the market rate of exchange at the beginning of May was more nearly between 200:1 and 225:1.[23]

The council tried to justify itself by pointing to its obligation to publish the rate of exchange under the law of the preceding December. "Would [anyone] desire of Council to publish what all the world knows to be false, and that under the sanction of an oath, by which they have solemnly engaged 'faithfully to execute their office, doing equal right and justice to all men, to the best of their knowledge and abilities, according to law'[?] The Council could not, without violating every principle of truth and veracity, declare the exchange to be 75:1, when there was not a single person in the city but must know to the contrary."[24]

The statement destroyed the the council's credibility and with it the convertibility that had existed between paper money and hard money in the city's markets. The next day the exchange dropped to between 500 and 700:1 specie for continentals and 4 and 6:1 for the state money, in effect halting the circulation of all paper currency.[25] Some holders of paper money in Philadelphia tried to pass it off in the countryside before news that it had ceased to circulate in the city arrived. Their opportunity to do so proved short because of the disorderly response of Philadelphia's seamen to the crisis on May 6 to 9.

During the preceding two months vessels arriving from the islands had filled the city with recently discharged sailors. Many had collected their wages in paper currency. When the money abruptly stopped circulating on May 5, the men rioted. As Levi Hollingsworth reported to a Virginia correspondent, "Our seamen have been Collected these three days last in a tumultuous manner & have broken off from all labour in consequence of the Money." Elizabeth Drinker's Diary noted on May 8 "the sailors getting together by hundreds with Clubbs, cursing the Continental Money, and declaring against it." The seamen's behavior echoed a smaller seamen's strike in January 1779, and, more ominously, the preceding January's mutiny of the Pennsylvania Line.[26] Its effects reverberated throughout the surrounding region, destroying the last remnant of value held by the paper currencies in Philadelphia's extended hinterland.

As part of Philadelphia's expanding trading orbit, Baltimore also felt the disorders. Maryland's congressional delegate, Daniel Carroll, warned Governor Thomas S. Lee that a "considerable amount" of the "old Continental money . . . has been forwarded to the Southward to be dispos'd of immediately. . . . As many individuals in our State . . . may be injured for want of Notice," Carroll urged that the "information . . . be made publick." News of Pennsylvania's currency debacle inevitably shook the confidence of Marylanders in continentals as well as in Pennsylvania's money. Thomas and Samuel Hollingsworth observed to their brother Levi that the "uneasiness in your Government & the late proceedings in the City tis feared will utterly complete the ruin of your State Money." Maryland's state currency was also affected by the disaster. Officials acting under commissions from the governor and Council of the state reported on its alarming loss of value and that the people were no longer willing to accept it.[27]

Monetary collapse seriously threatened the commercial revival that had been developing between Philadelphia and its hinterland. Pennsylvania's government—which bore the principal responsibility for the disaster—could but call the legislature back into emergency session and urge people to accept the new state money. The economic prospects of the entire mid-Atlantic region hung in the balance in May 1781. Defenders of the executive council accused their critics of disloyalty to the Revolution. On May 12, Philadelphians at a town meeting passed resolutions that called on the inhabitants to sign a pledge to receive the state money. The resolutions also recommended that the legislature empower the Supreme Executive Council to drive away "the disaffected," presumably those who refused to sign. Governor Reed clearly favored giving "private Interest some Check" and had recommended to Congress that it impose a general embargo and seize "outward bound Vessels laden with Flour." He promised the state's cooperation "in such a Case of Necessity," even though he acknowledged that the Assembly had deprived him of all power to pursue coercive measures on his own initiative.[28] Confrontation seemed imminent, leading either to a renewal of the regulation of 1779 or to the political disintegration of the state government whose resources had already been taxed to the limit.

Instead of suppression or disintegration, the commercially oriented Republican party seized the initiative and implemented a radically new program. Many developments converged in June 1781 to give them the upper hand beside the loss of what little credibility Reed and his followers still possessed in the currency debacle of the preceding month. Those championing a freer marketplace had an advantage in 1781 that they had lacked in 1779. The January mutinies in the continental army convinced many that the war had to be won in the next campaign or never. Early in 1781 Virginia had finally ceded enough of its western lands to win from Maryland grudging consent to the Articles of Confederation. Congress formally proclaimed their ratification on March 1, giving its authority—which had been in eclipse since 1778—a welcome boost. Even before the Confederation government was put into effect, Congress had elected the leader of Pennsylvania's Republican faction, Robert Morris, to the office of superintendent of finance.[29] But Morris refused to assume the onerous responsibilities of this post until he had attempted to reshape the local political landscape of his home base in Pennsylvania.

The preceding autumn Morris had been elected to the state's representative body for a one-year term. The governor's and council's call for an emergency June meeting of the Pennsylvania legislature gave Morris and his Republican allies a welcome chance to sort out the state's finances before he was sworn in as superintendent of the Confederation's finances. Morris realized that Philadelphia's reviving trade and the growing availability of hard coin presented him with a unique opportunity to challenge those, like Governor Reed, who looked to the coercive use of state power as the best way of providing for the army.[30]

During three weeks in June, Pennsylvania's legislature executed an about-face in its approach to supporting the army. On June 21 it repealed all remaining tender laws. In their place it provided for the equitable settlement of contracts entered into after January 1, 1777, according to their specie value at the time of the agreement. Then, on June 22, the Assembly passed a tax bill that would raise £200,000 in hard money during the next year. Against Morris's will, those who had taken an oath or affirmed their allegiance to Pennsylvania's constitution would be allowed to pay half of their tax liability in the state's most recent paper money emission, dated April 7, 1781.[31] However, the state had clearly embarked on a new policy that placed stimulating commerce ahead of coercive measures, such as embargoes and forced sales at fixed prices. The Assembly concluded its emergency session on June 25 with a series of resolutions that formalized how it proposed to support the war effort.

The resolutions empowered Morris to take responsibility for providing the state's quota of specifics requisitioned by Congress for the coming campaign. He also agreed to pay "into the continental treasury . . . so much of the paper bills of credit, emitted by other states, agreeably to the resolutions of congress, of the 18th of March, 1781, as will discharge to the united states, the balance due on the four-tenths of the quota of said bills, emitted and intended to have been emitted by this state." In exchange, Morris received a guarantee that none of the previous state paper emissions coming into the treasury from the collection of earlier taxes would be reissued, except the bills of the most recent emission, and those only by Morris's express warrant. The state thus placed the £500,000 currency emission of April 7 at his disposal.[32]

The results of the June legislative session set the stage for Morris's next step in putting the Confederation's finances in order. The cornerstones of his program were rigid economy in the conduct of the war and the creation of a national market with a stable national currency. Central to his quest for economy was provisioning the army by contract. He felt that this was the only way of ensuring that those purchasing for the army did everything possible to keep prices down and to take proper care of what they purchased.[33] Instead of escalating costs and shortages, contracts would allow the army to subsist at bargain prices guaranteed by the contractors. The alternative was reverting to requisitions in kind, which since 1780 had proved both ineffective and costly.[34] Morris subsequently argued that the failure of the legislatures to tax for money in a timely fashion, "instead of favoring their Constituents . . . [had] actually injure[d] them to an Amount of 25 to 50 per Cent," by forcing the authorities to do things in "an extravagant instead of a frugal manner."[35]

Morris believed in the superior efficiency of a market economy: "If every individual in the Country is left to dispose as he pleases of his property and compelled to pay his taxes in money . . . He will satisfy the tax by the sale of much less of that property, than in the case of a specific tax [which] must be taken from him to raise the same sum." However, taxing citizens who were already cash poor posed a political as much as an economic problem. Replying, as Morris initially did, that taxation would lead to the reintroduction of cash by creating a demand for it, did not really solve the problem.[36] He knew that effective taxation depended on an adequate money supply and that the most effective money would be a medium whose credit transcended the boundaries of regional markets.

Before he became superintendent of finance under the newly ratified Articles of Confederation, Morris had proposed the formation of a national bank capitalized at $400,000 specie to be subscribed in 1,000 shares valued at $400 per share. Congress passed a resolution authorizing subscriptions to the Bank of North America in May 1781, though the bank was not to start operations until its capital had been fully subscribed. From the beginning Morris and his advisers saw the Bank of North America as a means of restoring the reputation of paper currency by harnessing the private credit of monied men in place of the debased credit of the states and the continent.[37] At $400 a share Morris did not expect subscriptions from the common man. Instead, he hoped that the institution would become the repository for much of the private wealth in the nation and that bank notes issued against the backing of depositors' assets would provide a stable equivalent for specie that could circulate everywhere at a common value.

Morris realized that his grand vision of reform would take time to implement and that in the meantime he would have to rely on more parochial measures centered in Pennsylvania. In this connection he regarded Pennsylvania's currency as his principal domestic asset and declared his intention of appreciating its value.[38] An appreciating currency would buy more goods and services than a depreciating one could, diminishing the need for additional taxation and giving the public its money's worth for a change. In addition, those in possession of goods and services needed by the public would be eager to tender them for an appreciating currency. Appreciating Pennsylvania's state money would also demonstrate that a paper currency could through prudent management recover lost value, thus paving the way for the acceptance of the bank notes he hoped to issue.

Appreciating Pennsylvania's state currency remained a major problem, given the mistrust that now surrounded all paper money. Though Pennsylvania's recent emission had recovered in value a bit since the crisis of early May, it still stood at 5:1.[39] However, the challenge that Morris faced with Pennsylvania's currency was not as great as the one that Congress had confronted at the end of 1779 with the old continentals. Only a quarter of the new state money had been placed in circulation, and there were few public or private interests that would be injured by its appreciation. Since Morris controlled all but 30,000 pounds of the currency's future circulation, there was no danger of being swamped by warrants on the treasury that authorized its recirculation faster than it was recalled. Finally Morris had a tax measure in place that would bring in most of the state currency outstanding over the next year. The trick would be to control the outflow of the new money so as not to defeat the desired appreciation.

The obligation that Morris had assumed to meet Congress's warrants for four-tenths of Pennsylvania's quota of the new emission, which came to about $400,000, seriously complicated his task. Morris had to honor this debt or forfeit whatever credit he brought to his new office. If he honored it with Pennsylvania's new currency, he would double the number of bills outstanding and "most Probably depreciate [the currency's] Value further than already done." He chose instead to have recourse to "Continental Funds and Credit" because the "service of the United States is now intimately Connected with and dependent upon the Credit and Appreciation of the Pennsylvania paper Money."[40]

The "Funds and Credit" that Morris had in mind, since the continent was conspicuously devoid of both, were those that the French Court had promised for the campaign of 1781. Ambassador La Luzerne had played an influential role in getting the Articles of Confederation implemented. He had also gone out of his way to press Morris to accept the office of superintendent of finance. The French government preferred dealing with one sovereign instead of thirteen; experience had taught that their officials were altogether too likely to get into bruising confrontations with state authorities. La Luzerne had even provisionally authorized Morris to draw on a fund that had been established with the Parisian banking house of Messrs. Le Couteulx & Cie. for 500,000 livres as an inducement to accept the office.[41]

The sum would cover the warrants that Congress had issued on Pennsylvania's treasury. However, using French funds to meet one state's obligations and in the process to appreciate that one state's currency risked creating political problems both at home and abroad.[42] Morris also confronted difficulties in transferring funds in Europe to cover expenses in America. He had reason to expect that a large shipment of specie was on its way from France as part of the Crown's promised subsidy. However, Morris did not know when or where it would arrive, nor could he count on it until it actually was in hand. In the interval, he could sell bills drawn on the subsidy in Europe. But Rochambeau also relied on the sale of bills to finance his operations in North America, and Morris had to avoid doing anything that might hurt the campaign. If he flooded the markets with exchange, Morris risked further depressing the value of Rochambeau's bills as well as diminishing the value of the subsidy he enjoyed. He also risked forfeiting the confidence of the nation's only formal ally and the possibility of expanding his authorization to draw on Europe in the future.

Yet Morris had no choice but to draw such bills and sell them in Philadelphia for hard coin and state money. Though he had taken office on condition that he be absolved of providing for the campaign of 1781 beyond delivering Pennsylvania's specifics, he still had expenses. He explored a variety of strategies to escape competing with the French, but to little effect. The only other recourse he possessed for raising the money needed to retire the warrants was to sell the specific supplies he controlled. Buying state currency with specie while it stood at 5½ to 5:1 proved more advantageous than selling specifics, since creating a hard money demand for state money made it appear more immediately valuable. Before the end of the summer, Pennsylvania currency had risen from roughly 5:1 to between 2.5:1 and 2:1, the most substantial appreciation to take place during the entire war. In late August, Morris noted with satisfaction in his diary that he had managed to pay $154,074 due Congress "without taking One Dollar from the State Treasury." The appreciation also bought him time in which to pay off the remaining warrants. Many creditors were now prepared to wait for their money: the longer they did so the more it might be worth.[43]

Were Morris's efforts to appreciate Pennsylvania's currency justified? While the credit of the state currency remained too fragile to be of much use except in buying supplies within Pennsylvania, he further depressed the price of bills on France. During August the demands of the campaign brought French agents into competition with Morris's deputies in the primary markets of Boston and Philadelphia. As a consequence, bills passed at a ruinous discount. However, Morris could not withdraw from the market for long without bringing his operations to a standstill. He pleaded with the French to put the sale of their bills under his direction, inviting them to trade large bills for small ones in an effort to centralize their sale and keep all but those most in demand off the market.[44] Still, these strategies failed to address the basic reason for the low price of exchange, which grew out of the way the war shaped and limited the market for bills in America.

THE BANK OF NORTH AMERICA

In the late summer of 1781 the arrival of two large shipments of specie from France rescued both Rochambeau's and the Continent's finances. The French expeditionary force received the first, enabling it briefly to stop drawing bills on Europe. Rochambeau's agents could even repurchase some of the ones they had drawn at a discount with coin, partially balancing the losses they had recently suffered as sellers. The second shipment of 2.5 million livres in hard coin, the equivalent of 500,000 Spanish dollars, arrived at Boston on August 25, consigned to Morris. The money, along with an additional 2.2 million livres in supplies, was the fruit of Colonel John Laurens's mission to France earlier in the year. It freed Morris from having to devote so much of his energy to appreciating Pennsylvania's currency. Certainly 500,000 paper dollars paled beside 500,000 hard dollars in hand. The windfall gave Morris the power to support the state's money at whatever rate seemed desirable through specie purchases. It also gave him access to the mid-Atlantic region's recent harvest, which was the best in years.[45] But it did not solve his basic problem.

Five hundred thousand hard dollars was a drop in the bucket when it came to financing the war.[46] Since Morris had no immediate prospect of receiving further supplies of specie, the bank remained at the center of his blueprint for a functioning national economy. A bank could expand the money supply by issuing notes backed by specie in the form of subscribed capital and deposits made by individuals and the government. These notes in turn would make their way into general circulation through loans to the government—which would use them to pay contractors—and to private borrowers, either directly or through the discounting of bills on Europe. When the states raised taxes, the notes, along with coin and local currencies, would flow back into the hands of continental tax receivers.[47] In early November 1781, Congress authorized Morris to appoint a network of tax receivers more responsive to his orders than to the state-appointed loan officers. At Morris's behest, these officials could convert bank notes into coin or current money throughout the Confederation.[48] Morris could also instruct these officials to transfer funds in the form of bank notes wherever they were most needed at minimal cost and risk, allowing the Confederation's writ to run throughout the continent as it had not for some time.[49]

Capitalizing the bank proved to be Morris's biggest problem. Everywhere he turned for capital he ran into problems. Private subscriptions failed to materialize despite the growing availability of specie. Investors were not used to putting their cash in banks, particularly when commercial possibilities in the Caribbean looked so promising. Then the British captured a vessel carrying $620,000 in bills on France to Morris's agent in Havana. Morris had hoped that the authorities there would be interested in purchasing the bills as a way of transferring bullion to Europe during wartime. Only later did he learn that the Spaniards had assembled a heavily armed convoy in July to escort their treasure home. This relieved the Spanish court of the financial pressures that Morris had hoped to exploit. It also stymied his appeal to Cuba's governor for a specie loan. Morris had offered as collateral more than $120,000 of bills that Congress had drawn on John Jay, the American commissioner in Madrid, and had promised to pay off the principal in provisions. But neither the governor of Cuba nor the Spanish Court responded positively to any American overture for specie loans based on the exchange of provisions for bullion.[50]

That left Morris with no alternative but to use the $500,000 specie windfall that had just arrived in Boston to capitalize the bank. This involved him in two new complications, though. One grew out of Congress's indebtedness to the Bank of Pennsylvania. In the last half of 1780, the bank's subscribers had been called on for the full amount of the capital they had pledged to its operations.[51] Beyond depositing bills on Europe with the bank as a form of collateral, Congress had failed to compensate them in any way. Since the bank of Pennsylvania had been supported by many of the city's merchants, Morris felt that he had to offer its subscribers something if the new bank were to succeed. At the same time, paying off the old bank's debts and capitalizing the new bank were clearly beyond his means. Eventually he reconciled these competing objectives by offering to pay off subscribers to the Bank of Pennsylvania on condition that they transfer their shares to the new bank. Not all accepted his terms, and some who did tried to renege. Still, enough transferred their subscriptions that he was able to retire some of the debt due the Bank of Pennsylvania with the money he used to capitalize the Bank of North America.[52]

The other complication arose from the money's location in Boston. Despite the enormous expense involved in transporting the specie overland, Morris was determined that most of this fund be moved to the seat of the Confederation's government. In early September he instructed Tench Francis, his deputy for transporting the specie from Boston, to use some of it there to buy bills on France, then selling at a large discount. This spread around the benefits of the specie windfall while enabling Morris to sell the bills that Francis bought in Boston at a profit in Philadelphia, where exchange would rise once the specie arrived. But why did not Morris leave the money in Boston and issue orders payable on it there instead of going to the time, trouble, and expense entailed of transporting it to Philadelphia?[53]

Morris insisted on having the money moved to Philadelphia for two symbolic—but important—reasons. If bank notes were going to pass as the equivalent of specie, the specie and the bank had to be in the same place. If they were separated, people would have good reason to doubt whether the bank's notes were indeed convertible because of the absence of a fund with which to redeem them. Of course Morris might have divided the money and created two banks instead of one. Given the size of the Confederation and the hostility of American culture to centralization, it is striking that Morris insisted there be only one bank located in Philadelphia.

Morris protested publicly that several banks—as opposed to one—might obstruct the creation of a stable circulating medium for the nation. He argued that banks were new to Americans and that the failure of the first such institution might turn people against the credit of bank paper the same way they had turned against state and Continental paper currencies. If the notes of several banks were to circulate nationally, each would require drawing powers on the other. Without a thorough knowledge of each other's affairs, one bank might inadvertently force another into insolvency by drawing for more than its condition permitted.[54] However, Morris wasn't being totally candid in offering this defense of the monopoly that he claimed for the Bank of North America. He also hoped to use the tendency of a market economy to organize itself around a central place to reinforce the power of the government of the Confederation. If the specie and the bank remained in Boston, he feared that it would strengthen the periphery against the center.

The specie did not arrive in Philadelphia until the beginning of November, and even then more time was needed to assemble the required $400,000 in capital. The bank did not open its doors until the beginning of the new year. Meanwhile, Morris had to make do through various expedients. First he borrowed $20,000 from Rochambeau's war chest to pay the continental detachment ordered to Yorktown one month's wages in coin, pledging to repay the French when the continent's specie finally arrived from Boston. Although it took much longer than anticipated to move the money, Rochambeau remained well enough supplied with specie that La Luzerne allowed Morris to keep half the sum owed in Philadelphia subject to Rochambeau's orders.[55]

Morris also issued personal warrants on his treasurer, John Swanwick. These warrants specified that the bearer be paid one of several currencies or specie on demand. The currencies included Pennsylvania state paper of the latest emission, and "hard" currency, by which Morris meant any specie equivalent, including his own personal notes, which he intended should pass as specie until bank notes took their place. Morris encouraged the idea that his orders, notes, and eventually bank notes were all equivalent to coin by instructing Swanwick to make them exchangeable. But contrary to his instructions, his notes circulated at a discount.[56] Until the specie arrived in Philadelphia there was nothing to back it besides the specie that Morris raised locally by selling bills or borrowing privately.

THE "NEW" ECONOMIC ORDER

Some of the favorable developments that occurred after Robert Morris became superintendent of finance were beyond his direct control. Take, for instance, the declining discount at which exchange sold during the autumn of 1781. Morris boasted that he had helped manipulate the price of bills on France back to par by the end of the year.[57] The instruction to his agent, Tench Francis, to buy bills of exchange on France with some of the specie that had arrived in Boston marginally raised their price, which had been depressed by a shipping shortage. But the news that the French army would winter in the Chesapeake had more of an effect on their value by relieving French agents of the need to draw bills in the region. By the new year, bills in Boston were selling at only a 15 percent discount as supply came more into line with demand. The combination of rising demand for remittances on Europe with the diminishing likelihood that the French army would return to New England raised bills on France to an unprecedented 8½ percent discount by late April 1782. This discount persisted throughout the spring.[58]

Bills on France underwent an even more dramatic appreciation in the mid-Atlantic region. The principal factor here was the influx of specie, which freed both Rochambeau and Morris from having to sell bills. Admiral Comte de Grasse's arrival in the Chesapeake helped. Heeding La Luzerne's warning, de Grasse had brought a supply of bullion with him from Cuba. The proceeds of the Havana trade also brought specie into the region. However, the momentary naval superiority that de Grasse established in North American seas also affected the value of exchange. During the autumn it drew the continent's shipping disproportionately to the mid-Atlantic, stimulating overseas ventures. Consequently, the demand for bills as a remittance on Europe rose. In November, exchange began to push upward in the Philadelphia market, and by the end of the year bills occasionally sold above par. Area merchants seized on Britain's loss of the naval initiative in North American waters by launching winter voyages to Europe.[59]

Other felicitous events promoted Morris's objectives. The year 1781 proved to be a banner year for European and Caribbean imports. The flow of French bills into New England between July 1780 and June 1781 sustained the movement of European imports to Massachusetts Bay throughout 1781.[60] Philadelphia, in contrast, benefited disproportionately from imports from the islands in general and Havana in particular. Though each managed to share in a limited way in the other's good fortune, Philadelphia emerged less beholden to Massachusetts than Massachusetts was beholden to Philadelphia, as Morris wished. The lack of integration in New England's economy, underscored by the absence of a reliable currency, limited demand in the region and led its merchants to turn outward, first to New York, then to Philadelphia, and ultimately to Philadelphia's Caribbean market.[61]

New England merchants would have liked to establish direct commercial contact with Havana. However, their region lacked the supply of cheap, quality flour that Philadelphia enjoyed. The only other available cargo for Cuba was fish, but it was expensive. New Englanders also explored a trade with other Spanish American colonies. These ventures were not profitable. The best way for New Englanders to share in the island trade was to ship European imports to Philadelphia and exchange them for the flour so much in demand in the islands. However, if New

England merchants did so by land they had to pay inflated freights to Philadelphia and then consign the flour they had purchased on someone else's vessel, deducting 33 to 50 percent to pay for freight. If they tried transporting the imports by sea, they ran an additional risk of capture, particularly after de Grasse's departure for the West Indies in early November 1781. Insurance could cover these risks, but it reduced profits so much as to lose favor.[62]

Massachusetts merchants pursued both strategies. High-value, low-volume imports, such as Barcelona handkerchiefs, arrived by land. Bulkier and weightier ones came in eleven vessels—1,280 tons of shipping—that entered Philadelphia from New England ports during 1781. Massachusetts merchants also occasionally instructed their European correspondents to send goods on their account directly to Philadelphia.[63] Either way their desire to get some share of Philadelphia's booming new trade helped make the Philadelphia's dry goods market extraordinarily well stocked by the winter of 1782. The New Englanders, then, contributed to Philadelphia's emergence as the economic center of the Confederation at the end of 1781 because they remained secondary players in the Havana trade.

Morris did contribute to the improving economic situation in other ways, though. While he could not dominate the Confederation's economy to the extent he desired, his efforts at introducing creditable currency substitutes (orders and notes) facilitated provisioning the army by contract. More significantly, his policies helped to mobilize private capital for entrepreneurial ventures. A good deal of the hard coin that had been present in Pennsylvania at the war's beginning had been driven into hiding by the twin influences of the depreciation and the tender laws. In addition, the questionable loyalty of many wealthy Pennsylvanians led to the sequestration of considerable capital. Some of the disaffected, particularly the Quakers, remained alienated from the Revolution until peace came in 1783.[64] Others, who had not welcomed the Revolution, continued watchfully uncommitted. Morris's policies sometimes influenced them to join belatedly in the cause, as Stephen Collins's wartime career demonstrates.

Before the war Collins had been a major wholesaler of imports from

England. He spent the first four years of the struggle in semi-retirement. Apart from occasionally underwriting an insurance policy and participating in the public lottery, he engaged in little business besides defending the interests of his English mercantile connections. This required him, among other things, to discourage the payment of debts owed to his friends in depreciated currency and to remain in the city during the British occupation. Collins obviously felt ill at ease in the revolutionary economy. Only in late 1780 did he begin to consider the new commercial possibilities that were developing. The impetus behind his change of heart was not the lure of the Havana trade so much as the reappearance of hard money and the growing acceptance of the notion of hard money equivalency in Philadelphia's marketplace.[65]

Collins became an active participant in the Havana trade only after the legislature lifted all restrictions on the exportation of flour, in the middle of 1781. Once baptized, he pursued the trade like a fanatic. During the remainder of the year Collins consigned about one thousand barrels of flour to the Caribbean, three-quarters of it going to Havana and the rest divided among the various French islands, St. Thomas, and Puerto Rico. This entailed disbursing the equivalent of more than £1,600 in hard money, though not all of it was his own. He loaded some of the flour on the account of three New England correspondents who were owed money in Philadelphia from the sale of dry goods they had shipped there. His aggressive mobilization of capital during 1781 stood in marked contrast to his commercial inactivity prior to that year.[66] The rising tempo of exports to the Caribbean in 1781 make it unlikely that Collins was the only lukewarm patriot to be inspirited by the new opportunities. Collins's career illustrates one of the ways that Morris's policies, in tandem with expanding opportunities in the Caribbean, quickened the productive energies of the mid-Atlantic region during 1781.

The impact of Morris's policies, however, remained uneven at best. The role that the South occupied in Morris's plans for the campaign of 1782 reflected his recognition of the limits of his influence. He had initially declined to extend his system of contracting to provision the army in Virginia, citing the state's unwillingness to comply with Congress's requisitions. When Virginia responded by demanding contracts, Morris went through the necessary motions for political reasons. But his commitment seemed weak, since he tied the contract system in the state to concentrating the army there, a move that could be expected to complicate the contractor's task considerably. That does not mean that Morris was eager to write off the economy of the South as a complete loss in 1782. One reason for wintering the French army in Virginia was to give the lower Chesapeake an economic boost similar to the one that New England's economy had received the previous winter.[67] Morris hoped the French presence would, in turn, enable the region to support the operations of the southern army under Nathanael Greene's command.

Unfortunately, Virginia never proved an effective staging area for southern operations. Teams remained in short supply, making transportation a major problem that became even more severe as Greene attempted to recover South Carolina. The anticommercial character of Virginia's political leadership also posed a problem. Rochambeau's army tarried on the Yorktown Peninsula until July 1782, together with four French frigates—detached for the winter to protect the lower Chesapeake's commerce. But their presence failed to produce the same warm relationships that had formed between the French and the New Englanders, particularly the inhabitants of Newport. The absence of an indigenous mercantile elite meant that the small French squadron made less of an impression and that French money distributed in Virginia flowed to Baltimore and Philadelphia, having only a slight effect on the Virginia economy.[68]

Morris toyed with several other strategies for bringing distant southern states, such as South Carolina and Georgia, into what he hoped would become an expanding national economy. Ideally, he would have liked to extend the contract system to provide for Greene's army as well as Washington's. However, the stranglehold that the British continued to exercise over the South's commerce by virtue of their occupation of Savannah, Charleston, and Wilmington, North Carolina, made this goal unrealistic. In addition, British operations in the interior following the surrender of Charleston brought anarchy to the South. The attempt of American commanders to pacify the region by adopting a conciliatory policy toward the Tories met with little success, leaving the economy in an unpromising condition.[69]

Morris could do no more than make gestures toward integrating the deep South into the economy of the rest of the Confederation.[70] He briefly contemplated a separate fiscal system for the South, under which participating states would lay taxes to support the army and appoint federal tax receivers. The receivers would then issue notes in response to General Greene's warrants for specific supplies, and these notes in turn would be receivable for the taxes laid. In this way a form of paper money might come into circulation that could facilitate the army's purchase of local supplies. Morris was even prepared to dedicate a small portion of his precious specie reserves to garnishing the plan. But the Congressional delegates of the states involved objected to the requirement that the states collect taxes. So he dropped the proposal. Early in 1783, after the British withdrawal from Charleston, Morris finally attempted to provision Greene's army by contract, but without success.[71] South Carolina and Georgia—and to a lesser extent North Carolina—of necessity remained on the periphery of Morris's efforts to shape an expanding revolutionary economy. His limited resources and the higher priority of the northern theater of the war—because of the continuing British presence in New York—saw to that.

9

THE LIMITS OF
THE WAR ECONOMY

How significantly did the 1780–81 recovery in the Delaware and northern Chesapeake region affect the outcome of the Revolution? Whether there was a surplus of grain in the vicinity had little direct influence on France's decision to attack British General Cornwallis in the Chesapeake rather than General Clinton in New York. The comparative ease in gaining naval access to the Chesapeake, together with the limited amount of time that French Admiral de Grasse felt he could spare for North American operations, were more critical.[1] For a full year before the seven-week siege of Yorktown during the autumn of 1781, French officials had assessed the limitations of New England's regional economy. But the economic potential of the Chesapeake region looked equally unpromising. Beginning in the autumn of 1780, British operations against Virginia and Maryland had escalated, with predictable effects on the region's economy. Thus the Chesapeake did not present a compelling alternative to New York and New Jersey. La Luzerne, who paid the most attention to the problem of supplying the French expeditionary force, did prefer the Chesapeake to the Hudson on logistical grounds, though he urged de Grasse to come to the Chesapeake with money in hand to buy scarce provisions.[2] For the most part the French put little stock in the economic recovery of 1780–81, if indeed they were aware of it at all.

THE THIN MARGIN OF VICTORY

Nonetheless, the hitherto prostrate condition of the agrarian economy in conjunction with the revival of production that took place in the Delaware-Chesapeake region during 1781 decisively shaped the course of allied planning and the outcome of the war. The Chesapeake looked like a more promising theater for combined operations in the summer of 1781 than New York because dividing allied forces between the Hudson and the Chesapeake—rather than concentrating them in one place—would facilitate providing for armies in both locations. The supply services could collect the surpluses of the mid-Atlantic region more cheaply and efficiently on the Chesapeake than on the Hudson because land carriage between the Delaware and Chesapeake posed fewer problems than did land carriage between the Delaware and the Hudson, despite a shortage of teams that had developed in the Chesapeake well before the Yorktown operation commenced.[3]

Prior to de Grasse's arrival on September 1, enemy operations had taken a fearful toll in the Bay, particularly in Virginia, making the war-weary populace additionally reluctant to surrender precious teams to the army. After the French secured the Bay against British warships the demands for land and water transport still exceeded the area's capacities. While those in the Chesapeake who had been spared visits from the British had newly harvested surpluses, producers would not willingly relinquish them to the army. They preferred instead, as had been the case in New England and New York, to sell only to the French for cash.[4]

Fortunately, during the autumn of 1781 the expectation that the allied armies could take Yorktown helped persuade Maryland and Virginia residents to accommodate to the command policies of their states. Though French purchasers worked at cross purposes with their American counterparts, enough supplies moved toward the allied armies to sustain them until Cornwallis surrendered on October 19.[5] To judge from the shortages that afflicted Virginia after Cornwallis's surrender, however, the mid-Atlantic economy had only barely managed to sustain the seven-week siege. The state experienced considerable difficulty providing for the men who remained under arms through the ensuing winter.

As the continent's most extensive region, the Chesapeake's resources were also among the most dispersed. Had the roughly twenty-seven thousand men involved in the siege remained on the spot as winter set in, they all would have suffered as supply routes from the interior and the upper Bay shut down. Spreading the army around the region offered the best chance for comfortable accommodation but conflicted with General Rochambeau's desire to keep his force concentrated. The French chose to winter in the Williamsburg area.[6] They could do so only because their money—and the skillful management of the supply agents, Wadsworth and Carter—allowed them to supplement the limited supplies of the immediate tidewater area with commodities purchased in Baltimore and Philadelphia. Continental and state forces, together with British prisoners of war, could not afford such luxury and had to disperse.[7]

Fortunately, the tidewater region did not have to provide for more than the temporary needs of the French fleet, which sailed for the West Indies at the beginning of November. In addition, Washington hurried most of the continental regiments to South Carolina to reinforce General Greene, or to New York. However, some of Virginia's line contracted smallpox and had to wait until they had been inoculated and properly clothed. The 7,241 British prisoners of war presented the biggest problem.[8] If they were not guarded, they would disappear into the countryside, making it difficult to use them in future prisoner exchanges. If they were guarded, they had to be kept together, which meant providing for both prisoners and guards in the same place. At the time of the surrender, 1,500 of the British were too sick to move from Yorktown. Most capable of moving were marched to interior points like Hanover and Winchester, which could barely provision them. Dispersing the remainder in smaller units did not necessarily protect them from privation or even death. Still others simply "straggled" around the counties between Gloucester (near Yorktown) and the mountains, and sometimes beyond, hiring themselves out to civilians, who received them warmly.[9]

Were the difficulties experienced by the state forces and prisoners of war during the winter of 1781–82 in Virginia caused by supply or distribution problems? The French experienced little difficulty in procuring provisions. Their offer of cash had drawn so many cattle from Virginia's southeastern counties and from northeastern North Carolina that they could afford to refuse the scrawnier animals after the British had surrendered. Many of these cattle simply wasted away for lack of forage as Virginia's state troops starved at nearby Portsmouth. Supplying all other forces proved far more difficult because a popular backlash against impressment—which Governor Nelson, with the Council's support, had discontinued shortly after Cornwallis's surrender—led producers to withhold.[10]

Had Virginia and the continent possessed the financial resources available to the French, would there have been enough for everyone? Probably not. The damage inflicted by the British and guerrilla activity by loyalists during the previous year, combined with the burden of sustaining allied operations during September and October 1781, had left the region exhausted.[11]

Would the allies have fared any better had they moved against New York in 1781? Even assuming that de Grasse's naval force could have secured the Hudson as effectively as it did the Chesapeake, so long as the British retained control of adjacent portions of Long Island—free from large-scale hostilities after August 1776—Clinton would have enjoyed far greater staying power than Cornwallis possessed at Yorktown.[12] The allies would certainly have fared no better in surrounding New Jersey and New York, given the area's depleted condition after five years of war. The prostrate condition of Virginia after Cornwallis's surrender points to the narrow margin of resource sustaining the allies' triumph. At the same time it confirms the wisdom of the French in choosing to attack Yorktown instead of New York. Though the economic recovery of 1780–81 played a critical role in the campaign of 1781, the revival was weak and momentary.

Its fragility became evident in 1782. The harvest of 1782 yielded less wheat than had the harvest of 1781. The decline in production was partially the result of combined operations in the Chesapeake, which had disrupted the planting of winter wheat, just as British operations against northern Maryland, Delaware, and southeastern Pennsylvania had in 1777. In addition, in September 1781, President Joseph Reed and the Pennsylvania Council became convinced that the British were about to attack Philadelphia to relieve Cornwallis. Clinton had planned such an operation earlier in the year but dropped it in mid-July. Nonetheless, intelligence about the embarkation of a large detachment of British troops in New York led Governor William Livingston of New Jersey to conclude that an assault against the Delaware was imminent. Congress agreed with him and recommended that New Jersey and Pennsylvania mobilize three thousand militia each on September 10. Pennsylvania responded more decisively than New Jersey in detaching its quota of militia, though it delayed their march until the enemy's intentions became clearer. Robert Morris feared the effect that Pennsylvania's response to this alarm would have on his financial program.[13] He might with equal reason have been anxious about its effect on the next year's wheat supply, since the militia's mobilization also coincided with the planting season.

Other influences shaped the harvest of 1782 in the mid-Atlantic states. By September 1781, farmers knew enough about the island markets to realize that they looked better than they actually were. Even the size of Cuba and the Spanish military buildup there did not protect Havana against the price instabilities common to all island markets. Moreover, the embargoes and other restrictions imposed by French and Spanish authorities, particularly on vessels clearing from Cuba for the mainland, had put enough of a restraint on the Havana trade during the late summer of 1781 to induce merchants, millers, and farmers to approach the coming year with caution.[14]

Farmers had yet another reason for exerting themselves less in September 1781 than in September 1780. Most people understood that the outcome of the war would be determined at Yorktown. If the allies failed to force Cornwallis's surrender, the French alliance would collapse, as much from French as American exhaustion. A negotiated settlement would then take place. If the allies succeeded, the British eventually would abandon the war. Either way the war would probably wind down in the next year, ending both French and Spanish operations in the Caribbean. That prospect, together with uncertainties about the postwar world, encouraged restraint among producers.

Finally, farmers had less flexibility with regard to fallow lands than they had enjoyed in September 1780, when they could expand both acreage and yield by bringing recently idled land back into cultivation. In September 1781 the best way to stay ahead of soil exhaustion, since the tight wartime labor market made it difficult to open up new lands, was to cut back on wheat acreage. No steep rise in wheat prices occurred in Philadelphia during the planting season of 1781. This suggests that merchants and millers were less prepared to bid prices up and farmers were more willing to get on with their threshing at the expense of the next year's production than had been the case the year before.[15]

THE BLOCKADE OF 1782

The nation's struggling economy had to labor under another crippling burden during 1782. As the lucrativeness of the trade between the islands and the Delaware came to the attention of the British, it attracted enemy corsairs the way the tobacco trade had attracted them earlier in the war. French naval supremacy in North American waters kept the British navy on the defensive through the autumn of 1781. It also put a crimp in their privateering because the navy's urgent manpower needs led to the renewal of the press. Once de Grasse departed for the islands, followed a week later by a large British detachment of eighteen ships of the line under Admiral Samuel Hood, the pressure on New York's resources eased. Though it took a while for loyalist privateering to recover, the Royal Navy had four men of war near the Delaware Capes by the end of the year to intercept arrivals timed for just before the port froze up. Six years of warfare had taught them a lot about American strategies for eluding hostile cruisers.[16]

This small British squadron captured several vessels coming into

Philadelphia as well as five from a convoy of twenty clearing the Delaware Capes for overseas at the end of the year. Other Philadelphia-based ventures fared badly after clearing the coast. Merchant Stephen Collins reported the loss of forty merchant ships at the end of the year, most of them seized in distant waters. Six of thirteen vessels on which Collins had consigned flour to Havana between October and December came to grief in one way or another. These losses alerted the enemy to the importance of the island trade in general and the Havana trade in particular and ensured that the efforts of the Royal Navy to close off the Delaware would be seconded by loyalist privateers in the new year.[17]

British captures of two inbound prizes laden with money from Havana in conjunction with some outbound flour vessels led Rivington's New York *Royal Gazette* to proclaim in March 1782 that "our privateering again begins to raise its head." In the middle of the month the *Gazette* bragged that the arrival of four thousand barrels of prize flour in one day "evince[d] the attention of his Majesty's commanders and the sedulity of private cru[ise]rs in annoying the enemy's commerce." Rivington's reports of increasing captures in 1782 are corroborated by the comments of Philadelphians and by the city's rising marine insurance rates. After Stephen Collins had made his first successful ventures in the Havana trade, he insured his subsequent ones in slower sailors. As the capture rate rose during the new year, however, the cost of underwriting skyrocketed to the point that most if not all the value of a ship's cargo went to the insurer against the risk of seizure by the enemy.[18]

The city's merchants would not part with their newfound prosperity without a fight. They speedily commissioned a well-armed vessel, the *Hyder Ally,* to cruise against British privateers. Under the command of Joshua Barney the ship successfully cleared the lower Delaware of enemy intruders. In April 1782, Barney's vessel distinguished itself by taking the *General Monk,* an enemy privateer of superior armament, in a hard-fought action. Still, the *Hyder Ally,* which carried mostly six-pounders, could not challenge more heavily armed British frigates, several of which took station off the Delaware Capes at the end of March. During 1782, Philadelphia's overseas entries plummeted to only 37 percent of what they had been the year before. From April 1 to July 31, 1782—when the enemy's naval pressure was most intense—only twelve vessels entered the port of Philadelphia from outside the greater Delaware estuary. Of these, only nine had sailed from overseas.[19]

Clearing the coast was equally difficult. By early May, the British force at the Delaware Capes had increased to the point where it was seizing almost every vessel attempting to get out. From late May to late July 1782 a New England vessel that Collins had been instructed to load for the island trade—the *Enterprise*—made four unsuccessful attempts to clear the Capes in the company of numerous other vessels under convoy of the *Hyder Ally* before it finally succeeded in late July. It did so then only because the passage of a sizable French squadron from the islands—moving along the coast to Boston—obliged the British to relax briefly their pressure on the Delaware. During this three-month interval Collins was obliged repeatedly to make large advances to the master and crew and supply them with fresh provisions as well as pay multiple bills for the services of pilots.[20]

Why did it take the Royal Navy until March 1782 to mount the first effective blockade of the war against the Delaware? After their failure in the Chesapeake the year before, were they simply out for revenge? Undoubtedly, but this provides only a partial answer. The year 1782 was after all the first year that the navy was not required to support major army operations on the continent, leaving it freer than it had hitherto been. General Clinton, in New York, had been acutely aware of Philadelphia's recovery as an entrepôt in 1781 and of Morris's plan for the Bank of North America. The British had long realized that conquest by itself was futile. Their strategy had instead focused on finding pockets of loyalism on the continent and trying to energize them politically through military means. The chief grounds for believing that loyalism could be converted into a dynamic political force lay in the shambles into which the revolutionary economy had fallen. The British regarded the resurgence of Philadelphia's commerce and the Bank of North America as particularly unwelcome developments. In 1782 the loyalists, led by William Franklin, urged a temporary invasion of the region to seize or destroy the stock of goods that was reported to have accumulated in the city. They argued that such a blow would shake confidence in the new bank's notes.[21]

Parliament's resolve not to pursue offensive operations in North America in response to the surrender at Yorktown soon precluded this option, but not the close blockade of the Delaware. In mid-April, Admiral Rodney's spectacular victory over Admiral de Grasse's fleet near the Saintes, two rocky isles in the strait between Guadeloupe and Dominica, helped atone for the previous year's humiliation. Although it failed to confer decisive naval supremacy in the western Atlantic on the British, it did force the French to keep what naval force they retained in the Caribbean until the hurricane season, relieving the British navy in northern waters of any need to resume the press. In addition, Philadelphia's emergence as a major tobacco exporter and its continued prominence in the Havana trade whetted the appetites of the British officers and crews off the Capes of the Delaware.[22] Thus the vengefulness and greed of the Royal Navy and private adventurers ensured that the blockade would last until the conclusion of hostilities made the seizure of American property impossible.

For the same reasons, in 1782 the rest of the nation's Atlantic coastline experienced the closest blockade of the war. During the spring, pressure from Cape Henlopen, at the mouth of the Delaware, to Cape Fear, North Carolina, was almost as severe as that experienced off the Delaware Capes. Baltimore merchant George Salmon complained in early May about the vessels he had lost to enemy activity off the Chesapeake as they returned from the islands. John Banks, the business partner of James Hunter Jr., had extensive interests in Virginia and North Carolina. In mid-May he commented on the "amazing repeated losses we have sustain'd." Hunter and Banks felt fortunate when one of their small vessels arrived at Halifax, North Carolina, from St. Thomas; it was the only one out of a fleet of thirteen that had cut through the thick screen of cruisers off the coast. Other vessels eventually arrived from the islands, despite enemy pressure, but their arrival did not alleviate the firm's anxieties about investing in further ventures. The partners' initial response to enemy naval activity resembled that of many Philadelphia merchants, who declined to join in new ventures and sometimes tried to sell their shares in existing ones.[23]

The pressure to find profitable ways to employ their capital did not give merchants as much freedom to withdraw from the wartime economy as they seemed to want. Still, finding an attractive venture for investment remained a real problem throughout 1782. Baltimore's merchants had less difficulty in this regard than did merchants elsewhere. Substituting for Philadelphia as a port of entry gave them greater resources. They also benefited from the presence in Chesapeake Bay of the small squadron of French frigates that de Grasse had left with Rochambeau in November 1781. The largest of these frigates, the forty-four-gun *Romulus,* under the command of Chevalier de la Villebrune, remained in the Chesapeake until the end of the war.[24] The presence of even one such warship forced enemy cruisers in the Bay to be cautious and made the ports that the French used as a base—in this instance Baltimore—safer.

However, American merchants could not rely on the French sea force to protect their shipping, since French captains were subject to the orders of military commanders with priorities other than commerce. The limited French naval presence also had little effect beyond the Chesapeake Capes and did not prevent some of the less capitalized partnerships in the Bay from dissolving under the pressure of their losses. Nor did it lessen the difficulties that Bay merchants experienced both with assembling cargoes and with the low prices that these cargoes fetched in the island markets. Seeking to diminish risk and recoup losses, some merchants sent their vessels out on privateering cruises, thus temporarily withdrawing from legitimate commerce.[25]

The coast north of the Delaware experienced similar pressures. Commodore John Barry of the frigate *Alliance,* who was forced by a two-decker he had met at the Delaware Capes to bear off toward New London, reported he had been chased by two other frigates in the waters east of New York. Morris was anxious to send the *Alliance* back out as quickly as possible, but three enemy frigates hovered off the mouth of

New London harbor. Morris claimed the waters between Cape Cod and the Delaware contained the majority of the nineteen Royal Navy vessels that the British had deployed north of Cape Hatteras.

Even Massachusetts Bay felt the force of the blockade spearheaded by two Royal Navy vessels, one a fifty-gun ship.[26] The Boston mercantile firm of Codman & Smith had initially reacted to news of rising insurance rates in Philadelphia by boasting of the "preference" that Massachusetts Bay enjoyed in the "safety of our navigation on this coast not being confined to one port." This smugness quickly faded in May 1782 when the firm complained to its Philadelphia correspondent, Thomas Fitzsimmons, that the "risque upon our Coast is now greater than has been before during the War, scarce a vessel gets off safe."[27] The coast north of Cape Cod continued to enjoy an advantage, particularly when it came to entering. Yet everyone felt the pressure during 1782, and that pressure decisively affected other aspects of the war economy.

BENDING TO BRITISH POWER

The blockade of 1782 failed on two counts. It never completely closed down Philadelphia's navigation or cut off the region's access to foreign markets. While fewer vessels entered the port from overseas during 1782 than had entered during 1780, and while total tonnage entering from beyond the Delaware declined by 39 percent from 1781, total entries surged by 69 percent, from 184 to 312. Entries from coastal locations accounted for this surge. In 1781, coastal entries, including those clearing from ports in the Delaware estuary, had made up only 24 percent of Philadelphia's commercial entries and 23 percent of its estimated entering commercial tonnage. In 1782, coastal entries accounted for 82 percent of the entries and 52 percent of the tonnage, with the overwhelming number clearing from ports on the Delaware.[28]

Baltimore's experience differed from Philadelphia's. A complete listing of Baltimore's arrivals and clearances during 1782 can be assembled from records in the Maryland Hall of Records and the National Archives. Both sources point to an expanding commerce that challenged the lead that Philadelphia had established in 1781. Only entry figures

Table 9.1. Number and Estimated Tonnage of Commercial Vessels Entering Baltimore and Philadelphia, 1782

	Baltimore		Philadelphia	
	vessels	est. tons	vessels	est. tons
Overseas entries	95	9,265	46	5,180
European*	8	1,060	11	1,470
Islands	87	8,205	35	3,710
Coastal entries†	34	495	9	840
Local entries‡	352	14,255	257	4,825
Total entries	482§	24,135	312	10,845

*Includes the Atlantic Islands. †From beyond the Delaware (Philadelphia) and Chesapeake (Baltimore). All but four of the coastal entries for Baltimore are from North Carolina. ‡Includes all New Jersey and Delaware entries for Philadelphia and all Chesapeake entries for Baltimore. §One entering brig's port of origin is unknown.
Source: S 205 Naval Officer (General File), Hall of Records, Annapolis, Baltimore Entries, January 1–August 1, 1782; Records of the Baltimore Customs, August 1–December 31, 1782, Record Group 36, National Archives; PRI.

survive for Philadelphia, so we are confined to using them in comparing the two ports (table 9.1). During 1782, 170 more vessels and almost two and a half times the estimated tonnage entered Baltimore than entered Philadelphia. The two ports differed most in their entries from the islands (Baltimore enjoyed 2.4 times the number that Philadelphia received) and their entries from their respective rivers and bays. Baltimore also enjoyed a numerical advantage over Philadelphia in local entries, but in addition Baltimore's local entries averaged more than twice the tonnage of Philadelphia's local entries. The discrepancy arose from a small number of large-tonnage vessels that had been recently built in the northern Chesapeake and entered Baltimore to pick up their first outbound cargoes.

The most meaningful gauge of each port's activity, however, was the number of its overseas entries. Here again Baltimore enjoyed a decisive advantage over Philadelphia in both numbers and estimated tonnage. But Philadelphia's entries from Europe exceeded Baltimore's, both in numbers and estimated tonnage. The ratio of Baltimore's entries to its clearances also suggests that it did not completely take over Philadelphia's gateway functions during 1782. Baltimore's clearances for foreign ports exceeded its entries from foreign ports by almost a factor of 2. Its domestic entries outnumbered its clearances for domestic ports by a factor of more than 8.[29] These lopsided numbers suggest that Baltimore had become a collection point for exports from the Chesapeake far more than a distribution center for imports. Despite the drop in Philadelphia's overseas arrivals in 1782, the city remained an entrepôt for the mid-Atlantic region.

It did so because it had accumulated a large enough inventory of imports during 1781 to tide it over much of the following year. With so many people in the region beholden to Philadelphia for imports, it made little difference to the city's merchants whether a correspondent indebted to them in Baltimore or a more distant Chesapeake location shipped American staples to a foreign market on their account. In addition to being the principal owners of roughly 20 percent of the vessels entering and clearing Baltimore during the intervals for which we have records, Philadelphians undoubtedly held minority shares in many other Baltimore ventures.[30]

Admittedly, Philadelphia yielded to Baltimore as the center of the tobacco trade during 1782. Philadelphia also lost some of its ability to offer the highest prices for fresh flour, due to the decline in its overseas arrivals. Nonetheless, Philadelphia remained the center of a much larger trade than the entry figures suggest. As the year progressed, many vessels coped with the continued enemy presence in Delaware Bay by landing cargoes at Lewistown, Delaware, or in the Chesapeake, carting them to a safe point up the Delaware River and then shipping them by shallop to Philadelphia.[31] During 1782, shallops, boats, and ferries operating in the Delaware estuary constituted 73 percent of the city's entries.

The British blockade failed to cripple the mid-Atlantic region's economy, but it altered Philadelphia's role in it, another example of Britain's power to shape the revolutionary economy in fundamentally undesirable ways. The overall decline in imports and exports again led to an imbalance between the two. Prices dropped for exports and soared for imports in a manner reminiscent of the first years of the war.[32] More important, the blockade frustrated continuing attempts to integrate New England's regional economy with that of the mid-Atlantic region.

De Grasse's momentary superiority in the Chesapeake from September to November 1781 had led to some venturing by New England merchants to the mid-Atlantic states. Almost half the 1,280 estimated tons entering Philadelphia from eastern ports during 1781 did so after October 1. Between November 1 and the end of the year, 26 percent of Baltimore's recorded entries and 31 percent of its entering tonnage had cleared from the eastern states, apparently to pick up cargoes for the island trade. By contrast, between January 1 and August 1, 1782, only three vessels (totaling an estimated 320 tons) entered Philadelphia from New England ports, and only two vessels (totaling 200 tons) entered Baltimore. Four more New England-owned vessels (totaling 315 tons) entered Baltimore either from the islands or other Chesapeake ports during this interval. They represented a drop in the bucket when tallied against the more than three hundred other vessels entering Baltimore during the same period. The intensity of the blockade between Cape Cod and Cape Hatteras made land carriage from New England far safer than sea carriage.[33]

The blockade also ensured that the two regions would remain imperfectly integrated within themselves. Though the strategic network of inland water communications that defined the Delaware-Chesapeake region continued to elude enemy control, harassment from Tory refugees persisted as an unwelcome by-product of Britain's naval blockade. Complete interdiction was impossible, but the region's dependence on water communications made it vulnerable to a last burst of refugee marauding. The Chesapeake's continued dependence on slavery also made it possible for a relatively small force of raiders to disrupt its agriculture. The exposed eastern shore of Maryland and Virginia suffered most after the patriot effort to end loyalist buccaneering met with defeat at the Battle of the Barges at Cager's Strait on November 30, 1782. The patriots continued to dominate the western shore, though they could not protect plantations in discrete riverine locations.[34]

Britain's retention of New York as a base for enemy cruisers—right up until the end of the war—also devastated the commerce of southern New England and patriot-held New York. The British concentrated on southern New England during the autumn of 1782 with almost the same enthusiasm they had bestowed on the Delaware. Enemy exertions in Long Island Sound and beyond discouraged the use of water transport. If slavery was the Achilles heel of the Chesapeake, the absence of secure inland water routes that could replace open-sea ones was the weak spot of southern New England. Without them, the economic integration of the region lay at the mercy of British sea forces.[35]

During 1782, western New England and New York sold provisions to the Continental Army and briefly to the French army when it took station on the Hudson. But these regions did not earn enough to allay the growing feeling that they had fared far worse than either eastern New England or the mid-Atlantic region. Northern and eastern New England, like Virginia, felt less dependent on their neighbors to the immediate south and west than vice versa. Northern New England benefited from the French demand for spars. This, together with Massachusetts Bay's fleet of letters of marque, brought New Hampshire and—to a lesser extent—Maine into Boston's commercial orbit. However, even the more prosperous sectors of the New England economy experienced problems in assembling overseas remittances, and its merchants complained as much as Virginia did of being drained of specie.[36]

Finally, the blockade dramatically expanded the area of the Confederation that traded illicitly with New York, aggravating a long-standing and embarrassing problem. Advertisements in Rivington's New York *Royal Gazette* during the latter years of the war proclaimed that city to be the best-stocked market on the continent. As prices for domestic produce began to sag in Philadelphia in response to curtailed exports, the *Royal Gazette* reminded its readers that the specie price of produce in New York remained high, even in the face of a substantial influx of prize flour, while the specie price of imports in New York was comparatively low. This led to a flow of provisions and recently imported coin in that direction. The trade expanded beyond New York, coastal New Jersey and Connecticut, and Long Island—where it had flourished before

1782. Patriot authorities worried about produce moving toward New York from much greater distances. They were spurred to action by reports of the British trading by land with suppliers from as far away as Pennsylvania and by water with Massachusetts, Rhode Island, Maryland, and Virginia, often under flags of truce.[37]

Congress passed an ordinance against collusive captures and recommended that the states make it unlawful to import any British manufactures except prize goods. Most of the states complied with Congress's recommendation, but neither the measures of the states nor of Congress made much headway against market forces. The merchant communities in the principal ports were not to blame; they did their best to comply with regulations. They had no more desire to enhance the business of a nearby competitor in war than in peace. Not so the producers in the hinterland. Some states, like Connecticut, tried to turn the force of the market against trafficking with the enemy. Connecticut authorized anyone who had reason to suspect that certain goods were illegally imported to seize and libel them in the local Admiralty Courts, with half the value of the seizure going to the citizen making the arrest. Such measures, however, disrupted the peace of society more than the illicit trade.[38]

The illicit trade especially embarrassed officials like Morris, who were keenly conscious of the nation's continuing dependence on French aid. Morris tried to shift responsibility for trading with the enemy away from the patriots. "If the Commerce of this Country were protected and that of New York annoyed so that foreign Commodities [were] sold as cheaply here as there the contraband Trade in question would die away of itself." He also emphasized, in response to skepticism voiced by La Luzerne, the commercial benefit that France would extract from its alliance with the United States. Morris claimed that the only thing standing in the way of an expanding Franco-American trade was an extensive convoy system. Morris appealed to the French, who alone had the power to change the naval balance.[39] But the French were not in a position to undertake such a commitment after their naval defeat at the Saintes, and illicit trade flourished until the end of the war.

British pressure on the Confederation's commerce also posed a decisive challenge to Morris's attempt to shape a self-sustaining revolutionary economy. Morris believed that "no Country is truly independent until with her own Credit and resources she is able to defend herself and correct her Enemies." Accordingly, he sought a continental revenue that would free him from reliance on foreign subsidies. Early in 1781, Congress asked the states to amend the Articles and vest Congress with the power to lay an impost. Congress's proposal called for a tax of 5 percent of the value of imports to be paid in specie or its equivalents. The money raised would be used to pay interest on all debts contracted by the continent during the war. The tax would cease when the debts were paid.[40]

An impost was more likely than any other tax to win acceptance from a populace pathologically sensitive both to taxation and to the power of a central government. Importers would pay the duty at the point of importation, usually a commercial center, thus dispensing with the need for an elaborate bureaucracy of collectors. Merchants had access to hard money, both that spent by the French army in America and that entering the country from Havana. They could be relied on to pay because the money would come back to them either directly in the form of government expenditures or indirectly in a specie-backed currency, such as bank notes. Finally, the merchants could add the tax to the price of dutied goods that consumers purchased.[41]

Amendments to the Articles of Confederation required the unanimous consent of the states. During 1781, all the states—except Massachusetts, Maryland, and Rhode Island—acted on Congress's recommendation. Those that did not sanction the amendment nonetheless looked as though they would eventually do so. At the time it received Congress's proposal, the Massachusetts legislature was launching its own fiscal program.[42] Maryland's government had been distracted by the campaign of 1781 and had neglected to consider Congress's resolution until the end of the year. Then, it seemed in no rush to act, and Maryland's legislature did not get around to approving the plan until the following June.[43] For less convincing reasons Rhode Island postponed taking action on the impost during 1781, though Governor William Greene implied that the state would follow Massachusetts's lead. At the beginning of 1782, Morris felt confident that the impost would be implemented.[44]

The British blockade of 1782 helped harden political resistance to a continental impost. A cascade of imports into New England and the mid-Atlantic region during 1782 would have strengthened Morris's hand by enabling him to claim that implementing the measure would reestablish public credit. The decline in imports resulting from British naval pressure empowered dissidents by allowing them to argue that the revenue source was insignificant.[45] Though the Massachusetts legislature eventually endorsed the impost, the final authorizing legislation failed to conform exactly to Congress's recommendation. Virginia also partially rescinded its initial approval of the measure, though it left the governor free to certify the state's consent if and when the other states accepted it. Rhode Island acted more decisively. Under the leadership of its Congressional delegate, David Howell, it refused to adopt the federal impost, formally rejecting the measure at the end of the year. Shortly afterward Virginia revoked its qualified ratification.[46]

The blockade had even more of an effect on state compliance with Congress's requisitions. It compromised both the willingness and ability of the states to raise the specie revenues required of them, which, in default of an impost, remained Morris's principal domestic resource. Taxing in hard money was one thing if a thriving commerce made money relatively abundant, but quite another if commerce had been brought to a standstill and access to specie supplies abroad cut off. Most of the states replied to Morris's pleas for compliance with Congress's requisitions with excuses. They either claimed they were broke or said they had already contributed more than their share to the cause—or a combination of the two.[47]

Such attitudes affected compliance. In mid-May 1782, Morris complained he had received only £5,000 in specie from one state, a mere fraction of what was due. At the end of July his receipts stood at 1 percent of the requisitions laid. By the conclusion of the year the states had collected only $302,735 in specie, less than 4 percent of what Congress had budgeted.[48]

There was little that Morris could do about the states' failure to comply with requisitions. Liquidating and settling the accounts between the continent and the states—which alone would resolve the question of who owed what—promised to be time consuming and offered no immediate relief to the financial dilemmas he confronted. After seven years of bruising warfare, few of the state political systems were prepared to follow Pennsylvania's lead in subordinating themselves to Morris's master plan. And the blockade, by precipitating a credit crisis among Philadelphia's merchants that led to a rash of bankruptcies, posed questions about Pennsylvania's capacity to raise the specie taxes that Morris needed, even though the state was ostensibly willing.[49]

The blockade also compromised the operations of the Bank of North America. When Morris had subscribed public funds to its capital stock, he had expected to borrow them back, as indeed he had early in 1782. However, the blockade also led several of the state governments to seek loans from the bank as an alternative to taxing their hard-pressed citizens. In addition, Philadelphia merchants, squeezed in fulfilling contractual obligations, turned to the bank for discounts on bills that had been accepted but not paid. With its resources seriously pressed, the bank had to discontinue all discounting in late May. If private deposits had flowed in, the situation might have proved manageable. In early May, however, the blockade had set off a run on the bank. Only La Luzerne's deposit of 300,000 livres of the king's money eased the crisis. In the end, La Luzerne saved the bank but not its discounting operations. These remained suspended until mid-July, when they were resumed on a limited basis only.[50] The restriction of discounts neither helped to build public confidence in the bank's notes nor attracted private capital to the bank itself.

Thus the blockade forced Morris back to depending on foreign subsidies. The French had been reluctant to extend Morris's drawing rights beyond 1781. The combination of victory at Yorktown and the resignation of Louis XVI's finance minister, Jacques Necker, which dramatized France's financial plight, disposed the Court to deny subsidies to the

United States in 1782. It took Lafayette, a celebrity in Paris after distinguishing himself at Yorktown, to extract an additional credit of 6 million livres from the Crown.[51] Morris did not learn about this subsidy until April, and by then the closing of the Delaware had compromised his ability to benefit from it through the sale of bills on Europe.

The price of bills in the Philadelphia market had remained high through the winter of 1782 for several reasons. The success of the French in resupplying Rochambeau with specie in January 1782, the merchants' rising demand for exchange to accompany their spring orders on Europe, and Morris's limited success in drawing bills on Cádiz and Amsterdam rather than Paris had all helped. However, the abrupt cessation of Philadelphia's overseas trade in March 1782 quickly dampened the local demand for bills. By early May, as the effectiveness and duration of the British blockade became more evident, bills became difficult to sell at any price.[52] The Philadelphia market for exchange revived in July as the French army began its march north. Bills even momentarily approached par in early August with the brief relaxation of the blockade. But their price dropped again after the loss of 250,000 livres of specie in a French frigate attempting to resupply the army on the Delaware. The approach of peace also discouraged purchasers from buying exchange, making it impossible to negotiate large quantities of bills in Philadelphia at a discount of less than 13 percent.[53]

Morris felt too strapped by the demands he faced to accept such a discount. Instead, he looked around for a more favorable market in which to negotiate exchange. The departure of Rochambeau from New England in 1781 had diminished its access to bills. Though exchange continued to play an important role in New England's overseas commerce, bills now had to be earned by moving European imports southwest, toward New York and Philadelphia. The limited number of merchants engaging in the European trade in the Boston area, together with the seasonal nature of overseas ventures, kept bills at a 15 percent discount throughout the early part of 1782. However, by late April and throughout the rest of the spring New England's relative immunity from the blockade had increased demand, reducing the discount to 10 percent. Morris took as much advantage as he could of this circumstance, instructing James Lovell, the continental receiver in Boston, to sell 440,976 livres of bills for specie between May and the beginning of July, when Philadelphia was experiencing the worst of the blockade.[54]

The New England market had its limitations as well, however. Morris's directive to Lovell coincided with an increase in the intensity of Britain's naval blockade of the region. In addition, the region had never been much of a player in the Havana trade and so was not particularly rich in specie. Even if it had been, relying on New England failed to address Morris's objective of supporting the credit of the bank and maintaining centralized control over the war effort. New England specie would do so only if Morris paid the exorbitant costs of moving hard money to Philadelphia. In addition, the beginning of the peace negotiations in Europe canceled out the boost that the arrival of Vaudreuil's squadron might otherwise have given to commerce in Massachusetts Bay, depressing the demand for bills. However, reports that the French fleet was so cash rich that it would not have to rely on bills—together with uncertainties about the peace process—ironically helped push up exchange to within 7½ to 10 percent of par in Boston during the autumn.[55]

These prices anticipated Rochambeau's army marching from the Hudson to Boston to embark for Europe. This was expected to create an additional demand for bills as French troops sought a safe conveyance for their specie back home. When it became known that the army had been ordered to the West Indies, bills went into a slide as the army hoarded its specie. The price of exchange on France abruptly rose again after the French departed on Christmas Eve. Daniel Parker, one of the contractors for the northern army, claimed that he had manipulated the Boston bill market, first depressing it and then raising it. Though Parker was canny enough to anticipate these fluctuations, the truth was that forces eluding his or anyone else's mastery continued to shape exchange rates.[56]

Morris's inability to maintain French bills at par in turn affected the way his notes—and eventually bank notes—came to be valued in the revolutionary economy. With no private deposits in the bank and no state tax revenues, bills on France remained the only resource at Morris's disposal with which to redeem his currency substitutes. He tried vainly to defend the specie equivalency of his personal notes and bank notes beyond the immediate environs of Philadelphia, instructing his agents to receive them as such and urging the states to accept them in lieu of specie for all accounts, including taxes. Despite his efforts, most places discounted both because the farther one lived from Philadelphia, the less convertible notes were to specie at par. In the absence of state compliance with Congress's specie requisition of 1782, there were no funds locally available for redeeming Morris's notes. New York's reluctance to collect its quota of Congress's specie requisition left them unsecured in that state. In New England they passed at a 10 to 15 percent discount.[57]

The discount in turn contributed to the collapse of the provisioning contract that Morris had made for the main body of the army on the Hudson. Part of the problem stemmed from New York's resistance to Morris's revenue plan. As the threat of enemy attack receded, the people, whose property had been repeatedly seized to support its defenders, grew increasingly hostile to the army. In 1782, patriot New York elected a legislature that declined to receive Morris's bank notes at par with specie and seemed, at least from Morris's perspective, determined to sequester "their Quota of Taxes from the Public Service."[58] In addition, both producers and the state government withheld from the contractors, who were forced to pay a considerable premium both for future contracts with individuals and for the specific supplies raised by the state. Finally, New York's populace demanded ever higher prices for their produce in anticipation of a juncture between Rochambeau's and Washington's armies. When the rendezvous finally took place in September, Wadsworth & Carter, contractors for the French army, crowded the contractors for the Continental Army out of the local market, just as it had crowded Virginia's commissioners out of the Chesapeake. That left the contractors with no alternative but to import supplies from greater distances.[59]

Long before, the contractors had warned Morris that without adequate supplies of specie they would be unable to live up to their contractual obligations. The combined effects of the British blockade and the approach of peace left him unable to put his hands on enough specie to meet the contractors' needs along with his other obligations.

Anticipating the crisis, Morris had explored a variety of strategies for importing specie. He appealed to the French banker Ferdinand Grand, requesting he send 1.8 million livres under strong convoy to America.[60] Grand did not comply, but even if he had it would have taken months for the money to arrive. Timely help was more likely to come from negotiating bills on Europe in Havana. The blockade made Morris wary about the risk, however. In May 1782 he had tried dispatching the armed continental vessel *General Washington* and the frigate *Alliance* to the Caribbean as safe conveyances. The *Alliance* never got clear of the coast, despite La Luzerne's offer of a French frigate for an escort. Although the *General Washington* was more fortunate, it did not return to Philadelphia until the middle of July, and then it had too little specie to make much of a difference. Enemy pressure on the coast had convinced Morris's agents in Havana that a larger shipment was too risky.[61]

Morris's heroic efforts to raise specie proved unequal to the task of providing the contractors with enough cash to keep them going. By the middle of September 1782 he had exhausted all the strategies he had been pursuing as a hedge against the failure of the states to come through with their requisitions. Faced with the choice of surrendering the contract system or forfeiting his credit—on which he felt the Revolution depended—he chose to defend his credit.[62]

Fortunately, the army did not suffer as a consequence. Wadsworth & Carter took the original contractors' place in mid-October, after the withdrawal of Rochambeau's force to Boston. Since this contract had to be financed on Wadsworth & Carter's credit rather than Morris's, the continent paid a 33 percent advance for their services. The original contractors would have had difficulties even without the British blockade, which made it impossible for anyone but Wadsworth & Carter to negotiate the difficulties of providing for the army in war-torn America.[63]

CENTRIFUGAL FORCES

Although enemy naval pressure remained a major obstacle to the realization of Morris's economic vision until the cessation of hostilities on April 11, 1783, Morris also had to wrestle with intractable political prejudices against centralization. His program involved more than simply freeing commerce from the misguided regulations of state governments. Dispersing resources always remained a strategic option in responding to British pressure, as Nathanael Greene had brilliantly demonstrated in his southern campaigns. However, Morris believed that the nation's only hope of sustaining the war effort without foreign subsidies was to mobilize the continent's assets through a centrally managed national market.[64]

Though the parallel is seldom noted, Morris resembled Washington in his preference for centralization. Each responded to shortages in a way that ran counter to the mainstream of American political culture. As a result, both had to deal with the reluctance of the people they led. Of the two, Washington is remembered as the greater leader because of his greater success in managing this tension. Washington, however, could exploit the military convention of a centralized chain of command, while Morris could not. The only resource at Morris's disposal was the tendency of a market economy to organize itself around commercial centers.

Morris's efforts to strengthen the Confederation's economy by making Philadelphia its focal point had the ironic consequence of exposing his policies to two kinds of pressures. Until 1782, Britain had labored under the disadvantage of confronting an adversary that lacked a strategic center. To the degree that Morris succeeded in making Philadelphia that center, he also made the nation's economy vulnerable to the application of British naval power. The expansion of Baltimore's commerce in 1782 underlined the patriots' continuing ability to thwart British naval pressure through dispersing resources. However, Morris remained determined to limit that option.

In so doing he exposed himself to the charge of favoring Pennsylvania's interests. Morris vigorously rebutted such accusations by invoking a vision of a market-oriented war economy that would recirculate money raised from taxation and reestablish public credit through an impost.[65] Geography, alas, worked against him. Even after writing off the region south of the Chesapeake, Morris still found himself wrestling not with an integrated national economy but with two regional economies. So long as the British occupied New York, these two regional economies remained joined by only the most tenuous ties. Moreover, each of these regions contained a large state that spearheaded resistance to the centralizing implications of his policies.

Virginia gave him the most trouble. It remained the largest state in the Confederation, indisposed to taking orders from anyone, least of all a financier. At the beginning of the war the state had made establishing title to the extensive western lands it claimed as much a priority as supporting the Continental Army. In 1779, in response to Congress's heroic requisitions of that year, it had enraged the other states by establishing a land office to sell off large portions of these lands. Many suspected that it meant to spare itself the tax burdens that others faced.[66] The state continued its independent course by trying to obtain foreign loans when Europe's capital resources were already stretched to the limit. Virginia was not alone in doing so; every state felt strapped for funds at one time or another and had considered the possibility. As the largest suppliers of tobacco for the European market, Virginia and Maryland possessed more bargaining power than the other states. In 1782, Morris made a shocking discovery. The French government proposed to deduct a loan Virginia had secured in France from the desperately needed subsidy that the French Crown had given to Congress.[67]

Virginia's Governor Benjamin Harrison had the grace to acknowledge that his state's loan should not come at the expense of funds on which Morris depended. Still, Harrison quarreled with Morris over the financier's reluctance to extend the contract system to Virginia. Harrison also encouraged the legislature to resist Morris's program for laying specie taxes in 1782. The legislature blamed Morris for the state's economic difficulties, rejected his request that bank notes be receivable for taxes, and put their quarrel with him ahead of their support for the southern Army.[68] Finally, Harrison led the movement to block the execution of a contract that Morris had made to buy goods from civilian merchants within the British lines at the surrender of Yorktown with six thousand hogsheads of Virginia tobacco, which Congress had requisitioned from the state in 1781. Britain's success in disrupting Virginia's tobacco economy meant that six thousand hogsheads constituted a sizable proportion of the state's total crop. The legislature passed a series of resolves condemning the Yorktown tobacco contract, for, among other things, being beyond Congress's powers to authorize and contrary to Virginia's laws against trading with the enemy.[69]

Morris faced a less acerbic but no less significant challenge from Massachusetts, the commercial center of the northeast. At first glance that state's economic problems appeared to dwarf those of the other states. Massachusetts had contracted a large debt at the beginning of the war, to which the abortive Penobscot expedition of 1779 had dramatically added. However, Massachusetts also had assets that the other states lacked. In addition to being the second largest state in the Confederation, it was the target of little direct military pressure after 1776, aside from the 1779 British occupation of a post in eastern Maine.[70] Its Bay still provided the safest destination on the continent and remained the continent's premier center for privateering.

These assets emboldened the state's leadership—flushed with their success in winning popular ratification for the Constitution of 1780—to embark on a unique experiment during 1781 for funding the state debt. The legislature invited its individual creditors to subscribe to a loan that would "liquidate" their claims to specie value as they were presented. It then tried to raise a permanent revenue in specie or its equivalents to pay interest on this debt. It took time before the legislature hit on the right combination of taxes, but eventually an impost together with a variety of excise taxes produced the desired results. These measures eventually made Massachusetts's state debt negotiable at between 25 and 33 percent of its face value and therefore, at least to some extent, to answer as cash. Thus the state succeeded in partially realizing Morris's long-term objective of establishing public credit by consolidating and funding the debt.[71]

Morris responded to Massachusetts's initiative with skepticism. He and his supporters saw it as competing with his attempt to put the Confederation's finances on a sound basis. Massachusetts's impost would inevitably be compromised by a federal impost. Morris also feared that state's commitment to funding its own debt would interfere with its willingness and ability to comply with Congress's hard money requisitions. Massachusetts's actions had a limited impact on Morris's plans, despite the unpopularity of the financier in the Bay region.[72] The Massachusetts legislature conditionally sanctioned a federal impost despite the effect that the measure was likely to have on its own fiscal ambitions. In addition, the state's legislature had earlier authorized people to pay their taxes with the notes of the Bank of North America, incorporating it under the laws of Massachusetts. This effectively gave the Bank of North America a monopoly in the state for the duration of the war.[73] New York, Virginia, and Rhode Island behaved in more intransigent and confrontational ways.

Massachusetts's sins were ones of omission rather than commission. As leader of the region it failed to persuade Rhode Island to fall into line with Morris's bid for a continental impost. As the war wound down, Massachusetts contented itself with hedging its bets on the impost, leaving the state measure in place, at least until the federal one received the needed unanimous endorsement of the other legislatures. The wisdom of this strategy seemed borne out when peace finally came. Then Massachusetts found itself one of the few states in a position to reap a revenue windfall from the avalanche of overseas imports that came tumbling into the region's hungry markets.

Would Morris have been able to achieve his vision of an integrated national economy against such powerful centrifugal forces if the British had not done their best to disrupt his efforts during 1782? It is difficult to say, though British pressure certainly exacerbated localist impulses. At the end of 1782, Morris suddenly found himself at loggerheads with Pennsylvania over interest payments on subscriptions to the loan office made before March 1, 1778. Pennsylvanians held much of this debt and had grown accustomed to receiving their interest annually in bills of exchange on France. Morris had responded to a variety of pressures in terminating the payments, including a dispute with La Luzerne as to whether the French government had guaranteed these payments. Morris's realization that the blockade left him little alternative but to continue relying on French subsidies forced him to embrace every measure for limiting the amount of additional exchange in the American economy. He also hoped public creditors in the states that had resisted the continental impost would now bring pressure on their legislatures to support it as offering them the best prospect of being paid.[74]

On September 9, Congress announced the new policy that had been dictated by Morris. Pennsylvania's public creditors did meet and re-solve to bring pressure to bear on their legislature. However, the legis-lature responded to the creditors' petitions by threatening to divert its share of Congress's requisition for the following year to satisfying the creditors' particular claims instead of placing the money at the dis-posal of Congress.[75]

In the last days of the war, Morris and his coterie came to see enemy pressure as an ally in combating the intransigent localism of American society. As peace approached, they repeatedly expressed the wish that the war continue until Americans learned the lessons they wanted to teach them.[76] Morris and his supporters could not have it both ways, however. If British pressure provided the most convincing rationale for his nationalist vision of the economy, it also had subverted the effective-ness of the bank and his system of contracting for army provisions. During the last months of hostilities, some members of Congress joined with representatives of the army in the Newburgh Conspiracy to induce Congress to usurp the power of raising a continental impost. But sub-stituting the threat of a mutinous army for the threat of the enemy backfired. Morris was implicated in the plot but did all that was in his power to quiet the army, advancing it one month's pay.[77]

Morris's last service to the Revolution was to provide the army with an additional three months' pay, Washington's estimate of the minimum needed to get it to disband peaceably. Because of a dearth of funds, Morris had no alternative but to issue personal notes payable in six months to make this payment. He hoped that the notes would simply anticipate the Confederation's future income from requisitions. The states failed him almost completely, however, leaving foreign borrowing his only recourse. By this time the U.S. government possessed very little credit overseas. Morris nonetheless succeeded in cultivating a small co-terie of Dutch banking houses against whom he drew bills of exchange that in turn were sold for his notes. Though many of these bills were initially protested, a new Dutch loan in 1784 raised enough money to cover them and permit Morris to retire from office.[78] His grander vision of national economic independence would have to wait for the develop-ment of new political and economic structures in the young republic.

EPILOGUE

Only peace could resolve the many economic problems Americans struggled with during the Revolutionary War. Only peace could halt the wanton destruction of property and allow Americans to rebuild what had been lost. The cities that had been raided or occupied by the enemy bore the most visible signs of suffering, but desolation was everywhere.[1] Virginia encouraged its counties to tabulate the damage that each had suffered during the war, including losses arising from "obstructed Commerce." At least one county complied, listing among other things the abduction of slaves "during several invasions of the British forces."[2] It is impossible to tell whether the economy of New England suffered more from the loss of its shipping than from the burning of its towns in the raids on Bedford, New Haven, Fairfield, Norwalk, and New London. In 1783, Massachusetts Bay emerged from the struggle with vastly reduced tonnage despite the advantages it had enjoyed in wartime commerce and privateering.[3] Peace promised that the commerce of all regions would at last be again free to pursue a more spontaneous and fruitful course. The transition from war to peace proved almost as traumatic as the war itself, however.

"THE THUNDER-GUST OF PEACE"

In early May 1782, Americans learned of the fall of Lord North's government in response to the House of Commons' passage of a resolution condemning the further prosecution of offensive war against America. At the same time, they received a copy of an "American peace bill," which had been introduced in Parliament. So they had reason to assume that the war might begin winding down.[4] By 1782, however, a general peace depended not only on Britain's willingness to come to terms with the United States, but on France's, Spain's, and the Netherlands's willingness to negotiate with Britain. The process was bound to be complicated and time consuming.

Peace remained a real but indefinite prospect until early August 1782, when Washington received a communication from the two British commanders at New York, General Guy Carleton and Admiral Robert Digby. Their letter stated that negotiations for a general peace had already begun in Paris and that Britain's representative there had been empowered to acknowledge American independence without preconditions. The Carleton–Digby letter also announced that the British government had unilaterally taken the first steps toward a general exchange of prisoners of war by freeing Henry Laurens, a congressional peace commissioner captured while in transit to Europe, and returning to North America the many Americans imprisoned in Britain. Congress released this letter to the public on August 12, along with a series of resolutions warning Americans not to relax their efforts to prosecute the war until a peace treaty was formally concluded.[5]

Though a war-weary populace had reason to conclude that an end to the struggle was in sight, not everyone was jubilant. The last months of the war were perplexing ones for America's mercantile community. While merchants had many reasons for wanting the war to end, they were wary about the transition. Philadelphian Stephen Collins, for example, referred to the Carleton-Digby letter as the first "Thunder-Gust of Peace." In commercial centers like Philadelphia, the news had "totally stun'd Trade for the present." In mid-August, Collins characterized Philadelphia as having "no more Sale for Goods here than there is for Bibles or Warming Pans in the W. Indies." Local consumers had an interest in postponing as much consumption as possible until overseas commerce reverted to its normal, peacetime state. That, in turn, slowed the tempo of domestic commerce in the final days of the war. The following January, Collins concluded, "The War has broke one half of the Merchants here, the Peace is like to break the other Half."[6]

Weak markets were the least of the difficulties confronting American entrepreneurs. More threatening was the prospect of incurring wartime charges on goods that might have to be sold in a peacetime market. The merchants' desire to avoid this trap led them to back off from embarking on new overseas ventures after August 1782. Hard money, in turn, went back into hiding, and the bank found itself pressuring its debtors, including Morris, to repay their loans.[7]

The prospect of peace also hurt overseas markets. Before 1781, Amsterdam had been considered the best place to exchange American staples for European dry goods and tropical commodities like coffee and tea. When the Netherlands lost its neutral status, many Americans turned to France, where the price of manufactures had remained high. Rising American demand allowed French manufacturers to raise their prices even more. Throughout 1782, American merchants complained to their European correspondents about the high cost of French goods, but to little effect. The prospect of peace contributed to their dilemma by discouraging other European suppliers from entering the American market until the peace negotiations were concluded. Like their American counterparts, they feared having to sell in a peacetime market those goods that had incurred wartime charges. Their reluctance protected France's informal monopoly for the duration, though high prices and the prospect of peace limited orders from America. The westward movement of freight from France, never terribly robust, slackened during the autumn of 1782.[8]

Finally, the prospect of peace damaged trade with the islands, particularly Cuba. Despite George Rodney's victory at the Saintes, both Spain and France continued to maintain sizable forces in the West Indies during 1782, making their objective of taking Jamaica still seem a possibility. So long as the allies contemplated going on the offensive, Havana would continue to be a profitable market for American provisions. But the appearance of Vaudreuil's squadron on the North American coast in July 1782 signaled the allies' intention to postpone any major Caribbean initiative, at least until after the hurricane season. The focus of the naval war shifted to the eastern Atlantic, where Britain repulsed a Spanish assault on Gibraltar in mid-September.[9] Though the allied powers remained mobilized to campaign against British possessions in the Caribbean throughout the autumn and ensuing winter, American merchants realized that their inability to achieve a military decision in 1782 did not bode well for continued Caribbean operations in 1783. Thus they surmised that the lucrative island trade, which had been the principal force behind the recent expansion of the war economy, was likely to decline.

Although wary of new ventures, most American merchants were equally reluctant to let their capital lie entirely idle until peace came. Some had debts that compelled them to continue trading despite uncertainties about peace. Others doubted that the war would end, especially between mid-August and October 1782, when the negotiations appeared stalled. Still others shrank from the difficult adjustment that peace would require of them. Disarming their ships and reducing their crews presented few problems. However, their stake in new construction vessels—many of which were unsuited to peacetime commerce because they sacrificed carrying capacity to speed—posed a more serious problem.[10]

The investment of American merchants in newly constructed craft was substantial. The Baltimore Entry Records from November 1780 onward in the Annapolis Hall of Records and the National Archives are unusual in specifying when and where entering vessels had been built. They reveal that more than two-thirds of the vessels entering Baltimore during the last year of the war had been launched in the previous three years, undoubtedly embodying some if not all of the principles of the new construction.[11] Many of these vessels were Bay schooners that would be as useful in peace as war. But with one exception all of the vessels entering from overseas ports had been built since the beginning of the war, and the vast majority of these had been launched during 1782. They represented a major capital investment, in view of the average life expectancy of a dozen years for wooden vessels at the time, that could not so easily be disposed of.

American merchants tried to cope by resorting to a variety of strategies. Toward the end of the war John Peck had designed a vessel that was both fast and "nearly as capacious as the common Clumps in use before the War," but only a few of this design had been built. It was also possible to extend the principles on which Virginia-built sloops and schooners had been constructed to craft of larger tonnage. Only a few strategically placed merchants in Massachusetts Bay and the Delaware-Chesapeake were in a position to commission the construction of hybrid vessels that would be equally suitable for overseas commerce in war or peace before the end of hostilities. Short of that, one's next best course was to substitute unarmed clumps for sharp vessels of the new construction. Privateers had been more likely to bring in clumps than anything else, and the principal ports of America had come progressively to resemble ship graveyards. Merchants had cannibalized the clumps to equip their new-construction vessels, then left them to rot. By the end of the war most were in no condition to put to sea. The merchants' ability to replace new-construction vessels with clumps was further limited by the declining number of recent captures. Finally, the simultaneous pressure that everyone would be under to move from sharp to clump once peace was proclaimed would depress the price of the former and inflate the price of the latter.[12]

The ports in Massachusetts Bay that remained active in privateering until the end of the war had a slight advantage in adjusting to peace because they had a larger supply of recently taken clumps. New York captured the most new ships, but the majority of these were sharp vessels. Those that were not, the British would presumably requisition to evacuate the army. A merchant who did not have access to a suitable prize in Massachusetts or New York had fewer choices. Some merchants tried to modify vessels built for wartime conditions to the peacetime trade. Others exploited their overseas connections to pick up clumps at the end of 1782. Eventually, in 1783, American shipwrights began to produce the first postwar clumps. All of these strategies required capital. After more than seven years of war most American merchants felt strapped for capital. Those who were not nonetheless realized that they could ill afford major losses on the eve of the transition from war to peace.[13] Negotiating that transition would be one of the most difficult challenges the young nation's merchants faced.

PAINFUL TRANSITION

During the winter of 1782–83, the peace negotiations finally came to fruition. The United States and Great Britain did not agree to a preliminary peace treaty until the end of November 1782, after the onset of the winter westerlies. This made it unlikely that the news would reach North America before spring. The negotiations between Britain and the other powers remained in an uncertain state, making the continuation of war seem about as likely as a general peace. Only in late February 1783 did rumors begin to circulate in North America that a general European peace had been concluded. But these rumors were not confirmed until unofficial copies of the preliminary treaties arrived via a French sloop of war from Cádiz on March 24. On the same day, Congress directed Robert Morris to revoke the commissions of all American armed vessels and authorized the secretary of foreign affairs to approach the British commanders in New York about an immediate cessation of hostilities. Morris issued the order revoking commissions on the 25th. However, Carleton and Digby refused to respond to Secretary Robert R. Livingston's overture without explicit instructions from their home government.[14] That meant British armed vessels continued to hover off the American coast until April 11, 1783, the date that had been set in Europe for the cessation of hostilities in America.

The peculiar manner in which the war ended bestowed a lopsided advantage on Britain's merchant marine. With the exception of the few American merchants resident in Europe, British merchants had the best knowledge about the progress of the negotiations. They also knew the market well enough from before the war to choose appropriate cargoes. British merchants did not have to worry about converting their commercial vessels from a war to a peace footing. Britain's naval resources had enabled it to continue convoying large fleets of slow-moving clumps despite the widening war in Europe. Britain's merchant marine also benefited from the vigorous market for charter parties fed by the need to transport and provide for British forces in North America, the West Indies, the Mediterranean, and India.[15] If the British had occasionally found themselves strapped for tonnage by their far-flung commitments during the war, their resources were more than ample to taking advantage of the peace.

At the beginning of 1783 a few American merchants tried to position themselves in the Chesapeake to exploit a possible peace. They hoped to assemble cargoes of tobacco before March 1, when the first news from Europe was expected. In this way they sought to avoid the rising prices that everyone knew would result from producers gaining greater access to the European market than they had enjoyed during the war. Speculators also counted on taking advantage of the tobacco-starved European market. Boston merchant Daniel Parker attempted to form a syndicate in Massachusetts to charter an old French sixty-four-gun line of battle ship that would carry cheap tobacco to a dear market. Nor was the Chesapeake outdone by New England. In January 1783, taking advantage of an unusually mild winter, three vessels laden with tobacco cleared for Europe from Baltimore. The largest of these carried six hundred hogsheads for Amsterdam.[16]

Most American merchants did not have access to appropriate shipping. Even if they had, they would have experienced difficulty in launching spring voyages to Europe before peace brought the first British goods into the United States. Within days of the war's end, dry goods began arriving in the principal ports of North America. They came from New York, where British merchants had been stockpiling them since 1781. The first trickle of imports turned into a torrent as spring progressed, fed by a rising volume of shipping from Europe. This surge greatly affected the gateway port of Philadelphia, as the Pennsylvania Customs Records after May 1783 reveal.[17]

Throughout May many more vessels entered Philadelphia from France, the Netherlands, and Portugal, than from Britain. The most significant development during May was the dramatic rise in the number of entries overall. Only in June did the first hints of Britain's dominance emerge. In the two weeks between June 7 and 24, British vessels accounted for nine of the seventeen vessels entering from northern Europe, or 53 percent of the total and 70 percent of the cargoes measured by value.[18] Some of the vessels from Europe were American, but the profits of this lucrative commerce fell disproportionately to non-Americans. Not only did Europeans have more appropriate vessels, but naval hostilities had ceased in northern European waters well before they ended in the western Atlantic. American merchants could still approach their prewar correspondents in Britain about taking shares in European-launched ventures.[19] Such a strategy promised profit, but it was hardly a badge of economic independence.

As an avalanche of European imports, financed by the extension of cheap credit, flooded the new nation's ports during the spring and summer of 1783, few bothered to question the wisdom of admitting British vessels laden with long-desired commodities. Newspaper reports of the peace negotiations suggested Britain's willingness to grant its former colonies liberal trade concessions. The Shelburne government fell over the lenient terms granted to the United States in the preliminary peace treaty. Americans did not learn of this until word arrived of the general peace, however. The demise of Shelburne signaled that Britain might take a harder line with the republic's trade. Still, Congress was in no position to insist that Britain negotiate a commercial treaty with the United States before it would be allowed access to American ports. A mutinous detachment of the Continental Army at Lancaster, angered by Morris's failure to pay them, had forced Congress to take refuge in Princeton, New Jersey. This humiliation made it difficult for the confederation's legislature to muster a quorum, let alone deal with a commercial challenge from the former mother country.[20]

The state governments were also too weak to exclude British imports, fearing that they would have incurred the wrath of their constituents had they tried to stem the tide of importations. By easing access to overseas markets, peace raised the price of American exports in relation to imports to levels unknown in the war economy.[21] Frustrated consumers might not have even bothered to protest had the states tried to intervene. The public could just as well have ignored the government's injunctions and smuggled goods to and from more lenient neighboring jurisdictions along the nation's extended coastlines.

Under this combination of circumstances Americans went on a consuming spree. In the process they also went deeply into debt, undoubtedly assuming that the momentary rise in the value of American produce in the gateway markets of the continent would continue well into the postwar period. The credits extended by British merchants to American wholesalers were the normal ones: a third- to a half-year interest-free, with the opportunity for extensions at interest should they prove necessary.[22] This seemed to promise consumers plenty of time to scrape together remittances to pay for their impulse to satisfy pent-up demand.

In making their calculations, Americans ignored the high levels of public indebtedness incurred during the war. Some undoubtedly expected that much of that debt would be extinguished by default. Congress seemed to have set the precedent by allowing the old continentals to depreciate out of circulation. The war had also taught the American people that unpopular policies—such as the attempt to appreciate the currency in 1779—could be defeated by popular obstruction. They also assumed that the postwar world would be full of economic opportunities, both foreign and domestic, that would ease the transition from a wartime to a peacetime economy.[23]

In the end, the revolutionaries realized their brightest hopes for the American economy. The most promising emblem of the nation's future prosperity was the cession by Britain of an enormous expanse of territory between the Appalachians and the Mississippi. With such a large resource of land, the European population of the nation, which would increase by 80 percent between 1770 and 1790, now had plenty of room on which to accommodate its rising generation. The new nation thus solved one of the crucial problems that had precipitated the Revolution in the 1770s.[24] Still, the availability of land did not by itself guarantee economic growth as measured in rising per capita income.

Most economic historians agree that, beginning about 1790, such growth did take place and did lay the foundation for the modern industrial economy. They disagree, however, on why this change occurred. Some point to the expansion of the nation's foreign trade after 1793 and stress the nation's neutrality during the Napoleonic Wars. Not only did the wars accompanying the French Revolution create a demand for agricultural exports, but they also eventually enabled America's neutral-flagged merchant marine to surpass those of the maritime powers of Europe. Others argue that growth in per capita GDP predated 1793, that the benefits derived from an expanded foreign trade were unequally shared, and that the cumulative effects of an increasing foreign commerce were negligible.[25]

No one denies that there was a postwar recovery in the 1790s.[26] The important question is: How did the nation overcome the legacies of the war that obstructed long-term development? One such legacy was the effect that high levels of private indebtedness to European creditors had in depressing the value of American staples during the Confederation period. Though the credits that Europeans had earned in the United States led them briefly to bid up the price of American tobacco in 1784, this proved to be a temporary anomaly. Rising indebtedness had the more general effect of inflating the price of exchange on Europe and forcing the exportation of considerable quantities of specie. That in turn discouraged imports, which reduced the number of vessels looking for return cargoes to Europe. Diminished shipping to overseas markets depressed the price of American staples, complicating the repayment of private debts contracted in the first months of peace.[27]

Such cyclical and structural obstacles to retiring indebtedness abroad have always attracted less attention than America's exclusion from the colonial empires of the European powers—particularly their Caribbean possessions. Spain's termination of American trading privileges with its Caribbean and South American possessions took few by surprise. Though Spain had provided the revolutionary economy with critical assistance, its support of American independence, ambivalent at best, could hardly be expected to counter that nation's commitment to colonial monopoly.[28] The Franco-American Commercial Treaty of 1778 held out a better prospect for a flourishing trade with France and its possessions. Still, direct trade with metropolitan France continued to suffer from the reluctance or inability of French merchants to extend credit. In addition, the price of French manufactures remained high compared with Britain's. More important, French goods did not suit the American market. Finally, Americans encountered difficulties gaining legal access to France's island markets, which had been so important in revolutionary commerce.[29]

Beginning in 1784, the French government liberalized the restrictions on American merchants in both their home and island markets. This occurred over the opposition of powerful vested interests in the mother country. The effect of the government's actions remains in dispute. Some have argued that the liberalization had a significant impact on the American economy. Others believe that the lifting of legal restrictions was irrelevant, particularly in the islands, where American smugglers had ignored them all along.[30]

One area where liberalization was out of the question was the French tobacco market. The tobacco monopoly administered by the Farmers-General had an enormous potential for affecting the postwar economy. Its influence in raising or depressing the price of American tobacco has been disputed, then and now. The contract negotiated by Robert Morris with the United Farms in 1785 helped to swell American exports to France and its dependencies in 1786 and 1787. However, it did so at prices considerably lower than the postwar peak of 1784. More significantly, by the end of the 1780s tobacco had surrendered its claim to being the nation's leading export. Its decline paralleled the shrinkage during the Confederation period of French imports to America to about one-eighth of what they had been between 1781 and 1783 (including military expenditures). By 1789 the value of French exports to the United States amounted to only one-twentieth of British exports to the United States.[31]

The most unpleasant surprise of the immediate postwar period involved the restrictions imposed by Britain on the nation's trade. Americans rued the enthusiastic opening of their ports to all comers in the spring of 1783, when they learned, during the following autumn, that Britain had no intention of fully reciprocating. Instead of Parliament regulating Britain's trade with the United States, where the friends of America could make themselves heard, the British Crown undertook to do so through executive decrees known as Orders in Council. The regulations it promulgated suggested a former mother country bent on avenging itself rather than cultivating a mutually advantageous trade. The first order excluded American shipping from the carrying trade between the United States and Britain's possessions in the western Atlantic. Subsequent orders stopped imports of American fish and salt meat to the islands and whale oil to Britain's home market.[32]

Because the Articles of Confederation had failed to vest Congress with any power to regulate the new nation's trade, only the states were in a position to respond to such affronts. Virginia and Massachusetts alone made an attempt, though their efforts came to naught. To add insult to injury, the Barbary pirates started seizing American vessels in the eastern Atlantic, now that Americans were no longer under British protection, further clouding the already diminished commercial prospects of the republic.[33]

Exploring commercial opportunities outside Europe's principal commercial empires remained a possibility, but one fraught with hidden difficulties. One example is the opening of the China trade in the 1780s, which has been celebrated as the harbinger of a new commercial age. The voyage of the first American vessel to the Chinese market took over a year and cost five to ten times more than a comparable voyage to Europe. Few merchants possessed the capital required to undertake such a venture. In the short term, at least, this trade could not substitute for the commerce around which America's colonial economy had been structured.[34]

Restricted access to overseas markets in turn complicated dealing with the revolutionary debt, both of the states and the confederation. Although various forms of repudiation had been used during the war, they became less viable in peacetime as the plea of necessity ceased to ring true. In 1783 a wider sample of the population held the liquidated debt than at any prior or subsequent time, and that debt represented a significant portion of the nation's wealth. The notion that a debt, when properly funded, could serve as an asset as well as a liability had only begun to gain ground and still was not widely understood. Nonetheless, honoring the debt presented a superior moral alternative to repudiation, whatever the practical difficulties.[35]

A comprehensive debt settlement posed daunting problems, however. The most obvious one related to the mechanics of settling the accounts between the states and the continent. In 1782, Robert Morris had put the complex process of "liquidating" these accounts in motion, but it was far from complete as peace approached. Until it was completed, each state would continue to assume that it would be a creditor in a final settlement, having already done more than its fair share. Such attitudes hardly augured well for the states' future fiscal exertions or public credit.[36] The western lands offered little immediate prospect of fiscal relief. While the West's role in the nation's future development was evident, that asset could not be sold to pay off the debt in the near term because of the shortage of buyers with money. The lands would simply be engrossed by the few at a fraction of their potential worth.

In response to Morris's prodding, Congress forwarded the revenue plan it adopted on April 18, 1783, to the states within one week of the war's end. It renewed Morris's call for the states to grant Congress a permanent source of revenue, which would be raised from a federal impost. It also urged the states to lay additional taxes of their own and to appropriate them to paying interest due on the liquidated federal debt. Congress apportioned quotas among the states according to current population estimates so as to raise an annual fund totaling $1.5 million.[37] Because the quotas took no account of state debts, this approach invited political obstruction.

State creditors outnumbered federal creditors in every state. In any competition between the two groups, the states would pay their creditors before they paid those of the federal government, leaving a substantial segment of the revolutionary debt unfunded. Some states—such as New York and Pennsylvania, which benefited from a voluminous foreign commerce—raised large sums of hard money through local imposts. This enabled them to pay interest on their state debts. Where the state debts were small and the yields from the impost large, they could provide for their federal creditors as well, in the expectation of being compensated when a final settlement took place between the states.[38] Other states—such as Connecticut—were less fortunately situated, having large debts and meager revenues from imports. These states responded to the claims of their domestic creditors without addressing those of the federal creditors within their midst. Some states, after a prolonged political struggle between debtors and public creditors, decided to issue paper money in order to pay state debts. When Rhode Island's creditors refused the new paper money, the debtor majority in the legislature threatened creditors with draconian penalties.[39]

The burden of taxation proved sufficiently onerous in many states to compromise the postwar recovery of their economies. Taxation also complicated the task that private debtors encountered in paying for their initial postwar extravagance. Few states succeeded in converting their public debts into public assets by raising enough revenue to pay the going rate of interest on the face value of the principal. In Massachusetts, one of the states where this had happened, the government ignited Shays's Rebellion in 1786 by trying to defend the state's funding system from the challenge posed by the postwar depression.[40]

TOWARD FULL INDEPENDENCE

Human ingenuity eventually surmounted the political and economic challenges of the postwar world. The states responded to the problems of the Confederation's economy by resisting fragmentation and uniting under a new federal constitution that gave the central government sufficient power to fund the revolutionary debt. The first secretary of the treasury, Alexander Hamilton, had the vision to propose a plan for consolidating many of the remaining state debts with the federal debt. His approach relied on reducing the interest that would be paid on this consolidated debt, in turn making it possible to expand the principal funded by the federal impost. The impost was the most popular means of raising a revenue, and the yield from it promised to grow as the nation's foreign commerce increased. Consolidating the state debts with the federal debt guaranteed that the state creditors would cooperate in implementing the federal impost, ensuring that it would yield the maximum revenue.[41]

Both the newly consolidated debt and the impost were in place in time to take advantage of the economic opportunities created by the French Revolution in the early 1790s. The uncertainties of revolutionary Europe made the new federal republic seem a desirable haven in which Europeans could safely invest, leading to a substantial movement of capital—particularly from the Netherlands—to the United States. European investment quickly pushed the market price of the national debt above par, facilitating the use of U.S. securities as capital in the launching of other enterprises. Again, Hamilton led the way by proposing that investors be allowed to subscribe three-quarters of the proposed Bank of the United States' capital stock in the federal funded debt.[42]

After 1791 banks proliferated. There had been only four other banks at the time the Bank of the United States was incorporated. By 1800, there were twenty-eight, by 1811, ninety. The funded debt of the United States played little direct role in the capital subscriptions that launched these enterprises. The rash of new state banks drew more directly for capital on the wealth generated by the demand that the Napoleonic Wars created for American food staples and the services of neutral-flagged vessels, and after 1800 by the growth of U.S. cotton exports. This commerce made it possible for the republic to retire its foreign debt on schedule and to import an increasing quantity of commodities from overseas, swelling the yields from the impost beyond what had previously been imaginable.[43]

The new constitution also bestowed on Congress ample powers to address unresolved problems with other nations. These included securing of the western domain, negotiating commercial treaties with the great powers, and defending American vessels against North African piracy. The management of the nation's foreign relations proved more divisive than expected.[44] The political strife of the 1790s suggests that the United States was extraordinarily fortunate in having successfully strengthened its federal constitution at the end of the 1780s. If the new nation had had to cope with the pressures of the 1790s without the benefit of a fully empowered, legitimate central government—and without an effective settlement to the troubling issue of the revolutionary debt—its development might have pursued a very different course.

As it was, the republic proved able to defend its neutrality and reap the economic advantages of being a nonbelligerent well into the first decade of the nineteenth century. By then it had begun to win concessions from the great powers. For instance, the opening of the British East Indies to American traders in the Jay Treaty of 1795 laid the groundwork for the expansion of American enterprise in the Far East. After 1800, American neutral carriers, whose capital resources had dramatically increased since the 1780s, came to dominate Europe's lucrative commerce with the East Indies. The prolonged effect of the comparative prosperity between 1793 and 1807, uneven as it may have been, helped preserve the constitution and the revolutionary debt settlement despite the increasing pressures exerted by the principal belligerents on the young republic after 1805.[45]

The establishment of a federal legal order also provided a more promising setting for the entrepreneurial energy that had been so conspicuous in the revolutionary economy. Instead of repeatedly striving to surmount the structural limitations intrinsic to colonial economies, American entrepreneurs increasingly found themselves operating in a friendlier environment, where their energies could shape the economy of a prosperous, developing nation. Still, the memory of the revolutionary trauma continued to exert a powerful influence. The legacy of the war pointed to the desirability of developing national naval power, inland systems of transportation, and the capacity to arm and clothe forces without reliance on others. All of these had their advocates, and, since all were costly, they competed with each other. However, the nation's investment in turnpikes, bridges, canals, and eventually manufacturing, far exceeded its investment in a navy in the early years of the republic—for good economic as well as political reasons.[46]

Transportation and manufacturing improvements attracted private investors who had powerful incentives to push ahead with such enterprises, especially if they were granted the privilege of incorporation. In addition to direct returns on their investment, they could look forward to indirect returns, such as the greater integration of regional markets through transportation improvements and the freeing of female energies from the drudgery of manufacturing textiles in the home. By contrast, a navy was too expensive for any agency but a state to finance, especially since its principal benefits were confined to wartime. Some took the approach that the republic would be better served by being free of such a heavy burden.[47]

Complete naval impotence, however, invited the depredations of the North African pirate states. In response to the seizure of American ships by the Algerians, Congress authorized the building of six large frigates in 1794. When it declared a limited naval war against France in 1798, only three vessels were operational. Using expedients developed during the Revolution, such as modifying commercial vessels and taking them into the service, this sea force quickly expanded to fifty-four ships before the end of that contest. Some of these ships were subsequently deployed in bringing the North African states to terms in the early nineteenth century. Still, naval parity with the great European powers remained a luxury that the new nation could not yet afford. In 1812, when the republic went to war with Britain, its fleet—which then numbered nine frigates and eight smaller craft—acquitted itself with honor in individual actions against enemy vessels of comparable strength. But the navy was powerless to counter Britain's progressive extension and tightening of its blockade along the Atlantic coastline.[48]

The War of 1812 raised the specter of a replay of the Revolution. Besides confronting an adversary whose naval supremacy it could not hope to challenge, the U.S. government also encountered difficulties in mobilizing the nation's resources because of monetary problems. Still, there were important differences. The nation armed and clothed its armies on its own, partly due to emergent industries that had benefited from the embargo and subsequent nonintercourse measures of the previous decade. The United States also withstood the force of British power without the assistance of any European allies. Finally, it survived a three-year war without complete financial collapse. Never again would the republic have to depend on foreign powers for its survival. After the War of 1812, the young nation could celebrate the emergence of a truly national economy.[49] Twenty years later, when the republic next confronted a great European power, it no longer did so as the conspicuous naval inferior of its adversary.[50] Changes in the fabric of American life that we associate with industrialization gradually liberated the republic from the intractable dilemmas of Robert Morris and his generation. Though full economic independence had proved a good deal harder to achieve than political independence, the War of 1812 confirmed that the nation's economy had finally caught up with its political destiny.

APPENDIX

On Decoding the Hollingsworth and Lea Accounts

Significant business records spanning the revolutionary period are hard to find. My sketch of the revolutionary economy relies heavily on the surviving records of Levi Hollingsworth, a Philadelphia flour merchant, and Thomas Lea, a prominent Brandywine miller. Though the Hollingsworth records are more extensive than the Lea records, for the Revolution they are also more discontinuous and harder to interpret.

Hollingsworth kept most of his business records in bound folio volumes. Normally each folio covered a year's business, commencing on March 1 and ending the following February 28. With the disruption of the war, Levi turned his attention to running a local flour exchange between 1777 and 1783. For that period a Flour Journal, 1777–81 [really 1777–82] (540), and a Flour Ledger "B" [really "A" and "B"], 1777–80 (598), survive. These folios from the war years stand alone. Though there is a Journal (543) that seems to pick up where 540 leaves off on March 1, 1782, it makes no mention of flour transactions.

The display in the accompanying table is derived from entries in these two flour folios and a Flour Ledger (595, not of folio size) that records the flour Hollingsworth received between March and August 1774, from thirty-eight suppliers. During this six-month period, Hollingsworth processed 10,813 barrels of flour from the harvest of 1773. Since the interval spans the time when the mills resumed grinding wheat after the ice had broken on their races to the time when new wheat of harvest 1774 began to arrive, I assume that it represents roughly half of the total flour received from harvest 1773. My calculations assume the harvest year to begin on August 15 of each year, because that seems to be the earliest that new flour could be manufactured and transported to market.

Journal 540 records the flour transactions of the firm during a five-year period. Because it begins in mid-February 1777 and extends to the beginning of March 1782, its entries bear on six harvests, though only a portion of harvests 1776 and 1781 are reflected in it (again I assume one-half). Journal 540 does not always make it easy to distinguish between new flour being received and internal transfers of ownership, though that distinction is important to my argument. The distinction is more clearly recorded in 598, which also begins in February 1777 but ends roughly at March 1, 1780.

Though the entries in 598 should correspond to those in 540, there are minor discrepancies between the figures that I have derived from each source. Some of the discrepancies are the result of clerical error; others are undoubtedly the result of difficulties that I experienced in interpreting the entries. Journal 598 may be more accurate than 540 in the sense that 598 provided the basis for the settling of individual accounts and as such allowed Hollingworth's clients an opportunity to protest errors in the Journal. I nonetheless rely on 540 for estimates pertaining to harvest 1780 and 1781 in table 1.1 because 540 contains the best information about the arrival of harvest 1780—probably the most asymmetrical one of the war in the way it came to market (see Chapter 6)—and the only information about the first half of harvest 1781. For the other years covered by table 1.1 where 540 and 598 overlap, I have averaged the divergent values in calculating the percentages that appear in the display and in table 1.1.

Thomas Lea's Daybook and Journal together with a Ledger covering the same period seem to provide a more continuous and less problematic view of the economic activity of a prominent Brandywine miller throughout the war. The Daybook and Journal gives us a wide range of information about prices and volumes of wheat processed. But it also is a tricky document to interpret because of the idiosyncratic way the trans-

Quantities of Flour Received by Levi Hollingsworth from Harvest 1776–81

Harvest Year	1776	1777	1778	1779	1780	1781
bbl. of flour 598	5244		3061	3538	11411‡	
bbl. of flour 540	5245		3148	3703	11429	14670★
presumed annual supply in bbl.	10489★		3105†	3621†		
Percentage of estimated 1773 harvest; n = 21,626 bbl.	48.5		14.4	16.7	52.8	67.8

Sources: Flour Ledger (598) and Flour JOurnal (540), HFP.
Note: ★extrapolated; †averaged; ‡figure derived from 598 until March 1, 1781, supplemented thereafter by 540.

actions are recorded. One repeatedly finds entries out of strict chronological order, interspersed with earlier or later transactions. Though the Daybook and Journal was supposed to contain all the information that would go into the ledger, a few of the surviving ledger entries cannot be traced back to the Daybook and Journal.[1] In addition, several of the harvest year accounts contain summary notations about payments for freighting and measuring wheat that do not seem to correlate with the mill's wheat account.

For instance, in the harvest years 1774–75 the figures for freighting come to 22,784 and 18,977 bushels, respectively, for measuring 25,747 and 38,144. While these numbers reveal a wide discrepancy between the mill's wheat account in 1775 as represented in table 1.2 and Lea's total activity, it is not clear what the source of the discrepancy is. Perhaps both the freighting and measuring accounts carried over from previous years, or, in the case of freights, the same bushels passed through the hands of several handlers. While the freighting and measuring series is not complete for the war years, where values can be derived after 1776 they are in all cases less than the total of the mill and custom accounts. Given the uncertainty, not to mention the discontinuity, in these figures, I have omitted them from the display in table 1.2.

There are some additional peculiarities about the derivation of values in the display. The pagination of the Daybook and Journal is geared to the harvest rather than the calendar year. This particular Daybook and Journal begins in the middle of harvest 1774, on page 57, carrying over from a previous record that has not survived. Harvest 1774 continues through page 112 before beginning over again with page 1 of harvest 1775, and so on through harvest 1782. For reasons specified in the main text, Lea didn't begin to have access to harvest 1777 until July 1778. He then chose to keep the accounts for harvest 1777 open until the middle of October, two months longer than usual.

The accounts for harvest 1778 coincide with Lea entering into a partnership with John and Robert Morton.[2] The Mortons appear to have supplied much of the capital by which wheat was procured for Lea's mill during the rest of the war. In the early years of the partnership with John and Robert Morton, Lea did some of the work involved in gathering wheat; after harvest 1779 the partnership seems to have relied increasingly on jobbers who delivered wheat to the mill or to depots at key transportation points, like Head of Elk or Christiana Bridge. During the lean middle years of the war, most of the wheat came from a considerable distance. Journal and Daybook entries for locally produced grain virtually disappear from Lea's accounts for harvest 1778 and harvest 1779.

The Daybook and Journal poses a major problem when it comes to deriving the values for harvest 1780 that appear in table 1.2. As far as I can ascertain, this record omits all mention of 20,586.75 bushels of wheat that are recorded in the Ledger for harvest 1780 under "Mill in Comp. with Jno & Rob Morton." Most of the missing wheat relates to five special accounts with the jobber Nathan Newlin encompassing a total of 20,409.25 bushels, of which only 1,312.5 are recorded in the Daybook and Journal. In addition a net of 845 bushels (1,247 mentioned in the Ledger, 402 credited in the Daybook and Journal) belonging to Samuel Wallis fail to show up in Daybook and Journal. Finally, there is a reference in the Ledger to 645 bushels of wheat collected by John Wheeler and William Gaddis that I have been unable to identify in the Daybook and Journal, though this parcel may be subsumed in the Ledger entry referring to Newlin's account No. 3.[3] Even if we dismiss the two lesser discrepancies as minor mistakes, or acknowledge that accounts other than those strictly pertaining to the partnership between Lea and the Mortons were introduced into the ledger, the Daybook and Journal notes only 6.4 percent of the wheat that Newlin is credited with in the Ledger's reckoning of the partnership's accounts. That constitutes a major hole in the Daybook and Journal.

The Lea Ledger 1773–87 corroborates the impression given by the Daybook and Journal that the mill in company with the Mortons had been supplying Newlin with large quantities of cash to procure wheat since the spring of 1780.[4] An enigmatic entry in the Daybook and Journal on the final page of harvest 1780's accounts credits Lea and Joseph Tatnall, another Brandywine miller, with grinding 14,330 bushels of wheat at 50/ per hundred bushels.[5] Normally Lea did not figure grinding costs into the partnership's accounts, nor did he farm out his milling. But at the end of harvest 1782 the Daybook and Journal turns briefly into a mini ledger occupying four consecutive pages detailing the accounts of a Lea-Tatnall partnership during 1780–81. Here are recorded the freight charges for the movement of wheat to Tatnall's mill as well as his share of the grinding entry referred to above.

My guess is that Newlin's activities in connection with harvest 1780 created a problem. Most of his purchases had been made with continental money, probably at a considerable distance from the Brandywine. Much of the wheat appears to have arrived late in the season, just before new wheat from the harvest of 1781 was about to become available. Lea may have acted to free up his mill for harvest 1781 by farming out a portion of Newlin's wheat to Tatnall. The quality of the new wheat was clearly superior to the older wheat, and Lea processed 4,316 bushels from the new harvest before the end of September. In deriving a figure for the mill account in 1780, I have assumed that Lea ground 6,310 bushels of 1780 wheat that Newlin had purchased and farmed out 8,020 to Tatnall. That assumption still leaves 4,767 bushels of Newlin wheat unaccounted for in the Daybook and Journal entries. My best guess here is that this wheat was part of a parcel of 13,150 bushels that Thomas Starr is credited in the Ledger with shipping for the partnership of Morton and Tatnall and that it was disposed of elsewhere. In any case I have excluded the "missing" wheat from the totals entered for the mill's account in 1780 but included the Tatnall and Lea wheat.

Fortunately, no such problem exists with the Daybook and Journal for harvest 1781. Here the Ledger confirms the partnership's success in collecting and grinding a record of more than 50,000 bushels of wheat.[6] Local suppliers vied with jobbers buying at a greater distance in maintaining the continuing cascade of wheat recorded in the Daybook and Journal for this harvest year. But in harvest 1782, I encountered another problem that resembles that noted for harvest 1780. The activity of local suppliers fell off and the partners again relied disproportionately on the services of jobbers, particularly Thomas Jones, who seems to have used his own capital. Jones had begun purchasing cheap 1781 wheat in large quantities at the end of that harvest year, depositing it at the mill but holding it in anticipation of a price rise in 1782. He was not disappointed as the new wheat quickly climbed from 5/ to 6/ in mid-October to 8/ at the end of the following harvest year. Jones did succeed in maintaining a steady flow of wheat to the Brandywine mill throughout the entire harvest year, which was a jobber's principal function. Lea's Daybook and Journal corroborates the Ledger in crediting him in a summary notation with supplying the partnership with 40,591 bushels of wheat, or roughly 83 percent of the total for harvest 1782.[7] But I can find entries in the Daybook and Journal to account only for 22,101 bushels of the 1782 wheat. If we add the 1781 wheat that he deposited at Lea's mill during the previous harvest year, most of it at the end of that year, the total still comes to only 28,894 bushels of Jones's wheat, leaving 11,697 bushels unaccounted for. Nonetheless, because the Daybook and Journal and Ledger agree in their summary entries, I have added all of the Jones wheat to the mill account for 1782.

ABBREVIATIONS

I have relied extensively on abbreviations to designate locations, principal manuscript sources, and published collections of primary sources. The following list of abbreviations doubles as a bibliography, though it covers only collections and items cited more than once in the notes. It excludes newspapers, which are fully referenced. Preference in annotating has been given to the primary sources because of the undeveloped nature of the subject. Published monographs, scholarly articles, and dissertations are referred to sparingly.

ABBREVIATIONS

Locations

BA	Boston Athenaeum, Boston
BHS	Beverley Historical Society, Beverley, Mass.
BLHU	Baker Library, Harvard University Graduate School of Business Administration, Boston
CCHS	Chester County Historical Society, West Chester, Pa.
CHHS	Chicago Historical Society, Chicago
DSA	Delaware State Archives, Dover
HL	Huntington Library, San Marino, Calif.
HSD	Historical Society of Delaware, Wilmington
HSP	Historical Society of Pennsylvania, Philadelphia
LC	Library of Congress, Washington, D.C.
MAC	Archives of the Commonwealth of Massachusetts, Boston
MdHR	Maryland Hall of Records, Annapolis
MdHS	Maryland Historical Society, Baltimore

MHS	Massachusetts Historical Society, Boston
MNHP	Morristown National Historic Park, Morristown, N.J.
NA	National Archives, Washington, D.C.
NCSA	North Carolina State Archives, Raleigh
NEHGS	New England Historic Genealogical Society, Boston
NHHS	New Hampshire Historical Society, Concord
NYHS	New-York Historical Society, New York City
PEM	Peabody Essex Museum, Salem, Mass.
PHMC	Pennsylvania Historical and Museum Commission, Harrisburg
PLDU	Perkins Library, Duke University, Durham, N.C.
PRO	Public Records Office, Kew, London
PROC	Public Records Office, Chancery Lane, London
RIA	Rhode Island State Archives, Providence
RIHS	Rhode Island Historical Society, Providence
SCHS	South Carolina Historical Society, Charleston
WLCL	William L. Clements Library, University of Michigan, Ann Arbor

Principal Manuscript Collections

AGP	Arnold Greene Papers, John Carter Brown Library, Brown University
AHP	Andrew Huntington Papers, Connecticut Historical Society, Hartford
ALBLB	Anthony L. Bleeker Letter Book, 1767–87, New-York Historical Society, New York City
AM	Library of Congress photocopies of Archives de la marine antérieures à la révolution, Archives Nationales, Washington, D.C.
ANAE	Library of Congress microfilm of Archives Nationales, Affaires Estrangeres, Correspondance Consulaires, Washington, D.C.
CCLB	Christopher Champlin Letter Book, Newport Historical Society, Newport, R.I.

CLLB	Christopher Leffingwell Letter Book, Yale University, New Haven, Conn.
CP	Cabot Papers transcripts, Beverley Historical Society, Beverley, Mass.
CSLB	Codman and Smith Letter Book, Baker Library Historical Collections, Harvard University Graduate School of Business Administration, Boston
C&WLB	Chaloner and White Letter Book, Historical Society of Pennsylvania, Philadelphia
C&WP	Chaloner and White Papers, Historical Society of Pennsylvania, Philadelphia
DPLB	Daniel Parker Letter Book, Baker Library Historical Collections, Harvard University School of Business Administration, Boston
EBP	Ephraim Blaine Papers, Library of Congress, Washington, D.C.
EHDP	Elias H. Derby Papers, Peabody Essex Museum, Salem, Mass.
EWJ	Elkanah Watson, Journal, New York State Library, Albany
GMLB	George Morgan Letter Books, Carnegie Library, Pittsburgh
HFP	Correspondence and Business Records, Hollingsworth Family Papers, Historical Society of Pennsylvania, Philadelphia
HGP	Horatio Gates Papers, microfilm edition, Library of Congress, Washington, D.C.
H-GP	Hunter-Garnett Papers, Alderman Library, University of Virginia, Charlottesville
HHLB	Hugh Hughes Letter Book, New-York Historical Society, New York City
JDP	John Davis Papers, Library of Congress, Washington, D.C.
JHCL	John Holker Papers, William L. Clements Library, University of Michigan, Ann Arbor
JHLC	John Holker Papers, Library of Congress, Washington, D.C.

JJLB	Jonathan Jackson Letter Book, Lee Family Papers, Massachusetts Historical Society, Boston
JnWLB	Jonathan Williams Jr. Letter Books, Yale University Library, New Haven, Conn.
JoSLB	Josiah Smith Letter Book, Southern Historical Collection, University of North Carolina, Chapel Hill
JosT	Joseph Trumbull Papers, Connecticut Historical Society, Hartford
JTP	Jonathan Trumbull Papers, Connecticut State Library, Hartford
JWLB	John Welsh Letter Book, Baker Library Historical Collections, Harvard University School of Business Administration, Boston
JWNY	Jeremiah Wadsworth Papers, New-York Historical Society, New York City
JWP	Jeremiah Wadsworth Papers, Connecticut Historical Society, Hartford
LCTB	Library of Congress Transcripts, Great Britain, Washington, D.C.
LHLB	Levi Hollingsworth Letter Book, July 20, 1780–December 2, 1782, Business Records, Hollingsworth Family Papers, Historical Society of Pennsylvania, Philadelphia
MBL	Meletiah Bourn Letters, Houghton Library, Harvard University, Cambridge, Mass.
MRLB	Matthew Ridley Letter Book, Massachusetts Historical Society, Boston
MRP	Miralles Rendón Papers, trans. Aileeen T. Moore, Members of the Continental Congress Papers, Library of Congress, Washington, D.C.
NBCoP	Nicholas Brown Co. Papers, John Carter Brown Library, Brown University, Providence, R.I.
NBED	United States Navy Board, Eastern District Letter Book, New York Public Library, New York City
N&TSP	Nathaniel and Thomas Shaw Papers, Yale University Library, New Haven, Conn.

PCC	Papers of the Continental Congress, National Archives, Washington, D.C.
PMIR	Ezekiel Price Marine Insurance Records, Boston Athenaeum, Boston
PRI	Registry of Imports February 1781–April 1783 in Records of the Office of the Comptroller General, Pennsylvania Historical and Museum Commission, Harrisburg
RC	Rodney Collection, Historical Society of Delaware, Wilmington
RCLB	Robert Carter Letter Books, Perkins Library, Duke University, Durham, N.C.
R&FP	Reed and Forde Papers, Historical Society of Pennsylvania, Philadelphia
RHD	Robert Honeyman Diary, Library of Congress, Washington, D.C.
RMHL	Robert Morris Papers, Huntington Library, San Marino, Calif.
RMNY	Robert Morris Papers, New York Public Library, New York City
RRLP	Robert R. Livingston Papers, New-York Historical Society, New York City
SAP	Samuel Abbot Papers, Baker Library Historical Collections, Harvard University School of Business Administration, Boston
S-AP	Stone-Alcock Papers, Maryland Historical Society, Baltimore
SCLB	Stephen Collins Letter Book, Massachusetts Historical Society, Boston
SGP	Samuel Gray Papers, Connecticut Historical Society, Hartford
SHC	Southern Historical Collection, University of North Carolina, Chapel Hill
S&SLB	Sears and Smith Letterbook (microfilm), State Historical Society of Nebraska, Lincoln

S&WVP	Samuel and William Vernon Papers, Newport Historical Society, Newport, R.I.
TBP	Terrasson Brothers Papers, Perkins Library, Duke University, Durham, N.C.
WBP	William Bingham Papers, Library of Congress, Washington, D.C.
WDP	William Duer Papers, New-York Historical Society, New York City
WHP	William Heath Papers, Massachusetts Historical Society, Boston
WJMLB	Wallace, Johnson, and Muir Letter Book, New York Public Library, New York City
WPP	William Palfrey Papers, Houghton Library, Harvard University, Cambridge, Mass.
W&SLB	Woolsey and Salmon Letter Book, Peter Force Collection, Library of Congress, Washington, D.C.

Published Primary Sources

AA	Peter Force, ed., *American Archives* . . . 4th ser., 6 vols.; 5 ser., 3 vols. Washington, 1837–53.
ACRA	Howard C. Rice Jr. et al., eds., *The American Campaigns of Rochambeau's Army 1780, 1781, 1782, 1783.* 2 vols. Princeton, N.J., 1972.
AM	Bernard C. Steiner et al., eds., *Archives of Maryland.* 72 vols. Baltimore, 1883–1972.
BC	Brian N. Morton and Donald C. Sinelli, eds., *Beaumarchais correspondance.* 4 vols. to date. Paris, 1969–.
CVSP	William P. Palmer, ed., *Calendar of Virginia State Papers.* 11 vols. Richmond, 1875–93.
DA	*Delaware Archives.* 5 vols. Wilmington, Del., 1911–16.
DAJA	L. H. Butterfield et al., eds. *Diary and Autobiography of John Adams.* 4 vols. Cambridge, Mass., 1961.
DAR	K. G. Davies, ed., *Documents of the American Revolution, 1770–1783.* 21 vols. Dublin, Ireland, 1972–81.

DCG	John J. Meng, ed. *Despatches and Instructions of Conrad Alexandre Gérard, 1778–1780* Baltimore, 1939.
EAB	Charles B. Evans, comp., *American Bibliography . . .* 14 vols. Chicago, 1903–59.
FME	Benjamin F. Stevens, *Facsimiles of Manuscripts in European Archives Relating to America, 1773–1783.* 25 vols. London, 1889–98.
HPFA	Henri Doniol, *Histoire de la participation de la France a l'éstablissement des Etats-Unis d'Amérique.* 5 vols. Paris, 1886–92.
HSUS	*Historical Statistics of the United States, Colonial Times to 1970.* 2 vols. Washington, D.C., 1975.
JCC	Worthington C. Ford, ed., *Journals of the Continental Congress, 1774–1789.* 34 vols. Washington, 1904–37.
J&L	Kenneth W. Porter, *The Jacksons and the Lees: Two Generations of Massachusetts Merchants.* 2 vols. Cambridge, Mass., 1937.
JNS	Frances Norton Mason, ed., *John Norton & Sons, Merchants of London and Virginia . . .* New York, 1968.
LAR	Stanley J. Idzerda, ed., *Lafayette in the Age of the American Revolution . . .* 5 vols. Ithaca, N.Y., 1977–?.
LD	Paul H. Smith et al., eds., *Letters of the Delegates to Congress, 1774–1789.* 23 vols. to date. Washington, 1976–.
ND	William Bell Clark et al., eds., *Naval Documents of the American Revolution.* 10 vols. to date. Washington, 1964–.
OLGV	H. R. McIlwaine, ed., *Official Letters of the Governors of the State of Virginia.* 3 vols. Richmond, 1926–29.
OLMC	Charles O. Paullin, ed., *Out-letters of the Continental Marine Committee and Board of Admiralty . . .* 2 vols. New York, 1914.
PA	Samuel Hazard et al., eds. *Pennsylvania Archives, 1664 . . .* 9 series, 138 vols. Harrisburg, 1852–1949.
PAH	Harold C. Syrett et al., eds., *The Papers of Alexander Hamilton.* 27 vols. New York, 1961–87.
PBF	Leonard W. Labaree et al., eds., *Papers of Benjamin Franklin.* 34 vols. to date. New Haven, 1959–.

PJM	William T. Hutchinson et al., eds., *The Papers of James Madison.* 17 vols. Chicago, 1962–.
PHL	Philip M. Hamer, ed., *The Papers of Henry Laurens.* 11 vols. to date. Columbia, S.C., 1968–.
PNG	Richard K. Showman et al., eds., *The Papers of General Nathanael Greene.* 9 vols. to date. Chapel Hill, 1976–.
PPGC	Hugh Hastings and J. A. Holden, eds., *Public Papers of George Clinton, First Governor of New York* . . . 10 vols. Albany, 1899–1914.
PRCC	J. H. Trumbull and C. J. Hoadley, eds., *Public Records of the Colony of Connecticut, 1636–1776.* 15 vols. Hartford, 1850–90.
PRM	E. James Ferguson et al., eds., *The Papers of Robert Morris, 1781–1784.* 8 vols. Pittsburgh, 1973–.
PRSC	Charles J. Hoadly et al., eds., *The Public Records of the State of Connecticut* . . . 15 vols. to date. Hartford, 1894–.
PTJ	Julian P. Boyd et al., eds., *The Papers of Thomas Jefferson* . . . 26 vols. to date. Princeton, N.J., 1950–.
PWL	Carl E. Prince et al., eds., *The Papers of William Livingston.* 5 vols. Trenton, N.J., 1979–87.
RDC	Francis Wharton, ed., *The Revolutionary Diplomatic Correspondence of the United States* . . . 6 vols. Washington, D.C., 1889.
SAL	William W. Hening, *Statutes at Large; being a Collection of all the Laws of Virginia.* 13 vols. New York, 1969 (reprint).
TUSA	Hunter Miller, ed., *Treaties and Other International Acts of the United States of America.* 8 vols. Washington, D.C., 1931–48.
WGW	John C. Fitzpatrick, ed., *The Writings of George Washington.* 39 vols. Washington, 1931–44.

NOTES

PREFACE

1. John J. McCusker and Russell R. Menard, *The Economy of British America, 1607–1789* (Chapel Hill, 1985), 358.

PROLOGUE

1. See John H. Scheide, "The Lexington Alarm," *Proceedings of the American Antiquarian Society,* n.s., 50(1940): 54–57.

2. Bernard Bailyn, *Voyagers to the West: A Passage in the Peopling of America on the Eve of the Revolution* (New York, 1986), 26.

3. See John Adams's notes on a speech before the Congress by Samuel Chase, September 26–27[?], 1774, in *LD,* I: 103–4; see also ibid., I: 105, 111 on the issue of Britain's economic vulnerability; "To the Inhabitants of the British Colonies in America," July 15, 1774 in *AA,* 4th ser., I: 415. The military problems that Britain would encounter in sustaining such a force are mentioned in John Dickinson to Josiah Quincy Jr., October 28, 1774, in ibid., 1: 947, and "Americanus" in *Connecticut Gazette,* December 30, 1774.

4. *JCC,* I: 75–80; II: 67, 238–39, 268–69, 408–9.

5. The term has been given modern currency by Charles Royster, *A Revolutionary People at War: The Continental Army and the American Character, 1775–1783* (Chapel Hill, 1979), chap. 1. The moral basis of the *rage militaire* was rooted in the religious culture; see Harry S. Stout, *The New England Soul: Preaching and Religious Culture in Colonial New England* (New York, 1986), chaps. 13–14.

6. Mancel Alcock to Jas. Alcock, November 13, 1775, in S-AP; and Pascal N. Smith to Oliver Smith, May 18, 1776, in S&SLB. John Dickinson to Josiah Quincy Jr., October 28, 1774, in *AA,* I: 947.

7. See "Americanus," *Connecticut Gazette,* December 30, 1774; "Perseverance," *Independent Chronicle,* December 13, 1776.

8. *HSUS* provides figures that suggest that in 1770 the mainland colonies exported the equivalent of 604,836 barrels of flour, assuming wheat converted to flour at the rate of 5.14 bushels per barrel (458,680 bbl. exported × 5.14 = 2,357,615 bu. equiv. + 751,240 bu. exported = 3,108,855 total bu. / 5.14 = 604,836 bbl.). 604,836 bbl. would yield the equivalent of 118,547,785 rations. Technically, 1 barrel of flour was the

equivalent of two "long hundreds" (cwt) of weight, or 224 lbs. But an actual barrel seldom contained more than 200 lbs. of flour. It became common around the time of the Revolution to deduct 28 lbs. for the barrel, leaving 196 lbs. of flour (see Helen L. Klopher, "Statistics of Foreign Trade of Philadelphia, 1700–1860" [Ph.D. diss., University of Pennsylvania, 1936], 40). Theoretically, at 1 lb. of bread or flour to the ration, this would have been enough to supply an army of 324,788 with bread for a full year. But armies always consumed more rations than they had men because officers were issued additional rations in proportion to their rank and because of the presence of camp followers and support personnel. Allowing for 25 percent more rations than men, which was customary, the amount of exported flour still should have provided for an army of 243,591.

9. Or so "Americanus" argued, *Connecticut Gazette,* December 30, 1774.

10. See Nich. Cooke to the Governor of Martinique, December 28, 1775, and copy to the Governor of Guadeloupe, January 8, 1776, in "Revolutionary Correspondence of Governor Nicholas Cooke," *American Antiquarian Society Proceedings,* n.s., 36(1926), 299–300.

11. Royster, *Revolutionary People at War;* Richard Buel Jr., *Dear Liberty . . .* (Middletown, Conn., 1980).

12. The subject of America's economic vulnerability to British naval power was raised in the polemical literature preceding the Revolution by Myles Cooper, *A Friendly address to all reasonable Americans . . .* (New York, 1774), 39–42. Charles Lee dismissed the notion in *Strictures on a Pamphlet, entitled, A "Friendly Address to All Reasonable Americans" . . .* (Philadelphia, 1774), 5fn. Cooper assumed that the conflict, if it came to one, would be decided on land, and Henry Barry implicitly agreed in *The Strictures on the Friendly Address Examined . . .* (New York, 1775), alluding to the role of the British navy only in passing, 13. See also Alexander Hamilton, *The Farmer Refuted . . .* (New York, 1775), 59–70.

CHAPTER 1. THE GRAIN ECONOMY OF THE REVOLUTION

1. These themes have been canvassed in Charles Royster, *A Revolutionary People at War* (Chapel Hill, 1979), and Wayne E. Carp, *To Starve an Army at Pleasure: Continental Army Administration and American Political Culture* (Chapel Hill, 1984).

2. On the meat shortage, see John Chaloner to Ephr. Blaine, October 3, 1777, to Wm. Buchanan, February 3, and to Alex. Hamilton, February 12, 1778, in EBP. This was widely known at the time, though it has since been forgotten; see Corn. Harnett to Rich. Caswell, March 20, 1778, in Preston-Davie Collection, Southern Historical Collection, University of North Carolina, Chapel Hill; see also EWJ, 2: 31. Momentary flour shortages seemed to loom in December (see Ephr. Blaine to ?, December 16, 1777), but they were attributable more to problems with transportation and the reluctance of farmers in the region to thresh than to a real grain scarcity (see Blaine to the Executive Council of Pennsylvania, December 24, and John Chaloner to Wm. Buchanan, December 28, in EBP). In New England the commissariat felt threatened by a flour shortage in the late winter of 1778 but sought relief from outside the region; see

Peter Colt to Sam. Gray, February 20, 1778, and Asa Waterman to Gray, March 14, 1778, in SGP. For a secondary account of this and what follows, see Erna Risch, *Supplying Washington's Army* (Washington, D.C., 1981), 207ff.

3. For the commissariat's reliance on the middle district of Pennsylvania for flour, see Ephr. Blaine to Matthias Slough, January 20, 1778; to ?, January 27; memo following Blaine to Col. Patton, February 3; see also Blaine to Peter Colt, February 7; John Chaloner to Wm. Buchanan, February 27, and to Col. Lutterloh, March 4, and Col. Echart, March 8, all in EBP; General Orders, April 16, 1778, in HGP, reel 7. See also EWJ, 2: 31. On the alleviation of the meat crisis, see Hen. Laurens to Hor. Gates, April 20, 1778, in ibid. Also John Chaloner to Hen. Champion, March 1, 1778, in EBP.

4. For links between flour shortages and forage shortages, see, for instance, D. Creer to John Davis, March 8, 1779, in JDP. For the impact that a forage shortage might have on the meat supply, see Peter Colt to Hor. Gates, May 8, 1779, in HGP, reel 9. For other difficulties in substituting corn and rye for wheat flour, see Geo. Clinton to R. R. Livingston, January 7, 1780, in *PPGC*, 5: 447; also Wm. Christmas to Joshua Potts, April 7, 1781, in Revolutionary Commissary Correspondence, NCSA; and F. B. Morrison, *Feeds and Feeding: A Handbook for the Student and Stockman,* 20th ed. (Ithaca, N.Y., 1936), 328, 330. For Washington's repeated warnings between 1777 and 1781, see *WGW,* 10: 192, 198, 459, 463–64, 467–74, 491; 11: 117; 13: 466; 14: 82–82, 406; 16: 187, 188ff; 17: 87, 167, 244, 273–74; 18: 146, 332, 430; 19: 131, 136, 206, 393, 398–400, 462; 20: 105, 412, 447, 452–54; 21: 60, 120, 506; 22: 72.

5. See, for instance, Peter Colt to Hor. Gates, May 23, 1779, in HGP, reel 9.

6. See E. James Ferguson, *The Power of the Purse* (Chapel Hill, 1963), 132–33.

7. See Hor. Gates to Hen. Champion and Peter Colt, June 23, 1778, and Gates to Washington, April 12, 1779, in HGP, reel 7 and 9.

8. See Resolve July 9, 1779, in *JCC,* 16: 812–13.

9. See Udny Hay's response to Congress's resolutions, Hay to Gates, August 11, 1779, in HGP, reel 10.

10. See, for example, James A. Huston, *Logistics of Liberty: American Services of Supply in the Revolutionary War and After* (Newark, Del., 1991), who emphasizes the role of administrative, financial, and transportation difficulties; and Carp, *To Starve an Army,* who traces these administrative deficiencies back to colonial political culture.

11. 2,464,223 for purposes of calculation; extrapolated from "Estimated Population of American Colonies, 1610–1780," in *HSUS,* 1168.

12. Virginia Anderson, "King Philip's Herds: Indians, Colonists, and the Problem of Livestock in New England," *William & Mary Quarterly,* 3rd ser., 51(1994): 614; Margaret Visser, *Much Depends on Dinner . . .* (Toronto, 1987), 23.

13. Buckwheat is technically a bean rather than a grain crop, but it was used as a substitute for many of the grains and viewed as one for that reason.

14. My argument assumes the availability of cleared land. When cleared land was scarce, corn did better on partially cleared lands than did any of the European small grains; see Lewis C. Gray, *History of Agriculture in the Southern United States to 1860* (Washington, D.C., 1933), 1: 161.

15. Percy W. Bidwell and John I. Falconer, *History of Agriculture in the Northern United States, 1620–1860* (Washington, D.C., 1925), 260; Charles B. Kuhlmann, *The Development of the Flour-Milling Industry in the United States* . . . (Boston, 1929), 7; Max George Schumacher, *The Northern Farmer and His Market During the Colonial Period* (New York, 1975), 1, 63–64.

16. For milling times, see Chas. DeWitt to Wm. Duer, January 31, 1782, in WDP. On rye compared with wheat, see Bidwell and Falconer, *Northern Agriculture*, 91; Schumacher, *Northern Farmer*, 1; and Harry J. Carman, ed., *American Husbandry* (Port Washington, N.Y., 1964), 73, 79, 115. The overlapping schedules of wheat and rye led to specialization in one or the other. Crop choice was also influenced by ratios of seed to yield, which were influenced by soil and climate. For the market reaches of wheat compared to that of other grains, see Schumacher, *Northern Farmer*, 63–64. Corn producers living along rivers had a greater market reach than those living in interior areas; see Carman, *American Husbandry*, 185. Corn in the kernel possesses superior keeping qualities to meal, but it never rivaled wheat flour in this respect; see Visser, *Much Depends on Dinner*, 28. On price differences, see Anne Bezanson, *Prices and Inflation During the American Revolution: Pennsylvania, 1770–1790* (Philadelphia, 1951), 332–46.

17. Morrison, *Feeds and Feeding*, 277–79, 327. Wheat stalks, known as screenings, together with bran and middlings left over from the milling of wheat into flour were fed to animals but constituted much less of the total crop than was the case with corn. Nonetheless, volume for volume wheat and corn are comparable as feed; ibid., 336–39.

18. I use the figure 2,148,076 for population and 19,332,684 bushels of grain for purposes of calculation. An adult consuming wheat flour needed 9.6 bushels of wheat per year at 1 pound of flour per day but would consume 14.6 bushels of Indian shell corn if he or she subsisted exclusively on Indian meal (assuming 5 bu. shell corn = 125 lbs. meal). My estimate assumes that adults consumed on average 12 bushels per year, a mean between corn and wheat, and that children consumed half that per year. The 12-bushel figure was used at the time and is referred to by Robert Alexander in Edward C. Papenfuse Jr., "Economic Analysis and Loyalist Strategy During the American Revolution: Robert Alexander's Remarks on the Economy of the Peninsula or Eastern Shore of Maryland," *Maryland Historical Magazine* 58(1973): 194; James T. Lemon, "Household Consumption in Eighteenth-Century America and Its Relationship to Production and Trade: The Situation Among Farmers in Southeastern Pennsylvania," *Agricultural History* 41(1967): 69; David Klingaman, "Food Supplies and Deficits in the American Colonies, 1768–1772," *Journal of Economic History* 31(1971): 559 and fn. (Klingaman uses a slightly higher figure for annual consumption). Geoffery Gilbert, "The Role of Breadstuffs in American Trade, 1770–1790," *Explorations in Economic History* 14(1977): 385, and Bette Hobbs Pruitt, "Self-Sufficiency and the Agricultural Economy of Eighteenth-Century Massachusetts," *William & Mary Quarterly*, 3rd ser., 41(1984): 344–45, 358, use significantly lower figures for annual wheat consumption. My estimate of total demand also assumes that half the population be counted as children, following Gilbert's (385) and Klingaman's example (559–60). Males doing farm work would obviously consume an adult's ration long before reaching age sixteen or seventeen. On the other hand, women,

who matured more slowly in the eighteenth century than today, and slaves, who often complained of hunger, probably consumed less than a full adult ration even in early adulthood. Assuming half the population to be on adult rations and half on children's rations seems reasonable.

19. 5,667,022 bushels for purposes of calculation. Included in the tally are the following quantities based on the figures supplied by *HSUS* for 1770 exports taken from Customs 16/1, PRO, converted in the case of rice where figures for bushels are unavailable to bushels of wheat equivalents.

458,680 bbl. flour =	2,357,615 bu. wheat
	751,240 bu. wheat
578,349 bu. of ear corn =	289,175 bu. shelled corn★
	24,859 bu. oats
151,418 bbl. of rice =	2,084,701 bu. equivs.†
	8,200 bu. rough rice
4,430 bu. meal =	6,645 bu. shelled corn‡

Total: 5,522,435 bu. or equiv.

★Customs 16/1 does not specify whether the bushels are of ear or shelled corn, but it takes 2 bu. of ear corn to make 1 of shelled corn, Stephen J. Heimstra to Stanley Lebergott, July 29, 1968, copy in recipient's possession. It takes 1.5 bu. of shelled corn to make 1 bu. cornmeal. If the entries are for ear corn, then total grain exports came to 5,522,435 bu. of grain. If Customs 16/1 refers to shelled corn, as seems likely (see Nicholas P. Hardeman, *Shucks, Shocks, and Hominy Blocks* . . . [Baton Rouge, La., 1981], 234, 237), then total grain exports would rise to 5,811,609 bu. I use the average of the range (5,667,022).

†each bbl. of rice contained 525 lbs. (*HSUS*, 1163–64); a pint of rice weighs roughly 16 ounces (*PHL*, 11: 29); rice translated into rations at roughly 1 lb. rice = 1 lb. flour (*WGW*, 12: 361).

‡assumes 1.5 bu. ear corn = 1 bu. cornmeal (Helen L. Klopher, "Statistics of Foreign Trade of Philadelphia, 1700–1860," Ph.D. diss., University of Pennsylvania, 1936, 69).

Timothy Pitkin, *A Statistical View of the Commerce of the United States* . . . (Hartford, Conn., 1817), 22, also lists 7,964 bbl. shipstuff, equivalent to 41,000 bu. of wheat, which have been excluded from my calculations of grain exports.

20. 25,002,706 bushels for the purposes of calculation.

21. I have found Christopher Clark, *The Roots of Rural Capitalism: Western Massachusetts, 1780–1860* (Ithaca, N.Y., 1990), chap. 2, particularly suggestive in my thinking about this matter. See also Bruce H. Mann, *Neighbors and Strangers: Law and Community in Early Connecticut* (Chapel Hill, 1987).

22. Daniel Vickers, "The Northern Colonies: Economy and Society," in Stanley L. Engerman and Robert E. Gallman, eds., *The Cambridge Economic History of the United States* (Cambridge, 1996), 1: 221–22. Pruitt, "Self-Sufficiency," 363–64, is critical of the distinction between local and long-distance markets.

23. See Kuhlmann, *Flour-Milling*, 8, 22; Klingaman, "Food Surpluses and Deficits,"

557–58, 564–65. Klingaman excludes Connecticut from his definition of New England, though it seems likely that the western part of the state as well as Connecticut River farmers as far north as Massachusetts exported grain to distant markets; see Pruitt, "Self-Sufficiency," 359–61.

24. I use William S. Rossiter's estimates of the urban population of the five largest colonial towns in 1770, supplemented by Carl Bridenbaugh's estimate for the population of the fifteen smaller towns having a population of more than 3,200. These estimates are reproduced in Jacob M. Price, "Economic Function and the Growth of American Port Towns in the Eighteenth Century," *Perspectives in American History* 8(1974): 176–77. The Bridenbaugh estimates, with two exceptions, New Haven and Savannah, reflect population in mid-decade (1774–76) and have been adjusted downward by 15 percent as a guess at the 1770 population. In my calculations I project an urban population of 152,418 (roughly 7 percent of total population) consuming 1,371,762 bu. of grain annually.

25. 1,371,762 / 2 + 5,667,022 / 25,002,706 = 25.4 percent.

26. See Klingaman, "Food Surpluses and Deficits," 554.

27. John J. McCusker and Russell R. Menard, *The Economy of British America, 1607–1789* (Chapel Hill, 1985), 322. For the distinction between custom and merchant mills, see Kuhlmann, *Flour-Milling*, 26, 34; see also Victor S. Clark, *History of Manufactures in the United States* (New York, 1929), 1: 179. For the operations of a custom mill, see Charles Ridgely, Supplementary Ledger 691, in Charles Ridgely Papers, Maryland Historical Society, Baltimore.

28. On the evolution of merchant mills, see Kuhlmann, *Flour-Milling*, 23, 35. See also Peter C. Welsh, "The Brandywine Mills: A Chronicle of an Industry, 1762–1816," *Delaware History* 18(1956–57): 25. For the role that merchants played in organizing production to satisfy overseas demand, see John Smith to Murrell & Moore, February 2, 1774, in John Smith Letter Book, Maryland Historical Society, Baltimore. Millers and brokers continued to stress the importance of cash to their operations during the war; see Jesse Hollingsworth to Levi, August 19, 1780, Thos. May to Levi, September 10, and Jas. Black to Levi, September 11, 26, October 10, in HFP. David E. Dauer, "The Expansion of Philadelphia's Business System into the Chesapeake," paper delivered at the American Historical Association meeting, 1981, made the same point.

29. Clark, *Rural Capitalism*, 33, 67–69. Kuhlmann, *Flour-Milling*, 15, 23, 25. An undated memo in RRLP, the last document in 1780, reel 1, points to the regulative effect of cash in ensuring a continuous flow of wheat to the mills. Dauer, "Philadelphia's Business System," stresses the expanded area from which merchant mills had to draw wheat to secure adequate supplies to sustain their operations.

30. On the emergence of Philadelphia and the Brandywine, see Kuhlmann, *Flour-Milling*, 23, 34; Robert Proud, *The History of Pennsylvania . . .* (Philadelphia, 1797), 2: 225; and Arthur L. Jensen, *The Maritime Commerce of Colonial Philadelphia* (Madison, Wis., 1963), 7–8. Philadelphia's share of the flour market has been computed from statistics provided by Jensen (292–93) and Pitkin, *Statistical View,* 21–22, for 1770. Philadelphia accounted for only about 17 percent of wheat exports. Its share of wheat and flour exports combined, reduced to barrels of flour equivalents, came in 1770 to roughly 56 percent of

the total. New York also handled flour and wheat from eastern New Jersey; see Kuhlmann, *Flour-Milling,* 15–17; Virginia D. Harrington, *The New York Merchant on the Eve of the Revolution* (New York, 1935), 147. For the northern Chesapeake's emergence as a grain-producing region, see Paul G. E. Clemens, *The Atlantic Economy and Colonial Maryland's Eastern Shore: From Tobacco to Grain* (Ithaca, N.Y., 1980). For Baltimore, see Kuhlmann, *Flour-Milling,* 27–30, and G. Terry Sharrer, "The Merchant-Millers: Baltimore's Flour Milling Industry, 1783–1800," *Agricultural History* 56(1982): 144.

31. Chaloner and White, "Account of Provisions Purchased, 1778–1780," in C&WP. The firm used the conversion factor of 6.92 bushels of wheat to the barrel of flour for the harvest of 1778, reflecting the inferior quality of wartime wheat; see Chaloner and White to Patrick Ewing, December 17, 1778, in C&WLB. 4,666 bu. of wheat = 674 bb. flour for a total of 4,018 bb. flour plus a small parcel of bread. For the prewar comparison I used Jensen's figures from *Maritime Commerce of Philadelphia,* 292–93, converting tons of flour into barrels at 1:10 and bushels of wheat into barrels of flour at 5.14 bu. to the barrel. The annual average of wheat and flour exports from 1768 through 1772 came to 315,135 barrels equivalent.

32. The best genealogical account of the Hollingsworth family is *Hollingsworth Family and collateral lines of Gooch—Gilpin—Jamas—Mackall—Morris—Stewart* (Philadelphia, 1944). Henry's strategic position combined with his local prominence led to his appointment as deputy quartermaster general during the war.

33. Hollingsworth's career is discussed briefly in Thomas M. Doerflinger, *A Vigorous Spirit of Enterprise: Merchants and Economic Development in Revolutionary Philadelphia* (Chapel Hill, 1986), 124, 288. For an example of Levi's active involvement in contracting for flour, see his letter to Zeb. Hollingsworth, June 19, 1782, in LHLB. For reference to other contracts organized in the port towns, see Sam. Hollingsworth to Levi, July 25, 1780; and John and Thos. Ricketts to Levi, August 4, in HFP.

34. See Thomas Lea Account Book, 1773–1787, and Daybook and Ledger, February 20, 1775–September 27, 1783, in HSD; Samuel Canby, Diary, Yale University Library; William Brown's Account Book, DSA; Amos Brinton Grinding Account Book, 1775–1822; and Benjamin Hawley Diary, 1769–1782 (transcribed by Bishop's Mill Historical Institute) in CCHS.

35. Hollingsworth's Journal no. 540 reveals that more than 70 percent of the wheat he received from harvest 1780 came to him after March 1, 1781, for reasons discussed in Chapters 6 and 7.

36. Jensen, *Maritime Commerce of Philadelphia,* 292–93 (21,626 / 315,135 = 6.86 percent). See also Chaloner and White, "Account of Provisions Purchased, 1778–1780," in C&WP.

37. Cf. Doerflinger, *Vigorous Spirit of Enterprise,* 256. An account of the reasons for Hollingsworth's detention by the mob is in Henry Hollingsworth to Thomas Johnson, May 30, 1779, in Maryland State Papers, series A, MdHR. His arrest probably accounts for the absence of all entries in his Flour Journal 540 from July 15 to October 8, 1779.

38. An anonymous miller's "wheat account" (1772–80, intermittent), Eleutherian Mills Historical Library, Greenville, Delaware; Amos Brinton, Grinding Account Book,

1775–1822, CCHS; and Alexander Porter, Daybook and Journal, October 1, 1769–
November 1783, HSD, contain evidence congruent with that presented below for
Thomas Lea's mill. Levi Lewis, Flour Mill Account Book, 1769–1809, HSP, contains
evidence that describes a pattern exactly opposite that derived from the other accounts.
However, Lewis's accounts seem to tabulate flour sales rather than flour manufactured.

39. Peter C. Welsh, "Merchants, Millers, and Ocean Ships: The Components of an
Early American Industrial Town," *Delaware History* 7(1956–57): 321, and "Brandywine
Mills," 17, 19; John A. Munroe, *Colonial Delaware: A History* (Millwood, N.Y., 1978), 203.

40. The problems of interpretation presented by the surviving Lea records are discussed in the appendix.

41. The Daybook and Journal does suggest that he was involved in several grain
"adventures" during that year.

42. Welsh, "Brandywine Mills," 21–22.

43. Private speculators took his place, more often than not depositing wheat at the
mill to wait for favorable prices. Some of this activity began during harvest 1778; a good
deal more took place in connection with harvest 1781. This feature of the custom
account makes it particularly tricky to work with, since the expectation was that depositors would sell wheat to the mill in the future. I have tried to eliminate potential
redundancies by checking mill purchases against the deposits and carrying as "custom"
only what is not accounted for elsewhere in the Daybook and Journal.

44. Wheat from the harvest of 1781 fetched between 5/6 to 6/ at the beginning of
the harvest year. At the end of the harvest year it hovered around 5/. The pattern of
activity in the revolutionary grain economy that I am describing diverges from the
business cycles described in John J. McCusker, "How Much Is That in Real Money? . . ."
Proceedings of the American Antiquarian Society 101(1991): 360, table D-1. McCusker, using
the Brady-David-Solar series of consumer prices for the war years (see Paul A. David and
Peter Solar, "A Bicentenary Contribution to the History of the Cost of Living in
America," *Research in Economic History* 2[1977]: 1–80), identifies a peak in 1778, followed
by a weak trough in 1779, another peak almost comparable to that of 1778 in 1780,
followed by a deeper trough in 1781, and a final weak peak in 1782. Simply put,
McCusker's business cycles are defined by price movements while mine are defined by
grain volumes. Under normal conditions prices tend to correspond to volumes, but
during hyperinflations the relationship can be reversed.

45. The account books of the Patapsco plantation of the Jones Family suggest that the
harvests of 1778 and 1779 were relatively thin, while those of 1780 and 1781 were
stronger.

Bushels of Wheat Mentioned in the Jones Account Books, 1778–1782, by Harvest Year

	1778	1779	1780	1781	1782
bushels	200	101	385	299	112 (extrapolated)

Source: Jones Family Papers, Maryland Historical Society, Baltimore

See also William Brown Account Book, 1774–83, vol. 2, DSA; the data for Maryland's Upper Eastern Shore in Lorena S. Walsh, "Plantation Management in the Chesapeake, 1620–1820," *Journal of Economic History* 49(1989): 399; and Jean B. Russo, "A Model Planter: Edward Lloyd IV of Maryland, 1770–1796," *William & Mary Quarterly*, 3rd ser., 49(1992): 87–88.

46. Livingston Manor rent ledger, 1767–84, Livingston Family Papers, New-York Historical Society, New York City, reel 53. Other revealing accounts for the area are John Sanders, Ledger, 1749–1783, and Day Book, 1777–1807, also in NYHS.

47. For this and much of what follows I rely on Sung Bok Kim, *Landlord and Tenant in Colonial New York: Manorial Society, 1664–1775* (Chapel Hill, 1978), and Cynthia A. Kierner, *Traders and Gentlefolk: The Livingstons of New York, 1675–1790* (Ithaca, N.Y., 1992).

48. Totals include small parcels of rye as well as wheat and monetary rents when paid in wheat. When rent rate is not specified in the ledger, it is inferred by averaging payments in the two successive years closest to 1773.

49. For New England's growing dependence on grain imports, see Klingaman, "Food Surpluses and Deficits," 553–69. For the colony's continued production of flour, see Schumacher, *Northern Farmer*, 33. For the commissary's initial reliance on Connecticut, Hez. Bissell to Trumbull, May 12, 15, 1775, January 16, 1776; Thos. Mumford to Trumbull, June 24, September 18, 25, 1775, and January 2, March 27, 1776; Dan. Gray to Trumbull, November 17, December 26, 1775; Peter Vandervort to Trumbull, November 30, December 28, 1775; Samuel McClellan to Trumbull, January 17, 1776; Sam. Squire to Trumbull, April 2, 1776; Jab. Huntington to Trumbull, May 4, 1776; Chas. Miller to Trumbull, June 24, 1774; Peter Colt to Trumbull, September 28, and to Jere. Wadsworth, November 6, 1776, all in JosT. See also Jere. Wadsworth to Jos. Trumbull, June 15, August 19, September 3, September 17, and (quote) December 17, 1775; January 25, February 1, March 31, 1776, all in JWP.

50. See Jere. Wadsworth to Jon. Trumbull, September 4, 1776; Peter Colt to Wadsworth, September 28, October 3, 30, 1776; J. Drake to Jere. Wadsworth?, November 2, 1776, in JWP. Also Peter Colt to Jere. Wadsworth, November 6, 1776, and Colt to Jos. Trumbull, November 11, 1776, in JosT.

51. See Carp, *To Starve an Army*, 43.

52. The idea had occurred to Jos. Trumbull early on; see his letter to Jere. Wadsworth, June 27, 1775, in JWP. See also Ephr. Blaine to Wm. Buchanan, November 12, 1777, in EBP. According to Schumacher, Connecticut's economy was evolving in this direction in the late colonial period (*Northern Farmer*, 30–31).

53. See Richard Buel Jr., *Dear Liberty* . . . (Middletown, Conn., 1980), 160–62; Gray, *Agriculture in the Southern United States*, 1: 582.

54. James H. Levitt, "New Jersey's Revolutionary Economy," in *New Jersey's Revolutionary Experience* (Trenton, N.J., 1975), no. 9, p. 11; Kuhlmann, *Flour-Milling*, 17–18 and notes; Harry B. Weiss and Robert J. Sim, *The Early Grist and Flouring Mills of New Jersey* (Trenton, N.J., 1956), 13–14. For the Simcoe raid, see *PWL*, 3: 207; see also Washington

to Wm. Livingston, November 19, 1780, in ibid., 4: 92. For the unsettled conditions in East Jersey, see Wm. Livingston to Washington, May 1, 1779; Proclamation, August 18, 1779; John M. Goetschius to Livingston, July 29, 1780; Rich. Somers to Livingston, September 26, 1780; John Dennis to Livingston, December 26, 1780, all in ibid., 3: 81, 161–62; 4: 21–22, 65–66.

55. Sung Bok Kim, "The Limits of Politicization in the American Revolution: The Experience of Westchester County, New York," *Journal of American History* 80(1993): 883–85. The best extended account of what it was like to live in the contested areas is Adrian C. Leiby, *The Revolutionary War in the Hackensack Valley* (New Brunswick, N.J., 1962), esp. 48, 134, 224, 273, 275, 289fn, 303–4. See also Wm. Livingston to Gouv. Morris and Wm. Whipple, January 30, 1779; Washington to Livingston, August 26, 1780, in *PWL,* 3: 27; 4: 53.

56. Louis Morton, *Robert Carter of Nomini Hall . . .* (Williamsburg, Va., 1941), 143, quoting from Gray, *History of Agriculture in the Southern United States,* 1: 164. Also Kuhlmann, *Flour-Milling,* 31–32.

57. For references to the commissariat's expectations about southern flour, see Peter Colt to Wadsworth, July 15, 1778, in JWP; see also Chaloner and White to Jere. Wadsworth, November 16, 1778, in C&WLB. The illusion that Virginia grains could save the day persisted into 1780; see Clem. Biddle to Wm. Finnie, June 8, 1780, in HGP, reel 11. For the Virginia economy's actual performance, see Jas. Hunter Jr.'s account of flour purchases from harvest 1777 between December 1777 and February 1778, in H-GP; Chaloner and White to Jere. Wadsworth, December 1, 13, 1778, February 18, 28, 1779, in C&WLB. Wm. Aylett managed to get some flour out of the 1778 crop for the commissariat just before the harvest of 1779; see Chaloner and White to Aylett, June 19, 1779, and to Jere. Wadsworth, July 6, in ibid., but the quantity remained small. For the effect of the fly, see Zeb. Hollingsworth to Levi Hollingsworth, September 1, 1778; Hen. Hollingsworth to Levi, September 30, 1778; Alex. Porter to Levi, October 18, 1778, in HFP. Also Jere. Wadsworth to Jonathan Trumbull, November 1, 1779, in JWP; and Wadsworth to Hen. Laurens, September 6, 1778, in PCC, item 78, vol. 23, p. 561. Jere. Wadsworth commented retrospectively on the effect the fly had had on the Virginia and Maryland crops of 1778 in his letter to Jon. Trumbull, April 7, 1779, in JWNY.

58. For James Hunter's correspondence, see H-GP; RHD, 310, 316, 382. Cf. the value of corn in relation to wheat in Robt. Carter to Geo. Gordon, January 20, 1779, and to John Sutton, February 6, 1779, with price postings of January 1, 1780? [probably 1781] in RCLB. Also Benjamin Hill Account Book, 1773–1802, and Henry Fitzhugh of "Bedford," Stafford Co., Virginia, Ledger, in PLDU.

59. Morton, *Carter,* 65, 70, 179.

60. Robt. Carter to Hen. Morse, July 4, 1775; to Capt. John Lee, July 11; to Wm. Mathis, July 22; to John Shaw, August 5; to Lux & Bowley, September 8; to Rich. Parker, September 10; to Sam. Leighton, January 19, 1776; to Burgess Ball, March 5; to Thos. Jones, July 27; to Capt. Fitzgerald, August 6; to Wm. Taylor, August 12; to Wm. Carr, August 20; to Rich. Templeman, August 29, 30, and September 28; to Beckwith

Butler, September 15; to Chris. Lowndes, September 22; to Chas. Sanford, September 23; to Wm. Barber, November 21, in RCLB.

61. Rbt. Carter to Wm. Taylor, August 12; to Chas. Sanford, September 23, 1776; to Rich. Dozier, to Matt. Leonard, to Wm. Wroe, January 27, 1777, in ibid.

62. See RCLB, 1777–1780, esp. Rbt. Carter to ?, July 24, 1780; to Wm. Benson, August 2, 1781; to Wm. Rice, July 24; and to John Sutton, May 10, 1782.

63. Rbt. Carter to Wm. Taylor, December 30, 1775, and to Thomas, Lord Fairfax, May 14, 1776, in RCLB. Morton, *Carter*, 172–76; Walsh, "Plantation Management," 401.

64. Corn was too bulky in its unmilled state to be shipped overland from Virginia to the northern encampments and too susceptible to spoilage when ground into meal; see Rbt. Carter to Wm. Rice, October 12, 1781, in RCLB; Morton, *Carter*, 166–70, 181.

65. See *JCC*, 15: 1371, 16: 196, 18: 1011 for Congress's estimate of North Carolina's agricultural potential during the war.

66. See Mark Bird to John Davis, December 21, 1777, in JDP.

67. See Geo. Morgan to John Davis, May 6, 1778, and Davis to Jos. Brody, June 10, 1779, in ibid. Also Geo. Morgan to John Hancock, March 2, 1777, in GMLB, vol. 1. For the dynamics of the deepening grain crisis, see D. Grier to John Davis, June 4, 1778, and Dan. Brodhead to John Davis, May 21, 1779, in JDP. The rising cost of transportation also found reflection in the costs of hiring teams and drivers, particularly when the latter demanded payment of their wages in grain; see Jas. Johnston to John Davis, March 31, 1778, and Jos. Brody to Davis, April 18, 1779, in ibid. For the link between flour prices and the price of other grains, see Jas. Calhoun to John Davis, September 15, 1778, and D. Grier to Davis, March 8, October 14, November 3, 19, 1779, in ibid.

68. For word of price rises traveling rapidly over considerable distances, see D. Grier to John Davis, April 20, 1778, in JDP. For the effect, see Conrad Wederstrandt to Ephr. Blaine, December 27, 1779, in EBP. See also Geo. Morgan to Rich. H. Lee, February 3, 1777, in GMLB, vol. 1. Distillers stayed ahead of the market because grain in distilled form could be sold at profit over greater distances than could undistilled grain. For the threat they posed to procurement, see Davis to John Cox, September 4, 17, 1778; Grier to Davis, February 21, 1779; Davis to Owen Biddle, September 16, 1779; and John Johnston to Davis, October 2, 1779, all in JDP. For comments on the behavior of farmers, see Wm. Rippey to Davis, June 12, 1778; Davis to John Cox, September 4, 1778; Thos. Smith to Davis, January 11, 1779; Biddle to Davis, September 26, 1778; Nath. Greene to Davis, January 21, 1779; Davis to Sam. McCune, March 26, 1779; Grier to Davis, August 1, November 3, 1779; Thos. Buchanan to Davis, November 22, 1779; Thos. Collier to Davis, November 30, 1778; J. Heathington, February 14, 1779; Grier to Davis, October 5, 1779; and Matt. Wilson to Davis, November 8, 1779, all in JDP.

69. These areas used kegs and sacks on pack horses rather than barrels in wagons and vessels for transportation; see Geo. Morgan to Devereaux Smith, March 22, 1778, in GMLB, vol. 3. For their partial integration with other areas, see Geo. Morgan to John Hancock, February 12, 1777, in ibid.

70. See Nath. Greene to Ephr. Blaine, October 15, 1780, and David Duncan to Blaine, May 5, 1781, in EBP. See also Geo. Morgan to Board of War, March 23, 1779, in GMLB, vol. 3.

71. *HSUS*, table Z481–485; Pitkin, *Statistical View*, 22, is good on the comparative value of exports but way off on the quantities.

72. *HSUS*, 1164.

73. Russell R. Menard, "Economic and Social Development of the South," in Stanley L. Engerman and Robert E. Gallman, eds., *The Cambridge Economic History of the United States* (Cambridge, 1996–), 1: 281.

74. Assuming 525 lbs. to the barrel of rice in the late colonial period and deducting 25 percent for wastage.

75. *WGW*, 12: 361; Risch, *Supplying Washington's Army*, 190, 198, 221.

76. Plantation owners assumed that production would fall with the failure to deliver annual allowances of clothing; see Josiah Smith Jr. to Geo. Appleby, March 14, 1775, in JoSLB. See also Smith to John Moultrie, December 21, 1779, and to Geo. Appleby, December 2, 1780, in ibid.; and John L. Gervais to Hen. Laurens, August 17, 1778, in Gervais Transcripts, SCHS. The assumption that slave productivity depended on the master's ability to provide clothing was common throughout the South; see Dick & Stewart to Jas. Smith, May 15, 1776, and to Lux & Bowley, January 31, 1777, in Dick & Stewart Letter Book, PLDU.

77. Sylvia R. Frey, *Water from the Rock: Black Resistance in a Revolutionary Age* (Princeton, N.J., 1991), 64–66 and passim. See also Eliza Pinckney to Thomas Pinckney, May 17, 1779, in Pinckney Papers, SCHS.

78. Here I rely on Price, "Economic Function and Growth," 162–63. Menard, "Economic and Social Development," 279, gives a slightly different assessment of Charleston's capital resources. On the link between shipping and prices, see Josiah Smith to Geo. Austin, September 20, 1771, and to Jas. Poyas, March 18, 1778, in JoSLB; and Peter Manigault to Daniel Blake, January 27, 1772, in Peter Manigault Letter Book, SCHS.

79. For Livingston, who became the agent of Congress's commercial committee in Charleston, see *JCC*, 10: 114. For references to the port's prosperity, see Jos. Smith to James Poyas, July 25, 1777, and to the Rev. Dr. Rogers, March 5, 1778, in JoSLB. References to overland carting are in EWJ, 2: 32; see also Gray, *History of Southern Agriculture*, 1: 581.

80. See Wm. Ellery to Wm. Greene, March 2, 1779; Gouv. Morris to Chas. Pettit, May 1, 1779, in *LD*, 12: 138, 414–15; *JCC*, 13: 154; Ezekiel Cornell to Hor. Gates, May 14, 1779; Wm. Heath to Gates, May 15; and Gates to Washington, May 30, all in HGP, reel 9. See also Solomon Southwick to Peter Colt, June 24, 1779, in ibid.; Washington to Hor. Gates, May 21, 1779, in HGP, reel 9; and Fran. Lewis to Steph. Sayre, August 10, 1779, in *LD*, 13: 351.

81. Frey, *Water from the Rock*, 84ff.

82. John Holker was the son of a Jacobite of the same name who had fled England during the rebellion of 1745 and settled in Rouen, where he established himself as a

major textile manufacturer; see André Remond, *John Holker, manufacturier et fonctionnaire en France au XVIIIème siècle, 1719–1786* (Paris, 1946). The younger Holker's bilingualism admirably equipped him to serve first as unofficial agent of the French foreign minister, the Comte de Vergennes, and subsequently as agent for the French navy in North America. After encountering unexpected difficulties in getting accredited by Congress, he also became consul-general of France in Philadelphia; see *HPFA,* 2: 615–16, 626, 3: 172, 182, 183.

83. Peter Colt to Jere. Wadsworth, September 6, 1778; and Colt to Royal Flint, September 20, 1778, in JWP; Ephr. Blaine to Sam. Huntington, September 15, 1780, and to Chas. Stewart, May 15, 1781, in EBP.

84. See Jere. Wadsworth, undated memo between letters of March 29 and April 1, 1778, in JWP.

85. For the grain crisis, see Buel, *Dear Liberty,* 159–65.

86. The size of D'Estaing's requisition is inferred from Peter Colt to Wm. Heath, September 27, 1778, in WHP, and an undated, unsigned memo in the PCC, item 29, pp. 125ff, which also contains Congress's response.

87. The best estimate of the amount of flour D'Estaing received from the commissariat in Boston comes from Peter R. Dalton to Wm. Heath, October 11, 1778, in WHP. Dalton's report that he had delivered 1,100 barrels to the French came halfway through their refit, so I assume that they got about 2,000 barrels from him. This estimate is in line with Holker's claims in his letter to Thos. S. Lee, March 3, 1780, in *AM,* 43: 441. For the activities of D'Estaing's purchasing agent in the Boston area, see Washington to John Sullivan, November 18, 1778, in *WGW,* 13: 237; Peter Colt to Jere. Wadsworth, September 6, 1778; and Colt to Royal Flint, September 20, 1778, in JWP. For flour taken from the Delaware, see the notation on the undated memo, PCC, item 29, p. 125. For the Congressional estimate, see Whipple, Gouv. Morris, and Armstrong to Jere. Wadsworth, May 18, 1779, in C&WLB.

88. See Patrick Villiers, *Le commerce colonial atlantique et la guerre d'indépendance des états unis d'Amérique, 1778–1783* (New York, 1977), 298; Jonathan R. Dull, *The French Navy and American Independence* . . . (Princeton, N.J., 1975), 160; W. M. James, *The British Navy in Adversity* . . . (London, 1926), 146.

89. Ephr. Blaine to Jos. Reed, September 22, 1779, in *PA,* 1st ser., 7: 707.

90. For the Holker, Morris, Rumford affair see documents in PCC, item 96, pp. 27ff, item 114, pp. 125ff. See also my "The Committee Movement of 1779 and the Formation of Public Authority in Revolutionary America," in James A. Henretta, Michael Kammen, and Stanley N. Katz, eds., *The Transformation of Early American History: Society, Authority, and Ideology* (New York, 1991), 163–64; Ruth S. Hudson, *The Minister from France, Conrad-Alexandre Gérard, 1729–1790* (Euclid, Ohio, 1994), 154–55. Gérard had clumsily but successfully intervened with Congress on Holker's behalf, but this had done little to reconcile local authorities to Holker's activities; see *DCG,* 750, 753–58, 828–37, 851–58. For the continued antagonism stemming in part from this incident, see Jos. Reed to Holker, May 28, 1781, in *PA,* 1st ser., 9: 175–84, esp. 176.

91. Kathryn Sullivan, *Maryland and France, 1774–1789* (Philadelphia, 1936), 70.

92. Smith had lent only 500 barrels of flour to the continent; see John Holker to Thos. Lee, March 3, 1780, in *AM,* 43: 439–40.

93. Bezanson, *Prices and Inflation,* 336–37. The price of common flour increased to 4.6 times what it had been three months before (363 percent). The price of all other commodities roughly doubled during the same period—the major West Indian staples (molasses, rum, muscavado sugar, and loaf sugar) increased on average 117 percent, wheat 108 percent, and other American staples (corn, pork, bar iron, beef, and rice) on average 98 percent. The latter price increases can be attributed to a doubling of the money supply in 1779 (see Ferguson, *Power of the Purse,* 30), not the price of flour.

94. RHD, 309–10; also Jas. MacAllister to Hor. Gates, February 4, 1780, in HGP, reel 11; Ephr. Blaine's petition to the Continental Congress, October 29, 1779, with supporting testimony, in PCC, item 41, vol. 1, pp. 208ff.

95. Washington to Thos. Lee and Lee's Proclamation, December 29, 1779, are reprinted in Helen Lee Peabody, ed., "Revolutionary Mail Bag: Governor Thomas Sim Lee's Correspondence," *Maryland Historical Magazine* 49(1954): 6–7, 8; see Maryland Council to Chevalier de la Luzerne, January 24, 1780, in *AM,* 43: 66–67, for an official explanation of Maryland's policy.

96. The Maryland Council informed the state's congressional delegation on February 17, 1780, that seizure had yielded 8,000 barrels of flour exclusive of that found in the hands of French agents; see *AM,* 43: 89–90. At the same time, Holker claimed that Smith had purchased fewer than 12,000 barrels. See Holker to Thos. Lee, January 28, 1780, in ibid., 409. Holker's statement included the 2,256 barrels of flour and 129 barrels of bread that appear in Smith's tabulation of new flour exports to the French West Indies; see ibid., 436.

97. Calculations of Maryland's prewar exportable surplus take account of grain produced on the eastern shore that flowed largely to the Philadelphia market; see Carville Earle and Ronald Hoffman, "Staple Crops and Urban Development in the Eighteenth-Century South," *Perspectives in American History* 10(1976): 30; their estimates in turn are based on Robert Alexander's figures, reprinted in Papenfuse, "Economic Analysis," 194.

CHAPTER 2. THE BEGINNING OF THE WAR

1. Richard Buel Jr., *Dear Liberty . . .* (Middletown, Conn., 1980), 19–20.

2. For the debate in Congress, see John Adams's notes on remarks by Sam. Chase, Ed. Rutledge, and Thos. Cushing, September 26–27?, 1774, Silas Deane's Diary, October 6, 1774, in *LD,* 1: 103–5, 153–54; *JCC,* 1: 77.

3. For the Restraining Acts, see *Pennsylvania Gazette,* June 14, 1775, and supplement. Delaware was not mentioned in the supplementary restraining act, and Congress assumed that it was excluded; see *JCC,* 2: 125. For American expectations about a naval blockade, see Proceedings of the Pennsylvania Convention, January 23, 1775, in *Massachusetts Spy,* February 25, 1775, and various reports in ibid., April 6 and May 3. See also *Connecticut Journal,* April 20 and 26, 1775. For the Royal Navy's actions, see Narrative of Vice Admiral Sam. Graves, December 4, 1774; extract from the *Boston Evening Post,*

December 12, 1774; and Disposition of the Squadron under Vice Admiral Sam. Graves, January 1, 1775, in *ND*, 1: 4, 14, 47.

4. Sam. Graves to Phil. Stephens, January 8, 1775, in *ND*, 1: 59. The British did seize some small parcels of powder from incoming vessels and remove some powder from magazines on land. See Journal of His Majesty's schooner *Magdalen*, April 20, 1775; Jas. Montagu to Sam. Graves, April 26; extract from *New York Journal*, May 18; and Stephens to Graves, May 4, in *ND*, 1: 204, 228, 359, 463.

5. Commissioners of the Admiralty to Flag Officers and Captains of His Majesty's Ships, April 14, 1775; Phil. Stephens to Graves, May 4, in *ND*, 1: 453, 461; for reference to the effect of diplomatic pressures in Europe, see Elbridge Gerry to Jos. Gardoqui & Sons, July 5, 1775, in ibid., 818. Naval commanders on distant stations do not appear to have received timely notice of the colonists' activities; see Admiral Jas. Young to the President and Members of the Council at Antigua, August 14, 22, 1775, and to Phil. Stephens, August 30, in ibid., 1148–49, 1209–10, 1267–68. For the American response, see Thos. Johnson Jr. to Sam. Purviance Jr., June 13, 1775; John Adams's Notes on Debates, October 4, 12; and John Adams to John Hancock, October 7, in *LD*, 1: 483, 2: 109, 166, 136.

6. See Narrative of Vice Admiral Samuel Graves, May 15, 1775, in *ND*, 1: 338. The supply arrangements dried up slowly thanks to British pressure; see Ronald N. Tagney, *The World Turned Upside Down: Essex County During America's Turbulent Years, 1763–1790* (West Newbury, Mass., 1993), 158–60. It took about a month for Graves to order the seizure of American provisions; see Vice-Admiral Sam. Graves to Capt. Thos. Bishop, April 27, 1775; Graves to Capt. John Collins, May 14; Graves to Thos. Gage and to Phil. Stephens, May 15, all in *ND*, 1: 320, 329, 337. But others, like James Wallace of Newport, acted more promptly; see Jos. Wanton to Gage, April 27, in ibid., 232. Raids on coastal islands started in mid-May (see Abigail Adams to John Adams, May 24, ibid., 515–17), but didn't gather momentum until the end of summer (excerpt from *Massachusetts Spy*, August 2, 1775, in ibid., 1040). The policy of "lay[ing] waste" New England's seaport towns that were "not likely to be useful to His Majesty's Forces" appears to have dated from early September; see Sam. Graves to Thos. Gage, September 1, 1775, and Thos. Gage to Sam. Graves, September 4, 1775 (quote), in ibid., 1: 1281; 2:

7. The first action was taken by Wallace on his own initiative against Stonington, Conn., at the end of August; see Jas. Wallace to Graves, September 9, 1775, in ibid., 58–59. For Graves's expectations about chastising the coastal towns, see Graves to Hen. Mowat, October 6, and to Phil. Stephens, October 9, in ibid., 324–26, 372. The results were somewhat less spectacular but did result in the destruction of Falmouth; see Mowat to Graves, October 19, in ibid., 513–16.

7. See "Disposition of His Majesty's Ships and Vessels in North America . . . ," March 22, 1776, in *ND*, 4: 449, and Jas. Wallace to Molyneux Shuldham, April 10, 1776, in ibid., 746. For complaints about Wallace's activities, see Nathan Miller to Nich. Cooke, March 29, and excerpt from *Providence Gazette*, March 30, in ibid., 562, 576. For the terrorizing of Newport and Narragansett Bay, including the bombardment of Bristol, see Journal of HMS *Rose*, October 7, 1775; "Proposed Agreement Between Town of

Newport and James Wallace, October 13," in ibid., 2: 336, 440. For the extent of the fear that Wallace engendered in the neighboring population, see Matt. Griswold to Jon. Trumbull, October 20, 1775, in ibid., 536.

8. John White to Meletiah Bourn, September 4, 1775, in MBL; *PRCC*, 14: 415–16, 15: 14, 101, 105, 119, 135, 314, 413–14; *ND*, 4: 1479.

9. Congress acted through its Secret Committee formed on September 18, 1775; see Nathan Miller, *Sea of Glory: A Naval History of the American Revolution* (Annapolis, 1974), 185–86; Robt. Morris to Thos. Mumford, April 8, 1782, in *PRM*, 4: 542, 543fn. See also the clearance for the brig *Industry,* March 5, 1776, and the sloop *Florida,* April 10, in Outward and Inward Entries, 1776–83, Maritime Papers, RIA. See also the account of Capt. Packwood's powder voyage that began in February 1775, and Nath. Shaw to Jon. Trumbull, September 8, 1775, in N&TSP.

10. See "Estimate of the Loss on Income & the Trade of Cape Ann from April 1775 to April 1776" and "Estimate of the Loss on Income and Trade for the Town of Salem," April 30, 1776, in *ND*, 4: 1323–25.

11. *JCC,* 1: 75–79. Boston's port was legally closed by Parliament under the terms of the Boston Port Act passed in 1774 in response to the destruction of duty tea there in December 1773.

12. Matt. Ridley to Dun. Campbell, December 28, 1774, and May 13, 1775; to Thos. Hodges, December 29, 1775, in MRLB, vol. 1.

13. The entry list for the Annapolis District runs from April 6, 1756, to October 6, 1775. Most of this data, beginning with December 1, 1774—the day the nonimportation was supposed to go into operation—is republished in *ND*, 1: 1374–86; the original in MdHR is entitled "Port of Entry Records," MSA M1002. Entry data from Roanoke, North Carolina, spans the period December 1, 1774, to February 1776, republished in *ND*, 2: 1345–52. In addition, there is an entry series for Baltimore that runs from March 13, 1775, through March 16, 1776, tabulating 104 entries, reproduced in ibid., 3: 1367–70, original in LC, but the information in it fails to support any conclusions about the effectiveness of nonimportation, one way or the other. The committees of Edenton and Wilmington–New Hanover, N.C., acted in ways congruent with the Roanoke data; see Alan D. Watson, "The Committees of Safety and the Coming of the American Revolution in North Carolina, 1774–1776," *North Carolina Historical Review* 73(1996): 140.

14. The Patuxent and North Potomac series run from September 29, 1774, through September 29, 1775, and are abbreviations of the official records; see S205 Naval Officers, General File (oversized), MdHR. The Annapolis series runs from April 7, 1756, through July 19, 1775. The Roanoke figures extend into the early months of 1776. The James River records survive in the form of the Naval Office's manifest book spanning the period December 10, 1774, through September 9, 1775, which lists vessels and cargoes clearing only for Great Britain. These series are published in *ND*, 2: 1361–74, 1352–61, and 1387–94, respectively. Originals of the Roanoke series are in the James Iredell Papers, SHC.

15. Estimated tonnage associated with clearances for Great Britain recorded in the manifest book is 9,280 actual and 12,373 annual tons as compared with the 1772 figure of

5,151 actual tons for the year. The number of vessels increased from thirty to sixty-four, twelve of which succeeded in making a second clearance from the Customs House during the nine-month period. Cf. Customs 16/1, PRO, and James River Naval Office, Manifest Book December 10, 1774–September 9, 1775, in *ND*, 1: 1387–94. The above argument assumes that the James River Naval Office served both the Upper and Lower James Customs districts.

16. The tonnage referred to here and throughout the text, except where otherwise noted, is registered tonnage, which is distinct from measured tonnage and cargo tonnage. For a discussion of the differences between the three, see John J. McCusker, "The Tonnage of Ships Engaged in British Colonial Trade During the Eighteenth Century," *Research in Economic History* 6(1981): 74–80. See also Jean B. Lee, *The Price of Nationhood* . . . (New York, 1994), 118–19, 126.

17. The Annapolis series stops abruptly on July 19, 1775, preventing comparisons of multiple clearances and early September activity. Up to that point the total included 483,748 bu. of wheat at 5.14 bu. to the bb.= 94,114 bb. of flour and bread plus 51,139 actual barrels. All of this was from harvest 1774. Patuxent, North Potomac, and Maryland are included in the tally for 1769, Customs 16/1, PRO. Exports to coastal destinations are excluded.

18. *ND*, 2: 1360. Also, Watson, "Committees of Safety," 140.

19. The interval chosen is from January 6 to March 26, the season that most closely approximates conditions between September 10 to November 30. If we choose the interval between April 3 to June 23 for our comparison, the percentage rises to 19 percent.

20. See George III to Lord Sandwich, August 25, 1775; Lord Dartmouth to the Lords Commissioners of the British Admiralty, August 29; Lords Commissioners to Vice Admiral Graves, September 2, for the transmission of the orders, in *ND*, 2: 687, 694, 701. It took more than two months for them to reach America; see Journal of HMS *Rose*, November 5, 1775, in ibid., 2: 895.

21. Merrill Jensen, ed., *English Historical Documents*, vol. 9 *American Colonial Documents to 1776* (New York, 1955), 853. See also Matt. Ridley to Lux and Bowley, December 24, 1775, in MRLB, vol. 1.

22. Johnson to Sam. Purviance Jr., June 13, 1775, in *LD*, 1: 483. Congress formed a committee "to consider the State of Trade in America" on September 22; see Rich. Smith's Diary in *LD*, 2: 45. The issue was extensively debated during October; see John Adams's Notes on Debates, October 6, 7, 12, 13, 20, 21, 27, in ibid., 126–27, 130, 165–69, 173–74, 211–15, 221–24, 261–62; also Adams to Jas. Warren, October 7, 27, in ibid., 135–38, 206–7; and Robt. R. Livingston Jr.'s Notes for a speech, October 27, in ibid., 267–71.

23. *JCC*, 4: 229, 247, 256–59. Also John Adams to Hor. Gates, March 23, 1776, in *LD*, 3: 429; and Adams's Notes on Congressional debates, October 4, 1775, in *LD*, 2: 109.

24. See William B. Clark, *George Washington's Navy* . . . (Baton Rouge, La., 1960); Chester G. Hearn, *George Washington's Schooners* . . . (Annapolis, Md., 1995).

25. Graves had only twenty-one men-of-war on station at the beginning of hos-

tilities; by December 1775 he had fifty men-of-war in service manned by 7,460 men; see "The present disposition of His Majesty's Ships and Vessels in Sea Pay," December 1, 1775, in *ND*, 3: 1397–1401. Also Narrative of Samuel Graves, October 22, 1775, in *ND*, 2: 570, and Molyneux Shuldham to Phil. Stephens, January 15, 1776, in *ND*, 3: 793; Marriot Arbuthnot to And. S. Hamond, November 8, 1775, in *ND*, 2: 924; see also Shuldham to Phil. Callbeck, February 6, 1776, in *ND*, 3: 1144–45.

26. Of the forty-three ships under Shuldham's command on March 22 just after the comprehensive Prohibitory Act went into effect, only fourteen were cruising off the coast or attempting to blockade ports not held by the army; see "Disposition of His Majesty's Ships and Vessels in North America," March 22, 1776, in *ND*, 4: 448–50, with the Delaware River left untended. Once the evacuation of Boston was completed, the number of vessels cruising or otherwise on blockade duty rose to twenty-seven, with two stationed at the Delaware; see "Disposition etc.," April 24, in *ND*, 4: 1225–27. Howe responded to the new demands made on the Navy by slightly increasing the number of ships under his command to forty-five vessels and dramatically increasing the number of men manning them to 12,100; see *ND*, 5: 1357–63.

27. Compare Graves's list of seizures, June 1–December 31, 1775, in appendix D, *ND*, 2: 1373–77, and Shuldham's, December 28–March 25, 1776, with Gayton's Jamaica squadron's seizures in ibid., 4: 517, and Young's Leeward Island squadron's seizures in ibid., 4: 1375–77. Put another way, in comparable time intervals the ratio of captures to men-of-war was about 1:1 in northern waters, closer to 3:1 in southern waters.

28. Robert G. Albion and Jennie Barnes Pope, *Sea Lanes in Wartime: The American Experience, 1775–1942* (New York, 1943), 34, 36–38. Their assessment in turn has been echoed by William B. Willcox, "Why Did the British Lose the American Revolution?" *Michigan Alumnus Quarterly Review* 62(1956): 317, 319, 320, 321, 324, and by Miller, *Sea of Glory*, 180, 202. The issue was first raised in 1777 in response to the Howes's failure to crush the rebellion in one campaign; see Ira D. Gruber, *The Howe Brothers and the American Revolution* (Chapel Hill, N.C., 1972), 215ff. For the prize lists see *ND*, 2: 1373–77; 5: 113, 212–13, 330–31; 7: 428–29, 926–27; 8: 82–83, 161–62, 490–91, 637–38, 1053–63. (Howe's Prize List, March 31, 1777, is missing!)

29. In the James Iredell Papers, SHC.

30. For the Rhode Island series, Maritime Papers, RIA. Also Port of Philadelphia, Duty on Tonnage, September 6, 1775–August 27, 1776, in Records of the Office of the Comptroller General, Port of Philadelphia Accounts, 1774–1809, PHMC.

31. Between September 6 and March 1, an average of 25,718 tons of shipping entered Philadelphia from beyond the Delaware in 1772–73 and 1773–74; see PTD. Entries during this interval in 1774–75 increased by more than 30 percent for the same reasons that maritime activity in the Chesapeake increased prior to the cessation of most authorized commerce on September 10, 1775. Entries for 1774–75 accordingly do not play a part in the calculation of what would have been normal.

32. The evidence for French arrivals in American ports is spotty; see Miller, *Sea of Glory*, 193; Peter Elting to Rich. Varick, June 4, 1776, in *New York City During the American Revolution* (New York, 1861), 93–94. See also Thos. and Isaac Wharton to

Nath. Shaw, September 6, 1776, and Jos. Waters to Shaw, November 23, 1776, in N&TSP; RHD, 125, 130. For the tendency to avoid Philadelphia, see L. Rouzeau, "Aperçus du rôle de Nantes dans la guerre d'indépendance d'Amérique (1775–1783)," *Annales de Bretagne* 74(1967): 242; Thomas J. Schaeper, *France and America in the Revolutionary Era: The Life of Jacques-Donatien Leray de Chaumont, 1725–1803* (Providence, R.I., 1995), 209.

33. RHD, 92–93, 104, 118–19.

34. Tonnage is not supplied until the entries that begin in September, but the information can be extrapolated in many instances from the records of bonds posted by masters of vessels in Maritime Papers, vol. 3, RIA. The record of clearances lists owners for many vessels revealing a pattern of investment embracing the entire state including Newport. The same pattern is evident in the bonds recorded in ibid, vols. 3–6, under the heading of "Bonds, Masters of Vessels." Most of the vessels that appear in the Maritime Papers cleared from Providence.

35. The early clearances are partially reproduced in *ND*, 4: 1479–83. Thirty-six percent of cleared tonnage for overseas destinations was considerably less than the 45 percent average over the life of Customs 16/1, PRO.

36. Tonnage for the months March–August 1776, when tonnage figures are not entered in the Register of clearances, has been inferred by taking the average tonnage of clearances between September and December and applying it to the clearances for the earlier months. Rhode Island did commission forty-two vessels as letters of marque or privateers during 1776, some to out-of-state syndicates. Those issued to Rhode Island owners totaled approximately 2,115 tons that do not show up in the clearance data. Aggregating the letters of marque with the commercial clearances still leaves the state's merchant marine at 59 percent of its prewar tonnage. This was a larger percentage than for any other area we have information about, but it still represented a substantial reduction in maritime activity.

37. For instance, Rhode Island's prewar ratio of clearances to entries had hovered between 1.05 and 1, and 1.16 and 1. See Customs 16/1, in PRO.

38. The other brief list is for entries during 1780–81.

39. I have been able to identify only five Rhode Island vessels taken as prizes by Royal Navy men-of-war between May 19, 1776, and February 19, 1777. The information on many of the prize lists makes it hard to identify where a vessel came from, though. See *ND*, 5: 330; 7: 428, 926; 8: 490, 1053.

40. See Matt. Ridley to Capt. Thos. Moore, October 11, 1774, and March 14, 1775, in MRLB, I. Rouzeau, "Aperçus du rôle de Nantes," 232.

41. For those who were sent into Rhode Island, see "List of All Vessels Cargoes &c Brought into the Port of Providence and Libelled Tried and condemned in the Maritime Court AD 1776," in *ND*, 7: 642–47. However, the *Lady Washington* from Newport chose to libel the 265-ton ship *Marshall* in Boston's Admiralty Court; see Admiralty Notices in the *Boston Gazette*, October 24, 1776. Connecticut privateers also sent their prizes to the Boston market; see Josiah Waters to Nath. Shaw, August 2, 10, 1777; Paschal N. Smith to Shaw, March 21, 1778; and Peter Vandervoort to Shaw, September

21, 1778, in N&TSP; and notice of three vessels libeled by the Connecticut sloop *Broome* in *Boston Gazette,* September 12, 1776.

42. Anne Bezanson, *Prices and Inflation during the American Revolution: Pennsylvania, 1770–1790* (Philadelphia, 1951), 335; Secret Committee to Silas Deane, August 7, 1776; Hen. Laurens to John Rutledge, August 12, 1777, in *LD,* 4: 636, 7: 470. See also comments in *Massachusetts Spy,* March 23, 1775. Sam. Adams's Notes on Trade, [September 27? 1774] in *LD,* 1: 107–8.

43. See John Adams's Notes of Debates, February [16], 1776, in *LD,* 3: 260–61. Also Elbridge Gerry to John Wendell, June 11, in *LD,* 4: 187–88.

44. *JCC,* 2: 103. For the effect currency shortages had on colonial development, John J. McCusker and Russell R. Menard, *The Economy of British America, 1607–1789* (Chapel Hill, 1985), 237. McCusker and Menard argue that on the eve of the Revolution the money supply was adequate, 338. However, many Americans welcomed the greater availability of cash in 1775 and 1776.

45. For Congress's motives, see John Hancock to Jos. Warren, June 18, 1775, and John Adams to Jas. Warren, June 20, 1775; New Hampshire Delegates to Matt. Thornton, June 20; Washington to John A. Washington, June 20, in *LD,* 1: 508, 518, 524, 528. For the colonial experience, Fred Anderson, *A People's Army: Massachusetts Soldiers in the Seven Years' War* (Chapel Hill, 1984), 38, 51 and passim; Harold E. Selesky, *War and Society in Colonial Connecticut* (New Haven, 1990), 57–58, 69, 79, 132–34, 136–37, 139. Also excerpt from Silas Deane's Diary, June 13, 1775, and Caesar Rodney to Thos. Rodney, June 20, in *LD,* 1: 482, 525.

46. There were two currency emissions during 1776 before Independence totaling $9 million; see *JCC,* 4: 157, 164, 374, 380. Congress emitted $5 million more in August; its entrance into circulation coincided with the first hint of depreciation. David Ramsay, *The History of the Revolution in South Carolina . . .* (Trenton, N.J., 1785), 2: 81. For a comprehensive view of the depreciation, E. James Ferguson, *The Power of the Purse* (Chapel Hill, 1963), 32 and fn19.

47. Ferguson, *Power of the Purse,* 26–27, 31. The quantity explanation for the depreciation has been challenged by Charles W. Calomoris, "Institutional Failure, Monetary Scarcity, and the Depreciation of the Continental," *Journal of Economic History* 48 (1988): 56. He stressed instead the "decaying confidence in the ultimate redemption of the bills" arising from the failure of the revolutionary governments to back their credit instruments with taxation. Ron Michener, "Backing Theories and the Currencies of Eighteenth-Century America: A Comment," ibid., 682–92, attempts to defend the adequacy of the quantity explanation against Calomoris's challenge. Calomoris has replied in "The Depreciation of the Continental: A Reply," ibid., 693–98. For a comprehensive picture of currency finance in the Revolution, see Ralph V. Harlow, "Aspects of Revolutionary Finance, 1775–1783," *American Historical Review* 35(1929): 50–51, insert.

48. See Ramsay, *Revolution in South Carolina,* 2: 82; Buel, *Dear Liberty,* 84–85. The sterling price of commodities, both foreign and domestic, initially declined, reflecting

the premium attached to any currency that was thought to store value, see Hen. Laurens to John Rutledge, August 10, 1777, in *LD*, 7: 470–71.

49. See Chas. Carroll of Carrollton to Chas. Carroll Sr., June 2, 1777, in *LD*, 7: 164; Gouv. Morris's Proposals on Fiscal and Administrative Reform, June–July, 1778, in ibid., 204; Committee for Foreign Affairs to Commissioners at Paris, December 2, in *LD*, 8, 366; to Ralph Izard, February 5, 1778; Rich. H. Lee to Art. Lee, May 12, in *LD*, 9: 31, 653; Jon. Mathews to Thos. Bee, September 1, 1779, in Charleston Library Society, Charleston, South Carolina. Also Roger Sherman to Ben. Trumbull, October 20, 1778, in *LD*, 9: 491; Selesky, *War and Society*, 138. Chas. Carroll to Ben. Franklin, August 12, 1777, in *LD*, 7: 462. Oliver Wolcott to And. Adams, April 25, 1778, in *LD*, 9: 491.

50. Henry Laurens warned against dependence on the French, but largely because he feared they would take advantage of the Republic, see his letter to John Rutledge, August 12, 1777, in *LD*, 7: 471–72. He was also worried about the size of the debt the nation might accumulate in this fashion, see Laurens to John Rutledge, August 19, 1777, and to Lachlan McIntosh, September 1, in ibid., 511, 586. Ambassador Gérard discouraged all expectations about foreign loans, see his letter to Vergennes, March 4, 1779, in *DCG*, 555. For the early loans, see Ferguson, *Power of the Purse*, 40–41.

51. Robt. Morris to Silas Deane, January 29, 1777, in *LD*, 6: 161. Morris gave a similar account of the depreciation at the end of the war, see his letter to Francisco Rendón, March 5, 1782, in *PRM*, 4: 355; see also "T. S." in *Pennsylvania Packet*, June 22, 1779.

52. See John Adams, Notes on Debates, October 3[4] and 12, 1775, in *LD*, 2: 108, 166; also John Adams to Jas. Warren, October 7, 1775, in ibid., 2: 137. Hen. Laurens to John L. Gervas, September 5, 1777, in ibid., 7: 617. See also Ramsay, *Revolution in South Carolina*, 2: 112ff.

53. *JCC*, 5: 431, 576–89, 696, 709–10, 768–78, 884, 1057; for the clandestinely exported military supplies, see Miller, *Sea of Glory*, 193; for the commercial implications of naval superiority, see Robert R. Crout, "The Diplomacy of Trade: The Influence of Commercial Considerations on French Involvement in the Anglo-American War, 1775–1778" (Ph.D. diss., University of Georgia, 1977), 146, 170, 194, 219, 253.

54. Daniel Vickers, "The Northern Colonies: Economy and Society," in Stanley L. Engerman and Robert E. Gallman eds., *The Cambridge Economic History of the United States* (Cambridge, 1996), 1: 224.

55. See Harry J. Carman, ed., *American Husbandry* (Port Washington, N.Y., 1964), 37–38; Lewis C. Gray, *History of Agriculture in the Southern United States to 1860* (Washington, D.C., 1933), 1: 161. In addition less of the corn crop had to be set aside for the next crop's seed.

56. Max G. Schumacher, *The Northern Farmer and His Market During the Colonial Period* (New York, 1975), 1, 12, 40–41, 44. Carville Earle and Ronald Hoffman, "Staple Crops and Urban Development in the Eighteenth-Century South," *Perspectives in American History* 10(1976): 69, assume in their calculations that every farm laborer could produce 100 bushels of wheat in the course of a year. This seems to be a reasonable assumption if scythes, which more than doubled the acreage the average harvester could

cut in a day, were used. There are references to scythes in the principal wheat producing regions by the time of the Revolution, see Abraham Van Nest Day Book, October 2, 1775–November 18, 1779, in Firestone Library Manuscript Collection, Princeton University. But it is impossible to ascertain how widely they were being used. It seems safer to proceed as though the reaping bottleneck, which Schumacher emphasizes, persisted through the war and was only partially alleviated by the limited introduction of scythes, see reference in George Wall Jr., Daybook, November 14, 1778–November 8, 1784, under July 21, 1781, in Bucks County Historical Society, Doylestown, Pa. I use the smaller figure of forty bushels to the man in calculating the opportunity costs of raising the army. Farm journals of the period do show that reaping usually ended before the grain was all brought in, but efforts were made to sheave it immediately and get it under cover as quickly as possible. See Jones Account Books, 1779–1812 (for the years 1779–81), MdHS.

57. For wartime complaints about the effect of labor shortages on agriculture, see Jere. Wadsworth to Jos. Trumbull, September 4, 1776, in JWP; also Robt. Alcock to Jas. Alcock, October 26, 1778, in S-AP; Robt. R. Livingston to Wm. Duer, July 3, 1778, in RRLP; and "Publicola," in Connecticut Journal, March 5, 1777. Also Jos. Cooke to John Trumbull, August 9, 1776, and Trumbull to Cooke, May 13, 1776 (actually 1777) in JTP.

58. Exception has been taken to the authority of Knox's estimates by Charles H. Lesser in Lesser, ed., The Sinews of Independence . . . (Chicago, 1976), xxxiii–xxxv. Lesser is justified in questioning whether all of Knox's calculations were backed by hard data. On the other hand, Lesser's speculation that Knox had little beyond the returns of the army reproduced in Sinews to work with is less certain. Knox did have access to materials that were destroyed by a fire in 1800 as well as to living witnesses that could have clarified certain problems encountered in putting together his estimates. Knox's estimates are the only surviving attempt at a comprehensive calculation of who contributed what to the revolutionary mobilization. As such they are the best information we have to work with. My calculations omit the South Carolina and Georgia estimates which were probably the least accurate component in Knox's final tallies for reasons explained below, quite apart from the error noted by Lesser (xxxiv) in their subsequent republication.

59. The assumption that everyone in the ranks came from farms that produced wheat surpluses tends to overstate the adverse impact mobilization had on the wheat harvest. On the other hand, the error is muted by the exclusion of officers from these tallies, who were as likely to have been farmers as the rank and file. Staff and line officers in actuality accounted for between 8 and 12 percent of the continental formations; cf. Lesser, Sinews.

Knox's figures fail to record the militia's participation in the war effort. Though we have reasonably comprehensive figures for militia under Continental command, deriving a comprehensive estimate for the total militia is more difficult. The states raised sizable forces for local defense, and estimates of these forces are hard to establish because the state governments' authorizations bore very little relation to the numbers that actually served. The discrepancy between authorization, about which we have a fairly clear idea, and actuality, which remains largely inaccessible, minimizes the error resulting from the omission of state defense forces from our estimates. Certainly the larger, more disruptive militia mobilizations occurred in response to Continental levies. Since many Continental militia levies served for only a short time, the impact of their service on the economy has been weighted accordingly. Those who served for three months or less are discounted at 50 percent of the value in foregone productivity compared with those who served longer. The assumption here is that a short-term absence from a farm would have less of an effect than a long-term one. Farmers were more likely to find a replacement for short-term than long-term calls because most of the former came after planting and before harvest when the opportunity costs for not finding a substitute were greater. When a farmer was faced with a long-term loss of labor, he would be more apt to change his plans about planting.

60. No reference is made in table 2.1 to the opportunity costs of manning the state or continental navies on the assumption that those serving on their vessels were not previously part of the agricultural labor force. Figures on naval manpower are much harder to come by than force levels for the army. I have managed to construct estimates of manpower in the Continental Navy from a variety of sources, the most useful of which are Miller, *Sea of Glory,* 528–29, and *ND,* vols. 1–9. My calculations assume ten men per gun. Eight men per gun would give a more precise measure of the actual manning of the navy's vessels but would fail to take account of support personnel on shore. Attempts have been made to express values in terms of full-year equivalents to make the data congruent with that in table 2.1. At no time did total naval personnel exceed 10 percent of the army. However, the Continental Navy's mobilization peaked in 1777 rather than 1776.

Estimated Manpower in the Continental Navy

Year	1775	1776	1777	1778	1779	1780	1781	1782
Men	550	1910	4023	2840	2428	1726	1724	640

Exclusion of camp followers is more controversial if one credits the claim that there were as many of them as men under arms during the war, see Holly A. Mayer, *Belonging to the Army* . . . (Columbia, S.C., 1997), 1. Wagoners, servants, and slaves were the camp followers most intimately connected with agriculture, and their exclusion makes some of the extravagant assumptions behind the calculations in table 2.1 a little less extravagant. Privateersmen are also excluded for two reasons. First, the bulk of them, like the navy, came from sectors of the population only marginally involved with agriculture. Second, privateers and armed vessels pursuing commercial voyages had to turn a profit. If the cost of outfits, including wages and provisions, rose too high, owners would cut back. Overall, had the diversion of manpower and agricultural resources into cruising against the enemy not returned roughly what it took out of the economy, such enterprises would have been progressively abandoned as society's resources were exhausted.

61. There is a problem in doing so. The conversion ratio varied depending on the quality of the wheat. At the height of the wheat boom before the war, some merchants used a conversion ratio of 4.5 bu. to the bb., meaning that 270 lbs. of wheat yielded 196 lbs. of flour. On the other hand, when Congressman Robert Morris referred to the

harvest of 1776 as one of the "worst ever known," he had both quantity and quality equally in mind. In addition to the diminished number of bushels gathered, he expected more bushels of wheat would be required to make a barrel of flour (Robt. Morris to Wm. Bingham, February 16, 1777, in WBP, or so I infer from the commercial nature of Morris's communication; see also Morris to Silas Deane, December 20, 1776, in *FME*, no. 1396.

During the late colonial period the principal flour marts had developed elaborate grading systems consisting of two, sometimes three, categories of merchantable flour graded by fineness and whiteness. Arthur L. Jensen, "The Inspection of Exports in Colonial Pennsylvania," *Pennsylvania Magazine of History and Biography* 77(1954): 275–97 discusses the development of grading in both New York and Pennsylvania. The war ended most grading. Where producers were cut off from distant markets, there did not seem to be much point in maintaining them. Abandonment also allowed millers to increase yields in the short term, though the mixing of all grades, often with bran, seriously compromised the keeping qualities of what they manufactured. On perishability see Ephr. Blaine to Robt. Morris, March 20, 1782, in *PRM*, 4: 427. On cumulative neglect, see Washington's complaint about the degeneration of the quality of his wheat during the war in E. J. Kahn, *The Staff of Life* (New York, 1984), 174.

I assume that the quantity of usable by-products from a bushel of wheat remained roughly constant despite continued degradation, and I use the figure of 5.14 bushels to the barrel, as have other scholars of the period. Charles Ridgely's Ledger E in MdHS gives the yield from the 167,388 weight of wheat produced on his plantations during calendar 1781 as 89,839 weight of flour or about 6.1 bushels of wheat to the barrel. When middlings and stuff or bran are added to the computation, the conversion ratio becomes 5.2 bushels to the barrel.

62. To calculate available wheat flour that should have remained after deducting production foregone as a consequence of mobilizing the army, I take the annual surplus before the war = 604,835 bb., subtract the estimate of foregone production to yield the remaining potential surplus. I then multiply by 196 (the weight of flour in each bb.) for the number of rations and divide by 365 to derive the number of men that could be supported annually, minus 25 percent for wastage. When Knox's estimates are combined with my estimates for the navy, the peak mobilization of 1776 comes to 80,335; 1777's combined mobilization level to 55,198. The addition of the Convention Army for the last eleven weeks of 1777 brings the annualized total to 56,408.

63. In Chester County Archives, West Chester, Pa.

64. Robert Alexander also assumed only 25 percent of the improved land of the Delmarva Peninsula would be planted in grains each year, see Edward C. Papenfuse Jr., "Economic Analysis and Loyalist Strategy During the American Revolution: Robert Alexander's Remarks on the Economy of the Eastern Shore of Maryland," *Maryland Historical Magazine* 68(1973): 192. Labor shortages at harvest time that restricted specialization in wheat on larger farms should have had less effect on farms possessed of less acreage.

65. Bernard Bailyn, *Voyagers to the West: A Passage in the Peopling of America on the Eve*

of the Revolution (New York, 1986); Thomas M. Truxes, *Irish-American Trade, 1660–1783* (Cambridge, 1988), 235.

66. For instance, soil exhaustion seems to have played a role in Connecticut's decline as a provider of flour after 1775; see Mansel Alcock to Jas. Alcock, January 25, 1778, in S-AP.

CHAPTER 3. THE FRENCH CONNECTION

1. Jonathan R. Dull, "France and the American Revolution Seen as Tragedy," in Nancy L. Roelker and Charles K. Warner, eds., *Two Hundred Years of Franco-American Relations . . .* (Newport, R.I., 1978), 1–16, is the best exploration of the larger causes and consequences of France's intervention in the American war; see also Claude Fohlen, "The Commercial Failure of France in America," in ibid., 97–99, and Jacques God-echot, "Les Relations économiques entre la France at les Etats-Unis de 1778 à 1789," *French Historical Studies* 1(1958): 26, which emphasize the degree to which French political and commercial expectations were linked.

2. These two firms dispatched twenty ships, but only seventeen arrived. For vessels of Beaumarchais's firm, Hortales, Roderique et Cie., see Jonathan R. Dull, *A Diplomatic History of the American Revolution* (New Haven, 1985), 62. For the vessels of Reculès des Basmarein et Raimbaux, Cie., see Robert Castex, "L'Armateur de La Lafayette: Pierre de Basmarein d'après des documents inédits," *Revue des questions historiques,* 3rd ser., 6(1925): 91, 95, 96. Reculès des Basmarein et Raimbaux's fleet averaged 280 tons and included the *Duchesse de Mortemart* (18 guns) of 450 tons, *Le Meulan* (6 guns) of 260 tons, and *La Victoire* (6 guns) of 220 tons, on which Lafayette and his entourage made their way to North America. See also Paul Butel, "Le commerce atlantique français sous le règne de Louis XVI," in Jean de Viguerie, ed., *Le Règne de Louis XVI et la Guerre d'Indépendance américaine* (Dourgne, 1977), 83, fn19.

3. Simeon Deane to John Holker, May 30 and June 4, 1778, in JHLC. See also the report in *Virginia Gazette* (Dixon & Hunter), May 1, 1778. French vessels were also visible in other ports, see *Connecticut Journal,* March 25, 1778. For additional evidence of French commercial activity predating the formal announcement of the alliance, see John Bondfield to Robert Morris, March 4, 1778, in RMNY; Lony et Plombard to Sabatier fils, January 30, 1778, and Sabatier fils to John Holker, March 1, 1778, in JHLC; Peter Vandervoort to Nath. Shaw, March 17, 1778, in N&TSP. For the extent of the pre-alliance trade, see Edmond Buron, "Statistics on Franco-American Trade, 1778–1806," *Journal of Economic and Business History* 4(1932): 580. Also intelligence report of Capt. Macartney, March 18, 1778, enclosed in Richard Lord Howe to Phil. Stephens, May 9, in LCTB, Admiralty 1/488.

4. Jean Meyer, "Les Difficultés du commerce franco-américain vues de Nantes, 1776–1790," *French Historical Studies* 11(1979): 171ff, 180, argues that ports like Nantes estab-lished commercial relations with British North America before the Revolution in re-sponse to the declining profitability of France's colonial trade. For the *Fier Roderique,* see *PBF,* 25: 104, 27: 59fn; Thomas J. Schaeper, *France and America in the Revolutionary Era:*

The Life of Jacques-Donatien Leray de Chaumont, 1725–1803 (Providence, R.I., 1995), 51–52, 186. Gaston Martin, "Commercial Relations Between Nantes and the American Colonies During the War of Independence," *Journal of Economic and Business History* 4(1932): 815, claims that arming began as early as 1774. Some of the vessels, like the *Beaumont*—which had been built as a sixty-four-gun line-of-battle ship—carried forty guns; see Simeon Deane to John Holker, June 20 and 23, 1778, in JHLC. *La Dédaigneuse* also carried twenty-four guns; see Sabatier fils to Holker, March 1, 1778, in ibid. For the British assessment, see Extract of Capt. Onslow to Richard Lord Howe, March 2, 1778, in Howe to Phil. Stephens, March 16, 1778, in LCTB, Admiralty 1/488.

5. Quote from Paschal N. Smith to Hen. Crouch, June 30, 1778, in S&SLB. For the movement into cash, see Thos. Lawrence to John Reed, May 5, 1778, Thos. Bondy to Reed, May 19, 20, and Anth. Butler to Reed, May 24, in R&FP; Holker to Le Ray de Chaumont, August 25, 1778, in JHLC; and Josiah Waters to Nath. Shaw, April 30, May 13 and 21, 1778, in N&TSP. See also subsequent allusions to what had happened in "Walsingham" in *Pennsylvania Packet,* February 16, 1779, and Robt. Morris to Francisco Rendón, March 5, 1782, in *PRM,* 4: 354. For the brief appreciation of the currency, Holker to Le Ray de Chaumont, August 25, 1778, in JHLC; E. James Ferguson, *The Power of the Purse* (Chapel Hill, 1963), 32, fn19.

6. See Richard Lord Howe to Capt. Hyde Parker, September 22, 1777; Robt. Fanshawe to Howe, February 3, 1778; and Howe to Phil. Stephens, February 4, 1778, in LCTB, Admiralty 1/488. See also prize lists in London Gazette, December 2–6, 1777, with accounts of the seizure of the brig *L'Empereur,* June 2, and the snow *Triumville,* September 22; Théveneau de Francy to Beaumarchais, June 11, 1778, in *BC,* 4: 118; Castex, "L'Armateur de La Fayette," 98; Rich. Onslow to Richard Lord Howe, March 2, 1778, in LCTB, Admiralty 1/488. L. Rouzeau, "Aperçus du rôle de Nantes dans la guerre d'indépendance d'Amérique (1775–1783)," *Annales de Bretagne* 74(1967): 231, 239ff, 252–53, who cites a notirial record in the Archives de la Loire-Atlantique dated April 15, 1778, that suggests the first British seizure of a French vessel took place in July 1777. See also Patrick Villiers, "La Lutte contre la course Anglaise en Atlantique pendant la guerre d'indépendance des Etats-Unis d'Amérique, 1778–1783," in Commission internationale d'histoire maritime, *Course et Piraterie* (Paris, 1975), 2: 572.

7. For Britain's response to D'Estaing, see Richard Lord Howe to Phil. Stephens, February 4, 1778, in Admiralty 1/488; Jas. Gambier to Phil. Stephens, October 14, 1778, in Admiralty 1/489, both in LCTB; Robert W. Love Jr., *History of the U.S. Navy* (Harrisburg, Pa., 1992), 30. D'Estaing's brilliant prospects are detailed in John Holker to Sabatier fils, July 1778, in JHLC; Gérard to Vergennes, July 18, 1778, in *DCG,* 170. His early successes can be extrapolated from "Prizes taken by D'Estaing's squadron up to October 28, 1779," AM, B4 151. See also Jas. Gambier to Phil. Stephens, October 14, 1778, in LCTB, Admiralty 1/489; Michael J. Crawford, "The Joint Allied Operation at Rhode Island, 1778," in William R. Roberts and Jack Sweetman, eds., *New Interpretations in Naval History* (Annapolis, Md., 1991), 232–33. For D'Estaing's effect on the British blockade, see Wm. Smith to Holker, July 23, 1778, and Holker to Le Ray de Chaumont, August 14, in JHLC; Théveneau de Francy to Beaumarchais, June 11, 1778,

in *BC*, 4: 118. See also Richard Lord Howe to Phil. Stephens, July 26 and 31, 1778, in LCTB, Admiralty 1/489.

8. Richard Lord Howe to Phil. Stephens, August 17, 1778, in LCTB, Admiralty 1/489; Crawford, "Joint Allied Operation," 235; W. M. James, *The British Navy in Adversity . . .* (London, 1926), 106. Matt. Ridley wrote Wm. Carmichael, October 31, 1778, that D'Estaing appeared "close confined" in Boston; see MRLB, vol. 2.

9. Excerpt from London *Public Advertiser,* March 11, 1777, and "Instructions to Commanders of British Letters of Marque," March 27, in *ND*, 8: 662–64, 715–20; Lord Commissioners of the Admiralty to Mr. Gostling, March 10, 1777, in Admiralty 2/1059, PRO. Those from the Channel Islands were particularly active off the coast of France. See also Castex, "L'Armateur de La Fayette," 83. For Bermuda and the West Indies, see Lord Commissioners of the Admiralty to Mr. Gostling, June 25, 1777, in Admiralty 2/1059, PRO. For appeals to the High Court of Admiralty, beginning June 25, 1777, and thereafter, HCA 8/1, PROC. See also Villiers, "La Lutte," 575; Lambert Wickes to American Commissioners in France, August 31, 1777; Louis Charles Duchaffault to Gabriel de Sartine, September 19; Vergennes to Marquis de Noailles, September 27, in *ND*, 9: 617, 649–51, 666.

10. For the tactics of commerce raiding, see Villiers, "La Lutte," 580; Jon. Williams Jr. to John Williams, May 9, 1780, in JnWLB; Nathan Miller, *Sea of Glory . . .* (Annapolis, Md., 1974), 185, 255–57, 283ff.

11. Lord Commissioners of the Admiralty to Gostling, April 28, 1778, in Admiralty 2/1059, PRO. For evidence that there would be many volunteers, see Seddon to Lord Commissioners of the Admiralty, June 18, 1777, in ibid.; for the navy's alarm, Richard Lord Howe to Phil. Stephens, May 9, 1778, in LCTB, Admiralty 1/448. An embargo and a press provided a temporary remedy for the fleet's manpower problems; see Howe to Stephens, June 10, in ibid.

12. Both powers were reluctant to declare war against the other lest they forfeit treaty advantages with third parties in defensive wars. A minor sea engagement between a French frigate and the British channel fleet on June 16 is usually regarded as the official date on which hostilities began; see Dull, *Diplomatic History,* 99. For the prize list, see AM, B4 130. Villiers, "La Lutte," 575, uses the figure of 132 French vessels captured before the official declaration of war in June. Such lists were notoriously unreliable; see Meyer, "Les Difficultés du commerce franco-américain," 160–61. Rouzeau, working from notorial records, reports only forty-nine declarations of loss among the merchants of Nantes from August 1778 through May 1783, but he concludes from other sources that at least ninety-six vessels were seized by the British during this period; see "Aperçus du rôle de Nantes," 253, 277.

13. For reference to the heavy French losses, see Sabatier fils to Holker, October 9 and 31, 1778, and May 29, 1779, in JHLC; de Francy to Beaumarchais, June 11, 1778, in *BC*, 4: 118; Terrasson Brothers to Congress, January 27, 1784, in PCC, reel 56, item 42, vol. 7, p. 455ff. See also David Ramsay, *The History of the Revolution of South Carolina . . .* (Trenton, N.J., 1785), 2: 76. Privateers contributed substantially to the British naval effort, accounting for roughly 40 percent of the captures of French vessels making for

North Carolina in 1777–78 that were appealed to the High Court of Admiralty. See HCA, 32/267, Bundle 21, pertaining to the capture of the *Amphitrion,* April 19, 1778; HCA 32/322, Bundle 1, pertaining to the capture of the *L'Enfer,* July 10; HCA 32/323, Bundle 4, pertaining to the capture of the *L'Equivoque,* May 1; HCA 32/325, Bundle 15, pertaining to the capture of the *L'Este,* September 17, 1777; HCA 32/364, Bundle 1, pertaining to the capture of the brigantine *St. Jacques,* January 7, 1778; HCA 32/367, Bundle 7, pertaining to the capture of the *Jeune Hebrè,* August 7; HCA 32/456, Bundle 3, pertaining to the seizure of *Le Succès,* June 16, in PROC, photocopies in NCSA.

14. The *Beaumont,* renamed the *Lion,* loaded with six hundred hogsheads of tobacco, was seized by a twenty-gun British vessel off the Virginia Capes as it attempted to clear the continent; see Josiah Waters to Nath. Shaw, January 11, 1779, in N&TSP; Navy Board to the Marine Committee, January 14, 1779, in NBED. *La Dédaigneuse,* armed with twenty-four guns, may also have been taken while trying to get out; see Sabatier fils to Holker, October 9 and 31, 1778, in JHLC. Over 10 percent of Basmarein et Raimbaux's losses in 1777–78 were due to shipwreck; see Castex, "L'Armateur de La Fayette," 84. This was high for the eighteenth century. See also John Bondfield to Robt. Morris, August 20, 1778, in RMNY; Simeon Deane to John Holker, April 30, 1779, in JHLC. Meyer, "Difficultés du commerce franco-américain," 175, argues that some French captains were already familiar with the American coast. For the hazards of the westerly approach, see Patrick Crowhurst, *The Defense of British Trade, 1689–1815* (Folkestone, 1977), 77–78. Some of the trepidation that French mariners unfamiliar with the North American coastline felt about approaching it is captured in Marvin R. Cox, trans. and ed., "A French Sea Captain in Revolutionary Connecticut: Extract from the Memoirs of J. F. Landolphe," *Connecticut Historical Society Bulletin* 47(1982): 35–36.

15. My estimate of Basmarein & Raimbaux's losses from AM, B4 130, and "Etat des Compte d'armament . . . ," November 25, 1778, in JHCL, is slightly higher, but Robert Castex, "L'Armateur de La Fayette," 97, 98–99, 102, 127, repeatedly mentions the figures given in the text, apparently on the authority of Basmarein himself. For Hortales, Roderique & Cie., who were much more fortunate in their 1777 ventures than Basmarein & Raimbaux were to be that year, losing only one of their vessels to the enemy, see Dull, *Diplomatic History,* 61–62. Rouzeau lists eleven vessels that he claims Beaumarchais sent to America between January 1777 and March 1778, excluding the *Fier Roderique,* see "Aperçus du rôle de Nantes," 243–44.

16. Castex, "L'Armateur de La Fayette," 99–101, publishes an undated text of Basmarein's application to the Crown for a loan followed by the record of a long conversation with Necker on the subject (102–9). It should be read in light of the economic culture of cronyism that characterized the ancien régime; see Hilton R. Root, *The Fountain of Privilege: Political Foundations of Markets in Old Regime France and England* (Berkeley, Calif., 1994). For the commission issued on June 29, see Castex, 111–12. It only authorized the house to recover the cost of the vessels and cargoes of eleven ships seized by the British in European seas while the two countries were at peace; see also headnote in *PBF,* 26: 472–73, and Francis Montresor to Franklin, June 23, 1778, in ibid., 677–78. For the firm's

collapse, see Castex, 112–15; John Bondfield to the American Commissioners, February 16, 1779, in *PBF,* 28: 550. The firm had unwittingly confided in a British spy, which may explain some of its extraordinary losses; see note 2, ibid., 26: 472.

17. Castex, "L'Armateur de La Fayette," 97. French merchants were used to organizing overseas ventures as individual joint stock companies; see George V. Taylor, "Types of Capitalism in Eighteenth-Century France," *English Historical Review* 69(1964): 483. Jacob M. Price, *France and the Chesapeake . . .* (Ann Arbor, Mich., 1973), 2: 701, stresses capitals more than connections.

18. For Chaumont, see Schaeper, *France and America,* esp. 79–83, 159, 204, 304. Schaeper argues that Chaumont's involvement with and contribution to the American war effort was more significant and sustained than Beaumarchais's; ibid., 158, 186–87. Montieu had been a prominent arms supplier under Louis XV but fell from favor in 1773 after a scandal involving the quality of the goods delivered (see *PBF,* 20: 464fn; the editors speculate that he managed to sell many of the arms in question to Congress's commissioners). Montieu also owned a large number of ships and provided, in partnership with Beaumarchais, many of the vessels used to transport military supplies purchased on Congress's account to America in 1777–78 (see Schaeper, *France and America,* 82, 160; Jon. Williams Jr. to Ben. Franklin, May 20, 1780, in JnWLB).

19. Castex, "L'Armateur de La Fayette," 86–89.

20. Patrick Villiers, *Le commerce colonial Atlantique et la guerre d'indépendance des Etats Unis d'Amérique, 1778–1783* (New York, 1977), 276–94, 365–66, 415, 421; Paul Butel, *Les Négociants bordelais, l'Europe et les îles au XVIIIe siècle* (Paris, 1974), 246, 251. Affrètements royaux were sufficiently favorable to ship owners to stimulate a brief boom in maritime construction during 1781–82; see ibid., graphique 7. The loss rate on royal charters tended to be lower than those on other vessels; cf. Villiers, 352, 365. See also "Convois partis de France," in Villiers, 296, 298, 300, 302, 304, 365–66, for evidence of increasing reliance on royal charters as the war progressed. Rouzeau, "Aperçus du rôle de Nantes," 241, 255.

21. Sabatier fils to Holker, October 9 and 31, 1778, in JHLC; see Schaeper, *France and America,* 160, 294; Jean Meyer, *L'armement Nantais dans la deuxième moitié du XVIIIe siècle* (Paris, 1969), chap. 3 and p. 80, 81–82; Villiers, *Le commerce colonial,* 351–53. On the naval records of Nantes, see Villiers, "La Lutte," 582. For Bordeaux, see Butel, *Négociants bordelais,* graphiques 2 and 3; the archival record here is incomplete for the war years. Both ports suffered equally, to judge from the display "Commerce extérieur; Courbe générale," in Ernest Labrousse et al., *Histoire économique et sociale de la France* (Paris, 1970), 2: 503. However, Nantes trailed Bordeaux as the premier maritime center of France in the mid-eighteenth century, and it lost ground to its southern rival as a consequence of the American Revolutionary War; see Butel, 33–35, and Villiers, 163, 335. This should be borne in mind when making inferences from Nantes's experience.

22. Joshua Johnson to Thos. Johnson, April 21, 1779, in Maryland State Papers, ser. A, MdHR; *DAJA,* 2: 357–58. Nantes suffered the most during early 1779, losing twenty-three of twenty-nine vessels that had cleared from the West Indies in January and

February; see Villiers, *Le commerce colonial,* 299, 352. For Bordeaux, see John Bondfield to Robt. Morris, August 20, 1778, in RMNY. Rates rose to 80 percent out and back, referred to as "round," in the fall of 1778, and to 85 to 90 percent in mid-1779; see Sabatier fils to Holker, October 31, 1778, and July 20, 1779, in JHLC. See also Jon. Williams Jr. to David Waldo, February 20, 1779, and his other American correspondents throughout the year in JnWLB. Insurance to America was also influenced by intelligence about D'Estaing's failure to achieve and maintain superiority in North American waters and by his retiring to the West Indies.

23. Sabatier fils to Holker, October 9 and 31, 1778; Sabatier fils to Simeon Deane, February 7, 1779, in JHLC; Basmarein & Raimbaux to Holker, February 9, 1779, and bill of lading, January 25, 1779, for ship *Laclocheterre* and invoice of goods on ship *Le Docteur Franklin,* January 30, both on Basmarein & Raimbaux's account in ibid.; Sabatier fils & Després to Holker, December 7, 1778, and Basmarein & Raimbaux & Co. to Holker, February 9, 1779; de Meulan to Holker, April 10, 1779, in ibid.; Martin, "Commercial Relations," 826; Rouzeau, "Aperçus du rôle de Nantes," 271.

24. The limited convoys were known as *route patrouillée;* see Villiers, "La Lutte," 574. For the evolution of convois obligatoire, see Matt. Ridley to Geo. Digges and to Wm. Carmichael, October 31, 1778, in MRLB, vol. 2; Jonathan R. Dull, *The French Navy and American Independence: A Study in Arms and Diplomacy, 1774–1787* (Princeton, N.J., 1975), 122; Villiers, *Le commerce colonial,* 297, 575–77. They were obligatory only in the sense that vessels seized without a convoy were not entitled to benefit from insurance; ibid., 577. On early convoy losses, see Joshua Johnson to Thos. Johnson, April 21, 1779, in Maryland State Papers, ser. A, MdHR; Villiers, 298, 299. On requests for convoys, see Alexander Griffon to Holker, August ?, 1778, in JHLC; James, *British Navy,* 143. Americans asked for escorts to North America (see Rouzeau, "Aperçus du rôle de Nantes," 262) but usually were denied. There were exceptions, particularly after a French expeditionary force took station on the continent.

25. For the interception of the British fleet in 1780, Eduard Chevalier, *Histoire de la Marine française pendant le guerre de l'indépendance Américaine . . .* (Paris, 1877), 203. The event drew jubilant comment from Jon. Williams Jr. to his American correspondents; see his letters to Robt. Morris, September 3, 1780, and to Nath. Appleton, September 5, in JnWLB. The exact numbers seized are in dispute; see Jon. Williams Jr. to Jos. Wharton, October 17, in ibid. See also Jon. Williams Jr. to Holker, March 9, 1779; ? Biddle to Holker, September 21, 1782, in JHLC; David Syrett, *Shipping and the American War, 1775–83: A Study of British Transport Organization* (London, 1970), 79. For an account of what it was like to be part of a transatlantic convoy, see Logbook of the brig *Fame,* voyage from London to Quebec, February 17–August 21, 1780, in PEM. Villiers, "La Lutte," 581, argues forcefully for the effectiveness of convoys in limiting France's maritime losses in the latter years of the war.

26. Villiers, *Le commerce colonial,* 79ff, stresses eighteenth-century advances in French naval construction. Though naval vessels were more technically advanced than merchant vessels, Villiers argues that by 1780 the principles used in the former had been incorpo-

rated into the latter; see ibid., 86. See also "La Lutte," 582; M. D. Cabarrus to John Holker, May 21, 1779, in JHLC. I have been unable to identify what special technical features the *Souci* possessed, but I assume that if it had not had any its backers would not have invested as heavily as they did in it.

27. Raphael Charlet to Simeon Deane, January 28, 1779, and Simeon Deane to Holker, March 5, in JHLC. Deane did manage to salvage some of the vessel's cargo and sell what remained under water of the burnt hull for £500; Deane's Journal of Transactions re Souci, September 1, in ibid.

28. Sabatier fils to Holker, July 20, October 26, 1779, June 13, 1780, in JHLC; Jon. Williams Jr. to Chevalier Holker, September 26, 1779 (out of order next to letters of November 18) in JnWLB. See also Simeon Deane to Holker, January 23, 1779; Plantor Quemelo Co. to Holker, February 28, 1780; de Montigny de Montplaisir to Holker, July 31, and Bunel to Holker, November 17, 1781, in JHLC; Section 4 of the partnership agreement between Jean Berlié & Co. of Lyon and Terrasson Brothers, July 8, 1782, in TBP.

29. For price multiples, see Lony & Plombard to Holker, September 10, 1778; John Holker to Le Ray de Chaumont, November 24, 1778; Matt. Ridley to Holker, May 4, 1779; De Morel to Holker, July 13, 1780, and La Coste to Holker, July 18, 1780, in JHLC; de Francy to Beaumarchais, August 12, 1778, in *BC,* 4: 193. Consumers were deterred both by the high prices and the expectation that the terms on which they purchased imports would improve with the conclusion of the war. For the difficulties encountered by importers, Jos. de Valnais to John Holker, May ? (at end of the month), 1779; Wm. Turnbull to Holker, June 21, 1781, in JHCL. Many French adventurers preferred to sell their goods themselves, no matter how long it took, to judge from the example of a M. Robert of Amiens; see Lasseray to Holker, March 29, 1780, in ibid.; see also Edward C. Papenfuse, "An Uncertain Connection: Maryland's Trade with France During the American Revolution, 1778–1783," *La révolution américaine et l'europe* (Paris, 1979), 249–50. For the Scottish store system, see David Hancock, "Trade," in Michael Fry, ed., *Scotland and the Americas, 1600 to 1800* (Providence, R.I., 1995), 28. There is evidence of such stores being established by French merchants beginning in 1780; see De Morel to John Holker, August 18, 1780, in JHLC.

30. On the absence of financial instruments, see John Hall to Holker, August 11, 1778; Thos. Walker to Holker, October 10, 1779, in JHLC. De Francy found it advantageous to accept Lafayette's personal orders on France in 1778; see his letter to Beaumarchais, August 14, 1778, in *BC,* 4: 204. On the high price of American staples, see Holker to Le Ray de Chaumont, May 13, 1778, Simeon Deane to Holker, June 4, 1778, and January 23, April 24, 1779, in JHLC. See also EWJ, 1: 5.

31. For a cause célèbre shaped by the language problem, see Robt. Morris to Tim. Matlack et al., June 26, 1779, in Robert Morris Papers, Library of Congress, Washington, D.C.; Papenfuse, "Uncertain Connection," 249.

32. For the consular service's organization after 1780, Abraham P. Nasatir and Gary Elwyn Monell, *French Consuls in the United States . . .* (Washington, D.C., 1967), esp.

332–34. For consular provisions in treaties and conventions, see *TUSA*, 2: 26, 239. Fohlen, "Commercial Failure of France," 103–4, rightly stresses this point and attributes the delay to American sensitivity over possible French interference in domestic affairs.

33. There were rare cases in which Americans were willing, but just as often the French involved were not; see Benezet to Holker, August 13, 1780, in JHLC. Occasionally an aggrieved Frenchman would go to the trouble of securing a *lettre de cachet,* as Sabatier fils did against the Deane brothers over the *Souci;* see Sabatier fils to Holker, February 24, 1780, in ibid. However, it could not be executed in America.

34. For criticism of Deane, see Sabatier fils to Holker, October 26, 1779, and La Coste to Holker, December 6, 1780, in JHLC. De Francy, who was on the spot, was acutely aware of the vulnerability of the Bay ports to enemy raiding; see his letter to Beaumarchais, June 11, 1778, in *BC,* 4: 122. For the Langdon incident, see John Langdon to Silas Deane, May 8, 1778, and Holker to Le Ray de Chaumont, May 13, in JHLC. See also the discussion of the French consul at Baltimore's recommendations between 1781–84, in Papenfuse, "Uncertain Connection," 248–49.

35. Greg. Rouhlac to Holker, May 22, 1779; Sabatier fils to Holker, October 26, 1779, in JHLC; see also Jon. Williams Jr. to Simeon Deane, March 31, 1779, and to Matt. Ridley, to Campbell & Hooper, to John Deas, to Addams & Deane, to Wallace & Davidson, to John Holker, to Shaw & Brown, to John Langdon, and to Jon. Williams Sen., April 1, regarding a small invoice from Europe on Edward Bancroft's account "so that in whatever hands it falls the Bale may be received & taken care of," in JnWLB. Rouzeau, "Aperçus du rôle de Nantes," 272. As often as not, these were American houses.

36. The experience of the *Duchesse de Mortemart* in 1776, which sold its first cargo in Boston for 1.2 million livres but could get only a 16,000 livre return cargo, set the pattern; see Castex, "L'Armateur de La Lafayette," 117. For New England's staples, see Matt. Ridley to John Holker, October 16 and December 6, 1779, in MRLB, vol. 3. John Holker to Le Ray de Chaumont, August 14, 1778; Forsman and Chambas to Holker, and Lony and Plombard to Holker, September 10, 1778; Jos. de Valnais to Holker, April 22, August 19, September 29, 1779; John Bell to Holker, July 29, August 12, September 16, 23, 1779; January 27, 1780, in JHLC; Paul W. Bamford, "France and the American Market in Naval Timber and Masts, 1776–1780," *Journal of Economic History* 12(1952): 23, 25.

37. Tobacco accounted for 80 percent of French imports from the United States in 1778–80 and 93 percent in 1781–83; see Price, *France and the Chesapeake,* 2: 717.

38. Ibid., 2: 681, 683ff. Merchants in France were aware of the unrealistic nature of these contracts; see Jon. Williams Jr. to Jas. Cuming, May 17, 1780, in JnWLB. The farmers-general could still exercise considerable power over the European market; see Jon. Williams Jr. to Ed. Bancroft, May 6, 1780; to Jas. Cuming, May 17 and September 6; to V. & P. French & Nephew, May 29 and August 30; to John Nesbitt & Co., August 6; to Rich. Graham, November 30, in ibid. Another option open to the farmers-general was to buy tobaccos from other parts of the world; see Price, *France and the Chesapeake,* 2: 684–717 passim.

39. See Geo. Salmon to Steph. Steward, July 30, 1778, in W&SLB; Price, *France and the Chesapeake,* 2: 681, 705; Edward C. Papenfuse, "Uncertain Connection," 245.

40. Price, *France and the Chesapeake,* 2: 715, cites a table published in the *Political Magazine* 5(1783): 109, which depicts a 50 percent decline in the production of Virginia tobacco between 1773–74 and 1779–81. Price feels that this estimate is suspect, though. For Maryland, see Jean B. Lee, *The Price of Nationhood . . .* (New York, 1994), 113, 119–20, 152. See also Papenfuse, "Uncertain Connection," 260; Matt. Ridley to Josiah Johnston, October 2 and December 11, 1779, and to Messrs Barker, November 12, in MRLB, vol. 3. Geo. Woolsey to Steph. Tweard, July 30, 1778; to Phil. Moore, December 12, 1778, May 8 and August 7, 1779, in W&SLB. The rise in American tobacco prices surprised Geo. Woolsey; see his letter to Peter Moore, August 8, 1778; temporary declines in the West India market failed to affect American tobacco prices, Geo. Woolsey to Steph. Steward, July 30 and August 13, 1778; to Phil. Moore, August 15; to John Pringle, August 8, all in ibid.

41. For the tobacco ports, see Carville Earle and Ronald Hoffman, "Urban Development in the Eighteenth-Century South," *Perspectives in American History* 10(1976): 21–23; Jacob M. Price, "Economic Function and the Growth of American Port Towns in the Eighteenth Century," in ibid. 8(1974): 164–69. For wartime difficulties in assembling cargoes, see Matt. Ridley to John Holker, April 15, 1780, in MRLB, vol. 3; de Francy to Beaumarchais, June 11, July 22 and 31, 1778, in *BC,* 4: 158, 187–88; Matt. Ridley to Holker, December 6, 1779; April 24, 1782, in JHLC. Fredericksburg, Virginia, recommended itself as a safe place because its fortifications made it relatively invulnerable to attack from the sea; see LaCoste to Holker, July 18, 1780, in JHLC. But safe places could quickly become unsafe; see Ridley to Holker, June 2, 1781, in ibid. The Bay often was unsafe for water transport; see Matt. Ridley to Holker, August 1, 1780, and Wm. Smith to Holker, March 27, 1781, in ibid. Americans were as adversely affected as the French by this characteristic of the trade; see Wm. Pennock to Elias H. Derby, April 23, 1778, in EHDP. Martin, "Commercial Relations," 827fns; see also Castex, "L'Armateur de La Fayette," 119.

42. Matt. Ridley to Chris. Johnston, October 26, 1778, to Mark Pringle, November 14, and to Thos. Johnston, November 14, advised against shipping American commodities to Europe, though largely because he assumed money would rise against commodities. His warnings continued in 1779 (see Ridley to John Dorsey, February 24) and after he had returned to Maryland (Ridley to Messrs V. and P. French, October 2, 1779). In 1780 he was still worried about the profitability of tobacco ventures even after the threat of a currency appreciation had passed; see his letter to Josiah Johnston, March 1 1780, and to Jon. Williams, March 1, all in MRLB, vol. 3. See also Lony et Plombard to Holker, September 10, 1778, in JHLC.

43. John Holker to Le Ray de Chaumont, August 14, 1778, in JHLC. Twenty navigable rivers flowed into the Chesapeake; see EWJ, 2: 20–21. On the risks, see the complaints of Capt. Alex. Griffon to John Holker, August ?, 1778, and Capt. Raph. Charlet to Simeon Deane, January 28, 1779, in JHLC. Congress was aware of this aspect of the Bay from the beginning; see John Adams, Notes on Debates, October 4, 1775, in

LD, 2: 109. American adventurers also regarded it as a potential trap; see Wm. Patterson to Nath. Shaw, August 17, 1778, in N&TSP. The French navy occasionally sent frigates into the Bay, but they usually did not tarry long. The *Fier Roderique* had few peers, but it did not always provide a very effective convoy; see Matt. Ridley to John Holker, November 20, 1779, and to Josiah Johnston, December 14, in MRLB, vol. 3; Wm. Smith to Holker, November 20, 1779, and Cottrin & Frères to Holker, December 31, 1780, in JHLC.

44. Lony et Plombard to Sabatier fils, January 30, 1778, and Sabatier fils to Holker, March 1; Holker to Mons. Dupry, c/o Sabatier fils, September 4, all in JHLC. Basmarein & Raimbaux moved their North American headquarters from Charleston to New Bern, North Carolina, in 1778; see Castex, "L'Armateur de La Fayette," 97. On the navigational attributes of the harbor and the Carolina coastline, see EWJ, 1: 88, 2: 8, 10–17; Norman C. Delaney, "The Outer Banks of North Carolina During the Revolutionary War," *North Carolina Historical Review* 36(1959): 2, 3, 16.

45. See John Holker to Le Ray de Chaumont, August 14, 1778; Lony & Plombard to Holker, September 10, in JHLC. Matt. Ridley to John Holker, October 16, 1779, in MRLB, vol. 3. American owners routinely instructed the captains of their vessels to arrive on the coast in the late winter; see Nath. Shaw to Capt. Wm. Leeds, November 15, 1779, in N&TSP.

46. Sabatier fils to Holker, March 1 and October 9, 1778, in JHLC. Americans often responded in a similar fashion; see Jon. Williams Jr. to Jan Ingenhousz, April 13, 1779, in JnWLB. See also Ed. Bancroft to Holker, March 13, 1780, in JHLC; Jon. Williams Jr. to his father, November 4, 1779; to Ed. Bancroft, December 16, in JnWLB. Joshua Johnson to Thos. Johnson, April 21, 1779, in Maryland State Papers, ser. A, MdHR.

47. John Holker to Le Ray de Chaumont, November 24, 1778, in JHLC. Matt. Ridley to Josiah Johnston, February 22, 1780, and to Jon. Williams, March 1, in MRLB, vol. 3. For the desirability of a safe haven for foreign capital, see Robt. Morris to John Hanson, July 29, 1782, in *PRM*, 4: 63. For Holker's efforts to press for one, see Holker to Le Ray de Chaumont, March 10, 1779, in JHLC. Some American merchants tried remitting Congress's loan office certificates to France; see Nich. Brown to John Cooke, April 7, 1779, in NBCoP. References to loan office certificates also show up in the notorial records of Nantes, according to Rouzeau, "Aperçus du rôle de Nantes," 273.

48. Holker's ill-advised speculation in American loan office certificates is detailed in Holker to Le Ray de Chaumont, August 25, November 15 and 24, 1778, and John Holker Sr.'s affidavit, December 22, 1778, in JHLC. Also Schaeper, *France and America*, 295–302. For the scheme's persistence, see Couteulx & Co. to Holker, November 16, 1779, and unidentified correspondent in Paris (possibly Le Ray de Chaumont) to Holker, April 24, 1780, in JHLC. Holker was still receiving instructions early in 1780 to hold the proceeds of an importing venture in the funds (see Plantor Quemelo Co. to John Holker, March 1, 1780), and the de Meulan family was still hoping for an appreciation (see de Meulan to Holker, April 8, in ibid.). Americans in France claimed to be as surprised as the French by Congress's actions; see Jon. Williams Jr. to John Williams, July 24, 1780, in JnWLB.

49. See Matt. Ridley to John Holker, April 1, 1780; Ed. Bancroft to Holker, August 15, 1780; de Francy to Holker, September 10, 1780, all in JHLC. Jon. Williams Jr. to Joshua Johnson; to James Moylan, July 5, 1780; to Silas Deane, September 19, in JnWLB; Schaeper, *France and America,* 300–301.

50. For comments on the high prices of French goods, see Josiah Williams to Wallace, Johnson, and Muir, September 20, 1780 (?), and Wallace, Johnson, and Muir to Arch. Patson & Co., September 17, 1781, in WJMLB. See also Jon. Williams Jr. to Jas. Bowdoin, May 24, 1779 (out of order after August 15 letters) in JnWLB; Butel, "Le commerce atlantique," 77.

The American war affected the French economy, though not in uniform ways. Thus C.-E. Labrousse, *La Crise de l'économie française à la fin de l'ancien régime et au début de la Révolution* (Paris, 1944), vol. 1, focusing on wine production, stresses the collapse of agricultural prices after 1778. The price decline reduced wine's value in relation to volume and made it more difficult to find a vessel that would take it as freight during the war; see Jon. Williams Jr. to Robt. and Anth. Garvey, March 27, 1780, in JnWLB. But prices of industrial goods, including some specialty textiles used in the American trade, rose; see Williams to Jas. Bowdoin, May 24, 1779, in ibid.; Labrousse et al., *Histoire économique et sociale,* 522–23; *Esquisse du mouvement des prix et des revenues en France au XVIIIe siècle* (Paris, 1933), 2: 322; Françoise Bayard and Philippe Guignet, *L'économie française au XVIe, XVIIe et XVIIIe siècles* (Paris, 1991), 134.

On the quality of French manufactures, see Jon. Williams Jr.'s apology in his letter to Matt. Ridley, December 16, 1779; see also his letters to Thos. Peter, to Hugh Belcher, and to Jas. Mason, February 24, 1780, in JnWLB. Historians have attached considerable weight to the inferiority as well as cost of the goods first dispatched to the United States; see Godechot, "Relations économique," 29, 37, and Papenfuse, "Uncertain Connection," 246. Fohlen, "Commercial Failure of France," 111, accuses French merchants of trying to sell Americans "trash and rubbish."

French capitalists who ventured into the American trade were interested in speedy remittances; see Elkanah Watson to Josiah Hewes, December 14, 1779, to John Holker, December 18, and to Bossenger Foster, December 27, in EWJ, vol. 4. The longest credit that one could procure in the Chesapeake was four months; see Crockett and Harris to Wallace, Johnson, and Muir, August 20, 1781, in WJMLB.

51. See Wm. Turnbull to Holker, July 17, 1780, and June 21, 1781, in JHCL; Matt. Ridley to Holker, January 27, April 21, 1780, and to Jon. Williams, April 23, 1780, in MRLB, vol. 3. De Francy felt that the larger the cargo, the more likely the goods involved would be ill chosen; see his letter to Beaumarchais, July 31, 1778, in BC, 4: 178. See also Papenfuse, "Uncertain Connection," 263; Simeon Deane to Holker, June 4, 1778; Lony et Plombard to Holker, September 10, and Holker to Robt. Morris, October 6, in JHLC; Geo. Benson to Welcome Arnold, May 25, 1779, in AGP. See also EWJ, 1: 80–81, and comments in 3: 152. Lack of familiarity affected the popularity of goods from other foreign sources, such as Sweden; see Chris. Champlin to Hen. Greig, June 18, 1781, in CCLB, vol. 2.

52. Price, *France and the Chesapeake,* 2: 716. Before it became clear that the Franco-

American alliance had failed to make a decisive difference in the naval balance of power, de Francy had argued the virtues of the Chesapeake as a destination; see his letter to Beaumarchais, July 31, 1778, in *BC,* 4: 186. Compare "Etat des Raports faits au Consulate de Pensilvanie par les Capitaines de Navires, Marchandes Français qui ont abordé au Port de Philadelphia et autre endroits dans la Rivière de la Delaware, October 2, 1778-January 1, 1780" and "Etats des Présentations de Congés et Raports faits par les Capitaines des Navires Français qui ont abordé au Port de Philadelphia et autre Endroite dans la Rivière . . . 1780–1781," both in ANAE, BIII 445, with "Arrivée des navires depuis le 20 Avril 1777 jusque au 14 Novembre 1779," (Boston) in BI 209.

53. Five vessels were loading 750 hogsheads at Baltimore during the summer of 1779; Mitchel [Anseline J. Mitchele?] to Holker, September 11, 1779. See also Chevalier d'Annemours to Holker, July 23, 1779, in JHLC. Congress had pledged 3,000 hogsheads to Beaumarchais in January 1779; *JCC,* 13: 70. For the *Fier's* first convoy, see l'intendant du port de Rochefort to Sartine, October 3, 1778, cited in *BC,* 4: 258fn, and Beaumarchais to de Francy, December 6, 1778, in ibid., 284. For reports of increased enemy activity in the region, see Geo. Woolsey to John Pringle, September 12 and 26, 1778, in W&SLB. For Beaumarchais's plans, see Beaumarchais to de Francy, December 6, 1778, in *BC,* 4: 284–86.

54. Matt. Ridley to John Holker, November 20, 1779, in MRLB, vol. 3; James, *British Navy,* 435. For the effects of the winter of 1779–80 on the Bay's navigation, see Matt. Ridley to John Holker, December 29, 1779, January 20 and February 28, 1780; Ridley to Joshua Johnston, February 27, in MRLB, vol. 3. Terrasson Brothers to Holker, January 8, 29, 1780, and Robt. Smith to Holker, February 12, in JHLC. For de Francy's problems with Virginia, see Journal of the House of Delegates, November 24 and December 6, 1779; Journal of the Board of Trade, March 17 and 25, 1780, in *OLGV,* 2: 69, 73, 107, 113. See also Ben. Franklin to Chas. Dumas, June 22, 1780, in PCC, r127, i101, p. 36. For the last convoy, Matt. Ridley to Holker, April 21, 1780, and Boulangé to Holker, May 9, in JHLC; Ben. Franklin to Sam. Huntington, August 9, 1780, in PCC, reel 108, item 82, vol. 1, p. 263ff. Seven of these vessels were American; see Jon. Williams Jr. to Jas. Cuming, August 1, 1780, and to Jas. Ross, August 6, in JnWLB. For the subsequent closing of the Bay, Antoine Terrasson to Barthélemy, April 4, 1781, in TBP; Robert Fallaw and Marion W. Stoer, "The Old Dominion under Fire: The Chesapeake Invasions, 1779–1781," in Ernest M. Eller, ed., *Chesapeake Bay in the American Revolution* (Centreville, N.J., 1981), 453–69.

55. The *Fendant* (74) was detached briefly to the Chesapeake from D'Estaing's squadron after the withdrawal from Savannah and spent the winter of 1779–80 frozen into the James River; see Robt. Smith to Holker, February 12, 1780, in JHLC. For the lading of one of the supply ships, the flute *L'interessant,* see November 7, 1779, memo, n.d. but provenance suggests end of April 1780, and La Luzerne to Capt. Ethécart, July 15, 1780, in ibid. Holker also shipped small parcels of bread and flour to the islands via American vessels at the end of 1779; see list of such vessels at the end of the 1779 correspondence, ibid. There seems to have been some independent traffic in French vessels between the Chesapeake and the islands as well; see Chevalier d'Annemours to Holker, July 23, 1779,

and to De Vaivre, November 28, in ibid. For the force of frigates after Yorktown, see *ACRA,* 1: 65.

56. The Terrassons proposed to buy small, fast sailing vessels of fifty to eighty tons in Chesapeake Bay. They could load such vessels quickly with tobacco and other articles suitable for the island markets. Assuming that the Americans neutralized British privateering in the Bay, they could send these vessels between the islands and the continent in relative safety. The Terrassons envisioned undertaking these ventures in association with their American counterparts. They assumed that the Americans would have plenty of capital available since they were not investing heavily in fortifying strategic points in the Chesapeake. See Terrasson Brothers to Holker, August 19, 1779, in JHLC. For the Terrassons in general, see *PBF,* 26: 454–55; see also Rouzeau, "Aperçus du rôle de Nantes," 246–47. For the comments of others about the advantages of small-scale enterprises to the islands in wartime, see de Morel to Holker, August 28, 1780, in JHLC. De Francy to Beaumarchais, July 22, 1778, in *BC,* 4: 158; Sabatier fils to Holker, July 20, 1779, in ibid.

57. For instance, there were six French entries into Philadelphia and other minor ports on the Delaware between the British evacuation and the end of 1779, compared with eleven into Boston during the same interval, in each case half from the islands, the other half directly from Europe; cf. "Arrivée des navires depuis le 20 Avril 1777 jusque au 14 Novembre 1779," in ANAE, BI 209, fols. 16–17, with "Etat des Raports faits au Consulate de Pensilvanie par les Capitaines de Navires, Marchandes Français qui ont abordé au Port de Philadelphia et autre endroits dans la Rivière de la Delaware, October 2, 1778–January 1, 1780," in ibid., BIII 445. See also Nath. Greene to Jacob Greene, May 8, 1778, in *PNG,* 2: 381. For French anxieties, see John Holker to Le Ray de Chaumont, November 24, 1778, and Jos. de Valnais to Holker, March 16, April 17, April 22, August 19, 1779, in JHLC. Their impressions were confirmed by Wm. Palfrey to Thos. Reed, May 14, 1778, in WPP. Also Jon. Williams Jr. to Jas. Moylan, April 1, 1779, in JnWLB. For the persistence of the pattern, see Jos. de Valnais to Sartine, June 16, 1779, in Nasatir, *French Consuls,* 9; de Valnais to Holker, July 8, in JHLC. For the unusual 1781 convoy, see Jos. de Valnais to John Holker, April 23 and June 7, 10, 21, 1781, in JHLC. This convoy is also mentioned in "Journal en Campagne des Armées de Terre et de Mer, depuis le 22 Mars, 1781 . . . " in Smith Naval Collection, WLCL.

58. Jos. de Valnais to Holker, April 22, 1779; de Fagan et Roseau to Holker, June 19, 1779, and Holker to de Valnais, July 10; Fache Helloer to Holker, March 7, 1781, all in JHLC.

59. For the *Somerset,* see James, *British Navy,* 111. The wreck occurred just as the French fleet was about to depart; see Anne Rowe Cunningham, ed., *Letters and Diary of John Rowe, Boston Merchant . . .* (Boston, 1903), 323; Mansel Alcock to Jas. Alcock, November 8, 1778, in S-AP. For a summary of the difficulties that Massachusetts Bay presented to British naval commanders seeking to blockade it, see Richard Lord Howe to Phil. Stephens, February 20, 1777, in *ND,* 7: 1247; see also Howe to Stephens, June 5, 1777, in *DAR,* 14: 104.

60. See EWJ, 2: 8, 3: 136. William Almy, Log Book of the ship *Three Friends* on a

voyage from Rochefort to Boston, April 7, 1778, in William Almy Log Books, RIHS. See also the reproduction of "[Map of] New England, New York, New Jersey and Pennsylvania," *Atlas Minor,* 2nd ed. (London [1732]), Map 49, in Thomas M. Truxes, *Irish-American Trade, 1660–1783* (Cambridge, 1988), 108. For a discussion of navigational guides to the North American coast during the eighteenth century, see William P. Cumming, "The Colonial Charting of the Massachusetts Coast," *Publications of the Colonial Society of Massachusetts* 52(1980): 67–118. I rely on the underwater descriptions of F. R. Hassler and A. D. Bache that are appended to the 1852 map of the eastern seacoast of the United States, published in the 1880s, in NCSA. See also Richard Henry Dana Jr., *Two Years Before the Mast,* J. H. Kemble, ed. (Los Angeles, 1964), 2: 373.

61. Stephen Girard, residing in Philadelphia, formed a partnership with a M. Baldesqui in the French West Indies during 1780, only to find that his partner was confining the firm's ventures to Massachusetts Bay. Girard dissolved the partnership for that reason; see John B. McMaster, *The Life and Times of Stephen Girard: Mariner and Merchant* (Philadelphia, 1918), 1: 24, 31–33, 37. For efforts to resist the tendency, see Jon. Williams Jr. to John Holker, November 13, 1779, in JnWLB; Holker to Le Ray de Chaumont, August 14, 1778; see also draft of a contract for delivering goods from Europe on the account of Maryland, February 16, 1781, in JHLC. For the movement of the goods overland, see Jos. de Valnais to Holker, September 23, 1779, and Edward Bancroft to Holker, March 13, 1780, in ibid.

62. Neil L. York, "Clandestine Aid and the American Revolutionary War Effort: A Re-examination," *Military Affairs* 44(1979): esp. 29.

63. For the dissolution of the partnership with Poey, see Terrasson Brothers to E. Delabat, August 20, 1780, in TBP. For their involvement with La Luzerne in flour purchasing, see Antoine to Barthélemy Terrasson, April 10, 12, 23, 24, 30, May 14, June 25, 1781, in ibid. For Antoine's European trip via Cuba in 1781–82, see Antoine to Barthélemy, January 7, 13, August 24, 1782, and J. M. Perrin to Terrassons, June 19, 1782, in ibid. For an example of a contract that Antoine negotiated with a French dry goods firm, see the agreement between Terrasson frères and Jean Berlié & Cie. of Lyon, dated July 8, 1782, in ibid.

64. One of the few Franco-American firms to emerge during the war was LaCoste & Bromfield, at Fredericksburg; see LaCoste & Bromfield to Holker, July 18, 1780, in JHLC. The Bromfields were a prominent merchant family from Boston with extensive international connections; see Robert A. East, *Business Enterprise in the American Revolution* (Gloucester, Mass., 1964), 38–39, 60–61. For LaCaze & Mallot, see E. Delabat to Terrasson Brothers, April 18, 1780, in TBP; Mark Pringle to Holker, November 16, 30, 1781, in JHLC. For their ship purchasing, see Pringle to Holker, October 15, 19, 1782; Holker to ?, November 21, 1782, in ibid. LaCaze & Mallot had not begun their American career auspiciously, though; see *BFP,* 30: 88, fn2.

65. Beaumarchais found speculating on the Paris bourse more to his liking; see George V. Taylor, "The Paris Bourse on the Eve of the Revolution, 1718–1789," *American Historical Review* 67 (1961–62): 954; Schaeper, *France and America,* 84, 158, 186, passim; Rouzeau, "Aperçus du rôle de Nantes," 273–75; Villiers, *Le commerce colonial,*

304; and Butel, *Négociants bordelais,* 254–55. See also Godechot, "Les relations économiques," 37; and Meyer, "Les difficultés," 166, 177.

66. McMaster, *Stephen Girard,* chap. 1, recounts the many failed enterprises to which Girard was party during the war. He did better afterward, as a consignee for French merchants sending goods to Philadelphia. Commitment to America was also crucial to the success of Eleuthène Irénée du Pont de Nemours in founding the E. I. DuPont de Nemours Co. in the early nineteenth century; see *DuPont: The Autobiography of an American Enterprise* (New York, 1952), 3–22. For the difficulties experienced by French merchants in the American trade who stayed in France, see Meyer, "Les difficultés," 179ff.

67. For consular assessments of the French merchant community, see Létombe to Castries, October 27, December 9 and 19, 1781, July 18, 1782; Marbois to Castries, December 30, 1781, May 10, 1782, calendared in Nasatir, *French Consuls,* 13, 14, 17, 21, 148; Peter P. Hill, *French Perceptions of the Early American Republic, 1783–1793* (Philadelphia, 1988), 2.

CHAPTER 4. CONTENDING WITH ALBION'S MIGHT

1. *JCC,* 2: 189; John Adams to Jas. Warren, July 23, 1775, in *LD,* 1: 652. For the response to Congress's recommendation, see Louis F. Middlebrook, *History of Maritime Connecticut During the Revolution* (Salem, Mass., 1925), 1: 14–15; John W. Jackson, *The Pennsylvania Navy, 1775–1781: The Defense of the Delaware* (New Brunswick, N.J., 1974), 11, 39–40, 59–60. See also Charles R. Harte, "The River Obstructions of the Revolutionary War," *Annual Report of the Connecticut Society of Civil Engineers, Inc.* 62(1946): 1–53; Alan D. Watson, "The Committees of Safety and the Coming of the American Revolution in North Carolina, 1774–1776," *North Carolina Historical Review* 73(1996): 149. Some ports had taken the first step toward strengthening their defenses well before Congress's recommendation; see Frances M. Caulkins, *History of New London, Connecticut . . .* (New London, 1852), 517–21.

2. See Marine Committee to John Young, May 13, 1777, in *OLMC,* 1: 134.

3. *ND,* 1: 664.

4. Gardner W. Allen, "Massachusetts Privateers of the Revolution," Massachusetts Historical Society, *Collections* 77(1927): 19, mentions the seizure of HMS *Scarborough*'s tender, the schooner *Volante,* in April off Martha's Vineyard, as well as the recapture of two vessels seized in Vineyard Sound in May, before the better known incident at Machias involving the *Margaretta* on June 11. On June 7 the Provincial Congress formed a committee to consider the expediency of constituting a naval force but seemed hesitant to commit itself (see *ND,* 1: 622, 724), though on June 26 it commended the actions of the "brave men" of Machias (*ND,* 1: 759) and in early July offered a commission to any armed boat fitted out by the people there (ibid., 835). For the Machias incident, see Jack Coggins, *Ships and Seamen of the American Revolution* (Harrisburg, Pa., 1969), 13–16. The newly constituted House of Representatives continued to respond to local initiatives throughout the summer rather than take the lead; see *ND,* 1: 1163, 1195, 1212–13, 2: 236. For their decisive commitment to naval defense, see ibid., 2: 371, 450, 495, 503, 519,

620, 3: 291, 734, 1095, 1144. For Connecticut's naval policy, see *ND,* 1: 796. Charles O. Paullin, "The Connecticut Navy of the American Revolution," *New England Magazine* 35(1907): 715–16.

5. Coggins, *Ships and Seamen,* 102–6, gives a sketch of the various state navies. For the particular states, see Jackson, *Pennsylvania Navy,* 10, 11, chap. 2, appendix A; Charles O. Paullin, "The Massachusetts Navy of the American Revolution," *New England Magazine* 35(1906–7): 572; Joseph A. Goldenberg and Marion West Stoer, "The Virginia State Navy," in Ernest M. Eller, ed., *Chesapeake Bay in the American Revolution* (Centreville, Md., 1981), 201–2; Myron J. Smith Jr. and John G. Earle, "The Maryland State Navy," in ibid., 216, 247–60. The Marine Committee of Congress assumed that North Carolina was forming a naval force in 1776 (see Marine Committee to Ezek Hopkins, and to Governor and Council of North Carolina, October 23, 1776, in *OLMC,* 1: 41, 44), but this appears to have been a misunderstanding. North Carolina's program for defending Ocracoke Inlet is discussed in Norman C. Delaney, "The Outer Banks of North Carolina During the Revolutionary War," *North Carolina Historical Review* 36 (1959): 1–16. For Georgia's naval effort, see EWJ, 1: 51. Wm. Livingston made disparaging reference to "Capt. Heyler's gun boats (one of the first rates of New Jersey)" in the Raritan River; see his letter to Lord Stirling (January 11, 1782, in *PWL,* 4: 359), but they appear to have been manned by the local militia for the defense of New Brunswick and not subject to the governor's orders. Robert L. Scheina, "A Matter of Definition: A New Jersey Navy, 1777–1783," *American Neptune* 39(1979): 209–17, argues that the state's naval militia was a navy and lists sixteen vessels used by New Jersey forces during the war. For New England's naval advantage, see Allen, "Massachusetts Privateers," 51–52.

6. After commissioning the construction of two large vessels at the end of the seventeenth century, the Admiralty discouraged the North American colonies from building major warships during the eighteenth century, ostensibly because of the quality of North American oak; see Daniel A. Baugh, *British Naval Administration in the Age of Walpole* (Princeton, N.J., 1965), 257. There were two exceptions; see William M. Fowler, *Rebels Under Sail . . .* (New York, 1976), 9. James A. Knowles, "A Colonial Ship Model H.M.S. 'America' and the Building of the 4th Rate 'America,'" *Nautical Research Journal* 17(1970): 223–30. American shipwrights continued to build smaller vessels for the navy throughout the eighteenth century; see Nathan Miller, *Sea of Glory . . .* (Annapolis, Md., 1974), 205.

7. Jesse Lemisch, "Jack Tar in the Streets: Merchant Seamen in the Politics of Revolutionary America," *William & Mary Quarterly,* 3rd ser. 25(1968): 381–95, emphasizes the threat of impressment more than the legendary pugnacity of the Royal Navy. For the difficulties experienced in manning a naval force, see Richard Buel Jr., *Dear Liberty . . .* (Middletown, Conn., 1980), 35–38, 48. Still, it proved easier to raise men for naval duty earlier in the war than later; see Louis F. Middlebrook, *Exploits of the Connecticut Ship "Defence" . . .* (Hartford, 1922), 22, 26–27. For Congress's approach to the problem, see John Adams's Notes of Debates, October 6, 1775, and Adams to Jas. Warren, October 19, in *LD,* 2: 124, 130–31, 166, 205, 220–22.

8. John Hancock to George Washington, October 5, 1775; John Adams, Notes of

Debates, October 12, 1775, in *ND*, 2: 118–19, 165–66; Miller, *Sea of Glory*, 45–46; William B. Clark, *George Washington's Navy . . .* (Baton Rouge, La., 1960), 46–98. Henry Mowat was reported to be under orders "to destroy every Seaport between that [Falmouth] and Boston"; see Committee of Conference to John Hancock, and Ben. Franklin to Rich. Bache, October 24, 1775, in *LD*, 2: 244, 246. For the effect of the burning of Norfolk, see Sam. Adams to Jas. Warren and Sam. Ward to Nich. Cooke, January 7, 1776, in ibid., 3: 53.

9. Miller, *Sea of Glory*, 39–57; Fowler, *Rebels Under Sail*, 39–60, 248–52; *JCC*, 3: 425–27; John J. McCusker Jr., "The Tonnage of the Continental Ship Alfred," *Pennsylvania Magazine of History and Biography* 90(1966): 231; *ND*, 5: 1018–19. The actual dimensions of the *America* are hard to ascertain since the vessel was repeatedly modified. Jan Glete, *Navies and Nations: Warships, Navies, and State Building in Europe and America, 1500–1860* (Stockholm, 1993), 629, gives the *America*'s tonnage as 2,800. The frigates purchased from France were the *Deane*, the *Queen of France*, and the *Bonhomme Richard;* on the latter, see Samuel E. Morison, *John Paul Jones: A Sailor's Biography* (Boston, 1959), 187. The borrowed frigate was the *Pallas*. For a convenient list of the continental vessels, including the dates they were in commission, see Miller, *Sea of Glory*, 528–29. For the colonists' previous experience with privateering, see Carl Swanson, *Predators and Prizes: American Privateering and Imperial Warfare, 1739–1748* (Columbia, S.C., 1991); James G. Lydon, *Pirates, Privateers, and Profits* (Upper Saddle River, N.J., 1970).

10. Marine Committee to John P. Jones, February 1, 1777, in *OLMC*, 1: 68.

11. On the importance of seasoning, see Baugh, *British Naval Administration*, 242. "Double-decked" refers to the interior construction of a vessel; such a vessel is not the same thing as a "double decker," a warship that carried its guns on two decks. A double-decked vessel could absorb more recoil from its broadside than a single-decked vessel could; see United States Navy Board, Eastern District, to John Cotton, December 3, 1778, in NBED. "Clump" is a generic term referring to vessels of varying rig that were designed to stow the maximum cargo per measured ton at the sacrifice of speed.

12. Marine Committee to Livinius Clarkson and John Dorius, April 26, 1777, in *OLMC*, 1: 115; John J. McCusker, "Sources of Investment Capital in the Colonial Philadelphia Shipping Industry," *Journal of Economic History* 32(1972): 151. For U.S. reliance on foreign supplies for sailcloth, see Middlebrook, *Maritime Connecticut*, 1: 61. McCusker gives the average life of a vessel at 12.5 years (see ibid., 154), presumably for the hull. Sails, spars, and rigging would have to be replaced more frequently. Baugh, *British Naval Administration*, 241, estimates the average life of naval vessels to be fourteen years, perhaps because they were constructed and maintained with more care. For the role of iron in marine construction, see Fowler, *Rebels Under Sail*, 234–38. The Marine Committee thought that it would be easier to arm the *Raleigh* in France than in New England; see their letter to the American Commissioners in France, April 29, 1777, in *OLMC*, 1: 130.

13. Richard G. Stone Jr. refers to the state navies as an "unconscionable drain upon America's slender nautical resources" in "'The *South Carolina* We've Lost': The Bizarre Saga of Alexander Gillon and His Frigate," *American Neptune* 39(1979): 160.

14. See, for instance, Matt. Griswold to Jon. Trumbull, February 25, 1779, in JTP; Goldberg and Stoer, "Virginia State Navy," 180, 186; Smith and Earle, "Maryland State Navy," 214, 225; Middlebrook, *Maritime Connecticut,* 1: 30, 32–33, 84–85; Allen, "Massachusetts Privateers," 45.

15. For a good introductory discussion of the galley, see Spencer C. Tucker, *The Jeffersonian Gunboat Navy* (Columbia, S.C., 1993), 1–3. Howard I. Chapelle, *The History of American Sailing Ships* (New York, 1935), 54, argues that "light draft" was the distinguishing characteristic of a galley. For the unusual uses sometimes made of galleys, see Congress's attempt to requisition some of Maryland's and Virginia's fleets for an expedition against east Florida in the autumn of 1778, Marine Committee to John Barry, November 20, 1778, in *OLMC,* 2: 31. Goldberg and Stoer, "Virginia State Navy," 186, also lists the *Henry* and the *Caswell* galleys as carrying ten guns each, while the *Tempest* carried sixteen; ibid., 194, 199, 202. Jackson, *Pennsylvania Navy,* 14, states that the *Bull Dog* was launched three weeks after the Committee of Safety took responsibility for the defense of the river.

16. For the correlation between the size of a cannon and its range, see Middlebrook, *Maritime Connecticut,* 1: 194; Coggins, *Ships and Seamen,* 152. For galley tactics, see Marine Committee to Isaiah Robinson, April 18, 1777, in *OLMC,* 1: 99.

17. Naval Committee to Ezek Hopkins, January 5, 1776, in *ND,* 3: 638. The Naval Committee, created at the end of 1775, was subsequently absorbed into the Marine Committee.

18. This remained a preoccupation of the Marine Committee; see Robert Morris to John P. Jones, February 1, 1777, in *OLMC,* 1: 69. For Hopkins's achievements, see Miller, *Sea of Glory,* 98–99, 107–11.

19. The story has been most recently retold by Fowler, *Rebels Under Sail,* 97–99. See also Coggins, *Ships and Seamen,* 27–30; and Miller, *Sea of Glory,* 113–19, who stresses Hopkins's incompetence.

20. Wallace withdrew to Halifax, where he arrived on April 18, 1776; see *ND,* 4: 1211–12, and Miller, *Sea of Glory,* 132, 322.

21. In 1777 the committee started instructing captains to take newly commissioned vessels off shore and train their crews before attempting to engage enemy cruisers along the coast; see letters to Nich. Biddle, January 30, 1777, to Chas. Alexander, and to Jas. Nicholson, April 8, 1777, *OLMC,* 1: 63–64, 92, 93. Miller, *Sea of Glory,* 215–16.

22. Miller, *Sea of Glory,* 83, 128–32. For a complete tabulation of the captures, see Clark, *Washington's Navy,* 229–36. Ira D. Gruber, *The Howe Brothers and the American Revolution* (New York, 1972), 201, 291.

23. Clark, *Washington's Navy,* chap. 17; Gruber, *Howe Brothers,* 101–3, 141–42, 157, 201–5, 291–93. The revolutionaries were aware of the Royal Navy's difficulties; see Willing and Morris to Wm. Bingham, October 20, 1776, in WBP. John Hewes to Nich. Brown, November 4, 1776, in NBCoP; see also Marine Committee to Ben. Dunn, April 19, 1777, and to John Young, May 13, in *OLMC,* 1: 104, 134.

24. Jonathan R. Dull, "Was the Continental Navy a Mistake?" *American Neptune* 44(1984): 167–70, concludes that the navy was a bad investment. William S. Dudley and

Michael A. Palmer, "No Mistake About It: A Response to Jonathan R. Dull," ibid. 45(1985): 244–48, argue vigorously to the contrary.

25. The four frigates that were destroyed or captured before they put to sea were the *Congress* and *Montgomery* on the Hudson and the *Effingham* and *Washington* on the Delaware. The four vessels lost in the defense of the Delaware were the frigate *Delaware*, the *Andrew Doria* (12), the *Wasp* (8), and the *Fly* (8). Miller, *Sea of Glory*, 247. The *Hancock* was captured on July 8.

26. Miller, *Sea of Glory*, 302–3. William B. Clark, *Lambert Wickes: Sea Raider and Diplomat . . .* (New Haven, 1932). The two vessels arrived at L'Orient just after the loss of the *Lexington* (16) and the *Reprisal* (16), which had formed the core of Lambert Wickes's commerce-raiding fleet. The *Lexington* was taken by the British cutter *Alert*, and the *Reprisal* foundered at sea.

27. Miller, *Sea of Glory*, 224–27, 236–37; David Ramsay, *The History of South Carolina . . .* (Trenton, N.J., 1785), 2: 82. The Marine Committee had become concerned with the return on the continent's investment by the end of 1777; see their letters to Jas. Nicholson, November 6, 1777, and to the Commissioners of the Navy Board of the Eastern Department, November 12, in *OLMC*, 1: 167, 169.

28. Marine Committee to John Bradford, April 28, 1778, and to Commissioners of the Navy Board of the Eastern Department, May 8, 1778, in *OLMC*, 1: 232, 238–39; Miller, *Sea of Glory*, 316–18.

29. Marine Committee to the Navy Board of the Eastern Department, July 11 and 24, 1778, in *OLMC*, 1: 266–67, 270; Michael J. Crawford, "The Joint Allied Operation at Rhode Island," in William R. Roberts and Jack Sweetman, eds., *New Interpretations in Naval History . . .* (Annapolis, Md., 1991), 236–37, 239.

30. Marine Committee to Commissioners of the Navy Board of the Eastern Department, May 9, 1778, in *OLMC*, 1: 243.

31. Eastern Navy Board to Marine Committee, December 9, 1778, and April 17, 1779, in NBED; Marine Committee to Wm. Smith, Sam. Purviance et al., February 23, 1779, to Eastern Navy Board, April 27, to Sam. Tucker, June 2, to Sam. Nicholson, June 12, in *OLMC*, 2: 48, 67, 81, 86; Miller, *Sea of Glory*, 410–12. The cruises had to some extent been planned, though the plans were substantially modified; see U.S. Navy Board to the Marine Committee, February 20, 1779, in NBED. The *Alliance* also took the smaller frigate *Countess of Scarborough* while the *Bonhomme Richard* battled the *Serapis*. For the successes of American privateers, see tables 5.1, 7.1, and 7.3.

32. Board of Admiralty to Ben. Franklin, March 28, 1780, in *OLMC*, 2: 174; Charles O. Paullin, *History of Naval Administration* (Annapolis, Md., 1968), 27.

33. Those captured were the *Boston* and the *Providence*. The *Queen of France* was sunk. The Marine Committee had resolved to retire her as a fighting ship; see Marine Committee to Abra. Whipple and to Ben. Lincoln, February 22, 1780, in *OLMC*, 2: 159, 162.

34. For the *Confederacy*'s dismasting, see Board of Admiralty to John Langdon, February 15, 1780, and to Sam. Curson and Isaac Gouverneur, March 4, *OLMC*, 2: 158, 165; James L. Howard, *Seth Harding, Mariner . . .* (New Haven, Conn., 1930), 105–16. In April 1781, when two British frigates intercepted the *Confederacy* after it had become

separated from the *Deane* and the *Saratoga* in a storm, it surrendered to the superior force without a fight; see ibid., 144–46. For the *Trumbull*, see Miller, *Sea of Glory*, 424–25, 476.

35. Jackson, *Pennsylvania Navy*, 53–57.

36. The galleys were condemned for failing to dislodge the frigate HMS *Vigilant* in the final battle over Fort Mifflin, but Jackson argues that the criticism is unfair; see Jackson, *Pennsylvania Navy*, 259–69; also ibid., 271–74, 292.

37. Marine Committee to John Whereat, June 24, 1778, in *OLMC*, 1: 263; Goldberg and Stoer, "Virginia State Navy," 187–88, 189–96, 201–2; Smith and Earle, "Maryland State Navy," 233–34. Maryland built a shallow-draft naval force at the end of the war, concentrating on barges rather than galleys because its loyalist refugee adversaries were using such vessels. But when it came to a showdown off the eastern shore on November 30, 1782, the refugees emerged triumphant in the so-called Battle of the Barges; ibid., 243–44. A barge was akin to a galley but distinguished by a square stern; see Chapelle, *American Sailing Ships*, 54. It also tended to be of shallower draft and was less reliant on sails.

38. See the list of prizes taken by *Freedom, Republic, Tyranicide,* and *Massachusetts* in 1777, in Maritime Miscellany, vol. 157, in MAC. See also the account of various vessels sailing under Connecticut commissions in Middlebrook, *Maritime Connecticut*, 1: 28ff. For the losses at Penobscot, see *Connecticut Gazette,* August 9, 1780; *Independent Chronicle,* August 10, 1780; Miller, *Sea of Glory*, 413; Coggins, *Ships and Seamen,* 168. The *Protector* alone escaped, Coggins, 104. For states abandoning their navies, see Middlebrook, *Maritime Connecticut*, 1: 23–160; Jackson, *Pennsylvania Navy*, particularly chap. 15; Miller, *Sea of Glory*, 247.

39. For South Carolina, see Miller, *Sea of Glory*, 421; Coggins, *Ships and Seamen,* 102. The *South Carolina* carried twenty-eight 42-pound cannon, of larger caliber than the armament customary on a seventy-four-gun line-of-battle ship, in addition to ten 12-pounders and 450 men, making it far stronger than any frigate in the British service; see D. D. Huger Smith, "Commodore Alexander Gillon and the Frigate South Carolina," *South Carolina Historical and Genealogical Magazine* 9(1908): 211, 216, and Ramsay, *South Carolina,* 2: 73. Tonnage estimates vary; see *PRM*, 6: 103, fn32, whose figure corresponds to the ship's measurements. See also Glete, *Navies and Nations,* 284, who describes the *South Carolina* as a "super frigate" of 2,200 tons. The charter agreement for the vessel gave the owner one-quarter share in all captures; see Edward McCrady, *The History of South Carolina in the Revolution* (New York, 1901), 217–19; Stone, " 'The *South Carolina* We've Lost,' " 168–70, and Ramsay, *History,* 2: 72–75. For Virginia, see Goldberg and Stoer, "Virginia State Navy," 194–97; see also Paul Loyall, Thos. Brown, and Thos. Newton Jr. to Ben. Harrison, March 12, 1783, in *CVSP*, 3: 456.

40. Though rated for forty-four guns, the *Serapis* actually carried fifty—forty heavy cannon and ten lighter ones; the *Bonhomme Richard* had only forty guns, though it was rated for forty-two. The *Serapis* could throw 330 pounds of metal at an adversary per broadside; the *Bonhomme Richard* could throw 249 pounds. Miller, *Sea of Glory*, 372, 378–86; Fowler, *Rebels Under Sail,* 166–68. For its place in national folklore, see Walt Whitman, "Song of Myself," in *Leaves of Grass,* lines 897–944. John Paul Jones attracted

attention during the summer and autumn of 1776 for his solo cruises in the sloop *Providence* and the ship *Alfred,* which netted a rich haul of prizes, including the *Mellish,* which was loaded with uniforms for the British army. Miller, *Sea of Glory,* 128–32, 284–90, 291–92, 297–301; Clark, *Lambert Wickes,* chap. 8; William B. Clark, *Gallant John Barry* (New York, 1938), 139–53, 273–75; *PRM,* 6: 625.

42. Navy Board to Jere. Powell, December 7, 1778, and to the Marine Committee, December 9, 1778, January 6 and March 24, 1779, in NBED. See Swanson, *Predators and Prizes,* 218–19, for estimates of just how profitable privateering could be for individuals. Richard H. McKey Jr., "Elias H. Derby and the American Revolution," *Essex Institute Historical Collections* 97(1961): 177–78; undated "Discourse on Free Trade Between Nations," in Cushing-Orne Papers, MHS, for the nonmonetary advantages that privateersmen enjoyed. For examples of the sale of shares prior to a cruise, see EHDP.

43. Robt. Morris to John P. Jones, February 1, 1777, in *OLMC,* 1: 70; Octavius Howe, "Beverly Privateers in the American Revolution," Colonial Society of Massachusetts, *Transactions* 24(1924): 352, 378; Ralph D. Paine, *The Ships and Sailors of Old Salem* (Chicago, 1912), 81. On French deserters, see John Holker to Jos. Reed, June 21, 1780, in *PA,* 1st ser., 8: 347; Instructions to Colonel Nicola, July 18, 1780, in ibid., 422. See also Holker to Sartine, April 15, 1780, and Marbois to Castries, July 15, 1781, in Abraham P. Nasatir and Gary E. Monell, *French Consuls in the United States . . .* (Washington, D.C., 1967), 144.

44. Roland G. Usher, "Royal Navy Impressment During the American Revolution," *Mississippi Valley Historical Review* 37(1951): 685–88; Board of Admiralty to Jas. Nicholson, and to Chas. Miller, September 2, 1780, in *OLMC,* 2: 255–56. Congress declined to press for vesting its captains with greater authority; see Howard, *Seth Harding,* 100–4. For strategies pursued by state and continental authorities, see Miller, *Sea of Glory,* 228, 236. The *Randolph* had a complement of British POWs who threatened to mutiny (ibid., 221, 224), but that didn't stop J. P. Jones from making use of them on the *Bonhomme Richard* (ibid., 372). Barry also had troublesome British prisoners aboard the *Alliance* in 1781; see ibid., 458, 473–74. On occasion the navy accepted from the Continental Army soldiers who had been sentenced to death by court martial; see ibid., 409.

45. Board of Admiralty to John Langdon, December 28, 1779, April 14 and June 16, 1780; to Nath. Shaw, May 22, 1780; to Commissioners of the Navy Board of the Eastern Department, April 18 and July 7, in *OLMC,* 2: 144, 185, 187, 199, 210, 221. In the Boston area the price of vessels was as low proportionately as the price of other goods; see Matt. Ridley to John Holker, January 4, 1780, in MRLB, vol. 3. The *General Washington* had formerly been the *General Monk* (20) which was taken by the *Hyder Ally* in 1782. The story is best told by Hulbert Footner, *Sailor of Fortune: Life and Adventures of Commodore Barney USN* (New York, 1940), 102–16.

46. Fowler, *Rebels Under Sail,* 254; also Kenneth J. Hagan, *This People's Navy: The Making of American Seapower* (New York, 1991), 18. The *Deane* was one of the few ships in the navy that attracted deserters from privateers; see Paschal N. Smith to Sam. Nicholson, January 1, 1779, in S&SLB. Chapelle vigorously challenges the idea that French naval vessels were superior to British ones at this time; see *American Sailing Ships,* 78–85.

47. Fowler, *Rebels Under Sail*, 252.

48. R. J. B. Knight, "The Introduction of Copper Sheathing into the Royal Navy," *Mariner's Mirror* 59(1973): 301, 303. Coppering discouraged barnacles, enhancing a ship's speed and reducing the frequency with which vessels had to be cleaned by careening; see Fowler, *Rebels Under Sail*, 253–54; Coggins, *Ships and Seamen*, 48–49; Baugh, *British Naval Administration*, 343–45. There seems to have been some attempt to import copper toward the end of the war; see Robt. Morris to Sam. Huntington, June 22, 1781, and to Franklin, November 27; Diary, November 29, all in *PRM*, 1: 164; 3: 292, 300.

49. Miller, *Sea of Glory*, 372, 379. For the armament of British warships of the period by class, see Glete, *Navies and Nations*, 778, fig. 23:17. Board of Admiralty to Commissioners of the Navy Board of the Eastern Department, September 5, 1780, in *OLMC*, 2: 262. The *Confederacy* had earlier been authorized to try to get heavy cannon in Europe (see Marine Committee to Seth Harding, September 17, 1779, in ibid., 111) but was dismasted in mid-crossing (Howard, *Seth Harding*, 105–6). In gross numbers the Royal Navy had at its disposal in North American waters almost eight times the guns mounted by the Continental Navy; see Robert W. Love Jr., *History of the U.S. Navy* (Harrisburg, Pa., 1992), 22.

50. For the Marine Committee's initial ambitions, see their letter to Ezek Hopkins, August 22, 1776, in Harbeck Collection, HL. What they settled for was considerably less; see U.S. Navy Board to the Marine Committee, October 28 and December 9, 1778, February 26, 1779, in NBED. See also Marine Committee to Joseph Olney, February 10, 1779, in *OLMC*, 2: 42.

51. The only support that the Continental Navy provided to the French, aside from loans of naval stores for their 1778 refit in Boston, was to scout for the occasional small supply convoy attempting to clear the coast and to hold British naval prisoners; see U.S. Navy Board to the Marine Committee, December 9, 1778, in NBED. The Marine Committee sometimes appealed to others to provide a scout; see their letter to the President and Council of Pennsylvania, November 7, 1778, in *OLMC*, 2: 25. American naval vessels do not figure in any accounts of how the French established naval superiority in the Chesapeake during the autumn of 1781; see Miller, *Sea of Glory*, 480ff; Arthur T. Mahan, *The Influence of Sea Power upon History, 1660–1783*, 12th ed. (Boston, 1918), 388–93; James, *British Navy in Adversity*, 288–97.

52. In all, the British took six continental frigates into their service, acquiring the *Providence* and the *Boston* with the surrender of Charleston. The Royal Navy refused only the *Trumbull;* see Miller, *Sea of Glory*, 229–30.

53. Miller, *Sea of Glory*, 269–71, 273–74; Paine, *Ships and Sailors of Old Salem*, chap. 5; Martin Brimmer to Wm. Palfrey, August 21, 1780, in WPP. See also reference to the capture by two privateers of six provision vessels and one sloop of war in transit between New York and Penobscot at the end of 1779, in Jon. Williams Jr. to V. & P. French, February 29, 1780, JnWLB.

54. Summarized in Middlebrook, *Maritime Connecticut*, 2: 5. Lloyds also reported the capture of 215 (net) enemy privateers to (75) net British privateers. William B. Clark,

Ben Franklin's Privateers . . . (Baton Rouge, 1956), 40, suggests that Britain may have ruled European seas more tightly than it did American ones.

55. Goldberg and Stoer, "Virginia State Navy," 181; Smith and Earle, "Maryland State Navy," 206; Fowler, *Rebels Under Sail,* 93; Coggins, *Ships and Seamen,* 99–106.

56. *Acts and Resolves, Public and Private, of the Province of Massachusetts Bay* . . . (Boston, 1869–72), 19: 713–14. See also Maritime Miscellany, in MAC, 157: 1, 8, 17, 27, 31; Maritime Correspondence, in MAC, 292: 8, 26, 40, 49, 55, 60, 62, 69, 118, 129. Jon. Jackson to Thos. and Isaac Wharton, December 17, 1776, to Hen. Crouch, February 7, 1777, in JJLB. The same pattern was observable in Maryland; see Edward C. Papenfuse, *In Pursuit of Profit* . . . (Baltimore, 1975), 93. See also Charles C. Crittenden, *The Commerce of North Carolina, 1763–1789* (New Haven, 1936), 149–50; Robt. Morris to Jas. Duff, February 20, 1774, and to John Bondfield, October 10, 1777, in RMNY; Clarence L. Ver Steeg, *Robert Morris, Revolutionary Financier* (Philadelphia, 1954), 10–12.

57. See Stanley F. Chyet, *Lopez of Newport: Colonial American Merchant Prince* (Detroit, 1970), 158; John White to Meletiah Bourn, July 29, 1775, in MBL; Nich. Brown to Josiah Hewes, February 19, 1777, in NBCoP; Thomas Doerflinger, *A Vigorous Spirit of Enterprise* (Chapel Hill, 1986), chap. 3, passim and 197–99. Elizabeth M. Nuxoll, *Congress and the Munitions Merchants: The Secret Committee of Trade During the American Revolution, 1775–1777* (New York, 1985), chap. 4.

58. The most important marine insurance archive in eighteenth-century America is the Ezekiel Price Marine Insurance Records at BA. Price kept an insurance office in Boston between 1759 and 1781, and what appears to be a complete record of the policies posted at his office are contained in twelve bound volumes, three of which, vols. 17–19, pertain to the revolutionary period. On the back of many of the policies involving losses are accounts that show how claims were settled. There is also a small, less coherent body of Price insurance papers in the possession of the MHS. For the mechanics of making insurance, see also Jon. Williams Jr. correspondence—for example, his letters to Jos. Cordis, March 20, 25, and April 17, 1779, in JnWLB; see also Harrold E. Gillingham, *Marine Insurance in Philadelphia, 1721–1800* (Philadelphia, 1933), 31ff.

59. On the availability of insurance, see Jon. Williams Jr. to Duncan Ingraham, December 11, 1780, in JnWLB. Both Philadelphia and Boston experienced difficulty in providing insurance immediately after the British evacuations; see John Holker to Le Ray de Chaumont, August 14, 1778, in JHLC; Meletiah Bourn to Sam. Hinkley, December 10, 1776, in MBP; Robt. Morris to Ralph Forster, August 8, 1783, in *PRM,* 8: 406. On the other pitfalls of insurance, see Nich. Brown to Seth Barton, March 24, 1783, in NBCoP; Crowhurst, *Defense of British Trade,* 102. Insurers were wary of risks already covered by another policy (see notation on policy 2565, PMIR, vol. 17). See also Ramsay, *South Carolina,* 2: 75; Edward C. Papenfuse, "An Uncertain Connection: Maryland's Trade with France During the American Revolution," in *La révolution américaine et l'europe* (Paris, 1979), 248. For an example of an underwriter unable to honor his commitment, see Wm. Vans to Thos. Fayerweather, May 10, 1786, in Thomas Fayerweather Papers, NEHGS.

60. John Nesbitt to Wallace, Johnson, and Muir, April 8 and 10, 1781, and William Grahame to Wallace, Johnson, and Muir, July 23, in WJMLB; M. M. Hays to Welcome Arnold, June 3, 1782, in AGP. By the late eighteenth century, insurance between North America and Europe during peacetime had come down to 5 percent "round" (2.5 percent one way); see "Discourse on Free Trade Between Nations," n.d., in Cushing-Orne Papers, MHS. For armed vessels under threat of war, it ran about the same; see Manifest of the vessels *Le Dupré* and *Le Comte de Binulle,* June 21, 1777, in JHLC. During the war, rates rose to about 50 percent round and often reached 70–80 percent; see John Gray to Meletiah Bourn, September 5, 1777, in MBL. The highest rate recorded in policies posted by Ezekiel Price during the war was 80 percent round to the islands. But one-way insurance to and from the islands during the latter part of 1778 through 1779 routinely involved premiums of 50 percent; see PMIR, vol. 19. See also insurance policies in favor of Spooner and Davis, April 15 and 29, June 30, August 12, October 28, 1779, in Spooner Papers, Pilgrim Hall, Plymouth, Mass.

61. See Chris. Champlin to Geo. Hayley, November 12, 1774, in CCLB; Geo. Woolsey to Wm. Snell, December 8, 1774, in W&SLB. Cf. wartime policies on brig *Argo* from Cap François to Boston, September 5, 1778, in PMIR, vol. 19, with the declaration of Wm. Heyliger of Saint Eustatius, August 6, in Price Notarial Records, vol. 6, in BA. Underwriters often gave a return of 10 to 20 percent on the premium if the vessel was under convoy; see Paschal N. Smith to John Ramsay, July 23, 1779, in S&SLB. For wartime strategies in procuring insurance, see Elkanah Watson to Coussul, December 1 and 12, 1779, and to Nich. Brown, December 15, in EWJ, vol. 4; Jon. Williams Jr. to V. & P. French & Nephew, June 4, 1780, in JnWLB. Also cf. Matt. Ridley to Ribaud et LeVieux, May 4, and to Smith and Johnston Co., May 7, 1782, in MRLB, vol. 5; Wallace, Johnson, and Muir to John Nesbitt, April 8, 1781; and to Peter Whitesides, August 20, 1781, in WJMLB. John Welsh to Jacob Welsh, June 19, 1782, in JWLB; see also Franklin S. Coyle, "Welcome Arnold (1745–1798) Providence Merchant: The Founding of an Enterprise" (Ph.D. diss., Brown University, 1972), 125; Geo. Woolsey to John Pringle, December 26, 1778, and January 3, 1779, in W&SLB.

62. For the discriminatory practices of European underwriters, see Jon. Williams Jr. to Herman & Lewis, June 8, 1780, and to Jas. Cuming, August 3, in JnWLB; Wallace, Johnson, and Muir to James Grubb, June 3, 1781, to John Nesbitt, June 12 and 21, and to Arch. Buchanan, August 30, in WJMLB. For other difficulties, see Nath. Shaw to John W. Stanley, October 24, 1778, to Rouse and Helme, September 23, 1781, and Helme to Shaw, January 27, 1782, in N&TSP. Some claims took years to settle; see Paschal N. Smith to Dan. Phoenix, August 28, 1780, in S&SLB. See also the typescript of Thomas Rideout's Reminiscences, written in 1786, p. 24, in Brooks Papers, MdHS.

63. Shares of one-sixteenth appear to have been most common; see Paschal N. Smith to Jas. James, April 16, and to Isaac Sears, July 18, 1778, in S&SLB. A one-sixty-fourth share is mentioned in Peter Vandervoort to Nath. Shaw, March 27, 1778, in N&TSP. The high cost of insurance led merchants to cover only part of their risks; see Elkanah Watson to Nich. Brown, October 1, 1779, in EWJ, vol. 4. Occasionally a policy would note how much of the cargo and vessel was being covered; see the policy posted for the

ship *Marlborough,* June 17, 1779, in PMIR, vol. 19. Minority involvement in a voyage meant forfeiture of control (see Chris. Leffingwell to Cushing and White, January 1, 1779, in CLLB), but one ignored one's fellow investors at one's peril (Paschal N. Smith to Alex. Kennedy, June 12, 1777, in S&SLB); see also Chris. Leffingwell to John McCurdy, October 20, 1778, in CLLB.

64. Geo. Woolsey to Hugh Young, September 24, 1778, in W&SLB; Anth. L. Bleeker to Hercules D. Bize, December 27, 1777, in ALBLB; Elkanah Watson to Jon. Williams, January 1, 1780, and to John de Neufville, June 12, in EWJ, vol. 4; Paschal N. Smith to Messrs Daniel Commelin and Sons, October 21, 1778, in S&SLB. See also Jon. Williams Jr. to Jas. Carson, October 21, 1780, to Jon. Williams Sen., November 24, to Solomon Meyers Cohen, December 23, and to Jas. Cuming, December 28, in JnWLB; Welcome Arnold to Seth Russell, June 15, 1779, in AGP; Elias H. Derby's instructions to Captain Wm. Williams, January 28, 1778, in EHDP; And. Cabot to Jos. Gardoqui and Sons, May 3, 1777, in CP.

65. Brenton, Shattuck, and Jarvis to Elias H. Derby, January 15, 1783, in EHDP; quote from Matt. Ridley to Wm. Turnbull, January 16, 1780, MRLB, vol. 3. See also Ridley to Jean N. Ribaud, April 15, 1782, in MRLB, vol. 5; Elias H. Derby to Capt. Wm. Williams, January 28, 1778, in EHDP.

66. See log of the schooner *Scorpion,* March 23, 1778, and Journal of William Drame(?) on board the privateer *Belisarius* from April 28, 1781–July 26, 1781, pp. 29, 66, both in PEM; quote from Robt. Morris to Wm. Bingham, October 20, 1776, in WBP; Miller, *Sea of Glory,* 235.

67. Jon. Jackson to Robt. Jenkins, April 15, 1775, and to Thomas and Isaac Wharton, May 27, 1775, in JJLB; Chris. Champlin to Robt. Champlin, February 20 and May 4, 1775, to Messrs Murray & Wright, March 8, in CCLB; Chris. Champlin to ?, May 31, 1775, in Christopher Champlin Letters, Newport Historical Society, Newport, R.I.; Josiah Hewes to Wm. Vernon, September 21, 1776, in S&WVP. However, New Englanders experienced difficulties in disposing of unsuitable vessels; see Meletiah Bourn to John White, August 24, 1775, in MBL; Paschal N. Smith to Wm. Smith, August 2, 1775, and to Thos. Sanders, March 15 and March 30, 1776, in S&SLB; Ben. Goodhue to Captain R. Cook, May 11, 1777, in Goodhue Family Papers, PEM. Downsizing continued well beyond 1777, though; see Ben. Goodhue to Jos. Gardoqui, May 11, 1777, in EHDP. For cannibalizing, see Josiah Hewes to Wm. Vernon, April 19, 1776, in S&WVP; Barnabas Deane to Nath. Shaw, September 30, 1776, and Tim. Parker to Shaw, September 14, 1778, in N&TSP. U.S. Navy Board to Daniel Tillinghast, November 16, 1778, in NBED.

68. Cf. Chaloner and White to Gouv. Morris, July ?, 1779, in C&WLB, with entries for 1774 and 1776, in Levi Hollingsworth's Flour Inspection Book, 1774–77, no. 493, in HFP.

69. For the characteristics of Bermuda and Virginia sloops and schooners, see Howard I. Chapelle, *The Baltimore Clipper: Its Origin and Development* (Salem, Mass., 1930), chaps. 1–2. Also see McCusker, "Tonnage of Ships Engaged in British Colonial Trade," 77; Matt. Ridley to Joshua Johnston, October 2, 1779, and to Jon. Williams, June 9, 1780, in MRLB, vol. 3.

70. Mansel Alcock to Jas. Alcock, March 13, 1779, in S-AP. Though Massachusetts had enjoyed an advantage in divesting itself of clumps, that was to some extent neutralized by the disproportionate number of clumps seized by its privateers.

71. See John Nesbit to Wallace, Johnson, and Muir, April 8 and 10, 1781, in WJMLB.

72. For instance, the Cabots and Elias H. Derby; see Howe, "Beverly Privateers," 421–22, and McKey, "Elias Hasket Derby and the American Revolution," 167. Complaining about the war's newly rich was common; see U.S. Navy Board to the Marine Committee, February 26, 1779, in NBED.

73. The competitive advantage enjoyed by privateers for manpower is canvassed in the undated manuscript "Discourse on Free Trade Between Nations," in Cushing-Orne Papers, MHS.

74. Chris. Leffingwell to John Kirkland, Comfort Sage, John Foster, John Gellston et al., October 12, 1778, in CLLB; Elias H. Derby to Wm. Lamperell, February 9, 1779, in EHDP. Crews would sign on for what looked like a profitable voyage, even if it took them to a remote location, Jonathan(?) Glover to Massachusetts Board of War, February 25, 1778, in Board of War Letters, vol. 153, in MAC.

75. Marcus B. Rediker, *Between the Devil and the Deep Blue Sea* . . . (New York, 1987); Luther Little's career as recounted in Paine, *The Ships and Sailors of Old Salem,* chap. 6, is an exception to the general rule. Lemisch, "Jack Tar in the Streets," 101–4. For the increased risks associated with winter passages, see Matt. Ridley to John Holker, October 16, 1779, and to Joshua Johnston, December 11, in MRLB, vol. 3.

76. For the initial lucrativeness of privateering, see Mansel Alcock to Jas. Alcock, November 13, 1775, December 21, 1776, in S-AP. For references to its declining profitability, see Chris. Leffingwell to Cushing and White, February 28, 1779, in CLLB; John Kneeland to Sam. Abbot, March 14, August 8, and October 26, 1780, in Samuel Abbot Papers, BLHU; Paschal N. Smith to Jere. Platt, January 30, 1777, to John Grenell, March 2, 1778, to Thomas Hazard, October 8, 1778, and to Thaddeus Burr, November 5, 1778, and to John Grenell, January 14 and March 12, 1779, in S&SLB. Cf. Swanson, *Predators and Prizes,* 132–34. For privateering's persistence, see Jos. de Valnais to Holker, April 22, 1779, in JHLC; Howe, "Beverly Privateers," 407, 412–13.

77. For an example of some of the difficulties that could crop up, see Wm. & G. Hutchinson to Massachusetts Board of War, January 31 and March 23, 1778, in Board of War Letters, vol. 153, in MAC; see also Jon. Williams Jr.'s problems settling the accounts of the prize *Isabella,* taken by the *Mifflin* and brought into L'Orient, in his letters to Gourelade & Moylan, December 23, 1779, to Phil. Moore, January 20, December 3, 1780, to Thos. Greenleaf, May 10, JnWLB. Captains were instructed to send wood prizes on to the islands despite the problems associated with settling accounts in distant ports; see Elias H. Derby to Nich. Lamperell, November ?, 1779, in EHDP. Jon. Jackson to Thos. and Isaac Wharton, September 24, 1776, and to Jos. Gardoqui and Co., November 26, 1776, in JJLB. See also J. W. Cheekly to John Reed, March 9, 1779, in R&FP; Levi Hollingsworth to Wm. Stewart, December 2, 1782, in LHLB; Mansel Alcock to Jas. Alcock, November 8, 1778, March 13, 1779, in S-AP.

78. John Nesbit to Wallace, Johnson, and Muir, April 8 and 10, 1781, in WJMLB.

Some insurance policies in PMIR stipulated that the value of any prizes made by a letter of marque vessel would be deducted from the sums for which the underwriters were responsible in case of subsequent loss; see the policy on the ship *Marlborough,* May 31, 1779, which was subscribed at a premium 20 percent less than that posted for the brigantine *Janney,* June 1, 1779, in vol. 19. Howe, "Beverly Privateers," 353, 366. Under the ship's articles for the letter of marque schooner *Hawk,* the crew got 50 percent of the prizes taken after deducting charges, but no privileges with respect to the cargo; February 7, 1778, in Waite Papers, PEM.

79. In the period from June–November 8, 1777, the Council issued forty-one commissions to privateers and only eight to letters of marque. From November 12–July 14, 1778, it issued eighty commissions to privateers and only thirteen to letters of marque. But between July 18, 1778, and February 23, 1779, it issued sixty to privateers and thirty-one to letters of marque. Between March 2, 1779, and October 29, it issued seventy-seven commissions to privateers and eighty-one to letters of marque. Between November 1, 1779, and April 3, 1780, only fifteen privateers applied for commissions, compared with forty-three applications for letters of marque. From Massachusetts Council Papers, vols. 167–71, in MAC. Rhode Island's Maritime Records, on the other hand, do not make this distinction, listing all commissions as letters of marque.

80. Paschal N. Smith to John Nelson, October 19, 1780, in S&SLB; Elkanah Watson to Samuel White, January 7, 1780, in EWJ, vol. 4; Matt. Ridley to Thos. Johnson, November 14, 1778, and to de Francy, December 16, 1779, in MRLB, vols. 2 and 3.

81. Joshua Johnson to Hammon and Hudson, June 21, 1781, in WJMLB; Jon. Williams Jr. to Jos. Arden, May 8, 1779, to John Ross, May 26, and circular to John Hall, Shaw & Broom, Robt. Morris, Smith, Hovey & Southel, Jon. Williams Sr., and Tracy & Tracy, June 5, in JnWLB. For rates, see Jon. Williams Jr. to Jas. Williams, February 26, 1779, to Thos. Cushing(?), March 1, and to Jon. Williams Sr., March 8, in ibid. See Phripp & Bowdoin to Jas. Hunter Jr., September 3, 1778, Jas. Swan to Hunter, November 4, 1778, David Stodder to Hunter, October 13, 1779, in H-GP. For the factors influencing them, Cumberland Dugan to Caleb Davis, October 31, 1778, in Caleb Davis Papers, vol. 9B, MHS; Giles Alexander to Massachusetts Board of War, March 27, 1779, in Maritime Miscellany, vol. 157, in MAC; Steph. Collins to Thos. Jenkins, November 19, 1781, to Wm. Gray, November 5 and 20, to Jas. Seagrave, November 29 and December 4, in SCLB.

82. For peacetime primage rates, see undated essay "Free Trade Between Nations," in Cushing-Orne Papers, MHS. For primage in wartime, see Jon. Williams Jr. to John Bondfield, March 31, 1779, in JnWLB.

83. Jon. Williams Jr. to David Sears, May 8, 1779, to Jos. Arden, May 8, in JnWLB; Codman and Smith to Jos. Gardoqui and Co., July 15 and September 6, 1780, in CSLB. See also Levi Hollingsworth to Jacob Green, February 4, 1782, in LHLB; contract between Terrasson frères and Jean Berlié Cie., July 8, 1782, in TBP. Cf. Todd Cooper, "Baltimore Merchants," in Eller, ed. *Chesapeake Bay in the American Revolution,* 297, 301. Freight was estimated by taking 10 percent of the multiple at which invoices of European goods were currently selling in America.

84. The number of vessels for which Ezekiel Price posted policies declined from a peak of 102 in 1777 to 63 in 1778, rising briefly to 79 in 1779, before declining to 45 in 1780 and 7 in 1781; in PMIR, vols. 17–19. Gillingham asserts that Price retired from the insurance business in 1783, perhaps in response to John Hurd opening a Boston insurance office in 1781; see *Marine Insurance*, 112. For further evidence of the declining use of insurance during the war, see Jon. Williams Jr. to Chevalier Holker, September 26, 1779, to Daniel Waldo, July 29, 1780, and to Chris. and Chas. Marshall, October 18, in JnWLB.

CHAPTER 5. INTRACTABLE FETTERS

1. Carl Bridenbaugh, *Seat of Empire: The Political Role of Eighteenth-Century Williamsburg* (Williamsburg, Va., 1950), 29–32, and *Cities in Revolt: Urban Life in America, 1743–1776* (New York, 1971), 216–17. James H. Soltow, *The Economic Role of Williamsburg* (Charlottesville, Va., 1965), argues for the economic importance of the "Meetings of Merchants," which occurred in the town in the late colonial period.

2. James E. Vance Jr., *The Merchant's World: The Geography of Wholesaling* (Englewood Cliffs, N.J., 1970), esp. chap. 4, and *The Continuing City: Urban Morphology in Western Civilization* (Baltimore, 1990), 210, 251–52, 255; Douglass C. North, "Location Theory and Regional Economic Growth," *Journal of Political Economy* 63(1955): 250, fn57, 251. See also Michael P. Conzen, "A Transportation Interpretation of the Growth of Urban Regions: An American Example," *Journal of Historical Geography* 1(1975): 362; Gary B. Nash, *The Urban Crucible* . . . (Cambridge, Mass., 1979), 3. The initial administrative sites were chosen on the assumption that they would also serve as ports. This accounts for much of the continuity between early and late colonial urbanization; see Carville V. Earle, "The First English Towns of North America," *Geographical Review* 67(1977): 36. For late colonial urbanization, see Jacob M. Price, "Economic Function and the Growth of American Port Towns in the Eighteenth Century," *Perspectives in American History* 8(1974): 176–77.

3. Carville V. Earle and Ronald Hoffman, "Staple Crops and Urban Development in the Eighteenth-Century South," *Perspectives in American History* 10(1976): 7–11, 19, 29–31, 51ff. See also Earle and Hoffman, "The Urban South: The First Two Centuries," in Blaine A. Brownell and David R. Goldfield, eds., *The City in Southern History* . . . (Port Washington, N.Y., 1977), 45–51.

4. John J. McCusker, "The Current Value of English Exports," *William & Mary Quarterly*, 3rd ser., 28(1971): 624–27; James A. Henretta, *The Evolution of American Society, 1700–1815* (Lexington, Mass., 1971), 70–73; A. F. Burghardt, "A Hypothesis About Gateway Cities," Association of American Geographers, *Annals* 61(1971): 269–70. See also William Cronon, *Nature's Metropolis: Chicago and the Great West* (New York, 1991), 307.

5. Robt. Morris to Wm. Bingham, September 14, 1776, in WBP. See also Morris, "State of American Commerce and Plan for Protecting It," May 10, 1782, in *PRM*, 5: 150; James F. Shepherd and Gary M. Walton, "Economic Changes After the American

Revolution: Pre- and Post-War Comparisons of Maritime Shipping and Trade," *Explorations in Economic History* 13(1976): 399; Jacob M. Price, "What Did Merchants Do? Reflections on the Overseas Trade, 1660–1790," *Journal of Economic History* 49(1989): 273.

6. James F. Shepherd and Gary M. Walton, *Shipping, Maritime Trade, and the Economic Development of Colonial North America* (Cambridge, 1972), 78–80, 86–88; Shepherd and Walton make reduced inventory time largely a function of reduced port times. See also John Bondfield to Wm. Vernon, October 30, 1782, in S&WVP. Jacob M. Price, *Capital and Credit in British Overseas Trade: The View from the Chesapeake, 1700–1776* (Cambridge, Mass., 1980), is the best discussion of the role that British credit played in the American trade; see also Virginia D. Harrington, *The New York Merchant on the Eve of the Revolution* (New York, 1935), 99, 101–3, 179. For other advantages associated with an urban market, see Earle and Hoffman, "Urban South," 47–48; Lynne Withey, *Urban Growth in Colonial Rhode Island: Newport and Providence in the Eighteenth Century* (Albany, N.Y., 1984), 29–30. Price, "American Port Towns," 177–83, provides a survey of the functions performed by the larger gateway cities in his sectorial analysis of the populations of Boston and Philadelphia. However, Boston was losing its competitive advantage in shipbuilding to its outports by the late colonial period; see ibid., 145–48. This trend continued through the Revolution; see John Welsh to John Reynolds, September 3, 1782, in JWLB.

7. James T. Lemon, *The Best Poor Man's Country: A Geographical Study of Early Southeastern Pennsylvania* (Baltimore, 1972), 29–30, 118–22ff, esp. 137–39; Thomas M. Truxes, *Irish-American Trade, 1660–1783* (Cambridge, 1988), 109–11; Price, "American Port Towns," 155–56. Earle and Hoffman, "Urban South," 35, 36; Daniel B. Thorp, "Doing Business in the Backcountry: Retail Trade in Colonial Rowan County, North Carolina," *William & Mary Quarterly,* 3rd ser., 48(1991), 400–401.

8. There were five routes between the northern Chesapeake and the Delaware, but the portage between Head of Elk and Christiana Bridge was the most direct, and the traffic over it was sufficiently heavy to justify the maintenance of regular shallop service between Christiana Bridge and Philadelphia; see the extensive correspondence of Hen. Hollingsworth during the war years, in HFP. See also Earle and Hoffman, "Urban Development in the South," 33.

9. R. G. Albion, *The Rise of New York Port, 1815–1860* (Hamden, Conn., 1961), chap. 2; John Adams, Diary, June 7 and 9, 1771, in *DAJA,* 2: 27, 32; Price, "American Port Towns," 144–45, 162–63. Earle and Hoffman, "Urban South," 50–51, argue that Charleston embarked on a new era of expansion dependent on grain exports from the Piedmont after 1760.

10. Bernard Bailyn, *New England Merchants in the Seventeenth Century* (Cambridge, Mass., 1955), 81, 95, 96; Bernard Bailyn and Lotte Bailyn, *Massachusetts Shipping, 1697–1714: A Statistical Study* (Cambridge, Mass., 1959), esp. 19. For the discriminatory impact of the Navigation Acts, see Thomas C. Barrow, *Trade and Empire: The British Customs Service in Colonial America* (Cambridge, Mass., 1967), 179–85.

11. Henretta, *Evolution of American Society,* 45. See also Harrington, *New York Merchant,* 165–68.

12. For this and what follows, see Customs 16/1, PRO. James G. Lydon, "Fish for Gold: The Massachusetts Fish Trade with Iberia, 1700–1773," *New England Quarterly* 54 (1981):568, 573.

13. Based on Customs 16/1, PRO. For Rhode Island, see Withey, *Urban Growth*, 21, 22. Only the threat of a trade boycott by New York, Philadelphia, and Boston forced Newport reluctantly to adhere to the Non-Importation Association of 1768; see Elaine F. Crane, *A Dependent People: Newport, Rhode Island, in the Revolutionary Era* (New York, 1985), 117–18. Rhode Island cleared 5.5 times more tonnage for the West Indies than for Europe in 1772 and had 9.4 times more tonnage enter from the islands than from Europe. The comparable ratios for Boston were 1.3 and 1.2; for New York, 1.0 and 0.86; and for Philadelphia, 1.2 and 0.71.

14. Jacob M. Price, "The Economic Growth of the Chesapeake and the European Market, 1697–1775," *Journal of Economic History* 24(1964): 496; Earle and Hoffman, "Urban South," 35.

15. Earle and Hoffman, "Urban South," 41, 42–44, 49, and "Urban Development in the South," 21–24, 58. Price, *Capital and Credit*, 40; Edward C. Papenfuse, *In Pursuit of Profit . . .* (Baltimore, 1975), 6–8. Lois G. Carr, "The Metropolis of Maryland: A Comment on Town Development Along the Tobacco Coast," *Maryland Historical Magazine* 69(1974): 142–143; Price, "Economic Growth," 501ff, emphasizes the centralizing effect that French purchasing had on the organization of the tobacco market before the Revolution. James O'Mara, "Urbanization in Tidewater Virginia During the Eighteenth Century: A Study in Historical Geography," (Ph.D. diss., York University, 1979), 126, stresses the role of tobacco inspection legislation.

16. Earle and Hoffman, "Urban Development in the South," 28–31, 50, 74–78, and "Urban South," 46, stress Baltimore's role as a milling center more than does Clarence P. Gould, "The Economic Causes of the Rise of Baltimore," *Essays in Colonial History Presented to Charles McLean Andrews by His Students* (New Haven, 1931), 235, 242. Alexandria also emerged as a lesser grain port in the late colonial period; see Thomas M. Presser, "Alexandria and the Evolution of the Northern Virginia Economy, 1749–1776," *Virginia Magazine of History and Biography* 89(1981): 288–89.

17. Earle and Hoffman, "Urban Development in the South," 41–46; Price, "American Port Towns," 169–70.

18. Shepherd and Walton, *Shipping, Maritime Trade, and the Economic Development of the Colonies;* Henretta, *Evolution of American Society,* chap. 2; John J. McCusker and Russell R. Menard, *The Economy of British America* (Chapel Hill, N.C., 1985), chaps. 4–9, 13, and p. 354.

19. Ralph V. Harlow, "Economic Conditions in Massachusetts During the American Revolution," Colonial Society of Massachusetts, *Publications* 20(1920): 163–90; Lydon, "Fish for Gold," 556ff, argues that Boston was losing position in relation to its outports before the Revolution. Withey, *Urban Growth in Colonial Rhode Island,* 77–82ff. See also Bonds, Masters of Vessels, August 1776–December 1781, in Maritime Papers, vols. 3–6, RIA. Rochambeau's arrival at Newport in July 1780 led the British to maintain a squadron off Point Judith until a winter storm dispersed it in January 1781. Earle and

Hoffman, "Urban South," 48. Baltimore's good fortune during the war laid the basis for its postwar prominence; see Price, "American Port Towns," 171–72.

20. John W. Jackson, *The Pennsylvania Navy* . . . (New Brunswick, N.J., 1974), chap. 4; Thomas Lea Daybook and Journal, February 20, 1775–September 1783, entries after May 8, 1776, in HSD.

21. Geo. Woolsey to Capt. Jos. Dority, June 13, 1780, January 3, 1781, and to Capt. Craig, August 22, 1781, in W&SLB. See Woolsey to John Pringle, May 11, 1776, in ibid., for an early reference to this route; see also Steph. Steward to the Maryland Council, July 24, 1781, in *AM*, 47: 366.

22. Paschal N. Smith to John Blagge, October 2, 1778, and to Eleazer Miller Jr., February 15, 1781, in S&SLB; Peter Colt to Jere. Wadsworth, July 30, 1778, in JWP; Steph. Collins to Wm. Gray, December 4, 1781, in SCLB; Nich. Brown to Joshua Hewes, February 19, 1777, and Brown to Geo. Benson, September 30, 1779, in NBCoP; Wm. G. Hutchinson to Wm. Palfrey, April 29, 1779; Palfrey to Codman and Smith, July 7, 1780, and to his wife, October 30, in WPP; John Brown to John Langdon, April 14, 1780, in *OLMC*, 2: 185.

23. For carting from Charleston, see Lony & Plombard to Sabatier fils, January 30, 1778, in JHLC; RHD, 137. Even before the war, Charleston's market had a comparatively long reach into the interior; see Thorp, "Doing Business in the Backcountry," 400–401. For carting from New England, see accounts associated with an "Adventure to Boston," November 5, 1778, in R&FP; Steph. Collins to Jencks and Forrester, August 14, 28, 1782, in SCLB. The specie cost of wagonage in New England at the end of the war was 10d sterling per ton-mile, well over ten times the ton-mile cost of water transportation. The multiple of ten was standard; see Jon. Williams Jr. to Jas. Bowdoin, May 24, 1779, in JnWLB. See also Jared Tracy to And. Huntington, July 20 and August 20, 1778, in AHP. For the forage crisis between King's Ferry and Philadelphia in autumn 1781, see Wm. Heath to Robt. Morris, October 4, 1781, in *PRM*, 3: 21; the ton-mile rate for wagonage from Boston to Philadelphia accordingly climbed to 2/ hard money; see Wm. Turnbull to Holker, October 11, 1781, in ibid. Volatile forage prices led officials to utilize water transport as much as possible; see Thos. Fanning to Sam. Gray, September 15, 1778, in SGP.

24. See Chas. Stewart to Sam. Gray, November 28, 1777, in SGP; Chas. Clinton to John Davis, November 25, 1778, in JDP. As much as a third of the cargo space in a wagon might be devoted to hauling forage. The quartermaster corps organized wagons into brigades in an effort to maintain control, but not with much effect; see Mark Bird to Davis, May 24, 1777, in ibid. Some specially constructed, larger wagons carried considerably more than a ton of load; see John Else to Sam. Gray, August 25, 1778, in SGP. For other hazards, see Steph. Collins to Jencks and Forrester, September 18, 1782, in SCLB; Jas. Abeel to Nath. Greene, June 7, 1778, in James Abeel Papers, LC; Théveneau de Francy to Beaumarchais, July 22, 1778, in *BC*, 4: 133. Juan de Miralles, the Spanish agent dispatched to Charleston in 1778 to observe the Revolution, reported that the inland route north to Philadelphia was quicker despite being longer because of its fewer stream crossings; Miralles to Diego José Navarro, May 12, 1778, in MRP; Earle and Hoffman,

"Urban South," 40; Jacob Cuyler to Royal Flint, October 8, 1777; Peter Colt to Cuyler, September 20, 1778, in JWP. The speed of water transportation varied substantially depending on conditions but did not affect costs that much.

25. For a graphic description of the Charleston fire and its effects, see EWJ, 1: 21, 83; Josiah Smith to the Rev. Dr. Rogers, March 5, 1778, and to Jas. Poyas, March 18, in JoSLB. For the embargoes, see Smith to Poyas, January 10, 1776, in ibid.; John L. Gervais to Hen. Laurens, December 17, 1777, in Gervais Transcripts, SCHS; EWJ, 1: 12, 21; David Ramsay, *The History of the Revolution of South Carolina . . .* (Trenton, 1785), 2: 76–77.

26. Report of Welcome Arnold, May 21, 1778, in A-GP. For Massachusetts Bay's dominance in privateering, cf. tables 7.1 and 7.3. See also Gardner W. Alden, "Massachusetts Privateers of the Revolution," in Massachusetts Historical Society, *Collections* 77(1927): 65–331; William Fowler, "The Business of War: Boston as Navy Base, 1776–1783," *American Neptune* 42(1982): 28. Not only privateers but vessels from other state navies sent their prizes into the Bay; see Louis F. Middlebrook, *Exploits of the Connecticut Ship "Defence"* (Hartford, 1922), 23–24. For the problems of the Marine Committee, see Marine Committee to Commissioners of the Navy Board of the Eastern Department, May 20, 1779, in *OLMC*, 2: 75; John Brown to the Commissioners of the Navy Board of the Eastern Department, April 11, 1780, and to John Bradford, April 11, May 19, in ibid., 2: 182, 198. For the preference of importers, see Anth. L. Bleeker to John de Neufville, n.d., 1779, in ALBLB; see also Paschal N. Smith to Bleeker, July 14, in S&SLB. Massachusetts privateers occasionally seized incoming vessels; see Geo. Benson to Nich. Brown, September 20, 1780, in NBCoP; Joseph de Valnais to John Holker, April 24, 1779, and ? Bumel to Gregoire de Rouhlac, July 31, 1778, quoted in Rouhlac to Holker, April 13, 1779, in JHLC. See also Ben. Gowen to Massachusetts Council, July 29, and Wm. Hutchinson et al. to Massachusetts Council, August 12, 1778, Massachusetts Council Papers, vol. 169, in MAC; Protest of Pierre Talmin, captain of the *Marquis de Cassgny,* against Thomas Truxton of the privateer *Mars,* April 2, 1778, in Ezekiel Price, Notorial Records, vol. 6, 316, in BA. For late winter arrivals, see Nich. Brown to John de Neufville, May 8, 1779, in NBCoP.

27. John White to Meletiah Bourn, July 29, 1775, in MBL; Anne R. Cunningham, ed., *Letters and Diary of William Rowe Boston Merchant . . .* (Boston, 1903), 294, 295, 304, 309. Oscar Handlin and Mary Flug Handlin, *Commonwealth. A Study of the Role of Government in the American Economy: Massachusetts, 1774–1861* (New York, 1947), 7; Harlow, "Economic Conditions in Massachusetts," 172–73; Benjamin W. Labaree, *Patriots and Partisans: The Merchants of Newburyport, 1764–1815* (Cambridge, Mass., 1962), 58ff. See Lydon, "Fish for Gold," 564, 566.

28. Fowler, "Business of War," 35; Price, "American Port Towns," 173, 176. Geo. Woolsey to John Pringle, July 18, 1778, and April 3 and October 30, 1779, to Phil. Moore, August 8, 1778, and to Jas. Cuming, April 14, 1780, in W&SLB.

29. Paschal N. Smith to Jas. Jarvis, September 23, 1776, and to Francis Brown, November 9, in S&SLB. Also Steph. Higginson to Steph. Cleveland, November 23 and 26, 1776, in Higginson Family Papers, MHS. See also CP. For the Holland trade, see

John W. Tyler, *Smugglers and Patriots: Boston Merchants and the Advent of the American Revolution* (Boston, 1986); James B. Hedges, *The Browns of Providence Plantations* (Cambridge, Mass., 1952), 255. Welcome Arnold was involved in ventures to Sweden in the summers of 1777, 1778, and 1779, backed by Boston and Bedford investors; see Welcome Arnold to Russell and Howland & Co, August 2, 1777, to Jos. Russell, July 1, 1778, to Nich. Tillinghast, March 14, 1779, to Seth Russell, May 19, 1779, and to Sam. Bartlett, February 2, 1780, in AGP. See also Franklin Stuart Coyle, "Welcome Arnold (1745–1798) Providence's Merchant: The Founder of an Enterprise" (Ph.D. diss., Brown University, 1972), 97–98. For the developing European trade, see Paschal N. Smith to Jas. Jarvis, September 9 and December 29, 1778, and Smith to John Turner, September 29, 1780, in S&SLB. For notice of multiple arrivals from Europe in the latter part of 1780, see Smith to Sears, August 17, 1780, and to Eleazer Miller Jr., November 23, in ibid. See also Mary Foster to Isaac Foster, May 25, 1779, in Isaac Foster Papers, LC; Russell Sturgis to Meletiah Bourn, August 29, 1777, in MBL. Increased interest in the European trade is also evident in Chris. Champlin to John de Neufville, April 17, 1780, and to Henry Greig, May 10; and Champlin, Henry Hunter, and Geo. Gibbs to Greig, June 19, in CCLB. See also Smith's attitude toward the West Indies trade in his letter to John Turner, September 29, 1780, in S&SLB. Smith assigned his less desirable vessels to the Statia trade; see his letter to John Nelson, September 30, 1780, in ibid. For the price advantages of Boston's market, see Matt. McConnell to John Davis, March 10, 1779, in JDP; Steph. Bruce to Standish Forde, January 9, 1782, in R&FP; Wm. Palfrey to Susannah Palfrey, August 15, 1780, in WPP; Alex. Hamilton to Robt. Morris, April 30, 1781, in *PRM,* 1: 38 and 58n; John Brown to John Langdon, April 17, 1780, in *OLMC,* 2: 185.

30. Price, "American Port Towns," 149; John Welsh to John Caldwell, October 12, 1781, in JWLB.

31. If we take price convergence in the market area as a measure of its integration, as Winifred B. Rothenberg has suggested, (see *From Market-Places to Market Economy: The Transformation of Rural Massachusetts, 1750–1850* [Chicago, 1992], 53–54, 81ff, esp. 95), the New England region was highly unintegrated, with New York produce sometimes fetching twice the price in Boston that it did at home; see Geo. Clinton to Steph. Lush, April 17, 1779, in *PPGC,* 4: 732; Jas. Watson to Jere. Wadsworth, May 7, 1779, in JWP. For the persistence of some coastal trade, see Outward and Inward Entries, 1776–87, Rhode Island Maritime Papers, RIA; "Record of All Vessels Registered in New Haven, 1762–1794" (incomplete), in New Haven Customs Records, National Archives, Waltham, Mass. For the emergence of Norwich as a carting rendezvous, see AHP. For transportation and insurance rates, see Sam. Vernon to Wm. Vernon, October 23, 1781, in S&WVP; Chris. Champlin to Geo. Benson, October 15, 1780, in CCLB; Mansel Alcock to Jas. Alcock, November 28, 1778, in S-AP. For their effect on distribution, see Paschal N. Smith to Jas. Jarvis, July 27, 1780; Smith to John Broome, November 30, 1780, in S&SLB.

32. For the history of this Dutch island, see Barbara Tuchman, *The First Salute: A View of the Revolutionary War* (New York, 1988), chap. 2. Evidence for St. Eustatius's

entrepôt status during the war comes largely from the British and may be exaggerated; see J. Franklin Jameson, "St. Eustatius in the American Revolution," *American Historical Review* 8(1903): 699, 700–701.

33. Ypie Attema, *St. Eustatius: A Short History of the Island and Its Monuments* (Zutphen, 1976), 16–21, 30–31; for the kleine vaart, see Cornelius Ch. Goslinga, *The Dutch in the Caribbean and in the Guianas, 1680–1791* (Maastricht, 1985), 189, 204–5; Tuchman, *First Salute*, 21; Janet Schaw, *Journal of a Lady of Quality; Being the Narrative of a Journey from Scotland to the West Indies, North Carolina, and Portugal, in the Years 1774 to 1776*, ed. Evangeline W. Andrews (New Haven, Conn., 1923), 135, 136; Hedges, *Browns of Providence*, 48; Albion and Pope, *Sea Lanes in Wartime*, 54; Jameson, "St. Eustatius," 684, 687–88.

34. Albion and Pope, *Sea Lanes*, 52; Daniel A. Miller, *Sir Joseph York and Anglo-Dutch Relations, 1774–1780* (The Hague, 1970), 32, 56–57; Jameson, "St. Eustatius," 687–88; Simon Schama, *Patriots and Liberators: Revolution in the Netherlands, 1780–1813* (New York, 1977), 35, 59ff; F. C. Van Oosten, "Some Notes Concerning the Dutch West Indies During the Revolutionary War," *American Neptune* 36(1976): 165. On the Amsterdam connection, see Woolsey and Salmon to John Robinson, August 15, 1780, in W&SLB. N. W. Posthumus, *Inquiry into the History of Prices in Holland*, 2 vols. (Leiden, 1946), argues that Amsterdam's market was losing its competitive edge because of increasingly monopolistic practices (1: lxxv–lxxvi).

35. Schama, *Patriots and Liberators*, 54–55; see also Van Oosten's figures in "Some Notes," 163. For Statia's wartime advantages, see Jameson, "St. Eustatius," 686, 697; Matt. Ridley to John Holker, November 20, 1779, and to Joshua Johnston, December 11, in MRLB, vol. 3. On the time it took for messages to travel from Europe, see John Taylor to Wm. Palfrey, June 6, 1780, in WPP. For an analysis of Britain's strategic problems in the Caribbean, see Miller, *Sea of Glory*, 391; Alan G. Jamieson, "American Privateers in the Leeward Islands, 1776–1778," *American Neptune* 43(1983), 28. Jamieson argues that before France's entry into the war, American armed vessels had put the Royal Navy's small Leeward Island Squadron on the defensive (21–23). See also Richard Pares, *War and Trade in the West Indies, 1739–1763* (London, 1963), chap. 7.

36. Francisco Rendón to Diego José Navarro, July 11 and 12, 1780, in MRP; Lord George Germain to Sir Henry Clinton, April 4, 1781, and to Frederick Haldimand, April 12, in *DAR*, 20: 99, 109; Geo. Woolsey to Capt. Christian Bradley, December 19, 1778, in W&SLB; Light Townsend Cummins, *Spanish Observers and the American Revolution, 1775–1783* (Baton Rouge, La., 1991), 173–74. The British found quite a few British and Bermudian merchants at Statia when they seized the island on February 3, 1781; see Geo. B. Rodney to Phil. Stephens, March 6, 1781, in *DAR*, 19: item 466. See also And. Elliot to Hen. Clinton, January 9, 1779, in ibid., 17: 27–28; Wm. Reynolds to Geo. F. Norton, September 18, 1779; Moses Robertson to Jas. Withers, November 19, 1779, and Norton to Jas. Withers, November 29, 1779, in *JNS*, 427, 429, 431–32; Norman F. Barka, "Citizens of St. Eustatius, 1781: A Historical and Archeological Study," in Robert L. Paquette and Stanley Engerman, eds., *The Lesser Antilles in the Age of European Expansion* (Gainsville, Fla., 1996), 223, 238. Barka reports 3,551 arrivals in 1779 and 3,217 in 1780; ibid., 225. His figures are congruent with those supplied by Van Oosten, "Some

Notes," 163. The fleets originated sometime in 1779 (see Matt. Ridley to Thomas Leiper, December 6, 1779, in MRLB, vol. 3) and had become routine by the middle of 1780; see Geo. Woolsey to Plunket and Sterret, and to Capt. Jos. Dority, June 13, 1780, in W&SLB.

37. Geo. Woolsey to Steph. Steward, July 30 and August 13, 1778, to John Pringle, August 8, 15, 1778, in W&SLB; Todd Cooper, "Trial and Triumph, the Impact of the Revolutionary War on the Baltimore Merchants," in Ernest M. Eller, ed., *Chesapeake Bay in the American Revolution* (Centreville, Md., 1981), 293; John Taylor to Wm. Palfrey, April 2, 1780, in WPP; Matt. Ridley to Plunket and Sterret, March 8, 1780, in MRLB, vol. 3. The "shallowness" of the island markets had been a problem throughout the colonial period; see Richard Pares, *Yankees and Creoles* . . . (Cambridge, Mass., 1956), 64, 74, 85ff; Geoffrey N. Gilbert, *Baltimore's Flour Trade to the Caribbean, 1750–1815* (New York, 1986), 5. For Philadelphia's ability to absorb an unexpectedly large consignment of imports between June and December 1780, see Ben. Huntington to Nath. Shaw, June 12, 1780, in *LD*, 15: 303; Levi Hollingsworth to Sam. Harrison, December 5, 1780, and to Geo. Anderson, December 12, in LHLB. Those who visited the other islands often came away dissatisfied; see Geo. Woolsey to Wm. Van Wyck, November 5, 1778, to John Pringle, November [December?] 5, and to Capt. Christian Bradley, December 19, in W&SLB. Tortolean "pirates" also discouraged American vessels from making for the Danish islands; see Jean Louise Willis, "The Trade Between North America and the Danish West Indies, 1756–1807, with Special Reference to St. Croix" (Ph.D. diss., Columbia University, 1963), 136.

38. See *JCC*, 8: 725, 731; E. James Ferguson, *The Power of the Purse* (Chapel Hill, N.C., 1963), 36–39. The policy had limited potential because Congress could not offer prospective subscribers interest in bills on France without extending the same benefit to those who had already subscribed, limiting the amount of new debt that could be funded in this way.

39. *JCC*, 9: 956, 971. For the debtor's holiday in Massachusetts, for instance, see Harlow, "Economic Conditions," 164–65. For Maryland, see Jean B. Lee, *The Price of Nationhood* . . . (New York, 1994), 122, 127–28.

40. Ralph V. Harlow, "Aspects of Revolutionary Finance, 1775–1783," *American Historical Review* 35(1929–1930): 50–51; *JCC*, 9: 955–56. For the Springfield Convention, see Richard Buel Jr., *Dear Liberty* . . . (Middletown, Conn., 1980), 146. Ferguson, *Power of the Purse,* 34.

41. The Articles of Confederation were sent to the states on November 17, 1777; see *JCC*, 9: 932–34. Merrill Jensen, *The Articles of Confederation* . . . (Madison, Wis., 1940), chaps. 9–11; Ferguson, *Power of the Purse,* 209.

42. See Henry Laurens's anxieties about how a subsequent and much larger requisition would affect South Carolina, in Notes of Debates, May 19, 1779, in *LD,* 11: 494.

43. *JCC*, 9: 955; Buel, *Dear Liberty,* 146; Jon. Trumbull to the Delegates in Congress, December 8, 1778, in Massachusetts Historical Society, *Collections,* 7th ser., 2(1902): 319. This attitude persisted into 1779; see Wm. Whipple to Josiah Bartlett, May 21, 1779, in *LD,* 12: 504.

44. For contemporary discussions of this problem, see "T. S.," in *Pennsylvania Packet,* June 22, 1779; "7th Resolve of the Concord Convention," in *Boston Gazette,* August 2, 1779; Hen. Marchant to Wm. Greene, October 2, 1779, in *LD,* 14: 63.

45. For criticisms of a final settlement, see Ferguson, *Power of the Purse,* 204ff; Théveneau de Francy to Caron de Beaumarchais, July 31, 1778, in *BC,* 4: 175–77; Jas. Watson to Jere. Wadsworth, January 4, 1779, in JWP.

46. I have advanced this interpretation before in "Time: Friend or Foe of the Revolution?" in Don Higginbotham, ed., *Reconsiderations on the Revolutionary War* (Westport, Conn., 1978), 133, and in "The Committee Movement of 1779 and the Formation of Public Authority in Revolutionary America," in James A. Henretta, Michael Kammen, and Stanley N. Katz, eds., *The Transformation of Early American History* (New York, 1991), 155–56.

47. Buel, *Dear Liberty,* 140–44, 150–51.

48. See Ferguson, *Power of the Purse,* 30.

49. *JCC,* 13: 20–22; Ramsay, *History of South Carolina,* 2: 86–87. Buel, "Time: Friend or Foe," 134.

50. In December 1778, Silas Deane published his attack against the Lee family, two members of which were sitting in Congress; see "To the Free and Virtuous Citizens of America," in New-York Historical Society, *Collections* 21(1889): 66–76. Documents relating to the ensuing controversy, which continued into March 1779, are in ibid.

51. Wm. Livingston to Hen. Laurens, April 23, 1779, in *PWL,* 3: 67. Tender laws aroused controversy in the press (see, for instance, "Aristides" and "Honestus IV," in *Connecticut Courant,* January 19 and 26, 1779) before they came to Congress's attention in autumn 1779 (see John Fell's Diary, November 20, 1779, in *LD,* 14: 215). For creditor objections to tender laws, see Jon. Amory to John Amory, December 16, 1780, in Amory Family Papers, MHS; Steph. Collins to Jon. Amory, January 15, 1777, and to John Barrell, January 17, 1778, in SCLB. A public statute allowed Virginia debtors to tender continental money to the state loan office in exchange for a discharge of debts owed to Britons or loyalists; see *SAL,* 9: 379–80. For the rationale behind this law, see Jefferson's draft resolution "Concerning Money Due British Subjects," January 13, 1778, in *PTJ,* 2: 171–72. Jefferson's draft stresses the role that British naval power played in making money commercially useless.

52. Harlow, "Economic Conditions," 169. Congress alluded to these problems in its address "To the Inhabitants of the United States of America," May 26, 1779, in *JCC,* 14: 652–53. They had been discussed in the press earlier; see unsigned and "Cato," in *Connecticut Courant,* December 2 and 9, 1777. See also Jos. Reed to the Presidents of the Courts of Common Pleas, November 27, 1780, in *PA,* 1st ser., 8: 622. Jeremiads about declining civic virtue alluded to the general demoralization that also found expression in the rising incidence of thievery and banditry. See, for instance, Wm. Livingston to Washington, May 1, 1779, to Robert Harpur, June 22, 1778; Proclamation, August 18, Silas Condict to Livingston, July 20, 1781, and Livingston to Thos. S. Lee, October 29, 1781, in *PWL,* 3: 81, 118, 161–62; 4: 243, 323.

53. Ramsay, *History of South Carolina,* 2: 83, mentions the American speculators.

Popular hostility to appreciation is alluded to in John Chester to Jere. Wadsworth, November 24, 1778, John Lloyd to Wadsworth, December 1, Jas. Watson to Wadsworth, January 4, 1779, and Peter Colt to Wadsworth, June 3, 1779, in JWP. See also "Scipio," October 25, 1780, in *PWL,* 4: 77–78. "T. S.," in *Pennsylvania Packet,* June 22, 1779; the "7th Resolve of the Concord Convention," in *Boston Gazette,* August 2, 1779; Belchertown and Billerica Remonstrances, vol. 183, 292ff, in MAC, as quoted in Handlin and Handlin, *Commonwealth Massachusetts,* 14; Kenneth Scott, "Price Control in New England During the Revolution," *New England Quarterly* 19(1946): 468.

54. Ferguson, *Power of the Purse,* 34.

55. Cf. Wm. H. Drayton's Notes of Proceedings, February 15, 1779, in *LD,* 12: 71–73, with Gérard to Vergennes, February 15, 1779, in *DCG,* 521–22. See Francis Lewis to Geo. Clinton, February 24, 1779, in *LD,* 12: 109–10. John Pierce to Wm. Palfrey, February 20, 1779, in WPP. Gérard's request forced Congress to formulate negotiating terms that created internal controversy as well as tension between Gérard and the New England members of Congress over the fisheries; see John Fell's Diary, March 30, 1779, and notes; Jas. Lovell to Hor. Gates, [April 5, 1779], April 15, in *LD,* 12: 265, 299, 330. On the hoped-for naval victory by the allies, see the draft of a notice for a printer in the United States, between entries for June 7 and 16, 1779, and Jon. Williams Jr. to his father, March 6, 1780, in JnWLB.

56. For Congress's deliberateness, see Hen. Laurens, Notes of Debates, April 29, 1779, in *LD,* 12: 404–5. The stimulus that an appreciation of the currency might give to moneylending could work in a variety of ways; see John Collins and Wm. Ellery to Wm. Greene, June 4, 1779, in *LD,* 13: 24. Some still feared its effects, though; see Wm. Fleming to Thos. Jefferson, May 22, 1779, in ibid., 508. At the end of July 1779, Congress empowered the Board of Treasury to issue warrants on the treasurer who could endorse and forward them for payment to any state loan office; see *JCC,* 14, 904, 906. For the delegates' optimism, see John Dickinson to Caesar Rodney, May 21, 1779, in *LD,* 12: 501.

57. James, *British Navy in Adversity,* chap. 12.

58. Harlow, "Economic Conditions," 171; Amasa Keyes to Jere. Wadsworth, August 3, 1779, in JWP; Buel, "Committee Movement of 1779," 159–66.

59. See "Circular Letter from Congress of the United States of America to Their Constituents," September 13, 1779, in *JCC,* 15: 1052–62. Congress estimated the postwar debt would come to $300 million (ibid., 1056), which was hardly cheering news. Some members of Congress thought that this address to the public was a political error; see John Morin Scott to Ezra L'Hommedieu, June 6, 1780, in *LD,* 15: 271–72. Sometimes warrants were honored by the issuance of loan office certificates; see Ferguson, *Power of the Purse,* 54. For a schedule of the warrants drawn on the state treasurers between November 24, 1779, and February 28, 1780, see *PA,* 1st ser., 8: 121–22. Pennsylvania was not in a position to honor these warrants; see Joseph Reed to the Board of War, March 12[?], 1780, in ibid., 133. Buel, "Committee Movement of 1779," 163. For specific requisitions, see *JCC,* 15: 1311, 1371, 1377.

60. I use Ferguson's depreciation schedule in *Power of the Purse,* 32, as the basis for this argument. Difficulties in constructing such a schedule, as well as the reasons for seasonal

fluctuations, were canvassed in John M. Scott to Ezra L'Hommedieu, June 6, 1780, in *LD*, 15: 272–73; Chaloner and White to Peter Colt, August 13, 1779, and to Jere. Wadsworth, September 13, in C&WLB. Massachusetts had its own depreciation schedule, which reflected the tempo of economic activity along its extended seacoast. It was less seasonal, at least until winter 1779, than the congressional table. To judge from this piece of evidence, the committee movement in Boston and its environs had considerably less effect on the region's economy than the Philadelphia committee movement had on its region; see inside cover of Accounts of the Schooner *Eagle*, Amory Family Papers, bound vol. 14, MHS. For reasons why this may have been the case, see Buel, "Committee Movement of 1779," 165.

61. John Proud to Hor. Gates, September 6, 1779, in HGP, reel 10; Gates to Jon. Trumbull, September 6, 1779, in JTP; *JCC*, 15: 1108. Washington gave substance to the rumors by issuing a call for 12,000 three-months militia; see his letter to the governors of New York, New Jersey, Pennsylvania, Connecticut, and Massachusetts, October 14, 1779, in *WGW*, 16, 403–6.

62. Quotes from Peter Colt to Jer. Wadsworth, November 18, 24, 30, 1779, in JWP; see also John Lloyd Jr. to Wadsworth, December 1, 1779, in ibid., and John Tyler to Jon. Trumbull, November 24, 1779, in JTP.

63. Paschal N. Smith to Jas. Jarvis, March 30, 1778, in S&SLB; Geo. Woolsey to Dulap and McCreary, August 6, 8, 1778, and to Steph. Steward, August 13, in W&SLB.

64. Palfrey to his wife, August 1, 1780, in WPP. See also Geo. Woolsey to Dulap and McCreary, August 8, 1778, and to John Pringle, July 24, September 30, October 25, November 18, 1779, in W&SLB. PMIR contains an unnumbered specie policy for £400 dated February 25, 1780, for the brig *Phoenix*, in Business Records, vol. 22.

CHAPTER 6. CREATIVE MISFORTUNES

1. *EAB*, no. 15832. Arthur Lee to Foreign Affairs Committee, and copy to Jon. Trumbull, April 6, 1779, in PCC, reel 67, item 54, p. 275, and JTP; *PRSC*, 2: 358–60.

2. Kenneth Coleman, *The American Revolution in Georgia, 1763–1789* (Athens, Ga., 1958), chap. 7.

3. Christopher Ward, *The War of the Revolution* (New York, 1952), 2: 596–610, 638–47; Hugh F. Rankin, *The North Carolina Continentals* (Chapel Hill, 1971), 176, 213.

4. Jonathan R. Dull, *A Diplomatic History of the American Revolution* (New Haven, Conn., 1985), 107–10, 116–17; Ruth Strong Hudson, *The Minister from France: Conrad-Alexandre Gerard, 1729–1790* (Euclid, Ohio, 1994), 131–32. Expelling the British from the continent was something that the patriots had long realized they would have trouble effecting on their own; see Nath. Greene to Washington, December 3, 1777, in *PNG*, 2: 231–36, 237fn.

5. John Morin Scott to Ezra L'Hommedieu, June 6, 1780, in *LD*, 15: 270; Isabel T. Kelsay, *Joseph Brant, 1743–1807, Man of Two Worlds* (Syracuse, N.Y., 1984), chap. 14. Martha C. Searcy, *The Georgia-Florida Contest in the American Revolution, 1776–1778* (Tuscaloosa, Ala., 1985), 174ff; John S. Pancake, *This Destructive War: The British Cam-*

paign in the Carolinas, 1780–1782 (Tuscaloosa, Ala., 1985), 83ff; Henry Lumpkin, *From Savannah to Yorktown: The American Revolution in the South* (Columbia, S.C., 1981), 80ff; Jerome Nadelhaft, *The Disorders of War: The Revolution in South Carolina* (Orono, Maine, 1981), 50ff.

6. James S. Leamon, *Revolution Downeast: The War for American Independence in Maine* (Amherst, Mass., 1993), chap. 4. The abduction of Gold Selleck Silliman, on May 1, 1779, was the beginning of an escalating pressure that the loyalists applied along Connecticut's coastline; see Richard Buel Jr., *Dear Liberty* . . . (Middletown, Conn., 1980), 192, 222, 251–53, 259–60, 272. The kidnapping is recounted in Joy D. Buel and Richard Buel Jr., *The Way of Duty* (New York, 1984), chap. 6.

7. Only 10 of the 132 vessels appearing on William Tryon's "List of Prizes Taken by Letters of Marque, September 16, 1777–February 1, 1779," in CO 5/1109, were libeled before March 1778; see Court Minute Book, New York Vice-Admiralty Court, HCA 49/92, both documents in LCTB.

8. Tryon had obviously been lobbying for this power for some time; see Wm. Tryon to Lord George Germain, July 8, 1778, in *DAR*, 13: no. 1962. For his authorization, see Lord George Germain to Wm. Tryon, June 5, 1778, and Tryon to Germain, September 5, in *DAR*, 13: no. 1876; 15: 198. Most vessels took out commissions against both French and American shipping, but twenty-four did not; see Tryon's list in CO 5/1109, LCTB.

9. Tryon stressed exemption from impressment in his letter to Germain, October 8, 1778, in CO 5/1108, LCTB; James Gambier, *A Narrative of Facts Relative to the Conduct of Vice-Admiral Gambier During His Late Command in North America* (London, 1782), 13, 19. As admiral of the station, he received a percentage of all prizes condemned in the New York Vice-Admiralty Court.

10. Tryon to Germain, February 5, 1779, in *DAR*, 17: 51, claimed his letters of marque had brought in 142 vessels since he had been empowered to issue commissions. However, about half the vessels appearing on "List of Prizes Taken by Letters of Marque, September 16, 1777–February 1, 1779," in CO 5/1109, LCTB, had been captured before either Tryon had received authorization to issue commissions or Gambier had given the order about impressment. Between February 5 and July 27, 1779, letters of marque libeled an additional 143 prizes in the New York Court of Vice-Admiralty; see "List of Prizes Taken by Letters of Marque," February 5, 1779–July 27, 1779, in ibid. See also Robert M. Dructor, "The New York Commercial Community: The Revolutionary Experience" (Ph.D. diss., University of Pittsburgh, 1971), 230, 235, 645–724.

11. Cumberland Dugan to Caleb Davis, October 31, 1778, in Caleb Davis Papers, vol. 9B, MHS. Allusions to the heavy losses of late 1778 can also be found in "A Plebeian," in *Pennsylvania Packet,* June 28, 1779; Chaloner and White to Peter Colt, April 19, 1779, in C&WLB; and Geo. Woolsey to Milner and Haynes, September 20, 1778, and to John Pringle, September 26, 1778, in W&SLB. See also references to the success of the new policy in Rivington's *Royal Gazette* (New York), September 12, October 24, 28, November 4, 14, 21, 25, December 9, 16, 1778.

12. Quote from Chaloner and White to Jere. Wadsworth, July 14, 1778; also to Ephr.

Blaine, July 30, 1778, in C&WLB. Levi Hollingsworth appears to have counseled clients to hold off sending produce into the Philadelphia market until arrivals had reduced the price of imports; see Steph. Howard to Levi Hollingsworth, July 30, 1778, in HFP. But he made the same assumptions as Chaloner had. The patriots had waxed lyrical about the importance of Philadelphia on the eve of the British conquest; see Harry M. Tinkcom, "The Revolutionary City, 1765–1783," in Russell F. Weigley et al., eds., *Philadelphia: A 300-Year History* (New York, 1982), 134. See also Alice H. Jones, *Wealth of a Nation to Be* (New York, 1980), 303, who identifies the Middle Colonies as the richest in "nonhuman wealth."

13. The British evacuation did not halt naval surveillance; see Anne R. Cunningham, ed., *Letters and Diary of William Rowe . . .* (Boston, 1903), 310–12. The threat of invasion seemed real enough in 1778, when the British concentrated off Boston after D'Estaing had retired there to refit (see ibid., 321); see also John Sullivan to Wm. Heath, September 14, 1778, in WHP; Heath to Washington, September 15, to the Massachusetts General Assembly, and to Sullivan, September 16, in WHP. For Boston's ability to avoid food shortages, see Ezek Hopkins to Abra. Whipple, June 18, 1776, in Abraham Whipple Papers, RIHS; ? Moore, John Carter, and Adam Babcock to Arch. Mercer, February 27, 1778, in Langdon/Elwyn Papers, NHHS. Cf. Eben Wales to Josiah Batchelder, July 15, 1779, in "Shipping, 1750–1800," BHS. See also Ralph V. Harlow, "Economic Conditions in Massachusetts During the Revolution," Colonial Society of Massachusetts *Publications* 20(1920): 166, 178; Mansel Alcock to Jas. Alcock, December 26, 1776, in S-AP. Boston's economic recovery did not involve a full restoration of its prewar population; see Stanley K. Schultz, "The Growth of Urban America in War and Peace," in William M. Fowler Jr. and Wallace Coyle, eds., *The American Revolution: Changing Perspectives* (Boston, 1979), 130.

14. Geo. Woolsey to John Pringle, September 9, 1777, and March 5, 1778, and to And. and Jas. Caldwell, March 20, in W&SLB. John Pringle was deeply involved with the Baltimore firm Woolsey and Salmon in a number of ventures at the time of the British evacuation; see ibid., May–July 1778. See also Josiah Hewes to Nich. Brown, July 7, 1778, in NBCoP; Gérard to Vergennes, July 25, 1778, in *DCG*, 183; Elaine F. Crane, ed., *The Diary of Elizabeth Drinker* (Boston, 1991), 305, 306; John F. Watson, *Annals of Philadelphia, and Pennsylvania, in the olden time . . .* (Philadelphia, 1884), 2: 297; Hudson, *Minister from France*, 93. James T. Lemon, *The Best Poor Man's Country . . .* (Baltimore, 1972), 148. John Henry? to Richard Lord Howe, May 6–9, 1778, in Admiralty 1/488, LCTB; Report of the Philadelphia Committee, in *Pennsylvania Packet,* September 10, 1779.

15. Chaloner and White to Jere. Wadsworth, July 24, 1778, to Joseph Hugg, August 5, to Azariah Dunham, August 5, to Wm. Buchanan, August 11, to Ephr. Blaine, August 21, 1778 (quote), to Sam. Adams, December 10, 1778, in C&WLB. See also Alex. Porter to Levi Hollingsworth, November 13, 1778, in HFP.

16. "Walsingham," in *Pennsylvania Packet,* February 16, 1779. The comparative fortunes of Baltimore and Philadelphia can be traced in Thos. Hollingsworth to Levi Hollingsworth, August 25, 1778; Geo. Morris to Levi Hollingsworth, October 8, 1778; Thos. Hollingsworth to Levi, August 27, 1778; Jesse and Thos. Hollingsworth to Levi,

November 14, 1778, in HFP. Philadelphia buyers also invaded the smaller market towns; see Alex. Porter to Levi Hollingsworth, November 13, 1778, and Wm. Deacon to Hollingsworth, November 15, in ibid. Baltimore was blessed with four arrivals from the West Indies in the middle of September; see Jesse and Thos. Hollingsworth to Levi, September 15, 1778, in ibid. The illusion of plenty did not last for long, however, and Hollingsworth's correspondents were soon complaining again about the absence of arrivals; see Wm. Hammond to Levi, October 25, 1778; Thos. and Jesse Hollingsworth to Levi, October 31; and Thos. to Levi, November 26, in ibid. A small fleet did arrive in Baltimore at the beginning of December (see Jesse and Thos. to Levi, November 30, December 7 and 18), and this momentarily threatened to renew Baltimore's advantage in the market; see Geo. V. Mann to Levi, January 16, 1779, in ibid.

17. For reports about the urban markets, see Zebulon Hollingsworth to Levi Hollingsworth, August 4, 1778; Mathias Slough to Levi, July 29, August 6; Jesse Hollingsworth to Levi, August 26; Steph. Howard to Levi, July 30; Elijah Bolden to Levi, August 8, 1778; David Moore to Levi, August 21; Hen. Armistead to Levi, August 31; Wm. Hammond to Levi, September 5; David Moore to Levi, September 11; Amos Alexander to Levi, September 26; Hen. Hollingsworth to Levi, September 30; Caleb Rucketts to Levi, November 16, in HFP. See also Geo. Woolsey to John Pringle, September 19, October 10, 28, 31, in W&SLB. David Ramsay noted that the same thing happened in South Carolina; see *The History of the Revolution of South Carolina . . .* (Trenton, 1785), 2: 88.

18. Anne Bezanson, *Prices and Inflation During the American Revolution: Pennsylvania, 1770–1790* (Philadelphia, 1951), 336. For the swollen volume of arrivals throughout 1775, see PTD. Hostilities affected imports from the foreign West Indies more than from Europe, which had already been diminished by nonimportation. Merchants had also anticipated the latter more than the former by stockpiling European goods. The same pattern characterized the experience of other regions; see Bernard Mason, "Entrepreneurial Activity in New York During the American Revolution," *Business History Review* 40(1966): 198, 200.

19. Mansel Alcock to Jas. Alcock, March 26, 1777, January 25 and March 12, 1778, in S-AP.

20. Quote from *Pennsylvania Packet,* February 16, 1779; Bezanson, *Prices and Inflation,* 336; Mansel Alcock to James Alcock, March 26, 1777, in S-AP; Harlow, "Economic Conditions," 168–70.

21. This was also the case in Boston; see Harlow, "Economic Conditions," 177.

22. One encounters entries for hard money or hard money equivalency transactions with harvest 1778 in Thomas Lea's Daybook and Journal, February 20, 1775–September 27, 1783, HSD. The British occupation had led briefly to the creation of a hard money economy early in 1778 (see Willard O. Bishoff, "Business in Philadelphia During the British Occupation, 1777–1778," *Pennsylvania Magazine of History and Biography* 61 [1937]: 177), so the farmers knew some specie was around. See also John J. Jackson, *With the British Army in Philadelphia, 1777–1778* (San Rafael, Calif., 1979), 149, 151, 154. For bartering, see Thos. Lowry to Nath. Greene, January 17, 1780, in Nathanael Greene

Papers, WLCL. Bartering arrangements limited competition in the marketplace and were regarded as hostile to the public interest; see Sam. McClellan to Jere. Wadsworth, June 7, 1780, in JWP. For additional commentary, see Hen. Hollingsworth to Levi Hollingsworth, October 29, 1778, in HFP.

23. Hugh Hollingsworth to Levi Hollingsworth, November 20, 1778; Thos. Lowry to Levi, February 17, 1779, in HFP. Bezanson, *Prices and Inflation,* 336, 344; Chaloner and White to Ephr. Blaine, and to Jere. Wadsworth, both April 18, 1779, in C&WLB. Also Daniel Roberdeau's Speech to the Philadelphia town meeting in *Pennsylvania Packet,* May 27, 1779.

24. Hubertus Cummings, "Robert Morris and the Episode of the Polacre 'Victorious,'" *Pennsylvania Magazine of History and Biography,* 70(1946): 239–57; Richard Buel Jr., "The Committee Movement of 1779 and the Formation of Public Authority in Revolutionary America," in James A. Henretta, Michael Kammen, and Stanley N. Katz, eds., *The Transformation of Early American History* (New York, 1991), 161. The committee movement is best traced starting in the *Pennsylvania Packet,* May 27, 1779.

25. Quote from John and Thos. Ricketts to Levi Hollingsworth, June 12, 1779; see also September 22 and October 4, all in HFP. Memorial of Philadelphia Merchants, in *Pennsylvania Packet,* September 10, 1779; see also Rob. Morris to Tim. Matlack, July 17, in RMNY.

26. For the suspicion directed at the merchants, see Daniel Roberdeau to the Philadelphia town meeting, in *Pennsylvania Packet,* May 27, 1779; "Address of the Committee of the City and Liberties of Philadelphia," in ibid., June 29; Philadelphia Committee to Robert Morris, July 11, and "Report of the Philadelphia Committee," in ibid., July 24; "A Citizen," in ibid., August 28. The merchants defended themselves in the public prints; see "Address to the Inhabitants of Philadelphia," June 15, in ibid., July 2; "W. S.," in ibid., September 9; and "Memorial of the Philadelphia Merchants," in ibid., September 10, 1779.

27. John and Thos. Ricketts to Levi Hollingsworth, June 12, 1779. See also Thos. May to Levi, September 10, 1780, and Jos. England to Levi, November 29, in HFP. Charles B. Kuhlmann, *The Development of the Flour-Milling Industry in the United States . . .* (Boston, 1979), 32ff.

28. One of the objections to the attempts at legislative price regulation in 1777 had been that farmers responded by fattening their horses; see Jere. Wadsworth to Hen. Laurens, May 27, 1777, in JWP. The temptation to sell to distillers was particularly powerful because the demand for whiskey remained strong; see Mathias Slough to Levi Hollingsworth, December 18, 1778, in HFP. Chaloner and White to Jere. Wadsworth, October 6, 1779, November 2 and 3, in C&WLB.

29. In Hollingsworth's case, roughly 90 percent of it was brought to market after the beginning of 1780, and about half of that 90 percent after June 1; see Levi Hollingsworth, Flour Journal no. 540 and Ledger no. 598, in HFP.

30. New Jersey Assembly to Congress, October 7, 1779, in PCC, reel 82, item 68, 467ff; Azariah Dunham to Ephr. Blaine, December 20, 1779, in EBP; *PRSC,* 2: 567–68; *JCC,* 15: 1289–92. Roger Sherman to Jon. Trumbull Sr., December 28, 1779, and to

Andr. Adams, January 7, 1780, in *LD*, 14: 305, 325. The New Jersey legislature took the initiative in petitioning Congress for such a measure; see New Jersey General Assembly to Congress, October 7, 1779, in PCC, reel 82, item 68, 467ff.

31. Wm. Ellery to Wm. Greene, February 15, 1780, in *LD*, 15: 417–18. Regulation continued to have influential political supporters; see John Armstrong Sr. to Hor. Gates, February 16, 1780, and to Jos. Reed, March 15, in ibid., 423–24, 502–4; Jos. Reed to Caesar Rodney, November 16, 1779, in *PA*, 1st ser., 8: 10.

32. C. Page Smith, "The Attack on Fort Wilson," *Pennsylvania Magazine of History and Biography* 78(1954): 177–88; John K. Alexander, "The Fort Wilson Incident of 1779: A Case Study of the Revolutionary Crowd," *William & Mary Quarterly*, 3rd. ser. 31 (1974): 602–6. See also Steven J. Rosswurm, *Arms, Country, and Class: The Philadelphia Militia and the "Lower Sort" During the American Revolution* (New Brunswick, N.J., 1987), 209–17. For Congress's defensiveness about the expanding debt, cf. "An Address of the Congress to the Inhabitants of the United States of America, May 8, 1778," *JCC*, 11: 479, with "To the Inhabitants of the United States of America, May 26, 1779," in ibid., 14: 649–57. Congress had no choice but to take the issue head-on in its address of September 13, 1779, though; see ibid., 15: 1056. For British intelligence, see anonymous communication dated February 3, 1779, enclosed with Wm. Franklin to Lord George Germain, February 5, 1779, in *DAR*, 17: 52; see also information supplied by Daniel Gray of Stamford, February 7, 1780, and by an unidentified source, February 19, and by Peter Grant of Branford, March 27, in CO 5/1110, LCTB.

33. For the permanent army and the draft, see Buel, *Dear Liberty*, 105–18, 173ff, 197ff; Arthur J. Alexander, "How Maryland Tried to Raise Her Continental Quotas," *Maryland Historical Magazine* 13(1947): 184–96; Jonathan Smith, "How Massachusetts Raised Her Troops in the Revolution," Massachusetts Historical Society, *Proceedings* 55(1923): 345–70. The experience of Pennsylvania is chronicled in *PA*, 1st ser., 8: 32, 114, 179, 290.

34. November 1 and December 13, 1779, in Massachusetts Historical Society, *Collections*, 7th ser. 2 (1892): 450, 459. Trumbull was relying here on an expedient utilized by Massachusetts Bay in coping with the depreciation of its provincial currency during the 1740s (see Richard A. Lester, *Monetary Experiments: Early American and Recent Scandinavian* [Princeton, N.J., 1939], 153), as well as on commercial practices that developed in response to the revolutionary depreciation (see Thos. Fayerweather bond to Hall & Bishop and Wm. G. Hutchinson, September 26, 1778, in Thos. Fayerweather Business Papers, NEHGS).

35. By the time they made the acknowledgment, the depreciation had advanced further; see Wm. Floyd to Pierre Van Cortlandt, January 11, 1780, in *LD*, 14: 332; E. James Ferguson, *The Power of the Purse* (Chapel Hill, 1963), 51–52. Congress wanted the interest to be paid in bills of exchange on Europe—like the loan office debt—before March 1, 1778, but none of it ever was; see *JCC*, 16: 262–66; Robt. Morris to John Hanson, July 29, 1782, in *PRM*, 6: 61.

36. For problems with implementing the plan, see Jas. Madison to Thos. Jefferson, May 6, 1780; John Walker to Thos. Jefferson, June 13, 1780; New York Delegates to

Geo. Clinton, June 16; Sam. Holten to Geo. Partridge, June 21; Jos. Jones to Washington, June 21?; Ezek. Cornell to Wm. Greene, June 30; Sam. Huntington to Oliver Wolcott, June 14; Thos. McKean to Caesar Rodney, July 24; Ezek. Cornell to Nath. Greene, August 13; Whitmell Hill to Thos. Burke, August 20, 1780, in *LD*, 15: 92, 315–16, 337, 356, 361, 389, 448, 501, 572, 608; see also Sam. Huntington to Jos. Reed, April 23, 1780, in *PA*, 1st ser., 8: 202. Connecticut acted before Congress to emit a new paper currency on a par with specie while recalling the continental money (Buel, *Dear Liberty,* 217–18).

37. For the effect of the fall of Charleston on the new emission money, see John Mathews to Robt. R. Livingston, April 24, 1780, and Wm. C. Houston to Wm. Livingston, June 4, 1780, in *LD,* 15: 67, 246. Other explanations for the failure of the new currency in replacing the old have been advanced. For instance, Ferguson, *Power of the Purse,* 51ff, cites the size of the certificate debt and the willingness of certain states to accept certificates rather than old continentals in taxation.

38. Cf. the report of Jeremiah Wadsworth's agent, Oliver Phelps, to Wadsworth, July 3, 1780, with John Chaloner to Wadsworth, July 23, and Hen. Champion to Wadsworth, August 4, in JWP. See also Jos. Reed to John Holker, June 22, 1780, in *PA*, 1st ser., 8: 350; Wm. Floyd to Pierre Van Cortlandt, January 11, 1780, in *LD*, 14: 332. The new continental emission was scarcer by definition than the old, but the states that issued their own new currencies had also been careful to limit the quantities involved; see Buel, *Dear Liberty,* 217; *Pennsylvania Gazette,* March 29, 1780. For Congress's additional requisitions, see *JCC*, 15: 1147, 1150. For the states' response, see Ferguson, *Power of the Purse,* 53, fn13.

39. For the continental currency's various utilities, see Sam. Hollingsworth to Levi Hollingsworth, July 3, 1780; Joshua Gilpin to Hollingsworth, December 3, 1780; Thos. May to Levi Hollingsworth, December 4; John Page to Hollingsworth, January 8, 1781; and Elijah Bolden to Hollingsworth, January 12, in HFP. Jos. Reed to Caesar Rodney, November 16, 1779, to Washington, December 22, to the President of Congress, May 6, 1780, and to Thomas S. Lee, June 16, in *PA*, 1st ser., 8: 10, 55, 229–30.

40. Ferguson, *Power of the Purse,* 52, argues that the abandonment of any pretense of a specie equivalency for the old continentals by Congress actually led to an appreciation. I have found no concrete evidence of this, though some expected it; see Officers of the Pennsylvania Line to the Pennsylvania Assembly, December 19, 1780, in *PA*, 1st ser., 8: 693; Jos. Reed to the Congressional Delegates, January 15?, 1781, in ibid., 703–4. Sam. Hollingsworth commented on the paradox of the old continental's declining value in the face of scarcity; see his letter to Levi Hollingsworth, November 9, 1780, in HFP. Those who preferred continentals to coin often wished to evade certain legal restrictions; see Wm. Henry to Jos. Reed, December 12, 1780, and Jas. Irvine to Reed, December 18, in *PA* 1st ser., 8, 652, 661.

41. Jas. Madison to Jas. Madison Sr., March 20, 1780, in *LD,* 14: 524; the younger Madison observed that it reduced the currency debt from $200 million to $5 million. The apt phrase comes from Winifred B. Rothenberg, *From Market-Places to a Market Economy* . . . (Chicago, 1992), 123.

42. Robt. Morris to Hor. Gates, June 12, 1781, in *PRM*, 1: 145; John M. Scott to Geo. Clinton, May 12, 1780, in *LD*, 15: 117.

43. For accommodating the army, see *JCC*, 16: 344; Phil. Schuyler to Alex Hamilton, April 8, 1780; Sam. Holten to Geo. Partridge, April 11; Jas. Lovell to Sam. Adams, April 11, in *LD*, 15: 24, 29, 31. Quote from Resolutions of Congress, August 26, 1780, in *JCC*, 17: 784–85. See also President of Congress to Jos. Reed, September 3, 1780, in *PA*, 1st ser., 8: 534. Officials charged with procuring teams had proceeded in this fashion even before receiving authorization; see John Cox to Chas. Pettit, July 11, 1780, in ibid., 8: 406.

44. See Thos. McKean to John Dickinson, December 25, 1780, in *LD*, 16: 480. Massachusetts took the first tentative step in January 1781; see Harlow, "Economic Conditions," 183; Jos. Reed to President of Congress, May 6, 1780, in *PA*, 1st ser., 8: 229. See also Jesse Root to Oliver Ellsworth, August 4, 1781, in CHHS.

45. For Washington's initial reluctance to introduce a French expeditionary force onto the North American continent, see his letter to D'Estaing, September 11, 1778, in *WGW*, 12: 424. The idea had been broached by the American commissioners in Paris early in 1779, dropped, and then revived by Washington in the autumn; see Dull, *Diplomatic History*, 115–18. The fate of the French plan to invade Britain in 1779 with the support of Spain is recounted in W. M. James, *The British Navy in Adversity* (London, 1926), 173–85; see also Congress to La Luzerne, January 30, 1780, in *RDC*, 3: 485–86.

46. For Lafayette's welcome, see his letter to Adrienne de Noailles de Lafayette, May 6, 1780, in *LAR*, 3: 8–9. For his attempts to orchestrate the ensuing campaign, see Lafayette to Washington, April 27, 1780, and to Vergennes, May 20, in *LAR*, 3: 3, 26. See also Sam. Huntington to Certain States, June 5, 1780; Oliver Ellsworth to Jon. Trumbull, June 8; Robt. R. Livingston to Phil. Schuyler, June 9; and Sam. Huntington to Jon. Trumbull, June 10, in *LD*, 15: 253, 276, 280, 285–86. *JCC*, 17: 467. Lafayette to La Luzerne, June 3, 1780, in *LAR*, 3: 47.

47. American sensitivities to French troops was a major issue with the French Court, which Franklin declined to help with; see Lee Kennett, *The French Forces in America, 1780–1783* (Westport, Conn., 1977), 8–10. See also Committee at Headquarters to Certain States, May 25, 1780, in *LD*, 15: 190; Vergennes to Lafayette, June 3, 1780, in *LAR*, 3: 51; Committee of Congress at Camp to Pres. Reed, June 19, 1780, and Washington to the Committee of Congress, May 25, 1780, in *PA*, 1st ser., 8: 337, 267. Quote from Jedediah Huntington to Jere. Wadsworth, May 5, 1780, in Connecticut Historical Society *Collections* 20(1920): 150; Joseph Ward to Col. Peabody, July 19, 1780, in Joseph Ward Papers, CHHS.

48. Committee of Congress at Camp to ?, May 10, 1780, in *PA*, 1st ser., 8: 240. See also Lafayette to Jos. Reed, May 31, 1780, in *LAR*, 3: 44. For the meat crisis, see Ephraim Blaine to Jos. Reed, May 20, 1780, in *PA*, 1st ser., 8: 260. Reference to New York's crop failure are found in Committee of Congress to Jos. Reed, July 10, in ibid., 8: 404.

49. For references to the tax rebellion, see *PA*, 1st ser., 8: 80, 124, 125–26, 129–30,

170, 207, 208. For Pennsylvania's currency, see Jos. Reed to Christian Wirtz, April 18, 1780, and to Nicholas Lutz, April ?, in ibid., 192, 201. The Assembly's actions with respect to Congress's plan, in addition to the Assembly's own plan, are printed in *Pennsylvania Gazette,* March 29, 1780.

50. See Jos. Reed to John Holker, March 28, April 5, 1780; Christian Wirtz to Jos. Reed, April 15, 1780, in *PA,* 1st ser., 8: 149, 164, 187.

51. Board of War to Jos. Reed, March 7, 1780, in ibid., 8: 122–23. Jos. Reed to the Board of War, March 11–13?, 1780, to John Proctor, April 29, to Mich. Lyndemood, May 10, and John Gibson to Reed, April 18, 1780, in ibid., 8: 133, 185, 217, 236–37. Jos. Reed to Nath. Greene, July 10, and to Ephr. Blaine, August 7 or 8, 1780, in ibid., 8: 427, 494–95. Also Jos. Reed to Congress, July 30; Ephr. Blaine to Jos. Reed, August 3, 1780, in ibid., 8: 462–63, 479–80.

52. Washington to Jos. Reed, June 19, 1780, in ibid., 8: 339–40. Washington to Jos. Reed, April 12, 1780, in ibid., 8: 180. Reed to Congress, July 30, 1780, and to Washington, August 8, in ibid., 8: 464, 466, 482–83. The situation was further complicated by de Corny's attempt to procure horses in Pennsylvania for the French army.

53. Washington to Major Henry Lee, July 24, 1780, in *WGW,* 19: 248. For the state's grudging authorization, see Jos. Reed to Major Henry Lee, August 1, 1780, in *PA,* 1st ser., 8: 477. See also the reference to Lee's activities in Jos. Hart to Jos. Reed, August 14, 1780, in ibid., 8: 504. The quote is from Reed to Blaine, August 7 or 8, 1780, in ibid., 8: 494. John Lacey to Jos. Reed, August 15, 1780, in ibid., 8: 508.

54. Jos. Reed to Board of War, August 15, 1780, in ibid., 8: 509–10.

55. Lawrence Lewis, *A History of the Bank of North America, the First Bank Chartered in the United States* (Philadelphia, 1882), 17, 19–20. The list is from PCC, reel 41, item 34, 297. Thomas Paine later claimed credit for starting the subscriptions with $500 of his own salary as secretary of the Assembly; see "On Government; The Affairs of the Bank; and Paper Money" (1786), in W. M. Van der Weyde, ed., *The Life and Works of Thomas Paine* (New Rochelle, N.Y., 1925), 4: 251–53.

56. "Plan for establishing a Bank," undated in PCC, reel 29, item 20, vol. 2: 87–90; *JCC,* 17: 549–50.

57. "Plan for establishing a Bank," 88–90; *PNG,* 6: 51–52n.; Robt. Morris to Phil. Schuyler, May 29, 1781, in *PRM,* 1: 92. Washington to Nath. Greene, July 19, 1780, in *WGW,* 19: 212. Even after combined operations were abandoned, Lafayette thought that efforts like the bank would have been sufficient to sustain the campaign "had it been necessary"; see Lafayette to Vergennes, October 4, 1780, in *LAR,* 3: 188–89.

58. Wm. Ramsey and Guilliam Aertsen to John Mercier, June 14, 1784, in PCC, reel 28, item 19, vol. 4, p. 553; Jerry Grundfest, "George Clymer, Philadelphia Revolutionary, 1739–1813" (Ph.D. diss., Columbia University, 1973), 156–57. 5,436 bu. of corn translated into roughly 700 (196 lb.) bbl. of flour in terms of rations. For Pennsylvania's specifics, see Jos. Reed to Holker, March 13, 28, 1780; Committee of Congress to Jos. Reed, June 2; Reed to the President of Congress, July 30, in *PA,* 1st ser., 8: 134, 148, 294, 463. Thirty thousand men had been agreed on after the Wethersfield conference, September 22, 1780, as detailed in *LAR,* 3: 176.

59. Quotes from Jos. Reed to Nath. Greene, July 19, 1780, in *NGP,* 6: 124, and John Nixon and Geo. Clymer to Washington, end of August 1780, in *WGW,* 19: 376fn. See Alex. Hamilton to Jas. Duane, September 3, 1780, in *PAH,* 2: 413. Hamilton's assessment of the bank's activities is confirmed by the directors' repeated calls for subscribers to pay in their capital shares; see *Pennsylvania Journal,* August 9, 23, October 4, 25, and November 14, 1780. Washington was sufficiently impressed with the scheme that he encouraged the establishment of a similar bank of private merchants in the eastern states to supply the army with tents; see *WGW,* 19: 150.

60. Lafayette to Rochambeau and Ternay, July 9, 1780; Rochambeau to Lafayette, July 16, 1780, in *LAR,* 3: 69–75, 96.

61. James, *British Navy* , 233. Washington to Lafayette, July 31, and August 1, 1780, in *LAR,* 3: 120–21, 122–23 and note. Lafayette to Rochambeau and Ternay, August 9, 18, 1780, in ibid., 3: 135, 145. Rochambeau was happy to credit Lafayette's claim; see his letter of August 12, in ibid., 3: 140; William B. Willcox, ed., *The American Rebellion: Sir Henry Clinton's Narrative of His Campaigns, 1775–1782* (Hamden, Conn., 1971), 202–8, 446–52.

62. James, *British Navy,* 233, 236. Rochambeau to Lafayette, August 12, 1780, and Lafayette to Adrienne de Noailles de Lafayette, October 7, in *LAR,* 3: 140, 193.

63. La Luzerne had been unable to provide de Corny with much money. See Lafayette to La Luzerne, May 17, 1780; La Luzerne to Lafayette, May 28 and 31, in ibid., 3: 21–22, 40, 45.

64. Kennett, *French Forces in America,* 30–31; Buel, *Dear Liberty,* 241–42; Rochambeau and Destouches to Washington, December 22, 1780, in *LAR,* 3: 271.

65. Mason, "Entrepreneurial Activity," 195; Buel, *Dear Liberty,* 242–43.

66. Kennett, *French Forces in America,* 68; Buel, *Dear Liberty,* 243.

67. Kennett, *French Forces in America,* 78, 89; Arnold Whitridge, *Rochambeau* (New York, 1965), 103. Jere. Wadsworth to Joshua(?) Huntington, October 21, 1780, and contract between Wadsworth and Carter and Morgan Lewis and Daniel Parker, February 2, 1781; John Carter to Jere. Wadsworth, February 28, 1781, in JWP.

68. Lafayette to Ternay, August 9; to La Luzerne, August 11, 1780, in *LAR,* 3: 131, 136, 137–38. Arnold appealed to anti-French prejudices in justifying his treason; see "Address to the Inhabitants of America," October 7, 1780, in *EAB,* nos. 16701, 16789.

69. See Lafayette to La Luzerne, January 4, 7, and 14, 1781, in *LAR,* 3: 276–81, 288–89.

CHAPTER 7. THE SEEDS OF RECOVERY

1. However, the French government considered abandoning its commitment to full American independence in 1781; see Jonathan R. Dull, *A Diplomatic History of the American Revolution* (New Haven, Conn., 1985), 123–24.

2. Royal Flint to Jere. Wadsworth, July 17, 1780, in Massachusetts Historical Society, *Collections,* 7th ser., 3(1902): 66. Lee Kennett, *The French Forces in America, 1780–1783* (Westport, Conn., 1977), 10–12, 14.

3. Paschal N. Smith to Sam. Flagg, March 10, 1780, and to John Nelson, March ? [between the 17th and 31st], 1780, in S&SLB.

4. A typical French army bill was drawn for anywhere from 1,000 to 6,000 livres; see Steph. Collins to Wm. Gray, October 28, November 20, December 3, 1782, in SCLB; Jere. Wadsworth, Memo, July 8, 1781, in JWP. See also Alex. Hamilton to Robt. Morris, September 21, 1782, in *PRM,* 6: 413. Bills of smaller denominations were negotiated more easily; see Geo. Woolsey to John Pringle, December 31, 1774, in W&SLB; Peter Whiteside to Wm. Duer, March 27, 1781, in WDP. For the uses to which American merchants put French bills, see Steph. Collins to Wm. Gray, December 4, 1782, in SCLB; Jon. Williams Jr. to Ed. Bancroft, December 16, 1779, and to Matt. Ridley, April 16, 1780, in JnWLB; Paschal N. Smith to Wm. Lucas and John Nelson, April 10, 1781, in S&SLB; Codman & Smith to Geo. Meade, February 22 and April 4, 1781, in CSLB.

5. John J. McCusker, *Money and Exchange in Europe and America, 1600–1775: A Handbook* (Chapel Hill, N.C., 1977), 21–22. Bills were first presented to the payer for acceptance. In "accepting" them, the payer declared his intention of making the payment at the time specified in the bill. Once accepted, the holder of the bill could negotiate it at a slight discount and realize most of its value without delay.

6. Geo. Woolsey to Thos. Matthews, March 1, 1775, to John Pringle, November 8, 1775, January 3, and March 22, 1776, to Geo. Salmon, December 8, 1775, in W&SLB. McCusker, *Money and Exchange,* 186. The exchange also rose above par in Philadelphia at the end of 1782 for reasons that will be explored below; see Steph. Collins to Wm. Vans, December 25, 1782, in SCLB.

7. Paschal N. Smith to Eleazer Miller Jr., September 9 and November 3, 1776; to Moses H. Hays, March 18, 1779; to Eleazer Miller Jr., May 26, 1779, in S&SLB. According to eighteenth-century European convention, belligerents provided for their own men when taken prisoner. The attempt to use sterling exchange in providing for American prisoners and the refusal of British authorities to cooperate can be traced in Elias Boudinot to Lewis Pentard, May 5 and 22, July 27, and August 16, 1777; to Rich. Peters, June 30 and July 14, in Elias Boudinot Letter Book, 1777–78, in State Historical Society of Wisconsin, Madison. Americans accepted bills drawn by captured British officers on sterling accounts in Europe; see Jon. Williams Jr. to Jacob LeTillier, April 5, 1780, in JnWLB. For the rising paper price of sterling exchange, see Paschal N. Smith to Eleazer Miller Jr., December 9, 1778, and January 5, May 26, June 18, and August 25, 1779, in S&SLB. For continued difficulties in negotiating sterling bills, see Jon. Williams Jr. to Jon. Williams Sr., June 16, 1779, and John Swan, July 2, in JnWLB. However, some British merchants continued to honor their bills; see Williams to Titus Salter, June 16, 1780, in ibid.

8. McCusker, *Money and Exchange,* 7–8, 9, 10, 283. There were three livres to the petit or half écu, the standard French coin at this time. The Spanish dollar was roughly equal in value to two half écus.

9. Jon. Williams Jr. to Chas. Pettit, December 20, 1779, and January 20 and 25, 1780, in JnWLB. However, official bills occasionally encountered difficulties. The first such bill that Jon. Williams Jr. received, endorsed to Messrs. Hope & Co. in Amsterdam, was

refused acceptance, but Williams still expected it to be paid; see Williams to Messrs. Hope & Co., August 29, September 9, 1780, in ibid. The failure to accept a bill prevented the possessor from negotiating it; see Williams to Solomon Meyers Cohen, September 15, November 21, 1780, in ibid. Jonathan Williams Jr.'s correspondence reflects the role that bills on France, and particularly on the American commissioners, played in the development of Franco-American trade during 1779; see Williams to Simeon Mayo and John Merchant, March 7, 1779; to Nath. Appleton, and Willis Hall, and Samuel Parkman, February 28; to Nath. Appleton, Willis Hall, Sam. Barrett, Nathan Blodget, Gov. Greene, Dan. Waldo, Paschal N. Smith, Dan. Sears, Eliz. Perkins, and Thos. Cushing, May 26; to Sylvanus Hussey, Wm. Sever, Sam. Parkman, to Codman & Smith, to Job Prince and Jos. Barrett, August 12; to Thos. Cushing, Sam. Barrett, October 14, in JnWLB. For the growing demand for livre exchange, see Paschal N. Smith to Isaac Sears, November 9, 1778; to Hen. Newman, March 24, 1779; to John Grenell, May 26; to Isaac Sears, August 14, 1780, in S&SLB.

10. For the vessel shortage in early 1780, see Jon. Williams Jr. to Wm. Phillips, to Thos. Cushing, to Josiah Quincy, to Hannah Winthrop, to John Torrey, to Thos. Greenough, to Herman Brimmer, and to Lathrop & Coit, March 6, 1780; to John Mason, to Peter Boyer, March 8; to Nath. Appleton, to Sam. Perkins, March 30; to John Hodshon, April 4; to Ben. Franklin, April 21, in JnWLB. For the first French army bills in Boston, see Paschal N. Smith to John Broome, August 9, 1780, to John Nelson, September 8, in S&SLB. Large quantities of livre exchange did not show up in Europe until the arrival of the vessels that cleared the American coast in the late autumn; see Williams to Bradford, February 13, 1781, in JnWLB. For the use that New England merchants quickly made of livre exchange, see Paschal N. Smith to John de Neufville, October 2, 1780, to Eleazer Miller Jr., November 11, November 23, December 19, to David Crommelin & Sons, December 14, in S&SLB. Chris. Champlin to de Neufville, December 19, 1780, and January 4, April 1 and 21, 1781; to Chas. Sonderstrom, April 1; to Elkanah Watson, June 12; to Hen. Greig, June 18; and to Wanton Casey, June 28, in CCLB. French bills were not as negotiable in Spain, though; see Codman & Smith to Jos. Gardoqui, May 20, 1781, to Ingraham & Bromfield, June 19 and July 19, 1782, in CSLB. For the discount at which livre exchange sold, see John Bell to John Holker, August 10, 1780, in JHLC. See also Jere. Wadsworth to ?, January 13, 1782, in JWP.

11. For some of the factors affecting the price of bills, see Dan. Parker to Jere. Wadsworth, May 31, 1781, in DPLB; John Welsh to Richard Harrison, December 19, 1781; to Jacob Welsh, March 29, 1782, in JWLB. Bills could be sold in secondary commercial centers in the interior, such as Albany and Hartford, but not to so much advantage; see John Church to Jere. Wadsworth, August 11, 1781, in JWP. Before Rochambeau's arrival, Boston merchants had looked to Philadelphia for cheap exchange; see Codman & Smith to Wm. Turnbull, May 4 and 8, 1780; to Sam. Wells Jr., June 28; to Geo. Meade, June 29, in CSLB. After his arrival, buyers instead turned to Boston; see Codman & Smith to Geo. Meade, July 28, 1780, in ibid; Dan. Parker to Geo. Merrells, July 19, 1781, in DPLB. But during 1782 the Boston market sometimes was higher than Philadelphia's; see Parker to Ingraham & Bromfield, September 18, 1782, in

ibid.; John Welsh to Jacob Welsh, n.d. [provenance summer, 1782], in JWLB. Some Americans were interested in maintaining the price of livre exchange and sought out the highest rather than the lowest market; see John Church to Thos. L. Halsey, July 25, 1781, and to Jere. Wadsworth, July 25, in JWP. The behavior of both groups had the effect of minimizing price differentials over time; see John Church to Thos. L. Halsey, July 22, 1781, and to John Chaloner, August 14, in ibid.

12. Jere. Wadsworth to T. L. Halsey, July 3, 1781, in JWP; John Welsh to unidentified correspondent in Cádiz, July 12, 1781; to Richard Harrison, September 10, 1781, in JWLB; Robt. R. Livingston to François Barbé Marbois, June 4, 1781, in RRLP; Steph. Collins to Wm. Gray, November 20, 1781, in SCLB; Paschal N. Smith to Eleazer Miller Jr., March 13, 1781, in S&SLB; Dan. Parker to Ingraham & Bromfield, September 18, 1782, in DPLB; Lafayette's summary of the conference between Washington, Rochambeau, and Ternay at Hartford, September 22, 1780, in *LAR,* 3: 178.

13. Kennett, *French Forces,* 65–66, 67, 69. This was also true for the British, and Robt. Morris claimed that their costs were considerably greater than those incurred by the French; see Morris to La Luzerne, November 3, 1781, in *PRM,* 3: 134. See also Morris to the Governor of Cuba, July 17, 1781, in ibid., 1: 314.

14. John Welsh to Andr. Matthews, September 10, 1781, in JWLB. For the fisheries, see Daniel Vickers, *Farmers & Fishermen* . . . (Chapel Hill, 1994), 264–66, and CP, 1770–82. Fish did not disappear from Massachusetts Bay's trade during the war; see Jackson, Tracy & Tracy to Messrs. Joseph Guardoqui & Sons, November 26, 1776, in *J&L,* 1: 328. But much of it was prize fish; see lists of libels before Massachusetts Admiralty Courts in *Boston Gazette,* 1776–82. And the fisheries as such suffered severely; see document pertaining to Ipswich, Massachusetts, dated October 10, 1790, contrasting the state of the fishery in the town in 1767–75 with 1787–90, John Heard Papers, BLHU. Fragmentary evidence suggests that fish may have become a more prominent component of New England's commerce after 1780; see Codman & Smith to Geo. Meade, February 22 and May 10, 1781; to Jos. Soubies, March 1; to Messrs. Banere et Grand, June 14; to Silas Brenton, October 20, 1782, in CSLB; Elias Smith to Josiah Batchelder, February 22, 1782, in Batchelder Papers, BHS, perhaps as an alternative to privateering. See also James S. Leamon, *Revolution Downeast* . . . (Amherst, Mass., 1993), 135–36, 142. For the timber trade, see Jackson, Tracy & Tracy to Messrs. Lewis Ponset & Sons, December 7, 1776, and headnote in *J&L,* 1: 330, 338; Paschal N. Smith to John Blagg, July 29, 1778; to Godfrey Hutchinson, July 30, in S&SLB. For the triangular trade, see Paschal N. Smith to John Nelson, March 15, 1780, in ibid. This didn't prevent someone like Jon. Williams Jr. in Nantes from trying to encourage a triangular trade; see Williams to John Williams, December 2, 1780, in JnWLB.

15. Once the supply of livre exchange began to expand in the American economy, Jon. Williams Jr. expressed his preference for livres as a remittance from the more southerly ports that had access to traditional staples like tobacco; see Williams to Wallace & Davidson, October 4, 1780; to Young & Knox, November 30; to Bache & Shee, December 28, 1780, and January 11, 1781, in JnWLB. For the safety of bills, see John Welsh to Rich. Harrison, December 19, 1781, in JWLB; McCusker, *Money and Ex-*

change, 129–30. One still ran the risk that a bill might bear a forged endorsement or have some other irregularity; see Jon. Williams Jr. to Billy Franklin, August 29, 31, and September 9, 1780, in JnWLB. For the problems of westbound freight, see Welcome Arnold to John Turner, March 17, 1780, in AGP; Jon. Williams Jr. to John Holker, February 15, 1780; to Robt. and Anth. Garvey, March 27; to Jas. Coolidge, March 30; to Lathrop & Coit, April 2, in JnWLB; De la Lande & Fynje to John Barrett, April 1, 1781, in Wendell Papers, BLHU; Paschal N. Smith to Nich. and John Brown, December 17, 1778, in S&SLB. When the supply of shipping got really tight, as on the Atlantic coast of France in the first half of 1780, captains would accept only the highest priced goods, rejecting items like Rouen ware, the luggage of passengers, and even, on occasion, tea; see Jon. Williams Jr. to Mrs. Richard Bache, April 18; to Nathan Frazer, to Nath. Appleton, May 3; to Robt. and Anth. Garvey, May 11; to Thos. Hutchins, May 14; to Jos. Casson, June 8, in JnWLB.

16. For Holker's problems, see Jon. Williams Jr. to Chevalier Holker, May 11 and June 11, 1780, in JnWLB. Holker stopped drawing during summer 1780 (see Wm. Palfrey to Jos. Barrell, July 14, 1780, in WPP) but later resumed (see Steph. Collins to Wm. Gray, December 4, 1781, and to Jon. Amory, April 9 and 11, 1782, in SCLB). For French dependence on mid-Atlantic grain, see John Holker to Jos. Reed, September 10, 1780, *PA*, 1st ser., 8: 545. For French purchasing in New York, see Udny Hay to Clinton, November 23, 1780, in *PPGC*, 6: 443; Wadsworth to John Church, February 14 and March 8, 1781, and Church to Wadsworth, June 3 and July 6, 1781, in JWP.

17. Wadsworth & Carter's activities in providing for the French during their sojourn in New England is documented in box 153, Letter Book B, JWP.

18. Kennett, *French Forces*, 67; John Church to Jere. Wadsworth, June 8, 1781, in JWP. For the costs of transporting specie, see Steph. Collins to Robt. Rantoul, January 27, 1783, in SCLB. For the constriction of the coastal trade, see Martin Brimmer to Wm. Palfrey, November 12, 1779, and Nathan Bush to Wm. Palfrey, March 9, 1780, Wm. Palfrey to his wife, July 11, October 30, 1780, in WPP.

19. For the use of exchange between the two cities, see Wm. Palfrey to Codman and Smith, July 7, 1780, in WPP; John Welsh to Jacob Welsh, n.d. [summer 1782], in JWLB. For the Philadelphia speculation in Boston's market, see Levi Hollingsworth to Hen. Armistead, May 4, 1781, in HFP. For its consequences, see Jere. Wadsworth to John Carter, April 22, 1781, in JWP. Walt. Livingston to Comfort Sands, May 23, 1782, in Walter Livingston Letter Book, RLP. See also Paschal N. Smith to Eleazer Miller Jr., February 15, 1781, in S&SLB. For Philadelphia's prewar status as a market for exchange, see Geo. Woolsey to John Pringle, February 14, 1775; also cf. Woolsey to Pringle, July 15 and October 10, 1775, in W&SLB.

20. The two 1780 vessels were the *Katy*, a small brig that got into Providence, and the *Mars* (16); see Jon. Williams Jr. to John Thaxter or Rich. Dana, April 28, 1780; to Jas. Cuming, to J. Loring Austin, September 14; to Jon. Williams Sr., November 24; to Thos. Cushing, to Eben. Storer, December 2, 1780, in JnWLB. For the *Marquis de Lafayette,* one of the largest merchant ships in the world, see Jon. Williams Jr. to Messrs. James Seering & Sons, January 13, 1781; to John Hodshon, to Sigourney, Ingraham &

Bromfield, to John de Neufville, January 21, in JnWLB; the New England fleet soon expanded to six merchantmen escorted by the *Alliance;* see Williams to Silas Deane, February 14, 1781, in ibid. For Williams's difficulties in prosecuting the American trade from Nantes, see his letters to John Hall, July 17, 1780; to Jas. Cuming, August 1; to John Nesbitt & Co., August 6; to John Williams, August 18; to Matt. Ridley, October 14, in ibid. For his new ventures and the emphasis he put on remitting bills, see Williams to Wallace & Davidson, October 4, 1780; to Jon. Williams Sr., November 24 and December 5; to Messrs. Bache & Shee, December 28 and January 10, 1780; for his new willingness to ship before receiving remittances, see his letter to John Winthrop, November 21; to Thos. Chase, November 30; to Timothy Fitch, to Edward Jones, and to Thos. Cushing, December 2, in JnWLB.

21. Jon. Williams Jr. to Gardoqui & Sons, December 11, 1780; to de Neufville, December 28, in JnWLB. Williams Jr. circularized his European correspondents to this effect; see his form letter of January 30, 1781, to John Hodshon, to John de Neufville, to Jas.[?] Seering, to Francis Dana, to Sigourney, Ingraham & Bromfield, to Rich. Harrison, to Jos. Gardoqui, etc., in JnWLB. Some responded to the opportunity; see Williams to de la Lande & Fynje, February 20, 1781, in ibid.

22. *PRSC,* 3: 559–61, 562; for quotes from Udny Hay to Geo. Clinton, see November 23, 1780, in *PPGC,* 6: 443.

23. Washington to Clinton, November 27, 1780, in *WGW,* 20: 413; quotes from Washington to the President of Congress, December 22, 1780, in *WGW,* 21: 1, and George Clinton to Washington, December 15, 1780, in George Washington Papers, LC.

24. Disguising confiscation as sales had become customary in New York; see Jere. Wadsworth to Sam. Huntington, November 24, 1779, in PCC, reel 104, item 78, vol. 24, p. 192; Geo. Clinton to Washington, December 26, 1779, and February 21, 1780, in *PPGC,* 5: 430–31, 509–10; also Udny Hay to George Clinton, February 25, 1780, and the return of Hendrick Wykoff, May 1, 1780, in ibid., 512, 668. Quotes from Udny Hay to Geo. Clinton, November 23, 1780, in *PPGC,* 6: 443. See also "A General Return of Provisions purchased and delivered under the Direction of Udny Hay . . . from August 1780 to 1st of May 1781," in ibid., 820. The unpopularity of the state's method of procurement is documented in a resolution at a meeting of more than three hundred of the Inhabitants of the Manor of Livingston, January 6, 1781, RRLP, reel 15; Gouv. Morris to Robt. R. Livingston, January 18, 1781, in ibid., reel 2; Hugh Hughes to Maj. Wolfe, January 14, 1781, and Wolfe to Hughes, April 15, in HHLB, vol. 10. Also Cynthia A. Kierner, *Traders and Gentlefolk . . .* (Ithaca, N.Y., 1992), 234.

25. Contemporaries were more aware of the difficulties than the modest successes of New York's regime, detailed in Udny Hay to Geo. Clinton, July 20, 1780, and September 7, 1780, in ibid., 6: 26–29, 180–81; see also Hay to Robt. Morris, August 15, 1781, in ibid., 7: 208–9; and Hugh Hughes to Maj. Wolfe, April 15, 1781, and Wolfe to Hughes, December 9, in HHLB, vol. 10.

26. Gouv. Morris to Robt. Morris, June 4, 1781, in *PRM,* 1: 107. For their reliance on coercion, see copies of impressment warrants issued by Governor Clinton to Colonels Van Schaick and Van Rensselaer, July 31, 1780, and to Abra. Wemple and Hen.

Glen, October 19; List of Press Warrants for Provisions, July through September 11; Geo. Clinton to Jas. Clinton, November 20; Geo. Trimble to Udny Hay, June 1, 1781, in *PPGC,* 6: 69, 208–9, 324, 422; 7: 6–8.

27. Proclamation, July 10, 1781, in *WGW,* 22: 351–52; Kennett, *French Forces,* 132, 161–2; *ACRA,* 1: 78, 164; 2: plates 141–46.

28. Dan. Parker to Jere. Wadsworth, June 28, 1781; to Jas. Watson,. August 23, in DPLB. John Sanders of Schnectady paid freight to John J. Beekman for transporting some goods "I have of Baltimore" on January 10, 1780, but a subsequent entry noted the return of the money. Beginning in January 1781 one encounters references to commodities like buttons and Barcelona handkerchiefs in addition to salt, tea, and indigo in his Day Book, 1777–1807, in NYHS. New York's special economic problems led Robert R. Livingston to identify the French reliance on bills as a disadvantage both to them and the New York consumer, since bills in large denominations could not be used to finance personal consumption. Instead, he urged the French to concentrate on the importation of specie; see Robt. R. Livingston to François Barbé Marbois, June 4, 1781, in RRLP, reel 2. See also Peter Whiteside to Wm. Duer, March 27, 1781, in WDP.

29. Estimates in table 7.1 are made by the same procedures as used in table 5.1 except that New London libels are adjusted by 20 tons one way or the other if the rigs are described as "large" or "small." The total for Massachusetts Bay was 140,962 tons, for New London 21,993 tons.

30. None of these attempts was successful; see W. M. James, *The British Navy in Adversity* (London, 1926), 270–74; see also Washington to Comte de Barras, July 23, 1781, in *WGW,* 22: 403.

31. Though only barely; cf. table 7.3. I say "may" because the relevant estimates in tables 7.1 and 7.3 are derived in slightly different ways.

32. Frances M. Caulkins, *History of New London, Connecticut* (New London, 1852), 552–56, 565, gives an account of the destruction.

33. Glen Weaver, *Jonathan Trumbull, Connecticut's Merchant Magistrate* (Hartford, Conn., 1956), 12. Customs 16/1, PRO, shows that in 1768 the two rivers between them were shipping close to 10,000 barrels of salted meat to the West Indies annually.

34. Chester M. Destler, *Connecticut: The Provisions State* (Chester, Conn., 1973), 11, 19, 26, 31, 33.

35. Quotes from Hen. Champion to Sam. Huntington, November 22, 1779, in PCC, reel 93, item 78, vol. 5, pp. 421, 437; see also Champion to Huntington, December 3, and to Jere. Wadsworth, December 3 and 14, in ibid., reel 170, item 152, vol. 8, pp. 231, 265. The commissariat adjusted to the reduction in cattle from New England almost immediately; see Royal Flint to Washington, January 3, 1780, in *PA,* 1st ser., 8: 70.

36. As did Jon. Trumbull; see his letter to Sam. Huntington, May 1, 1780, in PCC, reel 80, item 66, vol. 2, p. 41. See also Jere. Wadsworth to Jacob Cuyler, March 16, 1779, and to John Chaloner, May 11, in JWNY.

37. Or so I infer from the difficulties that the northern Army experienced with meat during the spring of 1780; see Phil. Schuyler to Ezra L'Hommedieu, May 20, 1780; Committee at Headquarters to Certain States, May 25, 1780; Phil. Schuyler to Geo.

Clinton, May 26 and 28; John M. Scott to Ezra L'Hommedieu, June 6 all in *LD,* 15: 165, 187, 199, 202. Since annual consumption normally affected only 25 percent of a herd, there could still be plenty of cattle around and a meat shortage as well. The significant question was how many were "fit for use" in age and weight. The phrase comes from Champion to Huntington, November 22, 1779, in PCC, reel 93, item 78, vol. 5, p. 421.

38. See "Proprietary and Other Tax Lists of the County of Bucks," in *PA,* 3rd ser., vol. 13. See also James T. Lemon, *The Best Poor Man's Country . . .* (Baltimore, 1972), 198.

39. My tabulation of cattle in Bucks County, Pennsylvania, during the period 1779–85 is as follows.

	1779	1781	1782	1785
Cattle	12441	10356	9562	9468
Percentage decline		16.8	7.7	1

Lancaster County had a larger population of cattle in 1779 than did Bucks County, though not per capita. While the published tax lists for it allow us only to compare 1779 with 1782, and the lists seem incomplete, the information included suggests that the county's cattle declined by 13.5 percent over that three-year interval; see *PA,* 3rd ser., vol. 17. More significantly, the four townships in the county with cattle populations of over 1,000 head in 1779—Earl, Lebanon, Cocalico, and Drumore—suffered a 41 percent decline in their herds between 1779 and 1782.

40. Jere. Wadsworth to John Chaloner, May 11, 1780, in JWNY. See also Ephr. Blaine to Sam. Huntington, January 5, 1780, in PCC, reel 182, item 165, p. 312.

41. Jere. Wadsworth to Oliver Phelps, July 8, 1780, in JWP. See Washington to Jon. Trumbull, January 19, April 10, and July 1, 1781; to Oliver Phelps and Sam. Osgood, January 19; to Phelps, April 16; to Geo. Clinton, April 29; to John Stark, May 6; to Wm. Heath, May 9, June 8 and 15; Circular to New England States, May 10, all in *WGW,* 21: 116–17, 122–23, 442–43, 465; 22: 8, 41–42, 63–64, 68, 182, 217, 311. See also Committee at Headquarters to Congress, May 10, 1780, in *LD,* 15: 105.

42. Frances M. Caulkins, *History of Norwich, Connecticut . . .* (Norwich, Conn., 1845), 215–16, 234, 270, 307–10, 330–31; Caulkins, *New London,* 574.

43. For the weight losses associated with driving stock, see Hen. Champion Jr. to Sam. Huntington, April 6, 1780, in PCC, reel 93, item 78, vol. 5, p. 468; Hen. Champion to Ephr. Blaine, January 6, 1781, in ibid., reel 182, item 165, pp. 394–95. For its wastefulness, see Robt. Morris to Meshech Weare, September 24, 1781, in *PRM,* 2: 342; to Udny Hay, December 6, in ibid., 3: 340; Alex. Hamilton to Morris, August 13, 1782, in ibid., 6: 188. For naval supplies, see John Holker to La Luzerne, February 26, 1781, in Destouches Papers, HL; John Holker to Wm. Duer, July 19, 1781, in WDP.

44. For the character of Philadelphia's entrepreneurs, see Willing and Morris to Wm. Bingham, October 26, 1776, in WBP; Thomas M. Doerflinger, *A Vigorous Spirit of Enterprise . . .* (Chapel Hill, 1986), 134, 215, 221. For their sense of vulnerability, see

Robt. Morris to Silas Deane, December 20, 1776, in *FME*, no. 1396. For the defense effort, see John W. Jackson, *The Pennsylvania Navy, 1775–1781* (New Brunswick, N.J., 1974), chaps. 1–8. Philadelphia's remoteness from the sea seemed an advantage in defending itself; see Jackson, Tracy & Tracy to Thos. and Isaac Wharton, May 25, 1775, in *J&L*, 1: 302.

45. For the struggle over the Delaware in 1777, see Christopher Ward, *The War of the Revolution* (New York, 1952), 1: 373–77.

46. Geo. Woolsey to John Pringle, March 5, May 7, June 4, 1778, in W&SLB. On the *Holker*, see William B. Clark, "That Mischievous *Holker*: The Story of a Privateer," *Pennsylvania Magazine of History and Biography* 79(1955): 27–30; John A. McManemin, *Captains of the Privateers During the Revolutionary War* (Spring Lake, N.J., 1985), 310–12, 326–36.

47. The figures for privateering are derived from Letters of Marque Register, July 31, 1778–August 12, 1782, in Records of Pennsylvania's Revolutionary Governments, 1775–1790, Pennsylvania Archives, Record Group 27, reel 9. The Register does not distinguish between letters of marque and privateers. I have inferred the distinction from the ratio of crew size to tonnage. For instance, a schooner of fifty-one tons carrying a crew of sixty was ill equipped to prosecute a commercial voyage and has been classified a privateer. Vessels with more than one man per two measured tons are categorized as privateers, the others as letters of marque. Some of the register's entries for 1779–82 omit reference to tonnage, though crew size and carriage guns are entered. In these instances I have assumed that vessels carrying four men or more per gun were privateers, those with less than four men per gun letters of marque. Other entries list guns and tons but omit the number of men. These vessels are designated privateers if their ratio of guns to tons is five or less, otherwise letters of marque. The three vessels in the sample for which the Register supplies insufficient information to apply the above rules have been designated letters of marque. Total tonnage for each category was estimated by adding all tonnage figures that were given in a category and extrapolating a value for the complete set by simple proportion. Thus for letters of marque in 1781, 76 / 100 = 6,078 / x = 7,997. Some vessels show up in the Register more than once in a given year, others several times over the years. New commissions were sought with changes in name, dimension, rig, captain, or ownership. In most cases it is impossible to distinguish reregistrants from new ones. Consequently the figures in table 7.2 provide a better measure of investment activity than of tonnage under sail. See also Clark, "That Mischievous *Holker*," 29–30.

48. The twenty-eight vessels arrived between October 7 and December 16, 1779; see *Pennsylvania Packet,* November 18 and December 16, 1779. Though the first vessels entered Philadelphia after the riot, it is likely that riverboats had brought word of their appearance in Delaware Bay some days before. For the Fort Wilson incident, see *LD,* 16: 16fn; Steven Rosswurm, *Army, Country, and Class . . .* (New Brunswick, N.J., 1987), 184–99; Eric Foner, *Tom Paine and Revolutionary America* (New York, 1976), 176–78; Charles Page Smith, *James Wilson, Founding Father* (Chapel Hill, 1956), 131. President Reed referred to the regulation as "having ceased"; see his letter to Caesar Rodney,

November 16, 1779, in *PA*, 1st ser., 8: 10. For merchant attitudes, see Wm. Palfrey to Codman & Smith and to Jas. Swan, June 6, 1780, to Wm. Foster, June 10, and to John Rand, June 13, in WPP.

49. Estimates in table 7.3 are derived from two sources. Commercial arrivals for 1779 are culled from the lists of arrivals in the *Pennsylvania Packet*, November 18 and December 16, 1779, together with all other references in that paper to arrivals not covered in these two issues. Estimates for commercial arrivals during 1780 are derived from lists for January 10 to March 13, May 19 to June 16, and November 28 to December 30—the winter, spring, and fall fleets—that also appear in the *Packet*, supplemented by the same procedures used for 1779. Commercial arrivals for 1781 are fully tabulated in PRI. The authority of the commercial figures in Table 7.3 thus improves with time. All estimates about prizes, which include recaptures, is from admiralty court notices in the *Packet* for 1779–81. All tonnages are estimated as in tables 5.1 and 7.1, but the documents used to construct table 7.3 only specify tonnages for a few prizes in 1779 and the designations "large" and "small" are inapplicable. I use the figure 43,872, the average of 45,443 tons entering Philadelphia during 1770 and 42,300 entering during 1772 in Customs 16/1, PRO for this computation. Tonnage entering from New Jersey, Maryland, and Virginia has been subtracted, since coastal entries from the latter two provinces would have shown up during the war as vessels entering from the Delaware due to reliance on inland water routes. See also PTD.

50. From reports in the *Pennsylvania Packet* during 1780.

51. Since there are no entry figures for Boston during the war aside from the fragmentary records kept by the French consul ("Arrivée des navires depuis le 20 Avril 1777 jusque au 14 Novembre 1779," in ANAE, BI 209), we can only compare the proportion of privateers to letters of marque in the two jurisdictions. At a comparable point after the British evacuation of Boston, 42 percent of the commissions issued to Massachusetts vessels were still to privateers, see Massachusetts Council Papers, MAC, vols. 170–71.

52. Anne Bezanson, *Prices and Inflation During the American Revolution: Pennsylvania, 1770–1790* (Philadelphia, 1951), appendix 1, 332–46. Beef had played catchup to flour in 1779. Between July 1778, the first month after the British evacuation, until the end of 1779, common flour increased in price by a factor of 33, superfine by 29. In the same interval the price of beef rose by a factor of 24, pork by a factor of 27; see ibid., 336. In 1779, the price of common flour and middlings had increased 8.5- and 7.4-fold respectively; during 1780 their prices increased less than twofold. The price of superfine flour followed the pattern set by common flour and middlings—down from an 8.5-fold increase in 1779 to less than a twofold increase in 1780.

53. See Hugh Hollingsworth to Levi Hollingsworth, July 12, 1780, and Alex. Porter to Levi Hollingsworth, August 2, in HFP. Porter was complaining that his flour had not been valued more highly because the new crop was only one-third the normal size. For differing estimates of the harvest of 1780, see Wm. Smith to John Holker, July 8, 1780, in JHLC; Ephr. Blaine to Board of War, June 29, 1780, in EBP; and John Hanson to Phil. Thomas, August 4, and Ezekiel Cornell to Hor. Gates, August 20, 1780, in *LD*, 15: 541,

606. See also Joseph Ward to Artemus Ward, August 23, 1780, in Joseph Ward Papers, CHHS.

54. See Jesse Hollingsworth to Levi Hollingsworth, August 19, 1780; Sam. Ewing to Levi, September 2; Jas. Black to Levi, September 11 and October 10; Thos. and Sam. Hollingsworth to Levi, November 25, in HFP.

55. I use the 1770 figures of 45,443 tons from Customs 16/1, PRO, subtracting tonnage entering from New Jersey, Maryland, and Virginia that year to make the figure congruent with that for 1780.

56. Baltimore clearances in 1780 came to 32 percent of Patuxent clearances in 1770. The total in Customs 16/1, PRO, is 23,176 tons, from which I have subtracted 1,349 tons, representing clearances in that year for Pennsylvania, Virginia, and North Carolina, for a wartime equivalency of "beyond the Chesapeake." In 1770, however, Patuxent had served both Annapolis and Baltimore. Baltimore's 1780 clearances thus may represent a higher proportion of tonnage cleared in 1770 than Philadelphia's entering tonnage in 1780 represented of its 1770 entries. Paul K. Walker, "The Baltimore Community and the American Revolution: A Study in Urban Development, 1763–1783" (Ph.D. diss., University of North Carolina, 1973), 379, lists Entries, January 1 to November 1, 1780, for the Fourth Naval District (Baltimore), in the possession of MdHS. MdHS has confirmed that it was once part of its Scharf Collection but say that it was transferred to MdHR. The staff of MdHR has been unable to locate it for me.

57. During 1780, 87 vessels arrived in Philadelphia from overseas, 77 (80 percent) of which cleared from the West Indies. A little more than half of these, 42 (55 percent), had cleared from Statia. For Baltimore's clearances, see Rhoda M. Dorsey, "The Pattern of Baltimore Commerce During the Confederation Period," *Maryland Historical Magazine* 62(1967): 122; Dorsey's information comes from Records of the Bureau of Customs: Collector of Customs at Baltimore, Record Group 36, NA. That data should be compared with the list of clearances for the Port of Baltimore beginning February 1, 1780, in S 205 Naval Officer (General File), MdHR, nos. 20422–276, 20422-277. Entry statistics in MdHR begin in November 1780. Also Matt. Ridley to Jos. Johnson, July 30, 1779, in MRLB, vol. 3; Edward C. Papenfuse, *In Pursuit of Profit* . . . (Baltimore, 1975), 104–6. The mid-Atlantic's staples did not lend themselves to a direct trade with Europe; see Jon. Williams Jr. to Hen. Lutterloh, March 1, 1779, in JnWLB.

58. Jos. Wilkinson to Levi Hollingsworth, March 7, 1780; John T. Ricketts, March 21, April 20, and July 5; Elijah Bolden to Levi, April 4, in HFP. His correspondents still worried about the threat of a renewed regulation; see John T. Ricketts to Levi, February 18, 1780, in ibid.

59. Bezanson, *Prices and Inflation,* 332–33.

60. For an exaggerated estimate of the expanding supply of flour, see Thomas Rodney to Caesar Rodney, September 13, 1780, in RC. For Hollingsworth's skill in keeping supply adjusted to demand, see Thos. May to Levi Hollingsworth, October 24, and John Rawlings to Levi, October 25 and November 11, in HFP. For evidence of continuing flour shortages victimizing the army, see Washington to Tim. Pickering, December 29, 1780; Circular to New England and New York, January 22, 1781; to the

President of Congress, March 24 and April 12, 18–19; to Rich. Platt, April 26, in *WGW,* 21: 36, 130, 371, 448, 475, 506.

61. One of those benefits would have been the end of the war; see Juan de Miralles to José de Galvez, February 3, 1780, in MRP. Jon. Williams Jr. hailed the event as compensating for the loss of Charleston the month before; see Williams to Wm. McCrery, July 22, 1780, in JnWLB.

62. Thos. and Sam. Hollingsworth to Levi Hollingsworth, September 23, 1780, in HFP. The development also drew critical comment from Jonathan Williams Jr. in Europe; see Williams to Francis Dana, October 31, 1780, and to Chas. Williams, November 1, in JnWLB.

63. James A. Lewis, "Anglo-American Entrepreneurs in Havana: The Background and Significance of the Expulsion of 1784–1785," in Jacques A. Barbier and Allan J. Kuethe, eds., *The North American Role in the Spanish Imperial Economy, 1760–1819* (Manchester, U.K., 1984), 112; Light Townsend Cummins, *Spanish Observers and the American Revolution, 1775–1783* (Baton Rouge, La., 1991), 4, 59–60, 78–89.

64. For the bills, see Cummins, *Spanish Observers,* 166, 169–70. The Spanish Court did eventually honor most of the bills Congress had drawn on the American Commissioners in Europe in 1779 which Jay presented to them, but not before humiliating him with numerous postponements, evasions, and temporary refusals, using them to rebuff the other requests made by the United States; see John Jay to the President of Congress, November 6, 1780, in *RDC,* 4: 114, 119, 124–25, 127–30, 137, 138, 147, 148. See also Wm. Carmichael to the Committee on Foreign Affairs, September 25, 1780, and January 4, 1781, in ibid., 4: 69, 228. The Spanish Court's handling of the six-months bills made them unnegotiable in commercial circles; see Jon. Williams Jr. to Russel Sturges, November 30, 1780, and to Thos. Cushing, December 2, in JnWLB. For the POWs, see Dull, *Diplomatic History of the American Revolution,* 112, and *JCC,* 21: 854; for Washington's response to Spain's plan to send British prisoners of war to New York, see his letter to the President of Congress, July 10, 1781, in *WGW,* 22: 357.

65. See Rendón to José de Galvez, June 19, 1780, in MRP; Cummins, *Spanish Observers,* 171. Many of Spain's contributions, though not the economic one discussed below, are admirably summarized by Dull, *Diplomatic History,* 110–11.

66. Sam. Huntington to La Luzerne, July 8, 1780, in *LD,* 15: 409; Rendón to Navarro, July 4 and 12, 1780, in MRP; quote from Cummins, *Spanish Observers,* 172.

67. Silas Deane to Robt. Morris, February 21, 1781, in *PRM,* 1: 11; Ben. Franklin to Morris, November 5, 1781, in ibid., 3: 150. The last flota bearing treasure to Europe had left the Caribbean in 1778; see Francisco M. Padrón, *Journal of Don Francisco Saavedra de Sangronis . . .* (Gainsville, Fla., 1989), 105fn.

68. See the case of the *Nymph,* in *Pennsylvania Journal,* October 7, 1781; Kennett, *French Forces,* 67. Lewis, "Anglo-American Entrepreneurs," 118. Cuban restrictions and taxes on the export of bullion further recommended this option.

69. Rendón to Navarro, July 4, 11, 12, and August 21, 1780, in MRP. Some of the flour was loaded in Delaware; see Caesar Rodney to John Holker, August 9, 1780, in RC. Miralles had introduced other American merchants besides Morris to the Cuban

trade during his year and a half in the United States, but Morris was his most prominent business associate; see Cummins, *Spanish Observers,* 133, 173–74.

70. For American entrepreneurial expectations, see Sam. Hollingsworth to Levi Hollingsworth, August 1, 1780, in HFP; Steph. Collins to Davis, Pitt & Davis, April 15, 1782, in SCLB; *Pennsylvania Packet,* August 29, 1780. The Spanish authorities actually had as their first priority eliminating the British from the Gulf Coast, which they achieved; see Cummins, *Spanish Observers,* 113–14, 204. On Spanish efforts to facilitate this commerce, see ? to Rendón, September 10, 1780, in MRP. Two other vessels had cleared from Baltimore for Havana in late August (23) and early September (6) with smaller loads of flour, presumably to test the market; see Clearances from Baltimore, January–December 1780, in Records of the Bureau of Customs: Collector of Customs at Baltimore, Record Group 36, NA.

71. Pennsylvania had proposed an embargo on seaborne exports as early as November 9, 1779, in the aftermath of the Fort Wilson affair, but according to the Constitution of 1776 it could not go into effect until the next meeting of the Assembly on January 19, 1780; see *Pennsylvania Gazette,* November 24, 1779. The legislature did not act on a law to provide its quota of specifics for the army until March 2, 1780; see ibid., March 8. There are references to Maryland coordinating its embargo policy with Pennsylvania's in Maryland Council to Jos. Reed, June 23, 1780, in *AM,* 43: 203. For Delaware's embargo policy, see Caesar Rodney to Jos. Reed, March 13, 1779, in *DA,* 3: 1460. On the discrepancy between the various state embargo laws inviting evasion, see [?] Ricketts to Levi Hollingsworth, August 4, 1780, in HFP.

72. New York and Virginia failed to send delegates to the Convention in Philadelphia at the end of January 1780. Those who did attend decided that their efforts could not succeed without the two missing states, so they adjourned until the beginning of April; see *Pennsylvania Gazette,* February 16, 1780. There is no record of the Convention reassembling.

73. *PRSC,* 2: 569. New York was represented at the meeting but specifically exempted from the recommendation. Council of Maryland to the Governors of Pennsylvania and Delaware, July 21, 1780, in *AM,* 43: 225. Delaware followed a month later; see Ricketts to Levi Hollingsworth, August 17, 1780, in HFP. See also J. Rawlings to Levi, August 2, 1780; Joshua Gilpin to Levi, August 7; Jon. Rumford to Levi, October 17, 1780, in ibid.

74. Francisco Rendón to Diego Navarro, August 19, 1780, in MRP; Robert L. Brunhouse, *The Counter-Revolution in Pennsylvania, 1776–1790* (Harrisburg, Pa., 1942), 88–90. For the political fragility of the embargoes, see Jos. Reed to the President of Congress, May 6 and November 16–18?, 1780, to Merchants of Philadelphia, May 25, and to Thos. S. Lee, June 16, in *PA,* 1st ser., 8: 229–30, 266, 331, 609. Delaware had highlighted the fragility of the state embargoes the previous May when it briefly lifted its export restrictions.

75. During peacetime there had been hardly any variation in the price of wheat at planting time; see Bezanson, *Prices and Inflation,* 333–34.

76. See John Rawlings to Levi Hollingsworth, October 25, 1780, in HFP.

1. Reports of the hurricane began appearing in Philadelphia's newspapers in late November; see *Pennsylvania Packet,* November 25, 1780; *Pennsylvania Gazette,* November 29, 1780. See also W. M. James, *The British Navy in Adversity* (London, 1926), 221. For food shortages in the French West Indies, see LeRoumuray to John Holker, April 10, 1781, and unidentified correspondent from Martinique, June 28, in JHLC.

2. Jon. Rumford to Levi Hollingsworth, October 17, 1780; Maxwell to Levi Hollingsworth and Hen. Hollingsworth to Levi, December 6, 12, 1780, in LHLB; Eliju Cole to Levi, December 11, in HFP; Jos. Reed to President of Congress, November 16?, 17?, 1780, in *PA,* 1st ser., 8: 609. Francisco Rendón to Navarro, November 7, 10, and 14; and to Galvez, November 10, in MRP. Four vessels from Baltimore cleared for Havana on December 23, 1780; see Clearances from Baltimore, January–December 1780, in Records of the Bureau of Customs: Collector of Customs at Baltimore, Record Group 36, NA. Quote from Jos. Reed to Washington, May 17, 1781, in *PA,* 1st ser., 9: 145. The act became law on December 22, 1780. It is printed in *Pennsylvania Gazette,* January 3, 1781. The merchants had anticipated this decision; see Levi Hollingsworth to Geo. Anderson, December 12, 1780, in LHLB.

3. PRI. The entry data were the direct by-products of the Assembly levying a 1 percent impost on imports. This law passed on December 23, 1780, and was printed in the *Pennsylvania Gazette,* January 3, 1781. An account of the duties collected under this law between February 1 and June 13 is in the Correspondence of the Supreme Executive Committee, May 4–September 29, 1781, under June 13, in Pennsylvania Archives, RG 27. The monthly breakdown of the duties shows that cargoes entering did not pick up until April. The percentage of entries from Cuba corresponded to the percentage of tonnage from Cuba.

4. Steph. Collins to Wm. Gray, May 14, 1781, in SCLB.

5. Levi Hollingsworth to Capt. Mesnard, May 2, 1781, and to Capt. Harris, May 7, in LHLB; Steph. Collins to Capt. Aaron Palmer, July 2, 1781; to Capt. Palmer, October 12, 1781, in SCLB. See also Collins to Wm. Gray, July 23, 1781, and to Capt. Aaron Welsh, October 12, 1781, in ibid.

6. Quote from Jos. Reed to Washington, May 17, 1781, in *PA,* 1st ser., 9: 145. The legislature had originally adjourned in mid-April until September but was called into emergency session at the end of May; see Reed to Sam. Huntington, May 22, 1781, in PCC, reel 83, item 69, vol. 2, pp. 385–86. The law lifting the remaining restrictions on exports was printed in *Pennsylvania Gazette,* June 13, 1781.

7. See John T. Ricketts to Levi Hollingsworth, May 7 and 28, 1780; Zebulon Hollingsworth to Levi, May 30 and August 21; Thos. Hollingsworth to Levi, August 19; Thos. and Sam. Hollingsworth to Levi, August 26, September 4; Alex. Porter to Levi, November 15, in HFP; Geo. Woolsey to Capt. Craig, August 22, 1780, in W&SLB. New England did not benefit as much from the shifting focus of Britain's war effort because of the success of the British in maintaining their base in the Penobscot region.

8. Thos. and Sam. Hollingsworth to Levi Hollingsworth, September 9, 1780, and

Samuel to Levi, November 12, in HFP. For Baltimore's special difficulties, see Woolsey and Salmon to Capt. Jos. Dority, June 13, 1780, and January 3, 1781, in W&SLB; Alex. Cowan to Levi Hollingsworth, July 8, 1780; Hen. and Thos. Brown to Levi, July 11; Thos. to Levi, July 12, 15, and 19, August 5 and 19; Carter Braxton to Levi, October 12, 1780; Thos. and Sam. to Levi, August 26, September 4, October 17, 28, November 18, 25; Zebulon to Levi, November 11, 1780, in HFP; Daniel of St. Thomas Jenifer to La Luzerne, January 5, 1781, in St. George L. Sioussat, "France, Maryland and the Ratification of the Articles of Confederation by Maryland, 1780–1781," *Pennsylvania Magazine of History and Biography* 60(1936): 407–8; Maryland Council to Maryland Delegates to Congress, July 28, 1780, in PCC, reel 84, item 70, pp. 4, 6, 17. The effect of British aggressiveness on Maryland is documented in Thos. S. Lee, incoming correspondence beginning January 25, in *AM*, 47: 37–213 passim. For the effect it had on Philadelphia merchants, see Levi Hollingsworth to Marsden Smyth; to Geo. Anderson; and to Carter Braxton, October 31, 1780, in LHLB. See also Jean B. Lee, *The Price of Nationhood . . .* (New York, 1994), 146, 152. For Baltimore's clearances, see Clearance Records, January–December 1780, in Records of the Bureau of Customs: Collector of Customs at Baltimore, Record Group 36, NA, and List of Clearances, January–December 1781, in S 205 Naval Officer (General File), MdHR. I found one less clearance from Baltimore for 1780 than Rhoda M. Dorsey did; see "The Pattern of Baltimore Commerce During the Confederation Period," *Maryland Historical Magazine* 62(1967): 122. For the state's response to Cornwallis's movements, see Commodore Jas. Barron to Lafayette, July 31, 1781; Thos. S. Lee to gentlemen on the eastern shore, August 4; and Lafayette to Lee, August 6, in Revolutionary War Papers, MdHS; Jere. Yellot to Levi Hollingsworth, August 4, in HFP; Robert Purviance, *A Narrative of Events Which Occurred in Baltimore Town During the Revolutionary War* (Baltimore, 1849), 138.

9. Hen. Hollingsworth to Thos. S. Lee, February 7, 1781; Jon. Hudson to Thos. S. Lee, February 13, 1781; Sam. Smith to Lee, July 11, 1781, in *AM*, 47: 57, 69, 344. See also John Rawlings to Levi Hollingsworth, September 16, 1780; Wm. Buchanan to Levi, September 29; Alex. McFaden to Levi, October 7; Thos. Hollingsworth to Levi, October 9 and 30; Barnaby to Levi, October 23 and November 3; Jas. Black to Levi, November 8; Hollingsworth and Lony to Levi, November 25, in HFP; Levi Hollingsworth to Marsden Smyth, October 10 and 31, 1780, and to John Sterrett, March 19, 1781, in LHLB; Codman and Smith to Butler and Matthews, August 4, 1780, in CSLB. *Pennsylvania Gazette,* March 21 and May 16, 1781. Several of Philadelphia's entries from Statia at the end of 1780 were Baltimore letters of marque; see Jacob Ganiquis to Reed & Forde, December 21, 1780, in R&FP. For Philadelphia's resurgence in shipping during 1781, see Joshua Johnson to Wm. Patterson and Bros., June 21, 1781, to Hansen & Co., July 7, and to John Sterrett, July 8, in WJMLB. The process can best be followed in LHLB, beginning January 22, 1781. See also Sam. Hollingsworth to Levi, August 1, 1780; Robt. May to Levi Hollingsworth, December 28; and Hen. Hollingsworth to Levi, January 15, 1781; also Wm. Buchanan to Levi, September 29, 1780, and Thos. and Sam. Hollingsworth to Levi, April 28, 1781, in HFP. See Levi to Geo. Anderson, December 12, 1780, in LHLB, for comment on European arrivals beginning to appear in

the port. The comparison between the two ports is as follows: 139 entries from beyond the Delaware = 14,440 tons for Philadelphia during 1781, as in table 7.3; 26 entries = 2,282 tons from beyond the Chesapeake for Baltimore. The multiplier is 5.3 for the number of entries, 6.3 for the tonnage. The Baltimore figures are derived from entry lists, S 205 Naval Officer (General File), MDHR.

10. Maryland Council to Capt. Wm. Middleton, and to Jabez Garrettson, Wm. Smith, Daniel Bowley, and Sam. and Robt. Purviance, December 22, 1780; Wm. Wright to Thos. S. Lee, January 5, 1781; Wm. Matthews to Lee, January 23; Hen. Hollingsworth to Governor and Council, February 7, in *AM,* 45: 251; 47: 5, 33, 57. For requisitions of shipping, see Sam. Hollingsworth to Levi Hollingsworth, May 2, 1780, in HFP; Mordecai Gist to Lee, February 27 and March 4, 1781; David Poe to Gist, March 8; Robt. Morris to Lee, August 28; Geo. Dashiell to Thos. S. Lee, September 24, in ibid., 47: 89, 105, 112, 453–54, 501. For the impressment of horses, wagons, and clothing, see David Poe to Lee, April 1; Lafayette to Lee, April 17; Rich. Dallam to Lee, June 19; Phil. Casson to the Governor and Council, and Pat. S. Smith to Lee, June 20; Dan. of St. Thomas Jenifer to Lee, June 30, in ibid., 47: 156–57, 196, 302, 305, 306, 324. For the preference given the Philadelphia market, see Wm. Wright to Thos. S. Lee, January 5, 1781; Hen. Hollingsworth to Lee, January 18 and February 7; Mordecai Gist to Lee, February 27, in ibid., 47: 5, 28, 57, 89. All restrictions on the export of flour were removed in July 1781 on the eve of the new harvest's arrival on the market; see Dan. Bowley, July 19, in ibid., 47: 359. See also Thos. and Sam. Hollingsworth to Levi Hollingsworth, October 17, 1781; Jere. Yellot to Levi, September 15, 1781, in HFP; Anne Bezanson, *Prices and Inflation During the American Revolution: Pennsylvania, 1770– 1790* (Philadelphia, 1951), 337; Robt. Morris to the Board of War, June 6, 1781, in *PRM,* 1: 117.

11. For premonitions of an Anglo-Dutch war, see "Verbum Sapienti," in *Pennsylvania Packet,* September 30, 1780; see also Jonathan R. Dull, *A Diplomatic History of the American Revolution* (New Haven, 1985), 125–26. The *Pennsylvania Gazette,* March 21, 1781, carried simultaneously confirmation of Rodney's actions, the text of the British ultimatum of December 20, 1780, and the Crown's declaration of limited naval warfare against Dutch shipping. A convoy of twenty-seven vessels had cleared St. Eustatius for Europe two days before Rodney's descent but was overtaken by a detachment from his fleet and brought back. There is no precise tabulation of what was seized at Statia, though Rodney reported that he had taken 150 vessels. Statia had accounted for 53 percent of Philadelphia's entries and 58 percent of the tonnage entering from the islands during 1780. See also Levi Hollingsworth to Bristol Brown, March 16, 1781, in LHLB.

12. For 1780 the figures are forty vessels totaling 4,340 tons from Statia; for 1781, forty-four vessels totaling 4,440 tons from Havana. Out of thirty-six individual vessels that I can identify as entering from Statia in 1780, ten subsequently participated in the trade to the French and Spanish islands. I have identified only one Massachusetts vessel entering Philadelphia from Statia. On the other hand, eleven New England vessels, totaling an estimated 1,280 tons, entered the port during 1781 and may very well have cleared for the islands subsequently.

13. Approximately 80 percent of the vessels that cleared Baltimore for offshore destinations in 1780 carried tobacco as their principal cargo. The total amount exported came to 6,310 hogsheads; see Clearances from Baltimore, January–December 1780, in Records of the Bureau of Customs: Collector of Customs at Baltimore, Record Group 36, NA. Maryland exported more than 49,000 hogsheads of tobacco in 1769, an extraordinary year, and averaged slightly more than 38,000 hogsheads annually from 1769 to 1771; see Customs 16/1, PRO. Geo. Woolsey apparently had reason for his complaint to Phil. Moore in Boston that Baltimore's "commerce is now small [compared] to what they used to be and our markets high"; March 25, 1778, in W&SLB. In subsequent letters he complained of a chronic shortage of shipping; see Woolsey to Norton and Beall, March 18; to John Pringle, April 2; to Waddell Cunningham, April 15. Baltimore also experienced chronic shortages in rigging, canvas, and chandlery; see Woolsey to Pringle, April 9; to Norton and Beall, April 23; to Arch. Blair, May 5, in ibid. See also Wm. Buchanan to Levi Hollingsworth, September 29, 1780, in HFP. Baltimore's role as a tobacco entrepôt derived principally from having a fortified harbor; see illustrations in Ernest M. Eller, ed., *Chesapeake Bay in the American Revolution* (Centreville, Md., 1981), 284, 511; *ACRA,* 2: plates 81, 130. Seventy-three percent of Baltimore's island trade in 1780 had been with Statia; see Clearances from Baltimore, January–December 1780, Records of the Bureau of Customs: Collector of Customs at Baltimore, Record Group 36, NA. For the shortcomings of the island markets, see Steph. Collins to Wm. Vans, February 12, 1782, in SCLB.

14. For Hollingsworth's complaints about the currency, see his letters to Carter Braxton, November 4, 1780; to Marsden Smyth, January 20 and August 21, 1781; to Jas. Leatch, March 2; to Geo. Anderson, July 17; to Messrs. Lony and Russell, July 20 and August 13; to John Sterrett, July 27, in LHLB. For the use of book debts in the city markets, see Codman & Smith to Isaac Moses, August 16, 1781, in CSLB. For the countryside's thirst for money, see John T. Ricketts to Levi Hollingsworth, March 23, April 5, and May 12, 1780; Jas. Black to Levi, September 26, 1780; Hoffman and May to Levi, September 30, 1780; Sam. Hollingsworth to Levi, November 9, in HFP. See also John T. Ricketts to Levi, April 1, 1780; Marsden & Smyth to Levi, May 3; Carter Braxton to Levi, June 7; John Campbell to Levi, March 18 [filed out of order], in ibid. Bernard Mason notes Albany's depreciation rates lagged significantly behind Philadelphia's; see "Entrepreneurial Activity in New York During the Revolutionary War," *Business History Review* 40(1966): 206. For the threat posed by a dramatic depreciation, see Joshua Gilpin to Levi Hollingsworth, December 3, 1780, in HFP.

15. John Kneeland to Sam. Abbot, June 28, 1780, in Samuel Abbot Papers, BLHU; Geo. Benson to Nicholas Brown, December 21, 1780, in NBCoP for Boston; and Thos. Hollingsworth to Levi Hollingsworth, May 17, June 3, 22, 24, 1780, in HFP for Baltimore. The correspondents of Philadelphia merchants were hardly bashful in complaining about the ill repute of Pennsylvania's money; see Sam. Hollingsworth to Levi Hollingsworth, July 3, 1780, in HFP.

16. The Assembly tried to fortify the value of its £100,000 emission of April 1780 as well as its portion of the new emission continentals with tender laws passed on

December 19 and 23, respectively, though published in reverse order in the *Pennsylvania Gazette,* December 27, 1780, and January 17, 1781.

17. They did not get around to issuing new emission money until December 1780. See receipt of Thos. Smith given to Mich. Hillegas, November 13, 1780, and Smith to the Supreme Executive Council, November 29, in Supreme Executive Council Correspondence, November 21, 1780–May 3, 1781, in Pennsylvania Archives, RG 27. Though the Quakers participated in the tax resistance, it went well beyond them; see Anne M. Ousterhout, *A State Divided: Opposition in Pennsylvania to the American Revolution* (Westport, Conn., 1987), 283–85. David Rittenhouse to Wm. Moore, May 2, 1781, in *PA,* 1st ser., 9: 117. Rittenhouse's estimates are confirmed by the fact that the state was able to issue only $561,840 of the new emission at 20:1, a little less than half its quota as fixed by Congress; see the statute passed December 19, 1780, in *Pennsylvania Gazette,* January 17, 1781.

18. *Pennsylvania Gazette,* December 27, 1780.

19. Quote from Thos. Higgins to Hollingsworth, May 20, 1780, in HFP. For the real value of Pennsylvania's currency, see Levi Hollingsworth to Jos. Gamble, December 23, 1780, in LHLB. For the merchants' pledge, see Levi Hollingsworth to Marsden and Smyth, November 20, 1780, in ibid. For their reneging, see Levi Hollingsworth to Geo. Anderson, December 12, 1780, in ibid. See also Jos. Reed to Chas. Pettit and Clement Biddle, May 10, 1781, in *PA,* 1st ser., 9: 129.

20. For the February value, see Levi Hollingsworth to Sam. Harrison, February 6, 1781, in LHLB. "Reasons on Behalf of the Resolves of Congress of March 18, 1780," in *Pennsylvania Gazette,* January 17 and February 7, 1781. David Rittenhouse to Wm. Moore, May 2, 1781, in *PA,* 1st ser., 9: 117.

21. The effect that news about the fall of Charleston had in accelerating the rise of goods in relation to the continental currency had to some extent been checked by the shortage of currency; see Thos. Hollingsworth to Levi Hollingsworth, June 3 and 9, 1780, in HFP. For the impact of Statia's fall, see Levi Hollingsworth to Hen. Armistead, April 10, 1781, in LHLB; David Rittenhouse to Wm. Moore, May 2, 1781, in *PA,* 1st ser., 9: 117. Proclamation by his Excellency William Livingston, Esquire, April 28, 1781, in *PWL,* 4: 186–87; see also statement of the Supreme Executive Council, in *Pennsylvania Packet,* May 8, 1781. For the Boston speculation, see Levi Hollingsworth to Hen. Armistead, May 4, 1781, in LHLB.

22. *Pennsylvania Gazette,* April 25, 1781; General Assembly's resolve of April 10, in Correspondence of the Supreme Executive Council, Pennsylvania Archives, RG 27.

23. David Rittenhouse to Wm. Moore, May 8, 1781, in *PA,* 1st ser., 9: 117. The Council's action was published in the *Pennsylvania Evening Post,* May 4 and the *Pennsylvania Packet,* May 5, 1781. For the currency's real value at the time, see Elaine C. Forman, ed., *The Diary of Elizabeth Drinker* (Boston, 1991), 1: 387; *Pennsylvania Packet,* May 8, 1781. Also "Strictures on Timoleon," in ibid., May 19.

24. See *Pennsylvania Evening Post,* May 7, 1781; *Pennsylvania Packet,* May 8, 1781; *Freeman's Journal,* May 9, 1781.

25. Why the Council's statement had the effect it did is explained in "A Citizen of

Philadelphia," in *Freeman's Journal,* May 9, 1781. See also Levi Hollingsworth to Hen. Armistead, May 4 and 8, 1781, in LHLB; Elizabeth Drinker, *Diary,* 1: 387.

26. There had been thirty-one arrivals from overseas totaling an estimated 3,220 tons between March 1 and the date of the Council's action. Quotes from Levi Hollingsworth to Hen. Armistead, May 9, 1781, in LHLB and Drinker, *Diary,* 1: 387. Steven Rosswurm, *Arms, Country, and Class* . . . (New Brunswick, N.J., 1987), 166.

27. Quotes from Carroll to Lee, May 5, in *AM,* 47: 230–31 and Thos. and Sam. Hollingsworth to Levi, May 19, 1781, in HFP. For its effect on Maryland, Thos. and Sam. Hollingsworth to Levi, May 14, 1781, in ibid. Rich. Dallam to Thos. S. Lee, May 7, 1781; Hen. Hollingsworth to Lee, May 12; Baruch Williams to Lee, May 13; John Reed to Lee, May 27; John Bolton to Lee, May 31, *AM,* 47: 233, 239, 241, 255, 260.

28. The Council's lame apology was followed on May 11 by Governor Reed's even lamer proclamation, in *Pennsylvania Packet,* May 15, 1781. For the political response of the government's defenders, see *Freeman's Journal,* May 9, 1781; quotes from *Pennsylvania Evening Post,* May 12, 1781; Jos. Reed to Washington, May 17, 1781; and Reed to Sam. Huntington, May 22, in *PA,* 1st ser., 9: 146, 162.

29. For the opposition's market orientation, see Robt. Morris to Jacques Necker, June 15, 1781, and to Washington, July 2, in *PRM,* 1: 150–51. Merrill Jensen, *The Articles of Confederation* (Madison, Wis., 1948), 228–38, tells the story of the Virginia cession but questions its influence on Maryland's behavior. *JCC,* 19: 180, 213–23.

30. For the contrast in the approaches of the leaders of the two factions, see Jos. Reed to Washington, May 17, 1781, and to Sam. Huntington, May 22, in *PA,* 1st ser., 9: 145, 162; Robert Morris to John Hancock, July 2, 1781, in *PRM,* 1: 211.

31. *Pennsylvania Gazette,* June 13, June 27, and July 4, 1781.

32. *Pennsylvania Packet,* July 2, 1781. Only £130,000 of the state emission had been put into circulation. The legislature reserved £30,000 and placed it at the disposal of the executive council. See Robt. Morris to Ben. Franklin, July 21, 1781, in *PRM,* 1: 363.

33. Advertisements for the first contracts drafted June 30, 1781, for Philadelphia and Lancaster appeared in the *Pennsylvania Packet,* July 2, and *Freeman's Journal,* July 4, and for Reading and Fort Pitt, July 14, and for York, July 16, in the *Pennsylvania Packet,* July 17; in *PRM,* 1: 207–8, 299–300, 304fn, 307–8. The Philadelphia and Lancaster contracts were quickly negotiated in mid-July; see ibid., 1: 374fn, 2: 110fn. Morris began paying the contractors in September; see ibid., 2: 244, 304, 346. Morris felt that the terms of the contracts were advantageous to the public; see his letter to Phil. Schuyler, July 21, 1781, ibid., 1: 368. Morris to Oliver Phelps, March 30, 1782, in ibid., 4: 483. Morris claimed that the initial contracts had saved enough to provision 3,200 men; see Morris to Governors of the States, February 9, 1782, in ibid., 4: 195.

34. Some of its costliness was related to the storage problem; see Morris to Sam. Miles, November 20, 1781, in ibid., 3: 213. See also John Robertson to Ben. Harrison, February 3, 1782, in *CVSP,* 3: 52. The problem tended to be especially acute with cattle, which had to be fed and could become diseased (see Wm. Davies to Harrison, March 12, 1782, in ibid., 3: 97, and Ephr. Blaine to Morris, November 27, in *PRM,* 3: 294), but most supplies were susceptible to spoiling and had to be guarded (see Wm. Davies to

Ben. Harrison, May 9 and June 6; Rich. Yarborough to Davies, June 6; Rich. Graham to Davies, August 10; Wm. Roane to Davies, August 23; Wm. Hay to Ben. Harrison, September 18, in *CVSP,* 3: 159, 189, 188, 254, 267). For the advantages of the market, see Morris to Washington, July 5, 1781, in *PRM,* 1: 237; Gouv. Morris to Robt. Morris, June 4, in ibid., 1: 107; Diary, October 13, in ibid., 3: 50.

35. Quote from Robt. Morris to John Langdon, April 16, 1781, in *PRM,* 1: 8; see also Morris, Diary, July 5, 1781, and to Jos. Reed, July 14 and August 23; Morris to Dan. of St. Thomas Jenifer, March 12 and June 11, 1782, in ibid., 1: 235, 296; 2: 96; 4: 397; 5: 380.

36. Quote from Morris to Oliver Phelps, March 30, 1782, in *PRM,* 4: 484. Morris reiterated the point in Report to Congress of July 29, 1782 (see ibid.,6: 57), though by this stage he was urging Congress to avoid taxation that went "so far as to intrench on the Subsistence of the People" and preferred borrowing abroad instead. See also "Hints on Tax Notes from the Quartermaster General," July 24, 1782, in ibid., 6: 18. He advised a New Hampshire correspondent on ways its citizens could raise money for taxes by supplying the army with cattle and outfitting the line of battle ship *America* constructed at Portsmouth; see his letter to John Wendell, March 25, 1782, in ibid., 4: 453–54. See also Morris to Thos. S. Lee, July 29, and to Alex. Hamilton, August 28, in ibid., 6: 84, 271.

37. For Morris's proposal, see *PRM,* 1: 58–72. Hamilton should be given some credit for this strategy; see Alex. Hamilton to Morris, April 30, 1781, in ibid., 1: 31.

38. Morris to the Committee of the Assembly, June 25, 1781, in *Pennsylvania Packet,* July 2, 1781.

39. Robt. Morris to Jacques Necker, June 15, 1781, in *PRM,* 1: 150; Morris, Diary, July 20, 1781, in ibid., 1: 342.

40. See Morris, Diary, June 26 and July 19, 1781, to Washington, July 5, and to the Treasurer of Pennsylvania, July 16, in ibid., 1: 179, 181, 183, 237, 307, 338. Estimates of what was due varied; see ibid., 1: 338; Morris to David Rittenhouse, July 16, 1781, in ibid., 1: 307. For the sums already issued, see Morris to Franklin, July 21, 1781; for quote, see Diary, July 19, in ibid., 1: 307, 364, 338.

41. La Luzerne to Congress, May 25, 1781, in *RDC,* 4: 435–36. For La Luzerne's active role in getting the Articles ratified, see Jensen, *Articles of Confederation,* 236; Sioussat, "The Chevalier de la Luzerne and the Ratification of the Articles of Confederation by Maryland," 393–94; Kathryn Sullivan, *Maryland and France* (Philadelphia, 1936), 97–100. For his role in getting Morris to accept the office, see Morris to Ben. Franklin, November 27, 1781, in *PRM,* 3: 275; for the subsidy, see Morris to Franklin, June 8, 1781, in ibid., 1: 123–24. Morris claimed that this sum was increased to 1.5 million livres; see Morris to Franklin, November 27, in ibid., 3: 265.

42. Quite apart from what the French might think, Morris had to worry about appearing to be the hireling of a country that many Americans viewed with suspicion; see John Bigelow, *Beaumarchais the Merchant . . .* (New York, 1870), 7. He also had to get Congress's consent to the funds being placed at his disposal; see Morris to Sam. Huntington, June 4, 1781, in *PRM,* 1: 105.

43. See Diary, June 11, July 20, August 23, and August 27, 1781, in *PRM,* 1: 141,

341–42; 2: 94 quote, 109; Morris to Sam. Huntington, June 30, in ibid., 2: 205–6. Bezanson, *Prices and Inflation*, 345.

44. Morris to Washington, August 22, 1781, in *PRM*, 2: 92; also Diary, November 23, in ibid., 3: 239. For the competition with the French, see Morris to La Luzerne, August 2, 1781; Diary, August 3 and 7; Gouv. Morris to Morris, August 8; Morris, Diary, August 27, in ibid., 2: 6, 12, 27, 37, 109, 260. For the large discounts, see Morris to Washington, August 22, 1781, in ibid., 2: 92; Codman & Smith to Isaac Moses, August 16, 1781, in CSLB; John Welsh to Rich. Harrison, July 12, 1781, in JWLB. For efforts to minimize the discount, see Diary, August 11, 1781, in *PRM*, 2: 47; Morris to Marquis de Barbé-Marbois, July 4, 1781, in ibid., 1: 221–22, where he argued that making Philadelphia a central market for negotiating French bills of exchange would help to diminish the discount at which they passed.

45. John Kneeland to Sam. Abbot, August 31, 1781, in SAP. John Laurens was the son of Henry Laurens, a former President of the Continental Congress and currently a peace commissioner held prisoner by the British. Shocked by the mutinies in the Pennsylvania and New Jersey lines during January 1781, Washington had dispatched the younger Laurens to France to represent the urgency of the situation to the French Court and to plead for additional assistance. For the effect he had on the government at Versailles, see Vergennes to Lafayette, April 19, 1781, in *LAR*, 4: 47. The size of the harvest was evident before the event, see Tench Tilghman to Morris, May 17, 1781, in *PRM*, 1: 74.

46. These varied radically from over $10,000,000 per year to $3,600,000 per year, cf. Alex. Hamilton to Robt. Morris, April 30, 1781, with Morris to the Governor of Virginia, October 17, in ibid., 1: 39; 3: 69. The former estimate pertained to total net cost, the latter to daily fixed cost.

47. Hamilton to Morris, April 30, 1781, in *PRM*, 1: 46–54; Morris, Plan for establishing a National Bank in the United States of North America, May 17, in ibid., 1: 68–72; Francisco Rendón, "Memorandum on the Finances of the United States," April 20, 1782, in ibid., 4: 602, 616–17; Morris to Fred. A. Muhlenberg, February 13, 1782, in ibid., 4: 230.

48. Morris to Thos. McKean, August 28, 1781, in ibid., 2: 135. Congress empowered Morris to implement it in an ordinance dated November 2, in *JCC*, 21: 1091. For Morris's expectations about convertibility, see Morris to Jas. Nicholson, May 8, 1782; to Jon. Trumbull, May 15; to Moses M. Hays, May 20; to Tench Francis and Richardson Sands, May 29, in *PRM*, 5: 131, 184, 228, 284. Morris also expected his orders on John Swanwick to serve the same purpose; see Morris to Washington, March 20, 1782, in ibid., 4: 426.

49. Bank notes were less cumbersome and expensive to transport than silver coins, and they were superior to bills of exchange because the bank did not reserve the right to accept or refuse them. They also minimized the risk of theft, which had become a major problem. Although they could be stolen, they could also be canceled by advertising their serial numbers. Morris to Ed. Carrington, April 25, 1782, in *PRM*, 5: 58; Morris to Jon. Trumbull, January 22, 1782, in ibid., 4: 91; see also Morris to Governors of North

Carolina and Virginia, April 30; to James Lovell, May 4; Diary, May 15, in ibid., 5: 85–86, 110, 178, 182–83. The same logic applied to bills; see Diary, September 10, 1781, in ibid., 2: 224; Morris's circular to receivers of Continental taxes east of the Hudson, May 15, 1782, in ibid., 5: 182–83. See also John Chaloner to Jere. Wadsworth, April 27, 1782, in JWP. For the rising incidence of robbery, see Phil. Schuyler to Morris, August 31, 1781, in PRM, 2: 170; Morris to Wm. C. Houston, May 9, and Houston to Morris, June 15, in ibid., 2: 141, 415; Diary, June 27 and July 12, 1782; Morris to Geo. Olney, August 13, in ibid., 5: 488, 566; 6: 181. See also Hen. Skipwith to Ben. Harrison, October 21, 1782, in CVSP, 3: 350.

50. On the growing supply of specie in America, see Hamilton to Morris, April 30, 1781, PRM, 1: 35, 60fn; Circular on the National Bank, June 11, 1781, in ibid., 1: 142–3; Morris to John Hancock, July 2, 1781, in ibid., 1: 211; Lawrence Lewis Jr., A History of the Bank of North America . . . (Philadelphia, 1882), 19. Morris saw little of it, though; see Morris to Hor. Gates, June 12, 1781, in PRM, 1: 145, 212, fn3; Morris to Washington, July 2, in ibid., 1: 214. For the loss at sea of the bills, see ibid., 1: 148, fn2; 315, fn3; The flota had sailed on July 24; see Francisco Morales Padrón, Journal of Don Francisco Saavedra de Sangtonis . . . (Gainesville, Fla., 1989), 211; Ben. Franklin to Robt. Morris, November 5, 1781, in PRM, 3: 150. Morris had feared this development; see Morris to John Jay, July 15, 1781, in ibid., 1: 301–2. For Morris's loan schemes, see Morris to the Governor of Cuba, July 17, 1781, in ibid., 1: 313; Silas Deane to Morris, February 23, 1781; Morris to John Jay, July 4, and to Robt. Smith, July 17, in ibid., 1: 11, 228, 320; Morris also recommended that France procure its coin in the West Indies through similar arrangements with Spain; see his letter to Ben. Franklin, July 19, 1781, in ibid., 1: 340. Best of all would have been an outright loan from the Spanish Court in Caribbean specie, which Morris continued to press Jay to solicit; see Morris to John Jay, July 4, and to Sam. Huntington, July 9, in ibid., 1: 312–14, 222–31, 254. Spanish officialdom regarded the exchange of bullion for grain as a bad bargain, though strategically desirable; see Padrón, Journal, 106.

51. See Pennsylvania Journal, August 9, 23, October 4, 25, November 15, 1781.

52. Morris to Sam. Huntington, June 21, 1781, in PRM, 1: 161. The government initially subscribed $253,200 of the bank's capital. Private subscribers, many transferring their subscriptions from the Bank of Pennsylvania to the Bank of North America contributed the rest; see Lewis, History of the Bank, 135; Morris, PRM, 1: 72, fn5; Diary, July 4, 1781, in ibid., 1: 220–21; Diary, January 10, 1782, in ibid., 3: 521. Blair McClenachan, one of the largest subscribers to the Bank of Pennsylvania, seems to have had second thoughts about transferring his subscription (see Diary, February 4, in ibid., 4: 156).

53. Morris to Francis, September 11, 1781, in PRM, 2: 246; Diary, September 10, 1781, in ibid., 2: 222–23. The money did not arrive in Philadelphia until November 6; see ibid., 3: 157.

54. Queries and Answers on the National Bank, July 21, 1781, in PRM, 1: 362.

55. Morris, Diary, September 1–5, 1781; Morris to Comte de Rochambeau, November 15, 1781, in PRM, 2: 172–74, 3: 187–88.

56. Morris, Diary, October 3, December 22, 1781, in PRM, 3: 12, 427. See also

Morris to Ed. Carrington, April 25, 1782, and to the Governors of Virginia and North Carolina, April 30, 1782, in ibid., 5: 57, 85–86.

57. The boast was motivated by a conflict with La Luzerne over the extent of his drawing rights. Morris was eager to demonstrate that he was managing France's largess frugally. See Morris to Franklin, November 27, 1781, in *PRM,* 3: 264–83, esp. 278.

58. On the shipping shortage, see Geo. Benson to Nich. Brown, September 10, 1781, in NBCoP; Dan. Parker to Jas. Watson, October 10, in DPLB. On the effect of the French wintering in Virginia, see Geo. Benson to Nich. Brown, September 22, 1781, in NBCoP; Codman & Smith to Geo. Meade, November 27, 1781, in CSLB; Dan. Parker to Peter Colt, November 22, in DPLB. On prices in 1782, see Geo. Benson to Nich. Brown, January 1, March 15, April 26, 1782; Eaton & Benson to Nich. Brown, April 18, June 11, 1782, in NBCoP.

59. For de Grasse's success in collecting bullion in Cuba, see William C. Stinchcombe, *The American Revolution and the French Alliance* (Syracuse, N.Y., 1969), 140; Edward S. Corwin, *French Policy and the American Alliance of 1778* (Princeton, N.J., 1916), 312. Most of the money was lent by private merchants and landowners in Havana; see Padrón, *Journal,* 205–11. For the price of bills, see Steph. Collins to Wm. Gray, November 5 and 20, December 4, 1781, in SCLB. In 1781, 50 percent of the clearances from Baltimore and 43 percent of the tonnage clearing from Baltimore did so between November 1 and the end of the year; see List of Clearances for 1781, in S 205 Naval Officer (General File), MdHR.

60. Throughout 1781, Philadelphia had only ten entries directly from Europe, totaling 1,080 tons: four ships, three brigantines, and three schooners. Paschal N. Smith refers to eight vessels arriving in New England from Gottenberg and Amsterdam within ten days at the end of the preceding year; see his letter to Eleazer Miller Jr., November 23, 1780, in S&SLB. This was unusual, but Massachusetts Bay's entries were also boosted in 1781 by a nine-vessel French convoy from Europe; see Jos. de Valnais to John Holker, May 6, June 7, 10, 14, and 21, 1781, in JHLC. Alex. Hamilton to Robt. Morris, April 30, 1781, in *PRM,* 1: 38, attributed the advantage that Massachusetts enjoyed in commerce principally to the difficulties the British experienced in blockading it.

61. See John Kneeland to Sam. Abbot, September 4, October 15, 23, and 26, November 1, December 14, 1781, in SAP; Codman & Smith to Geo. Meade, November 2, 1781, in CSLB. For Massachusetts's currency deficiency, see Geo. Benson to Nich. Brown, August 28, September 22, 1781, in NBCoP. For the flow of New England imports to New York, see Dan. Parker to Cornelius Glen, May 14, 1781; to Zenas Lewis, May 31; to Wm. Duer, June 26, in DPLB; Codman & Smith to Peter R. Livingston, April 24, 1781, in CSLB.

62. Wm. Vernon to Sam. Vernon, February 23, 1782, in S&WVP; Codman & Smith to Butler & Matthew, January 9; to Geo. Meade, September 15 and November 2, 1781; February 22, 1782; to Steph. Codman, September 26, 1781, in CSLB. Steph. Collins to Wm. Gray, July 23 and August 20, 1781, in SCLB. Freight on the better vessels was 50 percent, but one could worry less about insurance; see Steph. Collins to Wm. Gray, November 5, 1781, in ibid. For the increased risk in 1782, see Codman & Smith to Geo.

Meade, February 20, 1782, in CSLB. In fact, only ten vessels from New England entered Philadelphia during 1781, seven from Boston (one of which was virtually in ballast), two from Rhode Island, and one from New London.

63. For the flow of imports from New England to Philadelphia, see Steph. Collins to Wm. Gray, December 4, 1781, and January 8, 1782; to Wm. Vans, December 25, 1781, and January 8, 1782, in SCLB; Codman & Smith to Geo. Meade, December 8, 1781, in CSLB; Robt. Morris, Diary, November 2, 1781, and Agreement with John Holker, November 2, in PRM, 3: 122–23, 127–28. Philadelphia's annual prewar entries from New England had averaged more than 4,000 tons of shipping a year between 1768 and '73, Customs 16/1, PRO and PTD. At least one of the 1781 entries was a packet in the service of the United States; see Morris, Diary, November 29, 1781, in ibid., 3: 300. For instructions to ship directly from Europe to Philadelphia, see Codman & Smith to Steph. Codman, September 26, 1781, in CSLB.

64. Robt. Morris to Nath. Greene, June 12, 1781, and to John Jay, July 13, in PRM, 1: 145, 287; Ousterhout, A State Divided passim.

65. For his early wartime activities, see his correspondence with Jon. Amory, Hayley and Hopkins, and Harrison and Ansley, November 20, 1776–December 12, 1780, particularly Collins to Amory, November 26, 1776, and to Amory, Taylor & Rogers, January 17, 1778, in SCLB. For the hard money source of his change of heart, see Collins to Akker and Heineken, December 11, 1780; to Wm. Gray, March 12 and May 14, 1781, in ibid.

66. Collins's entry into the flour export business coincided with news that the price of flour had broken in Havana; see Collins to Gray, June 17, 1781, in SCLB. Consequently, his first ventures were divided among a number of islands. By the end of July, though, he was convinced that Havana was the best market; see Collins to Gray, July 23, and other correspondence from June 30, 1781, in ibid.

67. Morris, Circular to the Governors of the States, February 9, 1782, in PRM, 4: 195. See also Ben. Harrison to Morris, March 27, 1782, in ibid., 4: 465, 5: 237n; Ed. Carrington to Wm. Davies, April 30, in CVSP, 3: 144; Morris to Ed. Carrington, April 25, 1782, in PRM, 5: 58–59. The editors of PRM feel that Morris's insistence on having the army concentrated reflected a desire to facilitate provisioning (ibid., 5: 237), but it would also almost certainly have compelled greater reliance on distant sources of supply. Morris subsequently fended off congressional pressure for an extension of the contract system further south; see Report to Congress on Contracts for the Southern Army, June 27, 1782, in ibid., 5: 492–93. On the French wintering, see Morris to Thos. Nelson, October 16, 1781, in ibid., 3: 68–69.

68. Rich. Claiborne to Ben. Harrison, May 1, 1782, in CVSP, 3: 145–46; John Pryor to Wm. Davies, May 18, in ibid., 3: 168; Dan. Yeates to Thos. S. Lee and Council, May 30, 1781, in AM, 47: 260. For Virginian attitudes toward the French, see Comte de Clermont-Crèvecoeur, "Journal of the American War," in ACRA, 1: 65. John Selby, The Revolution in Virginia, 1775–1783 (Williamsburg, Va., 1988), 312, stresses the courtesies extended to the French by the planter elite. See also Barnabas Deane to Jere. Wadsworth,

January 28, 1782, in JWP; Lee Kennett, *The French Forces in America, 1780–1783* (Westport, Conn., 1977), 156–57. Governor Harrison was nonetheless jealous of Philadelphia's and Baltimore's commercial prominence; see *OLGV*, 3: 221, 222.

69. Nath. Greene to Morris, March 9 and April 12, 1782, in *PRM*, 4: 383, 564; John S. Pancake, *This Destructive War: The British Campaign in the Carolinas, 1780–1782* (Tuscaloosa, Ala., 1985), 221; Jerome J. Nadelhaft, *The Disorders of War: The Revolution in South Carolina* (Orono, Maine, 1981), chap. 4.

70. He attempted to load Continental wagons—delivering military supplies to Greene in Georgia and South Carolina—with indigo on their return journey, offering specie warrants on Philadelphia in exchange; see Morris to Geo. A. Hall, January 18, 1782, and Diary, January 20, 1782, in *PRM*, 4: 63–64, 81. He also tried to seed a commerce between the West Indies and the South by directing a vessel to deliver to Georgetown, S.C., a cargo of salt and West Indian produce needed by the army. The vessel was then to take on a cargo for Havana; see Morris to Geo. A. Hall, January 22, 1782, and to Sam. Nicholson, February 11, in ibid., 4: 93–94.

71. For Morris's fiscal plan for the South, see his letter to Nath. Greene, December 19, 1781, and Circular to the Governors of North Carolina, South Carolina, and Georgia, December 19; Diary, December 22, in *PRM*, 3: 407–9, 412–15, 427. For his attempt at a contract system, see Contract with John Banks, February 15, 1783, in ibid., 7: 432–34 and notes.

CHAPTER 9. THE LIMITS OF THE WAR ECONOMY

1. Barbara Tuchman, *The First Salute* (New York, 1988), 223–26; Arnold Whitridge, *Rochambeau* (New York, 1965), 137–38. The Marquis de Castries favored avoiding New York because compelling it to surrender would require a much stronger force than a more modest operation elsewhere; see his letter to Lafayette, May 25, 1781, in *LAR*, 4: 132.

2. The Court at Versailles was well informed about American conditions and sensitive as to how they might affect military operations; see de Segur to Rochambeau, March 9, 1781, in *HPFA*, 5: 466–67. For another view of the difficulties they had to contend with, see Philip Schuyler to Washington, May 28, and to Robt. R. Livingston, May 30, 1780; the Committee at Headquarters plan for provisioning a possible assault on New York, June 2, 1780, in *LD*, 15: 204, 219–20, 225–32. For La Luzerne's preference for the Chesapeake, see William E. O'Donnell, *The Chevalier de la Luzerne: French Minister to the United States, 1779–1784* (Bruges, 1938), 176, 177, 181. For La Luzerne's assessment of the New England economy, see his letter to de Ternay, December 18, 1780, in Destouches Papers, HL.

3. See John Brown to Thos. Nelson, July 25, 1781; Rich. Claiborne to Nelson, July 31; Vanswearingen to Nelson, August 3; Chas. Russell to Wm. Davies, August 27; Rich. Claiborne to Wm. Davies, September 6, all in *CVSP*, 2: 248, 276, 288, 365, 397. See also Ed. Carrington to Thos. Nelson, September 7, 1781, in ibid., 2: 401.

4. David Ross to Thos. Nelson, September 15, 1781, and Wm. Davies to Nelson,

September 17, in ibid., 2: 445, 449. Various impromptu attempts were made to increase Virginia's capacity to ship supplies by water; see Geo. Mutter to Nelson, September 22, 1781, in ibid., 481. See also Jas. Calhoun to Thos. S. Lee, September 2; Chas. Stewart to Lee, September 17; Geo. Dashiell to Lee, September 24, in *AM*, 47: 471–72, 497–98, 501. For the resistance of wagon owners, see A. Rucker to Wm. Davies, September 9, 1781; John Swan to John Pierce, September 10; Hen. Lee to Wm. Davies, September 17; David Jameson to Thos. Nelson, September 26, all in *CVSP*, 2: 406, 407–8, 452, 496.

5. For the sense of urgency, see Thos. Lee to Thos. Nelson, September 7, 1781; and Geo. Nicholas to Nelson, September 13; John Pierce to the commissioners of the several counties, September 13, in ibid., 403, 421, 424. Some counties responded by promising more than was required; see Wm. Ronald to Wm. Davies, September 27, in ibid., 498. Spontaneous exertions also characterized the behavior of some Maryland producers; see Chas. Blake to Thos. S. Lee, September 8; Thos. Beall to Lee, September 10; Wm. Hawley to Lee, September 11; Wm. Deakins to Lee, September 13, *AM*, 47: 480, 483, 486, 490; Jean B. Lee, *The Price of Nationhood* (New York, 1994), 180. For the problems posed by French procurement, see Jas. Hendricks to Wm. Davies, September 20, 21, 29, and October 11, 1781, and Hendricks to John Pierce, September 21; Rich. Young to Wm. Davies, September 23; Rich. Claiborne to David Jameson, September 25, in *CVSP*, 2: 472, 476, 478, 483, 487, 505, 543. For the continued flow of supplies, see Eleazer Calander to Nelson, September 14, and David Jameson to Nelson, September 15; John Pierce to Nelson, September 18; Jas. Hendricks to Wm. Davies, September 18; Chris. Roberts to Nelson, September 19; Robt. Lawson to Thos. Nelson, September 29, 1781; Jon. Buckley to Wm. Davies, October 4; Hen. Garnett to Nelson, October 6; Sam. Lyle to Davies, October 9, in ibid., 433, 443, 457, 458, 464, 505–6, 524, 528, 536. Also John E. Selby, *The Revolution in Virginia, 1775–1783* (Williamsburg, Va., 1988), 298–99.

6. Ben. Harrison to President of Congress, January 21, 1782, in *OLGV*, 3: 131. For the forces involved, see Christopher Ward, *The War of the Revolution* (New York, 1952), 2: 886–87. Ward's tally excludes officers, staff, and those providing support services, which in the case of the British raised the total to 20 percent more than the rank and file. See also Selby, *Revolution in Virginia*, 311–12.

7. The French set up a market at York and purchased the supplies that suited their needs; see de Tarlé to Nelson, October 22, 1781, and Rich. Graham to Wm. Davies, December 8, in *CVSP*, 2: 565, 645. But Wadsworth & Carter still had to make supplemental provision for the French Army; see letters relating to the French contract, January–March 1782, in *JWP*, box 133. Wadsworth noted the difficulties arising from Virginia's demographic dispersion; see Jere. Wadsworth to Mable[?], November 17, 1781, in *JWNY*. In February the French detached Lauzun's six-hundred-man legion to Charlotte County Court House, ostensibly to keep the British guessing about Rochambeau's next move; see Wm. Davies to Ben. Harrison, March 12, 1782, in *CVSP*, 3: 97; Ashbel Wells to John Jeffery, February 20, and Peter Colt to Jeffery, February 28, in *JWP*. This significantly relieved the pressure on supplies in the Williamsburg area. But Elisha Abbe, deputized by Wadsworth and Carter to provide for the legion, found the resources

of Charlotte County so thin as to make his task almost impossible; see Abbe to Wadsworth, March 12, 23, and April 24, in ibid. See also Selby, *Revolution in Virginia,* 311; Ben. Harrison to Alex. Spotswood, March 23, 1782, in *OLGV,* 3: 180.

8. Jonathan R. Dull, *The French Navy and American Independence: A Study of Arms and Diplomacy, 1774–1787* (Princeton, N.J., 1975), 248. Subsequently, a dispute arose between Morris and John Holker over whether the continental commissaries in Virginia had delivered to the French fleet three thousand barrels of flour due them for supplies that the French had forwarded to the Continental Army on the Hudson; see Morris to Holker, January 18, 1782, in *PRM,* 4: 67. On smallpox, see Christian Febiger to Wm. Davies, November 6, 1781, in *CVSP,* 2: 584. Though the French and Americans divided the British prisoners between them for the purposes of exchange, most of the prisoners remained in Virginia; see David Jameson to Ben. Harrison, November 26, 1781, in *OLGV,* 3: 100.

9. Geo. Weedon to Thos. Nelson, October 20, 1781; David Jameson to Nelson, November 5, in *CVSP,* 2: 560, 578. By the middle of November all but five hundred had been moved to Fredericksburg; see Thos. Durie to Jameson, November 14, in ibid., 2: 598–99. The prisoners required a guard of thirty-two-hundred militia. They were to be distributed equally between Virginia and Maryland; see Thos. Nelson to Robt. Lawson in *OLGV,* 3: 88; Jos. Holmes to Wm. Davies, October 26 and November 6, 1781; A. Kirkpatrick to Wm. Davies, November 25; Dan. Morgan to Ben. Harrison, December 11; Ben. Lincoln to the County Lieutenant of Frederick, December 12; Jas. Wood to Harrison, December 27, in *CVSP,* 2: 569, 579, 623, 646–47, 653, 673. Provisioning the British prisoners was complicated by Virginia's determination to make the continent assume this expense; see Ben. Harrison to Virginia Delegates to Congress, December 1, and to Jas. Wood, January 1, 1782, in *OLGV,* 3: 103, 118. Wm. Lyne to Wm. Davies, December 8, 1781, in *CVSP,* 2: 645. The executive received complaints about stragglers and repeatedly issued orders for rounding them up; see Geo. Webb to Wm. Davies, November 6, Ben. Harrison to County Lieutenant of Hanover, December 11, and Harrison to Davies, December 15, in *OLGV,* 3: 95, 109, 112.

10. Thos. Newton Jr. to Thos. Nelson, September 17 and November 2, 1781, and Geo. Kelly to Nelson, October 12. See also Jere. Wadsworth to Chas. Stewart and Ephr. Blaine, November 8, 1781, in *CVSP,* 2: 450, 575, 546, 588; Thos. Nelson to John Pierce, September 20, in *OLGV,* 3: 64; Peter Colt to Aaron Burr, March 28, 1782, in JWP. Ephr. Blaine to Thos. Nelson, November 16, 1781, in *CVSP,* 2: 606. Several men in a detachment at Portsmouth reportedly died because of lack of supplies; see Alex. Dick to Wm. Davies, January 14 and 17, 1782, in ibid., 3: 20, 30. Orders dated November 6 to Gen. Lawson, Col. R. H. Lee, and Col. Barbour in *CVSP,* 2: 579. See also Capt. E. Read to William Davies, December 27, 1781, in ibid., 2: 672; Robt. Andrews to John Scott, November 5, and David Jameson to Ben. Harrison, November 26, in *OLGV,* 3: 94, 99–100. Edmund Read to Ben. Harrison, January 5, 1782, in *CVSP,* 3: 8.

11. Guerrilla activity persisted after the British surrender; see Alex. Dick to Wm. Davies, December 26, 1781, in *CVSP,* 2: 671. For Virginia's exhaustion, see Col. T.

Parker to Ben. Harrison, *CVSP,* 3: 92. Levi Pease, commissioned to purchase horses for the French army, had to seek them as far away as Lancaster Pennsylvania; see his letter to Wadsworth & Carter, March 31, 1782, in JWP.

12. One key to the allied success at Yorktown involved sealing off Cornwallis's ability to forage in Gloucester; see Selby, *Revolution in Virginia,* 305–6.

13. See references to the "shortness of the present crop" in Hen. Young to Ben. Harrison, September 25, 1782, in *CVSP,* 3: 326. For the attack on Philadelphia, see Jos. Reed to County Lieutenants and to Wm. Livingston, September 6, 1781, in *PA,* 1st ser., 9: 387–88; George W. Kyte, "A Projected British Attack upon Philadelphia in 1781," *Pennsylvania Magazine of History and Biography* 76(1952): 379–93; Wm. Livingston to Jos. Reed, September 8, 1781, in *PWL,* 4: 288; *JCC,* 21: 947; President of Congress to Jos. Reed, September 11, 1781; Reed to Robt. Morris, September 12 and 20, in *PA,* 1st ser., 9: 395, 397, 414. See also Diary, September 19 and 21; Morris to Jos. Reed, September 20 and 24, in *PRM,* 2: 297, 316, 309–10, 344.

14. The price reported for flour in the Havana market in June 1781 had dipped from $40 earlier in the year to $16 per barrel; see Steph. Collins to Wm. Gray, June 17, 1781, in SCLB. See also Matt. Ridley to Thos. S. Lee, April 23, 1781, in *AM,* 47: 202–3. At the end of June, however, it rose to between $25 and $27; see Robt. Smith to Lee, June 30, in ibid., 325–26, and it stayed at $23–25 for the rest of the year, though the recent volatility in prices gave no grounds for assuming that it would; see Collins to Gray, July 23, August 20, September 4, November 20, 1781, January 12, 1782, in SCLB. Between July 18 and October 11, 1781, only two vessels entered Philadelphia from Havana. If Stephen Collins's experience is any indication, the Cuban embargo helped bring the trade almost to a halt during the planting season. Collins consigned parcels of flour to Havana on ten vessels mentioned in his letters from May 22 to August 31. Then, except for a small consignment mentioned on September 19 and another mentioned on October 12 (originally scheduled to depart in July) he was not involved in another such venture until November. If other merchants behaved in a similar fashion, the demand for flour in the Philadelphia market during planting season would have declined. See also Geo. Salmon to Jas. Moore, April 10, in W&SLB.

15. The price of wheat did rise 4 percent in September and October, but nothing like the 50 percent witnessed the year before; see Anne Bezanson, *Prices and Inflation During the American Revolution: Pennsylvania, 1770–1790* (Philadelphia, 1951), 337.

16. Rivington's *Royal Gazette,* August 1, November 17, 1781, first took note of the extent and profitability of the Havana trade. Steph. Collins began complaining of enemy captures in his letter to Wm. Gray, September 4, 1781, in SCLB. W. M. James, *The British Navy in Adversity* . . . (London, 1926), 298. By 1782, American ship owners were instructing their captains not to wait for northwesters in attempting to get clear of the coast, "as then the Enemy keeps a close look out for Vessels leaving our bay & very seldom misses them," in Geo. Salmon to Capt. Littleton Houston, October 30, 1782, in W&SLB.

17. Rivington's *Royal Gazette,* January 2, 5, 9, 1782. Two privateers also took two smaller flour prizes between them; see ibid., January 12, 1782. In addition, HMS *For-*

tunée had taken two flour vessels in December; see ibid., December 22, 1781. Steph. Collins to Wm. Gray, January 8, 12, March 5, 18, 1782; and to Jas. Seagrove, March 2, in SCLB. Philadelphia remained ice-free longer than usual during the winter of 1781–82. To judge from the entry data, the port was closed only from the middle of January to the middle of February; see PRI.

18. Quotes from Rivington's *Royal Gazette,* March 2, 16, 1782; see also March 23, 27, 30, April 6, 13. For rising insurance rates, see Gouv. Morris to Robt. Morris, April 8, 1782, in *PRM,* 4: 549; Collins to Gray, November 5, 1781, and March 5, 18, May 20, 1782; and to Davis, Pitt & Davis, April 2, in SCLB.

19. Steph. Collins to Wm. Gray, April 2, 1782, and to Davis, Pitt & Davis, April 9, in SCLB; Nathan Miller, *Sea of Glory* (Annapolis, Md., 1974), 277–79. Data from PRI; there were 125 entries in 1781, 46 in 1782.

20. Only two of eleven vessels attempting to get out in early May eluded capture; see Steph. Collins to Wm. Gray, May 14, 1782, in SCLB. For Collins's difficulties with the *Enterprise,* see Collins to Davis, Pitt & Davis, May 28, June 5, 12, 19, July 24, 1782, in ibid. For the easing of the blockade, see Robt. Morris, Diary, July 29, 1782, in *PRM,* 6: 32; Steph. Collins to Davis, Pitt & Davis, August 12, 1782, in SCLB. The passage of the squadron offered temporary relief at best, and between August 1 and the end of the year only nineteen more vessels entered Philadelphia from beyond the greater Delaware; see PRI.

21. Germain to Clinton, October 12, 1781, in *DAR,* 19: item 1149. See also Piers Mackesy, "British Strategy in the War of American Independence," *Yale Review* 52 (1963): 547–48, 550–51; William B. Willcox, "British Strategy in America, 1778," *Journal of Modern History* 19(1947): 99; and "Why Did the British Lose the American Revolution?" *Michigan Alumnus Quarterly Review* 62(1956): 320–21, 323. For the loyalists, see Wm. Franklin to Germain, March 23, 1782, and to Shelburne, May 10, in *DAR,* 21: 49, 68.

22. For the aftermath of the Battle of the Saintes, see James, *British Navy,* 354–60; Theo. Bland Jr. and Jas. Madison to Ben. Harrison, June 4, 1782, in *CVSP,* 3: 185. See also the intercepted letter of Peter Whiteside to Wm. Hunter, July 23, 1781, in *Royal Gazette,* September 19; the report of a capture, in ibid., September 12; and the *St. James's* evasion of capture, October 17. See also ibid., January 23 and March 2, 1782.

23. Geo. Salmon to Jas. Moore, May 9, 1782, in W&SLB; Thos. Newton Jr. to ? [Wm. Davies], March 14; Davies to Ben. Harrison, April 8, in *CVSP,* 3: 99, 124. Quote from John Banks to Jas. Hunter Jr., May 13, 1782; Banks to Hunter, May 16, 18, 19, 24, 30, 1782; Isaac Smith to Hunter, June 5; Mease and Caldwell to Hunter, May 14; Hen. Banks to Hunter, May 25, 29, 1782, all in H-GP.

24. Geo. Salmon to Jas. Moore, July 10, 1782, claimed that the pressure on the Chesapeake was less than that on the Delaware, though in sailing instructions issued to Capt. Wm. Campbell, July 17, he warned that privateers were still watching the Virginia Capes (in W&SLB). The *Romulus* helped Rochambeau's artillery move toward Baltimore in July 1782. It was there in February 1783 with at least one other frigate, the *Guadaloupe,* which La Luzerne placed at Jefferson's disposal for his passage to France; see

Comte de Clermont-Crèvecoeur, "Journal of the American War," in *ACRA*, 1: 65, 73, 76; Thos. Jefferson to La Luzerne and to Robt. R. Livingston, February 7, 1783, in *PTJ*, 6: 227–28, 228–29. Boyd mentions a three-vessel squadron (see ibid., 236fn); Clermont-Crèvecoeur mentions a four-vessel squadron.

25. John Banks to Hunter, June 20, 1782, which noted the dissolution of Smith, Bowdoin, and Hunter as a consequence of the loss of four ships, in H-GP. See also John Banks to Hunter, May 12, 28, 30; Francis Bright to Hunter & Banks, June 3, 9; Thos. Gordon Co. to Hunter & Banks, June 4; Hen. Banks to Hunter, June 12; Wm. Lewis to Hunter, May 28; Robt. Andrews to Hunter, June 19, in ibid. Privateering appeared an attractive alternative in part because of the success that American cruisers were having off Charleston; see John Banks to Hunter, May 13, in ibid.

26. John Barry to Morris, May 16, 23, 1782, in *PRM*, 5: 198, 247; Morris to de Grasse, May 16, 1782, in ibid., 5: 195. See also Steph. Collins to Wm. Gray, May 14, 1782, in SCLB; Thos. Newton Jr. to Wm. Davies[?], March 14; and Davies to Ben. Harrison, April 8, 1782, in *CVSP*, 3: 99, 124. Morris to Ben. Franklin, May 18, 1782, in *PRM*, 5: 219.

27. Codman & Smith to Geo. Meade, February 20, 1782, and Thos. Fitzsimmons, May 30, in CSLB.

28. With the exception of 9,940 tons of commercial shipping entering Philadelphia from beyond the Delaware, the calculations here diverge from those in table 7.3, which include prizes and exclude coastal entries from within the Delaware. I estimate 6,020 tons of commercial arrivals from beyond the Delaware in 1782. Philadelphia's total commercial entries from all ports, including those on the Delaware, I estimate at 16,705 tons in 1781, 10,835 tons in 1782. Estimates are made from PRI using the same procedures as in tables 5.1 and 7.3, but ferryboats are counted as 10 tons.

29. From the Baltimore records used in constructing table 9.1, I make 386 entries to 46 domestic clearances. Rhoda M. Dorsey, "The Pattern of Baltimore Commerce During the Confederation Period," *Maryland Historical Magazine* 62(1967): 122, gives different totals but notes a similar disparity. Baltimore's prewar commerce had shown a similar though less extreme imbalance; see Customs 16/1, PRO. I get a disparity of 7.4 using estimated tonnage, 5.4 using registered tonnage.

30. Dorsey, "Pattern of Baltimore Commerce," 123. Philadelphia and Baltimore merchants invested heavily in each other's shipping; see Geo. Salmon to Phil. Moore, January 5, 1782, and to John Rechman, January 12, 19, and March 9, in W&SLB.

31. On Baltimore as tobacco center, see Levi Hollingsworth to Sam. Galloway, February 17, 1782, to Smyth, Bowdoin, and Hunter, March 1, to a Dr. [?] David, March 7, to Hoffman and May, March 9, to George Anderson, April 6, to LaCaze and Bromfield, April 16, to Rich. Glasscock, May 18 and July 11, to Harrison, July 2, and to Jas. Crump, July 11, in LHLB. On the erosion of Philadelphia's price advantage, see Levi Hollingsworth to Hen. Hollingsworth, April 23, 1782, to David Browley, April 29, to Rich. Glasscock, May 18, to Smyth, Bowden, and Hunter, May 28, in ibid.; see also Bezanson, *Prices and Inflation*, 338. On Philadelphia's persistence as an entrepôt, see Steph. Collins to Wm. Gray, August 29 and September 25, to Jencks & Forrester,

September 25, in SCLB; Wills Cowper & Co. to Jas. Hunter Jr., October 12, 1782, in H-GP.

32. Cf. Bezanson, *Prices and Inflation,* 338. See also Steph. Collins to Davis, Pitt & Davis, April 9 and 15, 1782, and to Wm. Gray, April 23, in SCLB. Levi Hollingsworth to LaCaze and Bromfield, April 16, to Robt. Johnson, May 8, and to Rich. Glasscock, May 18, in LHLB.

33. Dan. Parker to Eleazer Calendar, October 17, 1781, in DPLB; Codman & Smith to Geo. Meade, November 14, 1781, in CSLB. Steph. Collins to Wm. Gray, August 6, October 17, 1782, and to Jencks and Forrester, August 14, 28, in SCLB. See also Levi Hollingsworth to Wm. Stewart, December 2, 1782, in LHLB. There were in all seven New England entries into Philadelphia during 1782 totaling 720 tons.

34. John Harmanson to Wm. Davies, May 14; Chas. Dabney to ? [Wm. Davies], May 16, 1782, in *CVSP,* 3: 164, 167. See also John Cropper Jr. to Wm. Davies, May 2, December 6, 1782; Geo. Corbin to Davies, May 2; Davies to Ben. Harrison, May 16; John Harmanson to Davies, June 11; Wm. Roane to Davies, July 8; John Heath to Davies, July 29; Winder Kenner to Davies, September 20, in ibid., 3: 148, 391, 149, 165, 191, 210–11, 236–37, 316. The Battle of the Barges is discussed in detail in Myron J. Smith Jr. and John G. Earle, "The Maryland State Navy," in Ernest M. Eller, ed., *Chesapeake Bay in the American Revolution* (Centreville, Md., 1981), 241–44.

35. Codman & Smith to Ingraham & Bromfield, October 7, 1782, in CSLB; *Connecticut Gazette,* September 27, October 11, 18, November 1, 15, 22, 1782. Levi Hollingsworth to Wm. Stewart, December 2, in LHLB. Some water transport persisted in fast sailors, though; see Josiah Waters to Thos. Shaw, October 6, 1782, in N&TSP. For general assessments of the region, see Washington to Morris, August 5, 1781; Diary, September 20; and Tim. Pickering to Morris, February 13, 1782, in *PRM,* 2: 24, 304, 4: 233.

36. For comments about the lack of integration, see Morris, Diary, May 16; to Washington, June 12[13], 1782, in *PRM,* 5: 189, 392–93. Paul W. Bamford, "France and the American Market in Naval Timber and Masts, 1776–1786," *Journal of Economic History* 12(1952): 25, exaggerates when he claims that the French Navy got no masts out of America, but he is justified in minimizing the significance of this trade. For evidence of the mast trade in New Hampshire, see John Langdon to Elbridge Gerry, November 4, 1782, in John Langdon Papers, NHHS. Americans also were involved in mast contracts for the French on the upper Delaware and upper Connecticut rivers; see Wm. Duer to [?] Deane, February 5, 1780, in WDP.

37. For the economic forces behind the New York trade, see Wm. C. Houston to Morris, June 1, 1782, in *PRM,* 5: 313–14; Jas. Madison and Thos. Bland Jr. to Ben. Harrison, June 25, in *PJM,* 4: 364. Concern about the illicit trade predated the British blockade of 1782; see Wm. Atlee to Jos. Reed, March 8, 1780, in *PA,* 1st ser., 8: 125. See also John Bracca[?] to Thos. Lee, June 10, 1781, and Jos. Dashiell to Lee, July 5 and 17; Wm. Allen to Lee, July 11, in *AM,* 47: 278–79, 337, 353, 342–43; Wm. Livingston, Proclamation, October 9, 1781, in *PWL,* 4: 312; and Richard Buel Jr., *Dear Liberty . . .* (Middletown, Conn., 1980), 261ff. New York's supply of specie also dwarfed Philadelphia's; see Julian Gwyn, "The Impact of British Military Spending on the Colonial

American Money Markets, 1760–1783," Canadian Historical Association, *Historical Papers* 50(1980): 78, 80, 83. The illicit trade in Chesapeake tobacco was driven by the high price the commodity fetched in the New York market; see Deposition of Alex. Ogg, July 16, 1781, in *AM,* 47: 357–58. The price of tobacco in Philadelphia did not compare; see Sam. Smith to Lee, August 11, in ibid., 47: 410. Beginning in 1782, the movement of any American produce in the direction of New York was considered inherently suspicious; see Geo. Corbin to Ben. Harrison, May 11, 1782; Alex. Dick to Harrison, November 22, in *CVSP,* 3: 161, 378; Alex. Hamilton to Morris, August 13, 1782; Tim. Pickering to Morris, August 24, in *PRM,* 6: 188, 246–47. The French became suspicious about illicit trading by flags of truce before the local authorities did; see Wm. Mitchell to Ben. Harrison, May 29, in *CVSP,* 3: 182; Wm. Bradford Jr. to Jas. Irvine, January 4[?], 1783, in *PA,* 1st ser., 9: 731; Bernard Mason, "Entrepreneurial Activity in New York During the Revolutionary War," *Business History Review* 40(1966): 209.

38. *JCC,* 22: 341, 392–93. For examples of state action, see *SAL,* 11: 101–3; *PRSC,* 4: 161–62. For their effectiveness, see Morris, "State of American Commerce and Plan for Protecting It," in *PRM,* 5: 150. For merchant attitudes, see Steph. Collins to Wm. Gray, October 17, 1782, in *SCLB.* Connecticut stacked the legal deck against libelees in the illegal trade in other ways as well, but to little effect; Buel, *Dear Liberty,* 261–62, 286–88.

39. Morris to Wm. C. Houston, June 19, 1782, in *PRM,* 5: 449. In La Luzerne to Morris, November 4, 1781, in ibid., 3: 140 (translation, 141), La Luzerne questioned the commercial significance of the Franco-American alliance; Morris did not respond directly to La Luzerne until the following May in his "Statement of American Commerce and Plan for Protecting It," ibid., 5: 148–54; see also Morris, Diary, May 15, in ibid., 5: 179.

40. For the quote, see Robt. Morris to Ben. Franklin, July 13, 1781, and to Geo. Webb, October 28, 1782, in *PRM,* 1: 282, 6: 671–72. *JCC,* 19: 102–3, 105–6, 110–13.

41. The advantages of an impost had been succinctly summarized by Thomas Paine in "The Crisis Extraordinary," October 4, 1780, in Philip S. Foner, ed., *The Complete Writings of Thomas Paine* (New York, 1945), 1: 183.

42. Alex. Hamilton to Morris, April 30, 1781, in *PRM,* 1: 42; also ibid., 1: 396.

43. Thos. S. Lee to Morris, December 13, 1781, in *PRM,* 3: 385, 4: 537, fn4.

44. Wm. Green to Morris, November 3, 1781, to Ben. Franklin, November 27, to Pierre Landais, January 16, 1782, in *PRM,* 3: 138, 266, 4: 54.

45. Morris to Thos. Tillotson, May 20, 1782, in ibid., 5: 229–30. Morris realized other taxes besides the impost would be necessary to establish public credit; see Morris to Thos. McKean, August 28, 1781, in *PRM,* 2: 133; Morris to Ben. Franklin, November 27, 1781, in ibid., 3: 269; Morris to Navy Board of the Eastern Department, March 26, 1782, in ibid., 4: 461.

46. For Massachusetts, see Morris to Nath. Appleton, April 16, 1782, in *PRM,* 5: 4, 5fn2. For Virginia, see Morris to John Hanson, February 11, 1782, in ibid., 4: 205, 213fn13. For Rhode Island, see David Howell, "Objections to the Impost in Rhode Island," July 31–August 2, 1782, in ibid., 6: 113–14. Morris requested a summary of the state's objections, to which he replied but with little effect; see Morris to Wm. Greene,

August 2, in ibid., 6: 123–26, fn6. The state acted on November 1, but Morris did not learn of its action until the end of the month.

47. "Hints on Tax Notes from the Quartermaster General," July 24, 1782, in *PRM*, 6: 18; Robt. Claiborne to Ben. Harrison, February 16, 1782, in *CVSP*, 3: 64. See also Wm. C. Houston to Morris, July 6, 1782; Thos. S. Lee to Morris, July 12, in *PRM*, 5: 541, 575.

48. Morris to John Hanson, May 17, 1782, to the Governors of the States, July 29, in *PRM*, 5: 203, 6: 35, 7: 397.

49. "Liquidate" is here used in the eighteenth-century sense of reducing to specie equivalence. See Levi Hollingsworth to Smyth, Bowdoin & Hunter, May 28, 1782, in LHLB; Steph. Collins to Wm. Gray, March 23, 26, April 2, 9, May 27, July 17, August 6, November 20, 1782, to Davis, Pitt & Davis, April 9, 15, June 12, to Wm. Vans, March 18, in SCLB. See also Thomas M. Doerflinger, *A Vigorous Spirit of Enterprise . . .* (Chapel Hill, 1986), 214–15.

50. Morris, Diary, January 15, 1782; Morris to Jos. Nourse, January 16, February 5, March 7, in *PRM*, 4: 23, 24, 165–66, 366–67. For state attempts to borrow, see Morris, Diary, April 15, May 31, 1782; Dan. of St. Thomas Jenifer to Morris, May 31, July 5; Morris to Dan. of St. Thomas Jenifer, July 12, in ibid., 4: 576, 5: 298, 306, 537–38, 572. For the merchants, see Morris, Diary, May 18, 28, 1782; Morris to Rich. Butler, July 18, in ibid., 5: 217, 268, 598. When the bank discounted an accepted bill, it took it up for cash at a slight discount in the expectation of collecting from the drawee on the date that the acceptor specified it would be paid. For the bank's response, see Morris, Diary, May 18, 23, 1782, in ibid., 5: 217, 242. For difficulties with deposits, see Morris, Diary, May 4, 15, 1782, in ibid., 5: 107, 178; O'Donnell, *Chevalier de La Luzerne,* 191. For the limited resumption of discounting, see Morris, Diary, July 10, in *PRM*, 5: 555; Morris to William Duer, July 23, in ibid., 6: 13.

51. During Morris's first year (1781) in office the French advanced more to him than all the gifts and loans previously bestowed on the republic. In addition to an outright gift of 6 million livres, they had lent the United States 4 million livres and guaranteed a 10 million livre loan opened in Holland, advancing to the American commissioners in France that sum in anticipation of subscriptions; see E. James Ferguson, *The Power of the Purse* (Chapel Hill, N.C., 1963), 126–27. On Necker's resignation, see John Bondfield to Morris, August 10, 1781, in *PRM,* 2: 45. The resignation complicated the financial situation of his successors; see Robert D. Harris, *Necker: Reform Statesman of the Ancien Régime* (Berkeley, 1979), 240; Jonathan R. Dull, *A Diplomatic History of the American Revolution* (New Haven, 1985), 123. Lafayette to Washington, January 30; and to Ben. Franklin, February 25, 1782, in *LAR*, 5: xxii, 9, 15.

52. For factors raising the price of exchange, see Morris, Diary, January 15, March 25, 1782, in *PRM*, 4: 23, 448; Morris to Ben. Franklin, April 17, in ibid., 5: 13. See also John Chaloner to Wadsworth & Carter, March 1, 26, 31; Peter Colt to John Jeffery, February 28, in JWP. For the effect of the blockade, see Morris, Diary, April 13, May 8, 1782; Morris to Ferdinand Grand, May 18, to Robt. Smith, May 25, to John Hanson, May 27, in *PRM*, 4: 570 and fn; 5: 125, 220, 259, 271.

53. Morris, Diary, July 23, 1782, in *PRM*, 6: 12. Morris to Jas. Lovell, July 30, 1782,

and Diary, August 2, 7, 1782, in ibid., 6: 108, 120, 150. France's increased need to support its forces in North America by selling bills pushed their price down again. Jas. Madison et al. to Ben. Harrison, September 24, 1782, in *CVSP,* 3: 325. The *Aigle* had had 2.5 million livres on board, of which 10 percent was lost; see Morris to Washington, September 9, 1782, *PRM,* 6: 345, 381fn9, 538fn3, 565. See also Clermont-Crèvecoeur, "Journal," 79–80. For Morris's response, see his letter to Le Couteulx and Co., September 24, 1782, in *PRM,* 6: 424 and notes. Morris, Diary, September 25, in ibid., 6: 429, should be understood in this light. Bills for smaller quantities sold at a lesser discount; see Steph. Collins to Jencks and Forrester, October 29, 1782, in SCLB.

54. Codman & Smith to Geo. Meade, November 14, 1781, in CSLB. For factors depressing the price of exchange, see Geo. Benson to Welcome Arnold, February 25, 1782; Welcome Arnold to Ephr. Bowen, March 16, in A-GP. See also David Lopez to Aaron Lopez, May 1, 1782, in Letters of Boston Merchants, vol. 3, BLHU. For the rise in the market, see M. M. Hays to Welcome Arnold, June 3, 1782, in A-GP. Morris to Jas. Lovell, May 4, 1782, to Ferdinand Grand, May 4, June 13, July 3, in *PRM,* 5: 109–10 and fn4, 114–15, 403, 529.

55. Eaton and Benson to Welcome Arnold, September 27, 1782, in A-GP. Vaudreuil arrived in Boston at the beginning of August; see Dull, *French Navy,* 301. The naval advantage that Vaudreuil's squadron bestowed on the area was qualified by the arrival of Hood's squadron at New York on September 5; see James, *British Navy,* 360. For the Boston price of exchange, Dan. Parker to Ingraham & Bromfield, September 18, October 7, 29, 1782, in DPLB; Eaton & Benson to Chris. Champlin, October 2, November 11; Thos. Russell to Champlin, October 20, in Letters of Boston Merchants, vol. 3, in BLHU.

56. Rochambeau had initially led his army to believe that it was returning to France; see Clermont-Crèvecoeur, "Journal," 84–85. Dan. Parker to Corn. Glen, November 14, 1782, and to Wadsworth, n.d. [probably early December], in DPLB; Eaton & Benson to Chris. Champlin, November 25, in Letters of Boston Merchants, vol. 3, in BLHU. Morris understood the dynamics of Boston's bill market; see Morris to Jas. Lovell, December 31, 1782, in *PRM,* 7: 251.

57. Morris derived 3.5 times more income from the sale of bills drawn on France than he did from requisitions on the states; see *PRM,* 7: insert between 386–87. The average yield on the sale of bills came to 5.86 livres to the dollar. For his instructions, see Morris to John Langdon, March 26, 1782, to Ed. Carrington, April 25, in ibid., 4: 460, 5: 57. For the effect of distance on value, see Morris to Jas. Lovell, June 1, 1782, in ibid., 5: 311; Codman & Smith to Geo. Meade, February 20, 1782, in CSLB. Morris to Alex. Hamilton, October 5, 1782, in *PRM,* 6: 499.

58. On the provisioning of the army, see Morris to Wm. Heath, February 7, 1782, in *PRM,* 4: 182. On the problems with the contract, see Washington to Morris, March 28, May 17, June 16, July 30, 1782, in ibid., 4: 477–78, 5: 209–11, 418, 6: 106–7. On New York's politics, see Alex. Hamilton to Morris, August 13, 1782, in ibid., 6: 187–93. See also Morris, Diary, May 16, 1782, in ibid., 5: 189. Morris complained to Washington about the situation; see his letter of June 12[13], 1782, in ibid., 392–93.

59. Walter Livingston to Morris, June 29, 1782; Tim. Pickering to Morris, August 5, in *PRM*, 5: 504, 6: 139. Walter Livingston to Morris, May 26, 1782; Geo. Clinton to Morris, August 2, in ibid., 5: 267, 6: 130. Tim. Pickering to Morris, September 19, 1782; Sands Livingston and Co. to Morris, September 25; headnote to Contract with Jere. Wadsworth and John Carter, ibid., 6: 404, 436, 565. Walter Livingston saw the crisis coming early, as did Washington (see Livingston to Morris, June 21, 1782; Washington to Morris, July 3, in ibid., 5: 459, 528). The New York contractors signaled that they were approaching the end of their tether in mid-September; see Comfort Sands, Livingston, Wm. Duer, and Dan. Parker to Morris, September 13, 1782, in ibid., 6: 357–62. They faced, in addition to the approach of the French army, a seasonal drought that dried up the local mill streams.

60. Morris, Diary, April 17, 1782; Morris to Ferdinand Grand, May 18, in *PRM*, 5: 11–12 and notes, 220–21. See also Morris to Le Couteulx and Co., September 27, and to Franklin, October 1, 1782, in ibid., 6: 452–53, 470–71, and 425 fn1.

61. Morris to Robt. Smith, May 16, 1782, to Joshua Barney, May 18, to John Barry, May 24, in *PRM*, 5: 196, 217–18, 248–49, fn1. La Luzerne to Morris, May 23; John Barry to Morris, June 5, 12, in ibid., 5: 246, 248–49, 345, 395. Morris, Diary, July 17, 1782, in ibid., 5: 593.

62. Morris, Diary, August 1, 1782, in ibid., 6: 117–18. Shortly afterward, Morris began to warn Washington that he might have to abandon the contract, possibly forcing the army to feed itself through seizure; see Morris to Washington, August 29, September 9, 1782, in ibid., 6: 282–83, 345.

63. Ezekiel Cornell to Morris, October 5, 1782, in *PRM*, 6: 501–2; Lee Kennett, *The French Forces in America, 1780–1783* (Westport, Conn., 1977), 162. Morris had also borrowed from Wadsworth & Carter's Philadelphia agent, John Chaloner, and made paying that debt part of the agreement with Wadsworth & Carter to feed the army; see John Carter to Morris, October 9, in *PRM*, 6: 538. Morris's Contract with Jere. Wadsworth and John Carter, October 12, 1782, in ibid., 6: 565–72. The terms were generous enough to ensure that the army was well cared for; see Morris to Tench Tilghman, October 10, in ibid., 6: 554; see also ibid., 6: 357.

64. Morris to Marquis de Barbé-Marbois, July 4; Queries and Answers on the National Bank, July 21; Circular to the Governors of the States, October 19, 1781; Morris to Fred. A. Muhlenberg, February 13, 1782, in *PRM*, 1: 221, 362, 3: 88, 4: 226.

65. Morris, Diary, February 25, 1782, and Morris to Dan. Clark, May 30, in *PRM*, 4: 299, 5: 288. For his defense, see Circular to the Governors, July 25, 1781, to the Governors of Massachusetts, Rhode Island, New York, Delaware, Maryland, and North Carolina, July 27, in ibid., 1: 382, 397–400; to Francis Wade, December 28, 1781, in ibid., 3: 459. See also Morris to Wm. Greene, January 14, 1782, to Jon. Trumbull, January 22; Circular to the Governors of the States, February 9, in ibid., 4: 19–23, 91–92, 191, 5: 288–89, 290. Morris's letter to John Hanson, July 29, 1782, described by the editors of Morris's papers as his "report on public credit," in ibid., 6: 60ff.

66. Virginia voided the sale of all land purchased from Indians within the state's

chartered boundaries under the authority of the Crown. Doing so invalidated the title of a major land company created in the late colonial period backed by out-of-state investors; see Merrill Jensen, *The Articles of Confederation* . . . (Madison, Wis., 1948), 198–99. Pennsylvania claimed some of the same lands that Virginia was threatening to sell. With landless Maryland, New Jersey, and Delaware, Pennsylvania vociferously protested Virginia's policy. Congress passed a resolution recommending that Virginia reconsider its land office act. Still the law remained on the books, though the legislature subsequently prohibited the sale of lands north of the Ohio River on the grounds that they were reserved for soldiers' bounties. For suspicions about the state's intentions, see Gouv. Morris to the Public, [September 4, 1779] in *LD*, 13: 453–54; "A Citizen of Philadelphia," in *Pennsylvania Packet*, August 14, 1779. Jos. Reed to Pennsylvania Congressional Delegation, December 15, 1779, in *PA*, 1st ser., 8: 46–47. See also Virginia Delegates to Virginia House of Delegates, November 2, 1779, in *LD*, 14: 149; *JCC*, 15: 1223–24, 1226–30; *SAL*, 10: 50–65, 159.

67. Virginia's quest for foreign loans originated at roughly the same time the land office was established; see "Credentials for Peter Penet," July 15, 1779, in *PTJ*, 3: 36. For the initiatives of other states, see Resolutions of the Pennsylvania General Assembly, May 29, 1780, and Jos. Reed to John Adams, July 9, 1780, in *PA*, 1st ser., 8: 276, 399; Joshua Johnson to Thos. S. Lee, October 10, 1780; John Hanson and Dan. Carroll to Lee, December 4, 1781, in *AM*, 47: 79, 562; Edward C. Papenfuse, "An Uncertain Connection: Maryland's Trade with France During the American Revolution, 1778–1783," *La révolution américaine et l'europe* (Paris, 1979), 262. Massachusetts and South Carolina also sent agents to Europe, but Virginia and Maryland alone succeeded; see extract dated April 20 in Matt. Ridley to Morris, April 24, 1782, in *PRM*, 5: 54–55, 8: 509, fn2.

68. Ben. Harrison to Morris and La Luzerne, May 11, 1782, in *OLGV*, 3: 210–12; Ben. Harrison to Morris, March 27, 1782, in *PRM*, 4: 465–66. Ben. Harrison to Dan. Clark, May 9, 1782, to the Speaker of the House of Delegates, May 14, to the Virginia Delegates, May 18, to Rochambeau, May 22, in *OLGV*, 3: 206, 223, 227, 231. He sounded a more conciliatory note toward Morris (see his letter of March 28, 1782, in *PRM*, 4: 475–76), but that didn't qualify his and the legislature's resistance to the financier's program; see Morris to Washington, July 9, 1782, in ibid., 5: 552. Ben. Harrison to President of Congress, January 21, March 29, to Nath. Greene, January 21, March 4, to Robt. Morris, February 7, and to the Virginia Delegates, March 1, April 6, in *OLGV*, 3: 132, 185–86, 133, 170–71, 145, 168, 192–93. See also Morris to Dan. Clark, May 30, 1782, to Ed. Carrington, June 6, 11, in *PRM*, 5: 287–93, 351, 378. When Morris relented on the matter of contracts, Harrison recommended that Virginia admit bank notes for taxation, but not before; see ibid., 379fn. Greene to Harrison, July 25, in *CVSP*, 3: 229–30.

69. According to custom, the goods were regarded as private property rather than legitimate spoils of war. For the tobacco contract controversy, see Morris to David Ross, January 11, 1782, in *PRM*, 4: 7–8; Ben. Harrison to Morris, February 7, 1782, in ibid., 4: 186. Execution of the contract would also have provided a fund in New York City for American prisoners of war there; see Diary, February 6, 1782, in ibid., 4: 167. The

legislature's resolves are in ibid., 5: 273. For Morris's rebuttal, see Morris to Dan. Clark, May 30, 1782, in ibid., 287–93, esp. 292–93.

70. For the state's consolidated, liquidated debt, see *Address from the General Court to the People of the Commonwealth of Massachusetts* (Boston, 1786), 5–6. Massachusetts felt pressure from the British occupation of Bagaduce but was powerless to do anything about it and settled for an uneasy balance of forces in the region; see James S. Leamon, *Revolution Downeast* (Amherst, Mass., 1993), 120–34.

71. Richard Buel Jr., "The Public Creditor Interest in Massachusetts Politics, 1780–86," in Robert A. Gross, ed., *In Debt to Shays* (Charlottesville, Va., 1993), 49. "Liquidation" in this case also involved adding 6 percent annual interest to the specie value of the original claim. *Acts and Laws of the Commonwealth of Massachusetts . . .* , 13 vols. (Boston, 1890–97), 1: 525–33, 573–79, 2: 152–53. Nich. Brown to Moses Hayes, October 31, 1782; Eaton and Benson to Brown, November 13, 23, 1782, in NBCoP; Dan. Parker to Sands & Livingston, October 4, 1782, in DPLB; Morris to John Hanson, July 29, 1782, in *PRM*, 6: 62–64.

72. His unpopularity had two sources: Congress had resisted the state's attempts to get the costs of the Penobscot disaster credited to its account with the continent. More important, rumors circulated in Boston that Morris had been behind the speculation by a group of Philadelphia merchants in spring 1781 to buy bills of exchange in Boston with depreciated old continentals. Massachusetts merchants held Morris responsible for the subsequent collapse of the old continental currency in New England. This forced Morris to work overtime with his Boston correspondents to exonerate himself; see Morris to John Hancock, September 15, 1781, to John Hanson, February 11, to Nath. Appleton, April 16, to James Lovell, July 10, in *PRM*, 2: 281, 4: 205, 5: 4, 559. See also Alex. Hamilton to Robert Morris, April 30, 1781, in ibid., 1: 42, to John Hancock, July 2, 1781, to the Marquis de Barbé-Marbois, July 21, in ibid., 1: 211–12, 355. See references to the speculation in John Hancock to Elias Boudinot, October 28, 1783, PCC, reel 79, item 65, vol. 2, p. 225; Roxbury, Massachusetts, response to Wrentham's and Medway's instructions, see *Independent Chronicle*, March 25, 1784.

73. Norman S. D. Gras, *The Massachusetts First National Bank of Boston, 1784–1933* (Cambridge, Mass., 1937), 13.

74. For the dispute with La Luzerne, see Morris to Ben. Franklin, July 13, 1781, and Franklin to Morris, November 5; La Luzerne to Morris, May 25, 1782, in *PRM*, 1: 284,3: 151, 5: 261, 263. See "The Remonstrance and Petition of the Proprietors of the Loan Office Certificates in the City and Neighborhood of Philadelphia," July 8, 1782, in PCC, reel 57, item 43, pp. 177–86, for the political potential of this interest group.

75. *JCC*, 23: 555; *PRM*, 6: 54–55fn.

76. Gouv. Morris to Nath. Greene, December 24, 1781, to Matt. Ridley, August 6, 1782, in *PRM*, 3: 439–40, 6: 147–48; Robt. Morris to Ridley, October 6, 1782, to Washington, October 16, in ibid., 6: 512, 604.

77. Richard H. Kuhn, "The History of the Newburgh Conspiracy: America and the Coup d'Etat," *William & Mary Quarterly*, 3rd. ser. 27(1970): 187–220; *PRM*, 7: 328ff, 463.

78. Ferguson, *Power of the Purse*, 169–70, fn58.

1. For a visual representation of war damage that survived into the early Republic, see Benjamin Latrobe's sketch of the Nelson House, Yorktown, Va., reproduced in Edward C. Carter II, ed., "The Virginia Journals of Benjamin H. Latrobe, 1795–1798," in *The Papers of Benjamin H. Latrobe,* ser. 1, *Journals* (New Haven, 1977–80), 2: 488. See also Thos. Parker to Ben. Harrison, March 10, 1782, in *CVSP,* 3: 92; Frances M. Caulkins, *History of New London, Connecticut . . .* (New London, 1852), 574.

2. See notation of resolutions passed by the Virginia Assembly, May 28, 1782, in *CVSP,* 3: 181, and Isle of Wight County's schedule of losses; in ibid., 3: 389.

3. Samuel E. Morison, *A Maritime History of Massachusetts* (Boston, 1921), 30–31; Benjamin W. Labaree, *Patriots and Partisans: The Merchants of Newburyport, 1764–1815* (Cambridge, Mass., 1962), 58; and Labaree, ed., "Nantes to Newburyport: Letters of Jonathan Williams," Essex Institute *Historical Collections* 92(1956): 68. Much of this destruction was inflicted in 1782; see James D. Phillips, *Salem in the Eighteenth Century* (Boston, 1937), 433.

4. *Pennsylvania Gazette,* May 8, 15, 1782; quote from August 7, 1782.

5. Ibid., August 14, 1782; Jas. Madison, Theo. Bland, and Arthur Lee to Ben. Harrison, August 18, 1782, in *CVSP,* 3: 259.

6. Quotes from Steph. Collins to Wm. Gray, August 12, and to Jencks & Forrester, August 14, January 29, 1783, in SCLB. See also Levi Hollingsworth to Thos. Brown, August 17, 1782, in LHLB.

7. Geo. Salmon to Wm. Moore & Co., August 21, 1782, in W&SLB. See also Levi Hollingsworth to Mordecai Steftall, November 19, in LHLB. The pressure increased as peace came to seem more imminent; see Steph. Collins to Robt. Rantoul, February 11, 18, 1783, to Wm. Gray, February 12, in SCLB. French merchants were not so canny in responding to the challenges of peace; see L. Rouzeau, "Aperçus du rôle de Nantes dans la guerre d'indépendance d'Amérique," *Annales de Bretagne* 74(1967): 274. For the effect of the approaching peace on specie, see Morris to Rich. Butler, August 26, 1782, and Diary, September 3, in *PRM,* 6: 253–54, 305.

8. For the Amsterdam market, see N. W. Posthumus, *Inquiry into the History of Prices in Holland* (Leiden, 1946), 1: lxvi. For complaints about French prices, see Woolsey and Salmon to Jas. Cuming, July 12, 1781, to Cuming and McCarty, January 24, 1782, to Wm. Moore & Co., August 21, November 30, in W&SLB. See also Robt. Morris to Ben. Franklin, December 3, 1781, September 30, 1783, in *PRM,* 3: 320, 8: 558; Jon. Williams Jr. to Nath. and John Tracy, October 10, 1782, in Labaree, "Nantes to Newburyport," 72.

9. Steph. Collins to Wm. Gray, September 25, 1782, in SCLB. W. M. James, *The British Navy in Adversity* (London, 1926), 351, 356, 360, 372–76.

10. For the pressure to continue trading, see Geo. Salmon to Capt. Littleton Houston, October 30, 1782, and to Wm. Moore & Co., November 30, in W&SLB. Codman & Smith to Silas Brenton, October 20, to Jas. Russell, October 21, to Rich. Harrison, October 29, to Callendar and Henderson, December 5, in CSLB. However, they re-

mained pessimistic about the ventures' profitability; see Codman & Smith to Jos. Gardoqui, December 20, in ibid. For uncertainties about the peace process, see Jonathan R. Dull, *A Diplomatic History of the American Revolution* (New Haven, 1985), 148, 150–51; Geo. Salmon to Wm. Moore & Co., November 30, 1782, in W&SLB. For the problem posed by investment in the new construction, see Isaac Smith to Jas. Hunter Jr., September 15, 1782, in H-GP; Geo. Salmon to Geo. Moore, April 30, 1782, in W&SLB.

11. All but 64 of the 480 entries recorded for 1782 note the date and place where the vessel was constructed. Thirty-three of the 64 which omit that information were prizes, most of them taken with the surrender of Yorktown. Only 37, or 9 percent, of the vessels whose dates of construction can be ascertained had been constructed before the war, and most of these were coasters of small tonnage entering from another Chesapeake port. On the other hand, 383 of the 416 for which construction dates are available, or 92 percent of the sample, had been constructed after the commencement of the war, and 300, or almost 72 percent, had been constructed since the beginning of 1780. See Baltimore Entries, January 1–August 1, 1782, in S 205 Naval Officer (General File), MdHR; Records of the Baltimore Customs, August 1–December 31, 1782, Record Group 36, NA.

12. For the quote describing Peck's design, see Dan. Parker to Ingraham and Bromfield, October 7, 1782, in Daniel Parker Collection, Historical Collections, Baker Library, Harvard University Graduate School of Business Administration. For the extension of the principles embodied in Virginia sloops and schooners, see Howard I. Chapelle, *The Baltimore Clipper: Its Origin and Development* (Salem, Mass., 1930), chaps. 2–3. For the desire to sell new construction vessels, see Presson Bowdoin to Jas. Hunter Jr., September 23, 1782, in H-GP; Codman & Smith to Jas. Russell, October 21, to Capt. Cole, April 10, 1783, in CSLB; Geo. Salmon to Capt. Littleton Houston, October 30, in W&SLB. For the desire to buy clumps, see Steph. Collins to his loyalist brother Ezra, August 28, 1782, in SCLB. For the disposal of clump prizes, see Steph. Collins to Wm. Gray, July 23, 1781, in ibid. Morris found himself having to authorize the purchase of the fast sailor *General Washington* at $20,000, a sum that he felt was "if a Peace takes place . . . vastly more than her Value, if War Continues considerably less," so that Congress might have a reliable packet boat during the peace negotiations; see Morris, Diary, August 28, 1782, in *PRM,* 6: 266.

13. Massachusetts Bay libeled twenty-eight vessels of 100 tons or more between September and December 1782, most of which were probably clumps; see prize lists, *Boston Gazette;* see also Steph. Collins to Wm. Gray, October 2, November 6, 1782, in SCLB. For New York's prizes, see Geo. Salmon to Geo. Moore, April 20, 1783, in W&SLB. For the use of overseas connections in acquiring tonnage, see Geo. Salmon to Geo. Moore, April 30, 1783, in W&SLB; Dan. Parker to Ingraham and Bromfield, October 7, 1782, in DPLB. For the effect of capital shortages, see Stephen Collins's discussion of the Philadelphia-based partnership, Reed & Forde, in Collins to Wm. Gray, October 9, 1782, in SCLB. Collins's leniency in pressing the firm for payment in turn involved him in complicated subsidiary transactions that limited his options; see Collins to Gray, November 6, 27, in ibid. For the heightened fear of losses, see Steph. Collins to Robt. Rantoul, February 11, 18, 1783, to Wm. Gray, February 12, in ibid. George Salmon complained of his grievous loss when the brig *Duke,* carrying 125

hogsheads of his tobacco, was taken in the last days of the war; see Salmon to Wm. Moore & Co., May 10, 1783, in W&SLB.

14. For uncertainties about the peace, see Matt. Ridley to Robt. Morris, November 20, 1782, in *PRM,* 7: 95; Geo. Salmon to Wm. Moore & Co., November 30, 1782, in W&SLB. For developments leading to the suspension of hostilities, see Robt. R. Livingston to Ben. Harrison, March 24, 1783, in *CVSP,* 3: 460; *JCC,* 24: 211; Order to Officers of Armed Vessels Commissioned by the United States, March 25, 1783, in *PRM,* 7: 635; Virginia Delegates to Ben. Harrison, April 1, 1783, in *CVSP,* 3: 464.

15. David Syrett, *Shipping and the American War, 1775–83: A Study of British Transport Organization* (London, 1970), 131, 135, 137, 139, chaps. 4–5.

16. On the effect that peace was expected to have on Chesapeake prices, see Steph. Collins to Wm. Gray, April 9, 1783, in SCLB. For the New England ventures, see Dan. Parker to Ingraham and Bromfield, September 18, 1782, in DPLB. All three Chesapeake ventures involved investors from beyond the Bay in addition to local sponsors, but from the islands or Philadelphia rather than New England. See Port of Baltimore, Clearances 1783, in Record Group 36, NA.

17. This document is in Port of Philadelphia Accounts, 1774–1809, RG 4 Records of the Office of Comptroller, 1762–1810, PHMC. See also John F. Stover, "French-American Trade During the Confederation, 1781–1789," *North Carolina Historical Review* 35(1958): 403.

18. The *Pennsylvania Gazette* began publishing naval office notices in May, lending support to a subsequent claim that "Since the 3d of May near 200 vessels have arrived at this port from abroad, most of which have brought valuable cargoes." *Pennsylvania Gazette,* May 14, June 11, 1783. Samuel E. Morison, *The Maritime History of Massachusetts* . . . (Boston, 1961), 35, reports a similar pattern for Boston between May and December 1783. See Curtis P. Nettels, *The Emergence of a National Economy* (New York, 1962), 48, for British dominance of the South's import trade.

19. Hostilities ceased in northern European waters two months earlier than in the western Atlantic, and one month earlier than in southern European waters; see article 22 of the preliminary treaty with France, a translation of which appeared in *Pennsylvania Gazette,* April 16, 1783. The actual dates were specified in the King's Proclamation of February 12, 1783; see ibid., April 16, 1783. Also *TUSA,* 2: 112, 113. For the strategy of approaching European partners, see Geo. Salmon to Geo. Moore, April 30, 1783, in W&SLB. Salmon sent essentially the same letter to ten other correspondents in the British Isles on the same day. On June 1 he dispatched another letter to eighteen European correspondents.

20. For reports of Britain's commercial liberality, see *Pennsylvania Gazette,* May 7, 14, 1783; the change in the ministry, though not the reasons for it, was first noted in ibid., April 30, 1783. Merrill Jensen, *The New Nation* . . . (New York, 1950), 83. Congress's preoccupation with other matters can be followed in Jas. Madison to Ed. Randolph, June 10, August 30, 1783, in *PJM,* 7: 134, 296.

21. On the weakness of the state governments, see Richard Buel Jr., *Dear Liberty* . . . (Middletown, Conn., 1980), 239ff. On the prices of American staples in relation to

imports, see Anne Bezanson, *Prices and Inflation During the American Revolutionary War: Pennsylvania, 1770–1790* (Philadelphia, 1951), 338.

22. James F. Shepherd and Gary M. Walton, "Economic Change after the American Revolution: Pre- and Post-war Comparisons of Maritime Shipping and Trade," *Explorations in Economic History* 13(1976): 399; Jensen, *New Nation*, 184–88; Geo. Salmon to Waddell Cunningham, September 30, 1783, in W&SLB.

23. See John Hancock's Address, in *Independent Chronicle*, October 2, 1783.

24. For the importance of the western domain, see Robt. Morris to John Hanson, July 29, 1782, in *PRM*, 6: 71. For its economic significance, see James A. Henretta, "The War for Independence and American Economic Development," in Ronald Hoffman, John J. McCusker, Russell R. Menard, and Peter J. Albert, eds., *The Economy of Early America: The Revolutionary Period, 1763–1790* (Charlottesville, Va., 1988), 81–87.

25. The emphasis on exports is referred to as the Taylor-North thesis; see Claudia D. Goldin and Frank D. Lewis, "The Role of Exports in American Economic Growth During the Napoleonic Wars, 1793–1807," *Explorations in Economic History* 17(1980): 22, though its lineaments are clearly apparent in Nettels, *Emergence of a National Economy*, 222, 278, 324ff, 336, 393–96, 399. The principal critics of the Taylor-North thesis are Donald R. Adams Jr., "American Neutrality and Prosperity, 1793–1808: A Reconsideration," *Journal of Economic History* 40(1980): 713–35; and Golden and Lewis, 7–23. Shepherd and Walton, "Economic Change after the American Revolution," takes positions consistent with these critics; see 413, 419, 420.

26. Paul David, "The Growth of Real Product in the United States Before 1840: New Evidence, Controlled Conjectures," *Journal of Economic History* 27(1967): 154–94; Thomas Weiss, "U.S. Labor Force Estimates and Economic Growth, 1800–1860," and Winifred B. Rothenberg, "The Productivity Consequences of Market Integration: Agriculture in Massachusetts, 1771–1801," in Robert E. Gallman and John J. Wallis, eds., *American Economic Growth and Standards of Living Before the Civil War* (Chicago, 1992), 30–34, 316–18; Stanley L. Engerman and Robert E. Gallman, "U.S. Economic Growth, 1783–1860," *Research in Economic History* 9(1983): 18–19.

27. Gordon C. Bjork, "The Weaning of the American Economy: Independence, Market Changes, and Economic Development," *Journal of Economic History* 24(1964): 553, 556, 559. See also Ruth Crandall, "Wholesale Commodity Prices in Boston During the Eighteenth Century," *Review of Economic Statistics* 16(1934): 121, 179; and George R. Taylor, "Wholesale Commodity Prices at Charleston, S.C., 1732–1791," *Journal of Economic and Business History* 4(1931–32): 371, 372. Jacob M. Price, *France and the Chesapeake . . .* (Ann Arbor, Mich., 1973), 2: 744; Nettels, *National Economy*, 48–49, 60, 62, 63; Myra L. Rich, "Speculations on the Significance of Debt: Virginia, 1781–1789," *Virginia Magazine of History and Biography* 76(1968): 308; John J. McCusker, *Money and Exchange in Europe and America, 1600–1775: A Handbook* (Chapel Hill, N.C., 1978), 20, 22; Timothy Pitkin, *A Statistical View of the Commerce of the United States of America . . .* 2nd ed., (Hartford, 1817), 30; *HSUS*, 761.

28. James A. Lewis, "Anglo-American Entrepreneurs in Havana: The Background and Significance of the Expulsion of 1784–1785," in Jacques A. Barbier and Allan J.

Kuethe, eds., *The North American Role in the Spanish Imperial Economy, 1760–1819* (Manchester, U.K., 1984), 121–24.

29. Geo. Salmon to Wm. Moore & Co., May 10, 1783, in W&SLB; Jean Meyer, "Les Difficultés du commerce franco-américain vues de Nantes (1776–1790)," *French Historical Studies* 11(1979): 166ff; Paul Butel, "Le Commerce Atlantique sous le Règne de Louis XVI," in Jean de Viguerie, ed., *Le Règne de Louis XVI et la guerre d'Indépendance américaine* (Dourgne, 1977), 77; Jacques Godechot, "Les relations éonomiques entre la France et les Etats-Unis de 1778 à 1789, *French Historical Studies* 1(1958): 29, 37, 38; Claude Fohlen, "The Commercial Failure of France in America," in Nancy L. Roelker and Charles K. Warner, eds., *Two Hundred Years of Franco-American Relations* (Newport, R.I., 1978), 111; Geoffery Gilbert, "The Role of Breadstuffs in American Trade, 1770–1790," *Explorations in Economic History* 14(1977): 379.

30. Scholarly opinion is divided on liberalization, but I follow Edmond Buron, "Statistics on Franco-American Trade, 1778–1806," *Journal of Economic and Business History* 4(1932): 573–74; and Henri Sée, "Commerce Between France and the United States, 1783–1784," *American Historical Review* 31(1925–26): 736. See also Meyer, "Les Difficultés," 182; Price, *France and the Chesapeake*, 2: 740; Gaspare J. Saladino, "The Economic Revolution in Late Eighteenth Century Connecticut" (Ph.D. diss., University of Wisconsin, 1964), 155–57; Bjork, "Weaning of the American Economy," 553; Peter P. Hill, *French Perceptions of the Early American Republic, 1783–1793* (Philadelphia, 1988), 79–86.

31. The debate about the influence of the monopoly is summarized in Price, *France and the Chesapeake*, 2: 731, 737ff, 768–69, 786–87, 842. See also Bjork, "Weaning of the American Economy," 544, 553; Nettels, *National Economy*, 50; Shepherd and Walton, "Economic Changes after the Revolution," 411. For comparison between British and French imports, Sée, "Commerce Between France and the United States," 737; Stover, "French-American Trade," 406, 412; Buron, "General Table of Commerce," in "Statistics in Franco-American Trade," 580; Hill, *French Perceptions*, 46–47.

32. Bjork, "Weaning of the American Economy," 551. Parliament had authorized the Crown to act through Orders in Council; see *Pennsylvania Gazette,* September 17, 1783; John Lord Sheffield, *Observations on the Commerce of the American States . . .* 6th ed. (London, 1784), esp. 246–47, 332–33.

33. Virginia voted to grant Congress the power to exclude British vessels from American ports; see *SAL,* 9: 313–14. When it became clear that the other states were reluctant to do so, Virginia called for a convention of the states at Annapolis in 1786 to concert commercial measures against Britain; see Jas. Jones to Jas. Madison, June 12, 1785; editorial note and "Draft of Resolution on Foreign Trade," November 15, 1785; "Resolves of the House of Delegates," January 21, 1786, *PJM,* 8: 293, 406–10, 471. Massachusetts struck back with discriminatory duties (see *Acts and Laws of the Commonwealth of Massachusetts . . .* [Boston, 1890–97], 3: 453–57; *Independent Chronicle,* July 29, 1785) as well as a local embargo against the export of provisions in British ships; see ibid., July 7, and *American Museum,* 1: 18. The former had no appreciable effect; the latter led to a humiliating incident in which the captain of a British frigate publicly insulted the

governor; see *Columbian Centinel*, July 13, 16, 30, August 3, 6; *Boston Gazette*, August 15, October 3. For the North African pirates, see Jensen, *New Nation*, 211–12.

34. Foster Rhea Dulles, *The Old China Trade* (Boston, 1930), chaps. 1, 3. On the length and capital requirements of the trade, see Clarence L. Ver Steeg, "Financing and Outfitting the First United States Ship to China," *Pacific Historical Review* 22(1953): 8–9. Boston's *Columbia* subsequently took three years to complete its voyage; see Morison, *Maritime History*, 43. Yen P'ing Hao, "Chinese Teas to America—A Synopsis," in Ernest R. May and John K. Fairbanks, eds., *America's China Trade in Historical Perspective: The Chinese and American Performance* (Cambridge, Mass., 1986), 13, notes that up to 1800, on average only 7.4 American vessels annually made voyages to the Far East; see also ibid., 14.

35. Roger H. Brown, *Redeeming the Republic: Federalists, Taxation, and the Origins of the Constitution* (Baltimore, 1993), 48. Morris had argued the economic advantages of funding the debt in his communication to Congress, July 29, 1782, in *PRM*, 6: 63.

36. Brown, *Redeeming the Republic,* is the best treatment of the impost during the Confederation period. See Robert Morris, "Report to Congress on the Representation of the New Jersey Legislature," September 27, 1782, in *PRM*, 6: 444.

37. *JCC*, 24: 257–60. The impost had been redesigned by Congress in ways mentioned in Brown, *Redeeming the Republic*, 23.

38. Forrest McDonald, *We the People: The Economic Origins of the Constitution* (Chicago, 1958), 141–42, 324–25, was the first to emphasize the distinction between the interests of state and federal creditors. For instances in which states honored their federal creditors, see *Pennsylvania Gazette*, December 14, 1785; *Honesty Shewed To Be True Policy* . . . (New York, 1786), 15. New York used the yields from a state impost to construct a fiscal system based on a half-million-dollar land bank scheme. The state paid interest on the liquidated state debt and a portion of the continental debt held by its citizens in land bank notes backed by specie; see McDonald, *E Pluribus Unum: The Formation of the American Republic* (Boston, 1965), 51, 59–61; Brown, *Redeeming the Republic*, 36, 38, 64, 135.

39. Buel, *Dear Liberty*, 328–29; Brown, *Redeeming the Republic*, 64, 79, 93–95, 122, 132–33; Irwin H. Polishook, *Rhode Island and the Union* (Evanston, Ill., 1969), 60ff. Seven states adopted paper money approaches to the payment of their debts.

40. Some have questioned the role of private indebtedness in setting off Shays's Rebellion, pointing to the declining number of court executions issued against debtors in some Massachusetts counties during the second half of the 1780s; see Brown, *Redeeming the Republic*, 115; Forrest McDonald and Ellen Shapiro McDonald, *Requiem: Variations on Eighteenth-Century Themes* (Lawrence, Kan., 1988), 61–68. The significance of this development should be evaluated in the context of Jonathan M. Chu, "Debt Litigation and Shays's Rebellion," in Robert A. Gross, ed., *In Debt to Shays* (Charlottesville, Va., 1993), 81–99. Certainly no one denies that private indebtedness played a part in the rebellion, though not all put as much stress on it as David P. Szatmary, *Shays' Rebellion: The Making of an Agrarian Insurrection* (Amherst, Mass., 1980), has done. See also my "The Public Creditor Interest in Massachusetts Politics, 1780–1786," in Gross, *In Debt to Shays*, 50–56.

41. "Report on Public Credit," January 1790, in *PAH*, 6: 78ff. E. James Ferguson,

The Power of the Purse (Chapel Hill, N.C., 1963), 294. The impost depended on voluntary compliance and could easily have been subverted if importers had been so inclined. The advantages of a centralized fiscal system are explored in another context by John Brewer, *The Sinews of Power: War, Money and the English State* (New York, 1989), 22–23.

42. James C. Riley, "Foreign Credit and Fiscal Stability: Dutch Investment in the United States, 1781–1794," *Journal of American History* 65(1978): 675–76, 678. France also exported substantial sums of "coined money" to the United States between 1793 and 1795; see Buron, "Statistics on Franco-American Trade," 578. For the appreciation of the debt, see Ferguson, *Power of the Purse,* 329–30. For the relevant portion of Hamilton's Report on the Bank, see *PAH,* 7: 334.

43. Bray Hammond, *Banks and Politics in America . . .* (Princeton, N.J., 1957), 144–45; Benjamin J. Klebaner, "State-Chartered American Commercial Banks, 1781–1801," *Business History Review* 53(1979): 530–33; Douglass C. North, *The Economic Growth of the United States, 1790–1860* (Englewood Cliffs, N.J., 1961), chaps. 3–4; Adams, "American Neutrality," 728. Though skeptical of the claims made for neutrality that he attributes to North, Adams seems to go along with this point. The value of waterborne imports increased by a factor of more than six between 1790 and 1807; see *HSUS,* 761. Government revenues from the impost dipped slightly in 1792 and thereafter rose steadily, with the exception of a brief decline in 1799, into the next decade. In 1808 they were 3.7 times greater than they had been in 1791; see Davis R. Dewey, *Financial History of the United States,* 2nd ed. (New York, 1903), 110; Nettels, *Emergence of a National Economy,* 385. The Spanish debt was completely paid off and the French debt converted to longer maturities at higher interest early in the decade, payable in dollars rather than livres. The Dutch debt had to be paid in guilder, which were raised by selling U.S. bonds in the Netherlands; see Margaret C. Myers, *A Financial History of the United States* (New York, 1970), 63.

44. See John R. Howe Jr., "Republican Thought and the Political Violence of the 1790s," *American Quarterly* 19(1967): 147–65; Richard Buel Jr., *Securing the Revolution . . .* (Ithaca, N.Y., 1972); James R. Sharp, *American Politics in the Early Republic: The New Nation in Crisis* (New Haven, 1993).

45. Yen P'ing Hao, "Chinese Teas to America," 13, 15; North, *Economic Growth, 46–* 54. Neither Adams nor Goldin and Lewis have argued that these were years of depression.

46. Nettels, *Emergence of a National Economy,* 254–62.

47. Adams rightly points to the lack of naval armaments as one of the hidden costs of American neutrality; see "American Neutrality," 734. For anti-navy sentiment, see the speech of William B. Giles to the House of Representatives, March 10, 1794, in T. H. Benton, *Abridgment of the Debates of Congress from 1789 to 1856* (New York, 1857–61), 1: 480–81. See also Craig L. Symonds, *Navalists and Antinavalists: The Naval Policy Debate in the United States, 1785–1827* (Newark, Del., 1980), chaps. 2–3.

48. Robert W. Love Jr., *History of the U.S. Navy, 1775–1941* (Harrisburg, Pa., 1992), 52–53, chap. 5; Jack Sweetman, *American Naval History . . .* 2nd ed. (Annapolis, Md., 1991), 16–17, 18, 28–39.

49. Hammond, *Banks and Politics,* 149; Dewey, *Financial History,* 133–34, 137. In 1814

and 1815 the U.S. government raised more revenue through internal taxation than it had raised in this fashion between 1791 and 1813; see Nettels, *Emergence of a National Economy*, 385. For the articulation of Henry Clay's American system, see Robert V. Remini, *Henry Clay, Statesman for the Union* (New York, 1991), 174, 225ff.

50. In 1816, Congress authorized the construction of nine 74-gun line of battle ships as well as twelve frigates; see Sweetman, *American Naval History*, 39. The next confrontation with a great European power occurred in 1834–36, over the settlement of spoilation claims against France arising from the Napoleonic Wars. Britain moved to mediate this dispute, fearing the commercial consequences that could ensue from a prolonged naval contest between France and the United States. See John M. Belohlavek, *"Let the Eagle Soar!" The Foreign Policy of Andrew Jackson* (Lincoln, Neb., 1985), chap. 4, esp.122ff; Robert V. Remini, *Andrew Jackson and the Course of American Democracy, 1833–1845* (New York, 1984), 3: 201ff, 230ff, 274ff.

APPENDIX

1. For the relationship of a daybook to a ledger, I rely on the standard accounting treatise used in the eighteenth century; see John Mair, *Book-keeping Moderniz'd; or Merchant Accounts by Double Entry, According to the Italian Form*, 4th ed. (Edinburgh, 1786), 8ff.

2. See Thomas Lea, Ledger, 1773–1787, 35, 53, 81, 94, 97, 118, 126, in HSD.

3. Ibid., 162.

4. Ibid., 150, 157.

5. This is how I interpret an enigmatic entry on the last page of his 1780 accounts:

"Cash of Thomas Lea for Grinding 6310 bush wheat @ 50/
Ditto Grinding for Jon. Tatnall 8020 ditto ditto @ 50/"

14330

6. See entries under "Mill in Company with John & Robert Morton," in Thomas Lea Ledger, 1773–1787, 190–91, 200, 213.

7. Prices of wheat peaked at 9/ in the spring of 1783, see Ledger, 1773–1787, 240.

INDEX

De Grasse, Admiral Comte de, 207, 209, 212, 213, 215, 217, 220, 221, 225
Delano, Gideon, 156
Delaware River and Bay, 12, 14, 71, 73, 78, 80, 86, 89, 146, 176; British operations in, 55, 86, 89, 91, 114, 189, 217–18, 220, 221, 224, 231; French presence in, 27, 71, 163
Delaware (state), 31, 36, 79, 216; grain embargoes of, 183, 184, 186
Delmarva Peninsula, 16, 18
depreciation, 128; attempts to combat, 45–46, 122, 126, 128; causes of, 44–45, 122, 125, 126, 132, 193–94; economic consequences of, 24, 64, 68, 103, 107, 127, 132–33, 140, 165, 170, 178, 191–92, 208; military consequences of, 91–93, 127, 154; political consequences of, 143, 248, 251; seasonality of, 130–31, 146; social consequences of, 127–28, 195
Digby, Admiral Robert, 241, 245
distillers, 24, 142
Duc de La Luzerne (continental man-of-war), 93
Dutch West India Company, 119

Egg Harbor, N.J., 134
embargoes, 29, 33, 104, 146, 157, 196, 198, 216; linked to requisitions for specifics, 143, 183; repeal of, 147, 157, 165, 183–84, 186–87, 188, 192
Enterprise (New England brigantine), 219
Estaing, Comte D', 180; effect of failures, 26–27, 56, 61, 89, 132, 139, 144, 148; expeditionary force of, 55, 58, 125, 131; loses supremacy in American waters, 56, 136, 137; retires to Boston, 27–28, 56, 87–88, 160
European imports, 64, 69–70, 108–9, 121, 139, 161, 162, 163, 165, 168, 207, 242. *See also* military supplies; naval supplies

Falmouth, Me., 33, 80
Fair American (Pennsylvania privateer), 92
Fairfield, Conn., 118, 119, 167
farmers-general, 66, 250
federal constitution, 253, 254
federal impost, 228, 229, 237, 238, 239, 252, 253, 254
Fier Roderique (French armed ship), 54, 58, 67, 70
Fitzsimmons, Thomas, 222
Flora HMS, 85
Flour, 6, 8, 9, 14, 28, 31, 50, 97, 104, 112, 141, 152–53, 166–67, 178, 179, 185; exports to West Indies of, 35, 105, 120, 121, 182, 183, 184, 186–87, 188, 191, 207, 209; price of, 17–18, 29, 139–40, 179, 190
Flour millers, 11–12, 15–18, 139, 142, 146, 178, 180–84, 216, 217, 257, 258–62
Fort Mercer, 90
Fort Mifflin, 89–90
Fort Wilson Massacre, 142, 143, 175
Fox (American merchant vessel), 182
Fox HMS, 86
France, 96, 241; American prejudices against, 70, 159; Franco-American commercial treaty, 54, 64, 249; commissariat, 27–29, 148, 150, 154, 155, 159, 160, 161–62, 172; consuls, 64, 65, 75; Court (Crown), 59–60, 66, 122, 200, 201, 231, 236; extends loans to Congress, 46, 160
Franco-American alliance, 27, 40, 44, 53, 54, 55, 57, 125, 134, 135, 159, 174, 216–17
Franco-Spanish naval operations, 129, 148, 180, 182
Francis, Tench, 153, 204, 206
Francy, Théveneau de, 71
Franklin, Governor William, 219
Fredericksburg, Va., 22, 75, 112
freight rates; peacetime, 109; wagon,

Newport (*continued*)
British occupation of, 42, 85, 113,
115, 119, 131; Rochambeau's expeditionary force in, 149, 153, 154, 156,
165, 169
New York (state), 31, 36, 79, 143, 212,
213, 214, 215, 252; effects of command
economy in, 165–67, 226, 233; illicit
trade of, 27, 226–27; imperfect integration into New England economy,
118–19, 165, 167–68; opposes Morris's
policies, 233, 238. *See also* grain (cereal)
production
New York City 12, 55, 77, 83, 86; allied
designs against, 148, 153, 165; British
occupation (evacuation) of, 113, 115,
118, 131, 167, 211, 235, 244; as gateway, 108, 109, 110, 111, 246; illicit
trade with, 21, 27, 226–27; as loyalist
privateering base, 136–37, 217, 218,
225–26
New York *Royal Gazette,* 218, 226
New York Vice Admiralty Court, 136–37
nonexportation, 2, 16, 26, 31, 33, 35–36,
97, 101, 159. *See also* Continental Association
nonimportation, 2, 31, 32, 34–35, 159.
See also Continental Association
Norfolk, Va., 80, 112–13
North African (Barbary) pirates, 251,
254, 255
North Carolina, 31, 36–37, 65, 79, 109,
111, 112, 211, 215; interest of French
merchants in, 67–68
North, Frederick, Lord, 240
North Potomac, Md., clearances in 1775,
35, 36
Norwich, Conn., 109, 115, 118, 119,
170, 172, 173

Paine, Thomas, 79
Palfrey, William, 133
Parker, Daniel, 232, 246

Parliament. *See* Great Britain
Patuxent, Md., clearances in 1775, 35, 36
peace, 217, 240; negotiations, 241, 242,
243, 244–45, 248; news of in America,
245, 246–47; problems arising from,
232, 233, 239, 241–43; surge of imports accompanies, 238, 246–47
Peck, John, 213
Penobscot expedition, 88, 90, 237; British
base at, 136
Pennsylvania, 151–52, 215, 227, 238–39,
252; naval force of, 78–79, 83, 90; currencies of, 150, 192, 193–96, 199–200;
grain embargoes, 183, 184, 187, 188,
192; mobilizes militia, 151, 216; monetary policy in 1781, 192–93, 194–95,
196; political changes of 1780–1781,
187, 188, 192, 197–98; response to specific requisitions, 149–51, 153, 192; response to specie requisitions, 230, 238–
39; tax resistance in, 150, 192
Philadelphia, 27, 77, 101, 115, 129, 143,
173, 196, 214; British occupation
(evacuation) of, 14–15, 17, 107, 113,
118, 131, 137, 138–39, 173–74, 209;
committee movement in, 15, 129–30,
141–42, 174, 177; defense of, 86, 173–
74; effect of the blockade of 1782 on,
218–25, 230, 232; as gateway, 108, 109,
110, 111, 113, 118, 121; French bills in,
159–60, 161, 163, 202, 231; French
merchants in, 40, 74, 75; market of,
12–14, 15, 18, 29, 50, 138, 139–42,
177–78, 179–80, 184–85, 197, 209,
217, 224–25; merchants' speculation in
old continentals, 164, 194, 237; money
current in, 150, 191–96, 197, 209; privateering of, 174–75, 176, 189; recovery as entrepôt, 164, 176–78, 188–89,
190, 191, 208, 210, 219, 220, 224, 235;
riverine communications of, 12, 110,
114, 189, 224, 225; seaborne commerce of, 39–40, 187, 190, 222–24,